Fun and Games in Twentieth-Century America

D0068772

GV
53
.G56
2003

WITHDRAWN

Fun and Games in Twentieth-Century America

A Historical Guide to Leisure

Ralph G. Giordano

GREENWOOD PRESS
Westport, Connecticut • London

Library of Congress Cataloging-in-Publication Data

Giordano, Ralph G.
    Fun and games in twentieth-century America : a historical guide to leisure / Ralph G. Giordano.
      p. cm.
    Includes bibliographical references and index.
    ISBN 0–313–32216–3 (alk. paper)
    1. Leisure—United States—History—20th century.   2. Lifestyles—United
States—History—20th century.   I. Title.
    GV53.G56 2003
    790'.0973'0904—dc21   2003045533

British Library Cataloguing in Publication Data is available.

Copyright © 2003 by Ralph G. Giordano

All rights reserved. No portion of this book may be
reproduced, by any process or technique, without the
express written consent of the publisher.

Library of Congress Catalog Card Number: 2003045533
ISBN: 0–313–32216–3

First published in 2003

Greenwood Press, 88 Post Road West, Westport, CT 06881
An imprint of Greenwood Publishing Group, Inc.
www.greenwood.com

Printed in the United States of America

The paper used in this book complies with the
Permanent Paper Standard issued by the National
Information Standards Organization (Z39.48–1984).

10 9 8 7 6 5 4 3 2 1

Dedicated to
Matthew Giordano,
Jonathan Giordano,
Thelma Lynn Olsen,
and
Rock-it

CONTENTS

ACKNOWLEDGMENTS

First and foremost, I wish to thank Matthew Giordano, Jonathan Giordano, and Thelma Lynn Olsen. All of them have provided more inspiration and support for this book than they will ever know.

I thank both my mom, Phyllis Giordano, and my uncle Dominick Dattilo for reading the early drafts and providing insight and some interesting interviews; my grandmother Anna Dattilo, whose philosophy in life is what I continue to follow: she always said, "You treat others the way you want to be treated yourself"; my dad, Thomas M. Giordano, and my uncle George Leaver, who hopefully will read a copy of this book—up there somewhere. It was my Uncle George and Aunt Dolores who first introduced me to Coney Island in my youth.

I thank my good friend and fellow architect Steven M. Peterson, for without him I would not have had the opportunity to discuss the ideas of this book nor to digress and laugh at our common humor in life. I also thank my friend Jeff Benjamin for his valuable insight and support.

I thank Greenwood Publishing for offering me the contract to write this book. Special thanks go to my photo editor, Liz Kincaid, who did a great job in making the photograph inclusion a simple process.

I thank two mentors and friends, Professors Frederick Binder and David Nasaw, for their guidance in my initial scholarly writings and research. I also thank Angie DeMartinis who serviced the City University of New York interlibrary loan; she searched for and provided me with access to many of the volumes referenced within this work.

Thank you, Thomas Jefferson. It was my early writings on his life and architecture that inspired me to combine both my own architecture and scholarly historical research into a lifetime pursuit of happiness.

I thank my colleague and friend Karen Svenningsen. If she never taught me the "secret handshake," I never would have even started nor would I have finished my first book. A sincere thanks to Marc Sica and the band *Nashville Attitude*. Also my "Saturday night" dance friends Greg Kmit and Stella Benardello who provided a welcome relief to the rigors of writing this book.

On a personal note, I live in New York City and I had to deal with writing this book while bracketing the chaotic times of the attack on the World Trade Center on September 11, 2001. For this author, on August 28, 2001, just a few weeks before the attack, my partner-in-life Thelma Lynn Olsen and I attended a concert by country artist Tracy Byrd at the WTC plaza. The previous day we had also taken a ferry ride along with my mom Phyllis Giordano to visit both Ellis Island and the Statue of Liberty. Little did we know how much would change within a few weeks.

My brother Thomas Giordano, a New York City Fire Department Captain, lost his entire engine company and he spent many months sifting through the rubble; sometimes in the hope of finding a colleague or even the remains of Steve Lauria, who was both a friend of mine and a talented recreational runner. Prior to his loss, Steve was dating my dear and close personal friend Debra Mahr. It is with additional thanks that go to Debra, for she was instrumental in reading every word of this manuscript even through those difficult times as we both tried to placate our monumental losses by "burying" ourselves in this project.

It was also with deep heartfelt concern that my editor at Greenwood, Debby Adams, spoke to me immediately after the incident. Her patience and emotional support cannot be described in mere words. And on one particular day, about one

Ralph G. Giordano relaxes on a hammock at Breezes Resort in Runaway Bay, Jamaica. Courtesy of Thelma Lynn Olsen.

week after the WTC attacks, as my son Matthew and I ended our daily recreational run in Clove Lakes Park, near our home in Staten Island with military jets thundering overhead "for our protection," we were just glad that we were together, rather than trying to make sense of a senseless tragedy. It was most important to know that we were alive and that I would also witness my younger son Jonathan finish his 4-year Lacrosse career at Msgr. Farrell High School and be fortunate enough to make the time to attend all his games. For as I learned, we must cherish our leisure time, and even make as much additional precious leisure as we possibly can—especially with those we love—for we never know when it will be the last time.

INTRODUCTION

According to the *American Heritage Dictionary*, the definition of *leisure* is "freedom from time-consuming duties, responsibilities, or activities," or "when one has free time; at one's convenience" (723). Some might simply define leisure as how individuals choose to use their own time without any direction or interference from others. The literal definition of leisure has been debated and analyzed. Texts from the twentieth century have attempted to define it either directly, literally, or sociologically. Almost all scholars agree that leisure is an activity removed from the paid workplace. This text is an attempt to look at what twentieth-century Americans chose to do when they were not working. Therefore, a professional baseball player is not at leisure while playing baseball—yet a dozen children on a sandlot are. Whether a person decided to take a leisurely walk in the park, to paint their own home, read, shop, or do absolutely nothing during leisure time was a matter of choice. The all-encompassing question examined by this text might simply be "What did Americans choose to do on their own free time to either relax, have fun, play, or simply to forget the pressures of work or the reality of life?" Most of this book will search the empirical—merely observing and drawing on first-person experience of leisure time. This reference work, arranged in a chronological format of "eras," identifies how Americans spent their leisure time during the twentieth century. Each chapter will answer questions such as:

- How much leisure time did children, teens, and adults have?
- Did they spend this time together or separately?
- What activities were popular during this period and which lost popularity?
- What factors (political, economic, or social) influenced leisure time in general?
- What specific activities did Americans enjoy?

The twentieth century began with 45 states and 76 million inhabitants making up the United States. The century closed with 50 states and 281 million people in the Union. During the first decade of the twentieth century more than 14.5

million immigrants arrived (the most in the history of the United States). The new immigration brought new cultures that would shape later generations and their approaches to work and leisure.

Most of the early twentieth century history of leisure and play can be divided along gender and ethnic differences. Male activities were usually dominated by aggression and competitiveness with strict rules and an ultimate goal of winning. Feminine activities of play, especially for the young, were usually based on co-operation and sharing and led to stress release and fun. Sociologist John J. Macionis stated, "Children's games, for example, may seem like light-hearted fun, but through them we teach young people what our culture deems important" (73). In 1900, bicycle riding, which was previously a masculine endeavor, was a good example of an activity where a female rider would have posed a threat to gender definition.

Women began the twentieth century with neither the right to vote nor representation in Congress. Thanks to the Nineteenth Amendment, birth control, and Title IX, the turn of the twenty-first century saw a tremendous upsurge in female participation in both leisure and sports activities. During most of the century, however, women were severely restricted regarding behavior and attire at public events and amusement venues such as the beach. The Boston Marathon, which began in 1897, for example, did not officially recognize female runners until 1972. Katherine Switzer ran "unofficially" in 1967, and a race director tried to forcibly remove her. For many women, their activities were confined to the home and family. Within a home exhibiting traditional roles, the husband was at leisure on a comfortable chair reading the paper, yet the wife serving in a domestic role at the same time was not at leisure.

Many entertainment and leisure venues were not only segregated by gender, but also by race. Segregation and the Jim Crow mentality were cemented in place. The 1896 United State Supreme Court decision of *Plessy v. Ferguson* provided the basis for legal segregation and effectively nullified the gains of the American Civil War. Segregation caused a mass migration from the South to northern cities. The nation was also in the midst of a transformation from a rural to an urban, industrialized society. Within the cities, many different leisure activities arose, although many were differentiated by social and class barriers. The leading spectator sport was baseball. In 1883, the National League merged with the American Association, effectively forming what is now major-league baseball. As a result, baseball was now accessible to working-class fans. It was not until 1947, however, that Jackie Robinson broke the "color barrier" in baseball. Prior to that time, baseball had a separate Negro League. In effect, leisure baseball played by American youths was divided along the same racial divisions.

Transportation would make tremendous gains previously thought unattainable in the years before World War I. The introduction of electricity in the cities would provide for mass transit such as trolleys and subways. The automobile, first thought of as a plaything of the rich in 1900, would make an immediate impact upon all classes of society within the first ten years of the century. The airplane in the same amount of time would go from a short two-minute flight across the sands of North Carolina to a flight across the English Channel. The twentieth century saw rapid, seemingly impossible advances in transportation that would serve both for commercial and for leisure and recreational purposes. These major technological developments would make a significant impact on the individuals' ability to make alternative use of their free time for relaxation and enjoyment. As the twentieth century began, however, most Americans still relied on horses, and the technological marvel of the late nineteenth century, the "iron horse"—the railroad.

During the century, the United States was involved in two world wars and other wars in Korea, Vietnam, and the Persian Gulf. The century was also filled with countless military "interventions" in areas such as Central America, the Caribbean, and the Philippines to name a few. Americans' leisure patterns were shaped around either the patriotic support of the war efforts or the economic upturns and downturns that accompanied these military efforts. And with war came one of the realities of life—death. Many young lives were lost due to war. In addition, the great influenza epidemic of 1918–1919 took many lives of all ages. Within an 18-month period, more were killed than in the previous years of World War I. Disease and the late-century epidemic of AIDS shaped the way Americans interacted on a social level. Subsequently, certain medical and technological advances (such as the flu and polio vaccines) contributed to Americans' ability to partake in certain leisure activities.

Within an industrialized society, it is apparent that consumerism and capitalism shaped leisure activities. The effects of advertising and media, including Hollywood and television, shaped what many believed to be popular and acceptable and in some cases rebellious, or simply what was a fad. Certainly, the same analysis can be applied to either popular culture or what individuals (usually young teens) chose as what was popular within their time, such as jazz, the hula hoop, or even hip-hop. In this book, I will present certain compatible themes that maintained popularity throughout the century, one being baseball.

Some points that should be noted are that illegal activities were certainly not leisure pursuits, although some discussion on drug experimentation during the period is required; so is some discussion on the effects of alcohol and gambling. Activities taking place within forced incarceration, such as a prison, are not necessarily considered to have occurred during leisure time and therefore are not studied. Where appropriate, certain leisure behavior patterns will be presented in an attempt to point out those who have tried to ban a particular leisure action either by law, censorship, or religious pressure.

CHAPTER 1

THE PROGRESSIVE ERA AND REFORMERS: 1900–1914

CHRONOLOGY

1893–1898   The United States experiences economic depression.

1896   The Supreme Court decides in *Plessy v. Ferguson*, "separate but equal."

1897   Steeplechase Amusement Park opens in Brooklyn's Coney Island.

1900–1914   14.5 million immigrants come to the United States.

1900   Eastman Kodak introduces an inexpensive one-dollar camera.

1901   The first transatlantic radio signal is broadcast.

1902   The teddy bear is introduced.

1903   The first airplane flight takes place at Kitty Hawk; the first silent movie, *The Great Train Robbery*, is released; the first baseball World Series is played.

1904   The National Child Labor Committee is formed; the first comic book is released.

1906   Kellogg's starts selling Corn Flakes; San Francisco experiences an earthquake.

1907   The first electric washing machine appears; Oklahoma becomes the 46th state.

1908   The Supreme Court decision of *Muller v. Oregon* upholds the maximum workday for women.

1909   Plastic is invented; Henry Ford begins assembly line production of the Model T, and the Sunday drive begins.

1910   Boy Scouts and Campfire Girls are established; the tango dance catches on; the NAACP is founded.

1911   The Triangle Shirtwaist Factory fire occurs; the air conditioner is invented.

1912   Oreo Cookies are first introduced; parachutes are invented; the *Titanic* sinks; New Mexico becomes the 47th state, and Arizona becomes the 48th.

1913   The first crossword puzzle appears.

1914   World War I begins in Europe.

INTRODUCTION

The image of American leisure in the beginning of the twentieth century was an innocent time of family get-togethers, picnics, Sunday strolls, drives in a horse and carriage, or the new automobile. Although these events did in fact happen for many families, the leisure situation within the nation as a whole was changing in ways never thought possible.

The differences were as diverse as the bookend presidents of the period: Theodore Roosevelt and Woodrow Wilson. Roosevelt, known for promoting vigorous exercise, especially outdoors, approached leisure and recreation aggressively and encouraged lively play among his children, including wrestling and boxing. Wilson's approach appeared to be the direct opposite. He would use his leisure time to golf with his wife or spend time indoors in the evening with his family, usually reading to them.

Similar to the differences between Roosevelt and Wilson, the period saw a clash of the old-world "protestant ethic" of the Victorian age with the new-world immigrants, who were entering the nation at a rate of more than one million per year. The image of the "idle rich" enjoying leisurely pursuits such as golf and tennis was in direct contrast to the everyday lives of city immigrants. The average working man could not support his family by himself; therefore, all the children, daughters and sons included, had to work. Workdays were long and did not allow much time, nor was there much excess income, for leisure activities. In contrast to the more expensive leisure activities of the "idle rich," the working class continually sought inexpensive leisure pursuits.

PUBLIC INTEREST

Parks, Playgrounds, and Open Space

Within the crowded cities, open space was not always available for outdoor events. The idea of creating an urban park began in 1858 with the design of Central Park in New York City. For the working-class poor of the city, a trip to the park became an inexpensive outing that provided a retreat for whole families and other groups to picnic, stroll, bike, sit, read, relax, or do whatever they pleased. In later years, museums, zoos, playgrounds, and restaurants would be added to the park. Architectural historian Spiro Kostof said that "the precedent of Central Park forever changed the look of American cities" (222). Many of the Gilded Age rich, however, whose opulent Fifth Avenue mansions lined the park, objected to the open fraternization that the park encouraged. The wealthy class thought activities in the park should consist of cultural enlightenment and be characterized by refined manners. The working class believed activities in the park should include fun and games.

Many cities and communities adapted the model of Central Park. Communities that did not require such a large park designed smaller county parks and recreation centers. In 1895, Essex County, New Jersey, developed the first county park. In 1898, Boston built a small model playground that included a small play area for children, a sports field for youths, and garden areas for adults. The idea of parks and playgrounds for cities grew in appeal, especially to help children stay out of trouble. A judge in Philadelphia claimed, "The public playground is the greatest deterrent of juvenile delinquency and lawlessness among children." The Playground Association, guided in part by the leadership of Luther Halsey Gulick, established a national organization to help cities and towns develop parks and playgrounds so that individuals could make productive use of their leisure time (Kraus [1971], 199). Gulick was a notable figure in the history of leisure and recreation. He was active in the early years of the Young Men's Christian Association (YMCA), an early promoter of recreational activities for women and girls, and in 1914, founder of the Camp Fire Girls of America.

Parks and playgrounds began to sprout up in and around cities and towns from coast to coast. Historian Richard Kraus noted that Chicago developed "a large-scale network of neighborhood recreation parks . . . [with] facilities for outdoor play with field houses that included gymnasiums, clubrooms, . . . and branches of the public library" (Kraus [1971], 187). Within the parks, communities began to sponsor organized events such as dancing, concerts, and civic activities. Golden Gate Park in San Francisco was considered a prime example of a successful facility; the park was scenic with many flowers, trees, and groves. In addition to a museum the park contained a music conservatory, a zoological garden, and an aviary. Audiences numbering 10,000 or more would regularly gather to hear 50-piece bands perform (Braden, 61). Cities continued to build parks and playgrounds as leisure attractions, adding features such as carousels, band shells, picnic areas, pavilions, fishing piers, boating docks, and sheltered areas.

Planned Communities: Pullman's Model City

Around the same time that the idea of parks and playgrounds developed, some held the contradictory view that an entire city should be constructed with the idea of controlling both the working and leisure habits of the working class, thereby providing social stability and eliminating potential labor problems. During the 1890s and well into the 1920s, industrial cities were built with that idea in mind. Pullman City, Illinois, built in the 1880s by railroad tycoon George M. Pullman, was a prime example. For leisure and recreation, Pullman built a park and a lake with facilities for boating, racetracks, tennis courts, and fields for baseball, cricket, and football. Fields were flooded in the winter for ice-skating. Pullman sponsored athletic activities such as sailing, sculling, and track and field, among others, that drew large numbers of spectators. During the warmer spring and summer months, a band played concerts in the park. Adjoining the park was a large arcade that served as a community center and contained meeting rooms, a library, a theater, and shops (Buder, 41, 69).

Pullman City, as did most industrial cities, prohibited drinking and integration. The only saloon was part of a central hotel in the town square. Segregation was an accepted part of American life based on the landmark 1896 Supreme Court decision of *Plessy v. Ferguson* (in which the court ruled in favor of legalized segregation). Segregation extended to schools, parks, theaters, eating facilities, and almost all other public establishments and places of recreation. "Separate but equal" would become an American way of life and would directly affect the leisure and recreational pursuits of African Americans for most of the twentieth century.

Muller v. Oregon

The 1908 Supreme Court decision of *Muller v. Oregon* in effect produced similar negative repercussions for women as *Plessy v. Ferguson* had for African Americans. *Muller v. Oregon* upheld an Oregon law that established a maximum hourly workday for women (Foner, 123). On the surface, it appeared that this legislation would pave the way for more leisure time for women. In reality, the freedom from "industry work" actually provided more time for household work such as cooking, cleaning, and caring for children. The court's decision contended that women were the "weaker sex," and the government reserved the power to regulate work in order to maintain their maternal role in society. The Court stated that "the fact that woman's physical structure and the performance of maternal functions place her at a disadvantage . . . [and] as healthy mothers are essential to vigorous offspring, the physical well-being of woman is an object of public interest. The regulation of her hour of labor falls within the police power of the State" (http://supct.law.cornell.edu/supct/index.php, *Muller v. Oregon*, 208 U.S. 412 1908).

LIFESTYLES

Rural Life and the "One-room" Schoolhouse

Although most people in rural areas did not have an abundance of leisure time, the family usually spent what time they had visiting neighbors or attending church. At home, families would relax on the front porch in the evenings or on Sunday afternoons and talk with family, friends, or neighbors. Within the home, the kitchen was the center of family activity. Mothers would cook or sew; small children would play; older children might do homework or venture outside for creative play; and fathers would read the newspaper. Board games, stereoscopes, and trade card collecting were among the amusements that families shared. If the family lived close to a town, the men might visit a tavern.

Saturday afternoons were usually reserved for the family to load up the horse and wagon and go to town for shopping. Sometimes the trip would be for the specific purpose of attending a traveling circus or the annual county fair.

At school, children were usually allowed recess times ranging from 15 to 30 minutes, twice a day. Most children played games or made creative use of the natural surroundings. Most of the children were the sons and daughters of Norwegian, Danish, Swedish, Finnish, Hungarian, and German immigrants, and their games reflected the heritage of their parents. Baseball, derived from the British game of rounders, was popular in the spring and summer. Other games included jump rope, leapfrog, kite flying, ring-around-the-rosy, and chase and tag games (Braden, 88). Some chase and tag games included rover red rover, capture the flag, hide-and-seek, and winter games such as fox and geese, to name a few. Mexican children in Texas and other southwestern states played Mexican- and Spanish-influenced games such as coyote and hen (*el coyote y las gallinas*), endurance (*los aquantes*), and traditional singing games (Gulliford, 188–196).

The schoolhouses were not limited to recreational use of children; they were also an integral part of adult recreation. For most rural areas, the one-room schoolhouse also served as a community center, and more than 212,000 such schoolhouses were in operation in the country at this time. Events ranged from theatrical stage shows and special productions to educational events, meetings of literary societies, debates, socials, and dances (Gulliford, 189, 200). The dances were especially popular and were attended by almost everyone in the community, including entire families, young and old alike. Of the dances, Andrew Gulliford said, "[T]hose too small to dance played outside until it got dark and then played hide-and-seek games underneath the school desks while their parents [danced] the schottische, the butterfly, the polka, and the waltz" (202).

On Sundays, the one-room schoolhouse would serve as a Sunday school and sometimes as the site for church services. Many rural areas discouraged any leisure activities on Sunday that were not directly related to religious activities—even reading was discouraged unless one was reading the Bible. Historian John W. Dodds discovered that "some towns took pride in having persuaded the railroad not to run local trains on Sunday, and others even banished the Sunday Papers" (81).

For many rural communities, the continuous daily activities of maintaining a farm did not allow for daily leisure activities; therefore, holidays and special events were anxiously looked on as a much-deserved time of leisure. Sometimes the community would gather to build a barn, and they would turn it into a social event. After work was completed, people would share food, talking would commence, and sometimes dancing would follow.

Victorian Culture Meets Immigrant Culture

From 1890 to 1914 more than 14.5 million new immigrants arrived in America. These immigrants were almost exclusively southern and western Europeans of Italian, Russian, Hungarian, Polish, and Greek descent, among others, and were mostly Catholic and Jewish (American Journey, 591–593). The new immigrants settled mostly in northern cities, among them New York, Boston, Chicago, Baltimore, and Philadelphia, with New Orleans being an exception. The new immigrants' views and cultural practices were in stark contrast to those of the mainly rural, white, Victorian-era, Protestant United States population.

The Victorian-era culture of the 1880s and 1890s, or the Gilded Age as it is sometimes called, is often associated with the "idle rich." In a world filled with maids, butlers, nannies, house servants, tennis, golf, croquet, dance socials, opulent mansions, and summer resorts, many of the urban rich maintained a lifestyle that they simply took for granted. In 1900, prominent banker and financier John Pierpont "J. P." Morgan, for example, put on what was considered the social event of the season, his daughter's wedding. To accommodate more than 1,500 invited guests, he constructed a 3,500-square-foot, two-story extension to his mansion in New York City. To the social elite, weddings of this type represented a valued part of their leisure activity. For other members of the upper class, their vast wealth allowed them to have the much-desired time to pursue leisure activities.

In New York City, however, just a few short blocks separated the wealthy and the poor. In response to the plight of the urban poor, some middle-class reformers introduced the idea of settlement houses, such as Jane Adams's Hull House in Chicago and Lillian Wald's Henry Street Settlement in New York. These settlement houses provided classes in cooking, sewing, housekeeping, and classes in speaking the American language. For recreation, they provided drama performances and organized playgrounds (Tompkins [1996, *American Decades: 1900–1909*], 316). For individuals such as Adams and Wald, among many countless others, much of their own leisure time was devoted to activism for reform.

For immigrants used to "old world" cultural habits, the new Americanized leisure pursuits offered newfound leisure opportunities. In the densely populated cities, there were more people in a few blocks than in either their European homeland villages, or for that matter, entire territories in the western and midwestern parts of the United States. Social life in the cities, therefore, was often more communal and within a very short walking distance. Historian Kathy Peiss noted that among the working class "[e]ach family member sought recreation in different places outside the home, the father going to the saloons, adolescent daughters and sons attending dance halls, children flocking to the streets, with only the mother staying at home" (179).

George Bevan's 1913 study discovered that immigrant working-class men who worked the longest hours and had the least amount of leisure time visited the saloon more often than others (Peiss, 17). For many immigrants, drinking was common and served as a recreational pursuit. However, for Victorian-era non-immigrant Americans who preached for temperance, the drinking habits of many immigrants were viewed as "sinful." The critics of drinking equated the idleness of socialization at saloons with laziness and unproductive work ethic. By the 1910s, there was an increase in the number of women in saloons, yet standing at the bar was not acceptable female behavior.

For many men, inexpensive leisure habits encompassed a wide array of activities. According to historian Cindy Aron, men found amusement

> in saloons, fraternal lodges, and clubs. Gambling, prizefighting, boxing, wrestling, and cockfighting captured the attention of urban working-class men and the scorn of pious reformers and middle-class moralists. Some men played more innocent sorts of sports, such as baseball; and in some cities large audiences of working-class men attended theaters. (Aron, 185)

Not all working-class and immigrant men had the income to enjoy leisure away from their neighborhoods. Therefore, they spent time on stoops or street corners talking and socializing. Many immigrants played simple games brought from their homelands. Italians, for example, played card games such as *scopa*, or a simple street game called *morra*. In *morra*, two players quickly threw one hand forward

Street fairs, such as this one in Vicksburg, Mississippi, served as a way for working-class and middle-class families to socialize. Courtesy of Library of Congress.

extending from one to five fingers and simultaneously called out a number from one to ten. The number of fingers held out was added together and the player who guessed closest to the total number won. Sometimes the game was just to pass time; other times it was played to gamble money. *Scopa* was a simple card game in which two or more players put down a card and whoever had the card with the higher number would "scoop" up the other cards.

Bevan's study further revealed that immigrant men spent more leisure time with their families than American-born men. Hungarian immigrants regularly socialized with family and neighbors within the home. Many immigrants took part in communal social gatherings, sometimes impromptu, outside in the street or tenement yard. One individual in New York's Lower East Side described it this way:

> [T]hey would play dance music, and all the girls and boys in the [apartments] would go in the yards and dance. How the people did enjoy that music! Every one would be at their windows listening. Sometimes they would play old song tunes, so soft and so beautiful. Then the people would clap their hands. (Peiss, 15)

The middle class had both time and money to go out but chose to spend most of their leisure time within the home and with family—some with the Bible, some tinkering, reading, and gardening—mainly pursuits that were considered in good moral standing (Nasaw, 15). For middle-class women in particular, gardening had a wide appeal and was considered morally acceptable. Middle-class women also did "fancy work." Fancy work consisted of needlepoint, painting, waxwork, and leatherwork, among other decorative crafts, whose products were intended to be displayed within the home (Braden, 87).

Outside the home, the middle class often chose "respectable" organized activities. According to Nasaw, "[t]here were lyceums and lecture halls, libraries, churches, and church-affiliated associations, such as the YMCA, that sponsored musicals, concerts, travelogues, even an occasional magician or illusionist" (15).

Time for leisure was not the only factor; so was money. According to Peiss, "the designation of the breadwinner's spending money as *personal* [Peiss italics] allowed men to pursue a social life based upon access to commercial, public recreation. Married women, however, received no spending money of their own" (24). Many married immigrant women simply stayed indoors or engaged in stoop gossip with neighbors while the children played sidewalk or street games. Neighborhood activity was sometimes filled with street amusements such as organ grinders and musicians in addition to numerous vendors peddling their wares in street carts. In New York City, in particular, church celebrations of saint's days such as San Gennaro (a carryover from Neapolitan tradition in southern Italy that is still a popular yearly festival), provided for weeklong festivities and the opportunity for socialization. Family leisure activities such as Sunday picnics usually became work for the women, as they were the ones who prepared the food, cleaned up, and monitored the children.

Young children and unmarried daughters did in fact work and contribute to the family income. (Many young women worked as seamstresses and in clerical positions. Boys sold newspapers and shined shoes, and many worked in factories and industry.) At that time, women and children together represented over 40 percent of the nation's labor force. Mary Harris Jones (also known as Mother Jones), an early-twentieth-century social activist, brought public attention to child abuse in the workforce. In 1912, Congress established a Children's Bureau and created laws for mandatory education and a minimum working age that produced a decline in the number of children in the workforce from almost 20 percent to less than 5 percent by 1920 (American Journey, 679).

In the cities, mandatory education laws increased the number of children in the schoolrooms and were an attempt by reformers and nativists to "Americanize" the immigrants and instill "proper" morals. African Americans were segregated in almost all southern schools and many northern schools. Native Americans were forced to give up their culture and accept American standards in special federally mandated Indian schools. On the West Coast, especially in San Francisco, a push to segregate Asian children in the school system began around 1905.

Progressive school reformers throughout the nation widely used the infamous *M'Guffey's* (sometimes spelled *McGuffey's*) *Reader* to institute proper ideals and morals. For example, one story in a second-grade reader, "The Little Idler," stressed the idea that idleness and play were bad, stating, "There are some little boys who do not love their books, nor their schools, but spend all their time in idleness and play. . . . As his play-mates knew him to be idle and a bad boy, none of them would have any thing to do with him" (American Studies, 42:1 Spring 2001: 1). The story stressed the idea that work was more important than play.

In place of idleness, reformers encouraged active sports as a method of creating better industry workers and as a means of social control. Physical education programs, therefore, were mandated within the schools, most with structured-play sports such as baseball, football, and basketball. Physical education was also promoted for female students, although it was less strenuous in nature. Basketball was popular among girls; however, they played a less physical version of the game with a different set of rules than boys. The school, therefore, was directly responsible for teaching the youth in the proper use of leisure time that in turn would make them better citizens. The intent was outlined in a report issued by the National Education Association: "The unworthy use of leisure impairs health, disrupts home life, lessens vocational efficiency and destroys civic-mindedness. . . . Education for the worthy use of leisure is of increasing importance as an objective" (Kraus [1971], 200). Cities began to mandate the addition of open-air playgrounds as part of new school construction. Other supervised leisure activities resulted in the formation of the Boy Scouts, Campfire Girls, Boy's Clubs, YMCAs, and social centers.

Legislators, reformers, and parents were also concerned about unmarried women (especially in their pursuit of leisure). In 1900, over 80 percent of working women were unmarried and worked an average of 10 to 12 hours per day. In 1912, the standard work time was a 9-hour day with a 54-hour workweek. In their time away from work, many young, unmarried women preferred the theater, concerts, and dancing. For almost all unmarried working-class women, leisure usually ended with marriage (Peiss, 34, 187).

In rural areas, for example, rumors abounded that innocent young women would be lured into lives of prostitution. A popular novel of the time, *Sister Carrie* (1900), told the story of the downfall of a small-town young woman who moved to Chicago. These stories were mainly based on Puritan fears of sexual activity and the growing realization that women (mostly middle-class women), led by the crusade of Margaret Sanger, were beginning to practice birth control.

ENTERTAINMENT

The Fourth of July, Wild West Shows, the Showboat, and Ice Festivals

Holidays such as the Fourth of July provided an opportunity for a community parade or family picnic. The Fourth was a day of carefree summertime fun such as venturing to a local swimming hole, picking berries, romping in a haystack, fishing, or playing baseball. In 1882, in connection with a Fourth of July celebration planned for the town of North Platte, Nebraska, a truly American entertainment fascination was born—the Wild West show (Lewis, 488).

William "Buffalo Bill" Cody brought the idea of a "frontier extravaganza" featuring exaggerated tales and fictionalized reenactments of the Old West to the Nebraska town. Roping, riding, and shooting exhibitions thrilled the crowds, making a legend of figures such as Annie Oakley. The Wild West shows toured and remained popular for more than 30 years. By 1914, with the saturation of literally hundreds of such shows and the onset of war, the public at that time simply lost interest. An offshoot of the Wild West show was the rodeo.

In 1897, the first of the big-time rodeos, Cheyenne Frontier Days, was held in Cheyenne, Wyoming. Cheyenne incorporated some features of the Buffalo Bill shows such as the stagecoach holdup. Rodeos proved to be extremely popular in the warmer months, especially in the plains states, and remained popular throughout the entire twentieth century. Summertime would also bring traveling theaters and shows. For those living near large rivers, especially the Mississippi, the arrival of a showboat provided for a special treat.

The showboat began as a popular form of entertainment after the Civil War and continued until the late 1920s. Showboats traveled up and down rivers within the United States, most notably the Mississippi, serving as traveling floating theaters, bringing various forms of entertainment that included popular plays, vaudeville, concerts, and circus acts, among others. The highly ornate boats so prevalent in the popular image of American culture were not always the reality. The boat itself was sometimes nothing more than a floating barge that could accommodate an improvised stage. Other showboats were large steam-powered boats with large wooden paddle wheels located either on the sides or rear of the vessel. The theatrical performers were usually the owner/captain of the boat's relatives. Town members were sometimes hired as extras for one performance or even for a few days. However, with the onset of winter, when the rivers ran cold, the showboats would disappear.

For the most part, during winter indoor activities remained the same; the out-

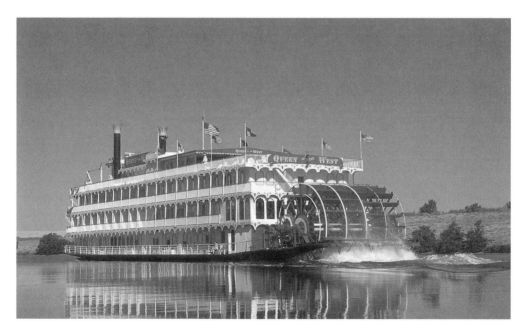

The *Showboat*, a floating theater, traveled up and down rivers within the United States bringing various forms of entertainment, which included popular plays and vaudeville, to rural areas. Courtesy of America West.

door activities were reflective of the climate. The early 1900s saw not only a continued interest in ice skating, but also skiing, sleighing, and tobogganing. Based on Scandinavian traditions, Americans adopted the winter institution of ice festivals. In areas such as St. Paul, Minnesota, the entire city (estimated at 200,000 people) took part in the festivities—no small feat when the average winter temperature was 40 degrees (Fahrenheit) below zero. The festivals would begin with parades, followed by events and demonstrations, among them sliding down man-made snow mountains and ski jumping. As technology advanced, motorized sleds (the forerunners of snowmobiles) came into use. This popular event spread to colleges and universities, and in 1911, Dartmouth College in New Hampshire sponsored the first of many collegiate ice festivals (Bruccoli and Layman [1996, *American Decades: 1910–1919*], 194).

Newspapers, Magazines, Advertising, and Books

In 1900, America had 1,600 daily newspapers. That number would increase to 2,600 by 1910 with circulation increasing from 2.8 to 24.2 million (Hofstadter, 145–147). As newspapers began to change from small-town, local, personal ventures into corporate journalistic endeavors, the leisure tradition of reading the Sunday-morning paper began. To garner a wide audience, newspapers began to include gossip columns, travel and leisure advice, color comics, and sporting results. Most important, newspapers, along with magazines, carried advertising. The inclusion of advertising would allow publishers to lower the newsstand cost, and circulation increased as a result. By 1906, newspapers such as the *New York Times* and the *New York Herald Tribune* advertised vacations and instituted Sunday travel sections (Aron, 207).

In 1900, magazine subscriptions to families numbered around 200,000. The number of magazine subscriptions would continue to rise and would eventually reach more than 32 million in 1950 (Braden, 83). Some magazines, geared specifically for women, among them the *Ladies Home Journal*, *McCall's*, *Good Housekeeping*, and the *Woman's Home Companion*, advised women on how to improve the home, marriage, and child rearing and how to properly spend their idle time. Magazines such as the *Saturday Evening Post*, *McClure's*, *Atlantic*, *Harper's*, the *Century*, and *Munsey's*, to name a few, provided stories geared toward both sexes in the middle and working classes. The magazine stories began working hand-in-hand with the advertisers. For example, a magazine would carry a story on the pleasures of the new phonograph and also an advertisement for a phonograph by Victor Talking Machine.

Magazines also introduced parlor games, collectibles, and contests. Trade cards were introduced for younger children that contained a variety of images including faraway, exotic places and celebrities, and of course an advertisement. Magazines also contained adult parlor games centered on advertising. The host of a "social party" would cut away any wording from an ad, and the guests would have to guess the product simply by looking at the pictures and/or logo.

Magazines also presented images that led to fads and fashions. The most popular fashion of the period was that of the Gibson girl. Illustrator Charles Dana Gibson first drew the "ideal" American woman for *Life* magazine in 1890. (This magazine was different than the general interest magazine, also titled *Life,* which began in 1936.) Gibson presented an image of an active woman who rode bicycles, drove an automobile, danced, and played golf and tennis. Women between the ages of 15 and 30 dressed and styled their hair as the Gibson girl did and actively began to pursue the same leisure interests. Men also became enamored with her image and even patterned their hairstyles and fashion attire in the same manner as the men in the Gibson girl ads. A reporter for the *New York World* wrote, "As soon as the world saw Gibson's ideal female, it bowed down in adoration, saying 'Lo, at last the typical American girl'" (Time-Life Books, *This Fabulous Century: 1900–1910*, 183).

At this time, less-expensive binding techniques and the introduction of a mass market increased readership of books, and the concept of the best-seller emerged. Many novels of the time were geared toward women with stories of romance with joyful plots; they were termed "happiness novels." Some other popular novels included Frank Baum's *The Wizard of Oz* (1899) and Jack London's *The Call of the Wild* (1903) and *White Fang* (1906). The books of Owen Wister, who set the basis for the western novel in 1902 with *The Virginian*, appeared during this era. Works by Carl Sandburg and poetry books sold well, as did Teddy Roosevelt's popular tale of *The Rough Riders* (1899) and other tales of travel and history.

As with all periods of American literature, novels reflected the social problems of the time. *The Jungle*, by Upton Sinclair (1906), uncovered abuses in Chicago's meatpacking industry and initiated the government's creation of the United States Department of Agriculture (USDA). Thomas Dixon praised the "righteousness" of the Ku Klux Klan in *The Clansman* (1905). The book sold more than 400,000 copies in a scant ten days. The reality of life in segregated America was reflected by Booker T. Washington's autobiography *Up from Slavery* (1901) and W.E.B. DuBois's *The Souls of Black Folk* (1903).

Animal Dances and Charity Girls

Dancing was not new to the twentieth century. Rural communities had sponsored dances for many years. The social elite attended dance functions at elaborate pavilions and resorts, where it was considered proper etiquette for a socialite to have a dance card. The card listed the order and type of dances played during the evening. Next to each dance was a blank line for the young lady to write in the name of a gentleman that asked her for a dance. Smooth-flowing, dignified, sedate dances that emphasized a strict erect carriage between the partners such as the waltz, two-step, and Lanciers (similar to a square dance, it dates from the Civil War era) were encouraged. Immigrants brought traditional folk dances from their native countries, such as the Italian tarantella, Jewish hora, and Greek *syrtos* and *pidiktos*, to name a few. Immigrants danced, young and old, male and female, mostly at communal events such as weddings.

In the first decade of the twentieth century, many of the working class attended dances in small neighborhood social clubs, mostly patronized by unmarried men and women. The young women ranged in age between 12 and 25. The males tended to be a bit older. In New York City alone, there were more than 500 neighborhood dance halls; Chicago had more than 400; San Francisco 300; and Cleveland 130 (Peiss, 88). After 1910, large ballrooms that accommodated almost 3,000 patrons, such as Roseland in New York, began to replace the small neighborhood dance halls. Roseland remained open past 1:00 A.M. during the week and until dawn on the weekends. Similar ballrooms opened in cities such as Chicago, Cleveland, Des Moines, Kansas City, Milwaukee, Newark, Philadelphia, and St. Louis. Kansas City alone had 49 dance halls (Nasaw, 111). Most of the dances were in response to a new form of music called Ragtime, the popular music format that began to replace the barbershop quartets and Sousa military bands.

With ragtime came a concern over the dances that accompanied the music. The music had a faster dance beat that younger adults enjoyed, and of course, older adults objected. The dances had names such as the Turkey Trot, Chicken Scratch, Monkey Glide, Grizzly Bear, and Bunny Hug, and were called *Animal Dances*. These dances initiated close contact, fast movement, and spieling and were considered vulgar and obscene by older adults. Spieling, which was to spin a dance partner, was particularly discouraged since it created physical excitement and was thought to arouse sexual tendencies. Many dance teachers ridiculed the newer dances, mainly because they were easy to learn and did not require intricate and expensive dance lessons. Ragtime, however, was lucrative, and business owners encouraged the new dance craze.

After 1913, the tango also caught on among the young. The sensuality and closeness of the new dance infuriated moral reformers and many cities banned the dance outright (http://www.mixedpickles.org/20cdance.html). Most of the other popular dances of the time were introduced from Broadway and theater. A production in New York's Harlem called *Darktown Follies* (1911) popularized dances such as "Ballin' the Jack," Cakewalk, and Texas Tommy. Dancing, however, as with almost all aspects of American recreation and leisure at this time, was segregated by race.

Many African Americans congregated in segregated jook joints, honky-tonks, and after hours places to enjoy dancing. Jook joints and honky-tonks were usually small, downtrodden places in undesirable parts of town that served alcohol and offered music for entertainment and dancing. *Jooking* was a slang term among African Americans for any social form of singing, playing, or dancing. Some differentiated that a jook joint was located in a remote, rural area and a honky-tonk was closer to an urban area. In either case, they were places that African Americans could go to eat, drink, and dance (Trotter, 359). Honky-tonks and jook joints would continue to be popular throughout the century, often distinguished by low-income clientele of all races. Patrons enjoyed dancing at these establishments regardless of their race, gender, or class for the reason that the dances were fast moving, simple, and fun.

Moral reformers, however, claimed that the dance halls in the cities were areas of vice and moral corruption, and concerns also arose over so-called charity girls. A charity girl was a young woman who would go on a date and provide her male partner with flirtatious glances, or sometimes even sexual favors, in return for the cost of the date. Most young working-class women were not financially able to afford the cost of going to a nightclub or a ballroom dance; therefore, the only opportunity for social participation was as a charity girl. As a result, the concept of a man "treating" (paying for the cost of the date) started at this time. The mere mention of sexual immorality, however, was cause for immediate censure and sometimes closure of an establishment.

In response to the numerous vice raids and increasing public attention, many establishments refused entry to unescorted women. (Society viewed an unescorted woman in public, especially at night, as a prostitute.) It was also improper for a man to ask a woman sitting at a different table than him to dance. The idea was continually stressed to enter, dance, and leave together as a couple. One couple, the professional dance team of Vernon and Irene Castle, maintained the same idea in order to make dancing socially acceptable.

On Broadway in 1912, the Castles first introduced the Castle Walk (a graceful walk that was a version of the two-step). They were an instant success and quickly gained popularity. The Castles applied ingenuity and grace to create a dance style that effectively toned down the "vulgar" effect of the animal dances. Newspaper and magazine articles featured photographs and illustrative dance steps so that everyone could dance the "Castle way." They also popularized the Fox-trot, a dance that would become a ballroom standard throughout the century. Irene was one of the first celebrities to influence clothing and hairstyle fashions on a nation-wide scale. Young women cut their hair in a short bob haircut with a beaded headband and searched for similar dresses to wear. Men likewise copied Vernon's fashion.

In 1914, the Castles published *Modern Dancing*, a popular instructional dance book. Included were chapters on how to host the proper dance, the clothes to

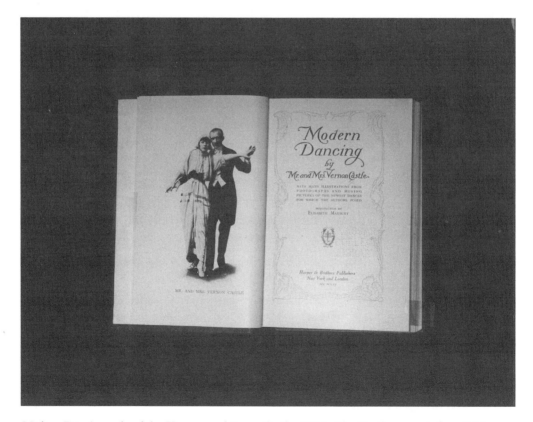

Modern Dancing, a book by Vernon and Irene Castle, 1914. The Castles were influential in encouraging people to learn to dance. Author's archives.

wear, and the music to play. The book claimed that "the modern dances properly danced are *not* vulgar" (Castle, 32). In support of the book, Elizabeth Marbury, a well-known literary agent and producer of the time, wrote, "If we bar dancing from the world, we bar one of the supreme human expressions of happiness and exultation. . . . therefore, I say that the best course in the interest of morals is to encourage dancing as a healthful exercise and as a fitting recreation" (Castle, 21–29).

Despite moral objections, dancing was a favorite leisure pursuit among all classes, especially among young women. The fun of dancing allowed working-class people to forget the realities of poverty and allowed the opportunity to escape the rigid family structure.

Board Games

Some of the most popular board games of the time included chess, checkers, and backgammon. These games had been popular since the Civil War and remained popular for the entire century. Four major companies produced most of them: Milton Bradley, McLoughlin Brothers, Parker Brothers, and Selchow & Righter. For the adult middle class, the Ouija Board was introduced and became a popular parlor game. For children, Erector Sets and Tinkertoys were introduced.

Card playing, although frowned on by religious groups and moralists, was popular in many American homes. In 1900, for example, more than 16.5 million decks of playing cards were sold (Rosenberg and White, 419).

Fairs and Amusement Parks

The inspiration for the creation of amusement parks came from the 1893 Chicago World Columbian Exposition. In Chicago, the concept of a *midway*, an entertainment zone of amusements, games, and concessions, was first introduced. One of the most popular sites and attractions was the Ferris wheel, a ride that rose to a dazzling height of 250 feet. The Ferris wheel was also at the 1904 St. Louis World's Fair, which had its own version of a midway called "The Pike." It was at St. Louis that Americans were first introduced to fast food as they walked and ate hot dogs and ice cream cones (Tompkins [1996, *American Decades: 1900–1909*], 308). World's fairs, however, would only last from six months to about a year, and when they were dismantled, they were gone for good.

Inspired by a first-hand visit to the midway at Chicago, George Tilyou opened a permanent site for an amusement area, Steeplechase Park at Brooklyn's Coney Island, in 1897. Steeplechase was an active attraction filled with fun houses, circus-quality side-show attractions, and mechanical rides, among other fascinations. A feature that dominated the landscape of the park was the Wonder Wheel, a half-scale version of the Ferris wheel. One of the most popular rides was a mechanical horse on a fixed metal rail that ran down a long, undulating slide. The thrill ride was one thing; the dismount at the end was another. A circus clown and a dwarf would chase people around as air jets blew women's skirts into the air, a scene that titillated crowds of onlookers. Needless to say, it was quite risqué for that time (Eaton, n.p.). Critics gasped at rides and attractions that in their view promoted promiscuity and immoral behavior. They were appalled by attractions with names such as "Barrel of Love," "Wedding Ring," and "Razzle Dazzle" that encouraged close contact and interaction among total strangers of different genders. Despite the critics, the public loved the rides and could not get enough.

Improvements in mass transportation such as the electric trolley and the improving subway systems connected the amusement parks at Coney Island with the rest of the city, allowing accessibility to the working class. A one-day summer excursion to Coney Island was a special treat for the working class and became a mecca for family entertainment. By 1900, it was reported that on any given weekend day or holiday 300,000 to 500,000 people came to Coney Island (Peiss, 124). During the 1909 season in particular, more than 20 million people visited (Nasaw, 3). American entertainer Jimmy Durante recalled the diversity of the summertime crowd that attended Coney Island: they were "young people—husky men and pretty girls in cheap finery; shipping clerks or truckmen or subway guards escorting their sweethearts [who] didn't have much to spend but [knew that at Coney Island one] could go a long way on a few dollars."

Two other amusement parks would open in Coney Island—Luna Park (1903) and Dreamland (1904)—that also contained thrill rides, attractions, and entertainment. Each park was illuminated by literally millions of light bulbs—a marvel in its own right at a time when electricity was just beginning to light city streets. The glittering array of entertainment and the popularity of the amusements also attracted the attention of the wealthy classes.

Coney Island's amusement parks added to the three already-present horse racing tracks. Frequented by the wealthy and fashionable, daily crowds averaged 40,000 horse racing fans including politicians, Wall Street barons, railroad men, society leaders, actors, and actresses. No other area in the country could boast three racetracks that provided continuous racing from May through October. After the completion of the day's races many of the wealthy would venture out for an evening's entertainment among the amusement parks. Gambling and racetracks, however, had been a concern among some for quite some time. As a result of mounting pressure from reformers and new state laws prohibiting gambling, all of the tracks were closed by 1910 (Stanton, n.p.).

The popularity of the amusement park spread throughout the country. By the start of World War I, almost 2,000 amusement parks existed in many cities across the country such as New York, Pittsburgh, Chicago, Ohio, and Denver (West, 30). Kansas City, with a population of only 250,000 residents, had five amusement parks that drew an estimated two million visitors during the 1911 summer season (Kraus [1971], 195). Atlantic City, billed as a "Mecca for Millions," contained many features similar to those at Coney Island. Adjacent to the beach was a seven-mile-long boardwalk with myriad carousels, peep shows, hotels, nickelodeons, bazaars and amusements, and arcades of all sorts. The West Coast was not without beachfront amusement parks. In San Francisco, the long stretch of Ocean Beach from Golden Gate Park to Seal Rocks contained amusements and rides and was dominated by Cliff House, an elegant entertainment venue for dining and dancing. Also along Ocean Beach was Playland, a park that contained literally miles of amusement rides and attractions. The park continued to gain popularity, reaching its height during the 1940s (www.cliffhouse.com).

Dreamland, pictured here, combined with Luna Park and Steeplechase at Coney Island in Brooklyn, New York, contained thrill rides, attractions, entertainment, and a glittering array of millions of light bulbs. Courtesy of Library of Congress.

By World War I, almost 2,000 amusement parks existed nationwide. Long Beach Amusement Park in California, pictured here, contained a beachfront boardwalk with amusements and entertainment venues for dining and dancing. Courtesy of Detroit Publishing.

MUSIC AND THEATER

Vaudeville and Broadway

In the early 1900s, vaudeville was the most popular form of entertainment, presenting audiences with a combination of variety acts including comedy, short plays, dance acts, animal acts, juggling, musicals, burlesque, and minstrel numbers. Vaudeville theaters were in cities of all sizes across the country. The theaters offered from two shows a day to continuous shows all day. The audience attended for one simple reason: to be entertained. The content was monitored by the show's producers to make sure all acts and dialogue adhered to an acceptable code of behavior, and the acts were intended to appeal to as wide a range of audience members as possible. In an article published May 6, 1906, the *New York Times* reported that a "chain of vaudeville houses from Boston to San Francisco" existed with "over a hundred first-class vaudeville houses where the higher class acts are sure of continual and profitable booking, besides hundreds of smaller houses."

Although married women and children were more likely to attend legitimate theater productions, the women represented almost one-third of New York vaudeville audiences and over 45 percent of San Francisco vaudeville audiences (Peiss, 143). Vaudeville managers recognized the need to attract and keep female audience members. To do so the prices were kept low and special matinees and "ladies nights" advertised either a special admittance fee or sometimes free entry. To attract men to the theaters, managers would advertise an array of attractions that would appeal to them such as baseball players, wrestlers, and tennis players. Nasaw noted "[f]emale swimmers were especially prized because they could appear in their swimsuits" (27).

As for the audience, almost everyone who could pay the admission price was allowed in, with two notable exceptions being Asians and African Americans. Asians tended to self-segregate and rarely left their communities in search of public entertainment. Racial segregation and stereotypical racial attitudes persisted in the vaudeville productions. On stage, almost every ethnic group was slandered and stereotyped, including African Americans, Asians, Italians, and Jews (Nasaw, 47).

Although many of the vaudeville performers were African Americans, the audiences were usually white; when African Americans were allowed into the theaters at all, they were usually restricted to undesirable segregated sections and the balcony. Those theaters without a balcony or separate areas usually barred them totally. Some vaudeville entrepreneurs saw in African American audiences an opportunity to make money and some attempted to provide specific days for African Americans only. In the South these owners were usually physically threatened, attacked, or had their theaters burned by vigilante groups. Some business owners in the North had limited success. Vaudeville was so popular and prosperous that African Americans sought to provide this entertainment for themselves. In 1904 in Chicago, Illinois, for example, a group of African American businessmen opened the Pekin Theater in 1904 (Nasaw, 50, 172). Regardless of audience members' race or gender, vaudeville would remain a popular form of entertainment until the 1930s. A slow decline in attendance began around 1910 as vaudeville began losing audience members to Broadway and the motion picture.

After 1910, Broadway theater grew in popularity as a purely American art form and became a favorite leisure pursuit of the wealthy and middle class. During this time before television and movies, Broadway produced new fashion trends, fads, and dance steps. The attraction of Broadway was described as follows:

> Theatergoers were thrilled to feel that they were in on things, and they knew that they would be the first to hear Irving Berlin's latest hit and would see—and also soon be imitating—[the latest] new dance step. Women copied the gowns, mannerisms and hairdos of ballroom stylist Irene Castle. Men picked up racy patter [slang] from Eddie Cantor or homespun humor from Will Rogers. (Time-Life Books, *This Fabulous Century: 1910–1920*, 260)

Broadway could not compete with the motion picture on a national scale or in offering low-priced admission, but it did not have to.

The Motion Picture

Prior to the introduction of the motion picture, still pictures were popular as a form of entertainment. Many photographic images could be viewed through home stereoscopes and in public penny arcades. The arcades would feature amusements such as phonographs, fortune-telling machines, kinetoscopes, and sometimes slot machines (Peiss, 145). Penny arcades were inexpensive and located within urban neighborhoods, which allowed married women and children without ready access to transportation to attend. Around 1905, the arcades began sectioning portions in the back of the facilities for the projection of the newly developed motion pictures. Because tickets for a show cost five cents, the arcades showing motion pictures became known as nickelodeons.

The nickelodeons represented an inexpensive form of entertainment. As a result, the motion picture grew in popularity very quickly. By 1907, more than 200 nickelodeons were in operation in Manhattan alone. The features were silent images, lasting only five or ten minutes, with live musical accompaniment, usually a piano. The nickelodeons were makeshift affairs, often converted storefronts. The *New York Herald* described a typical nickelodeon in 1908 as "a long, narrow room. . . . At the rear a stage is raised. Across it is swung a white curtain. Before the curtain is placed a piano. . . . Packed into the room as closely as they can be placed are chairs for the spectators who number from one to four hundred" (Uschan, 38).

Large theaters (used for vaudeville and stage productions) also began to show motion pictures. The makeshift nickelodeons and large elegant theaters had one thing in common: they were usually overcrowded, and the limited number of exits were usually locked. A tragic example of what could go wrong in these overcrowded spaces occurred in 1903 when a fire in Chicago's Iroquois Theater killed more than 600 people in a mere 15 minutes. Even after that fire, many theater owners continued to disregard safety requirements, and municipalities waged an ongoing crusade against them.

SPORTS AND GAMES

Baseball, Boxing, and Professional Sports

Baseball as a professional sport dated to 1883 with the formation of the National League. The American League was formed in 1900. In 1903, both leagues agreed to play the first World Series, a championship game between the top teams in each league. More than 100,000 spectators attended the eight games of the 1903 series. Between the years 1903 and 1908, attendance doubled at major-league baseball stadiums. Attendance, however, was not based on low prices. Tickets averaged more than 1 dollar per ticket and were considered expensive. Due to ticket pricing the notorious "cheap seats" in the bleachers (usually 25 cents) were occupied by working-class immigrants, mainly Irish and German families. African Americans, when allowed in at all, were relegated to undesirable segregated sections (Nasaw, 97, 100). The rise in the number of spectators was aided in part by the construction of new stadiums close to intersecting trolley lines in cites such as Philadelphia, Pittsburgh, Boston, Chicago, Manhattan, and Brooklyn.

Popular players in the early part of the century included Ty Cobb, Cy Young, Honus Wagner, and Shoeless Joe Jackson. These players were so popular that an American tobacco company, in order to boost sales, issued the first baseball cards. Card collecting became an instant leisure time activity among young men and boys. By the start of World War I, baseball was firmly entrenched as America's most popular spectator sport and was earning the title of America's national pastime.

Between 1903 and 1908, attendance at major league baseball stadiums doubled. By 1909, the date of this photo, baseball was fully entrenched as America's national pastime. Courtesy of Library of Congress.

Boxing, also known as prizefighting, had conflicting appeal. (It was not included in the 1912 Olympics because it had been outlawed in Sweden.) Many of the Ivy League colleges stressed boxing as a participatory gentlemen's sport and activity event for young men. Rules and regulations varied from state to state (and some states outlawed it completely). During this period, bare-knuckle fighting was still popular. Some cities, such as New Orleans, had a requirement for the contestants to wear gloves and limited rounds to three minutes (Tompkins [1996, *American Decades: 1900–1909*], 492).

Boxing did not necessarily ban African Americans from participation; it was usually segregated just as the rest of society was. America's racism was readily apparent when Jack Johnson became the first African American heavyweight world champion in 1908. The country's attitudes toward African Americans kept him from fighting against the top white fighters. Johnson had to travel to Sydney, Australia, to defeat Canadian Tommy Burns, the world champion. His victory created much racial tension within the nation (Trotter, 361-362).

Segregation extended from professional sports to recreational centers and leisure sports. For example, basketball separated both the genders and the races. Baseball had an unwritten rule to not only eliminate African Americans but also other ethnic groups, such as Jews and Italians, as well.

Horse racing was popular among the wealthy and eventually spread to become popular with all classes of people. The main appeal was not appreciation of competition or Thoroughbred, but gambling. Automobile racing also began to become a popular spectator event. Carmakers began to produce racing cars, mainly to create interest in their new automobiles and to capitalize on the growing American fascination with speed. The first permanent, enclosed spectator track was opened at Indianapolis, Indiana, in 1909, and the first of its famous Indy 500-mile races attracted more than 80,000 spectators, providing the thrill of speed, endurance, and distance all in one event (Braden, 233).

The appeal of endurance and distance captured the public's imagination. Marathon events that included bicycle riding and footraces drew large crowds. The bicycle events consisted of teams that would cycle on an indoor track called a "velodrome" for up to six days. Events in New York's Madison Square Garden drew tens of thousands of spectators and remained popular into the 1920s ("Cycling" Encarta Encyclopedia [2000], n.p.). The modern marathon was conceived to increase interest in the resurrection of the modern Olympic games in Athens, Greece, in 1896 and encouraged the Boston Athletic Association to sponsor the first annual Boston Marathon in 1897. Continued interest in the marathon encouraged promoters to put on a series of professional marathon races; the first was held at Madison Square Garden in November 1908. Marathoning shifted from a mainly spectator sport at the beginning of the century to a major participation leisure activity by the end of the century.

Active Participation, Tennis, Surfing, and Bocce

At the beginning of the century, tennis was a highly popular sport and leisure activity. Tennis, however, was almost exclusively played by affluent white adults, or "idle rich," who had a large amount of leisure time, and it was mainly part of expensive and exclusive country clubs that also sponsored golf. Private country clubs refused to admit African American members, and female participation in both tennis and golf was slowed by discrimination. Even wealthy women were under restrictions at their own clubs. For example, female members of New Jersey's Upper Montclair Country Club, founded in 1901, were restricted to playing golf only on Saturday mornings and Sundays after 3:00 P.M. (Tompkins [1996, *American Decades: 1910–1919*], 550).

After 1910, mainly due to inclusion of hard surfaces such as clay and asphalt at city parks, tennis's appeal to the middle class grew. In addition, municipalities began to open public golf courses. Although many people played golf and tennis, they remained mostly amateur sports. Other popular sporting activities were canoeing, rowing, walking, gymnastics, and basketball. Basketball was considered an acceptable activity for young female immigrants; however, to ensure that the activity was not too strenuous, a complete set of rules (dated from 1891) especially for women remained in effect for the first half of the century.

The 1912 Olympics in Stockholm, Sweden, generated American interest in sports, thanks mainly to Native American Jim Thorpe who won both the decathlon and the pentathlon. The Olympics in Stockholm served as an impetus for increasing the respectability of more than a few sporting activities. Due to exposure at the Olympics, swimming became more popular and was considered acceptable for women. At the same Olympics, a little-known swimmer from Hawaii made a lasting impression on American leisure.

At the Stockholm Olympics, Duke Kahanamoku won both a gold and silver medal. More important, Kahanamoku (known simply as "Duke") would become known as the "father of modern surfing," as he, along with others, rediscovered an ancient Polynesian sport known as wave sliding (Library of Congress, n.p.). Surfing would become a major leisure pursuit on the West Coast, especially in southern California, and in Hawaii in the late 1950s and 1960s.

Many immigrants, however, could not understand the American fascination with sports. For most immigrants, the value of an activity was determined by whether it was productive or harmful to the immediate family, and to be emotionally involved in sports was seen as madness. Immigrants, therefore, often developed conflicts with their own American-born children over the value attached to sports. Sports, however, were important aspects of some immigrant cultures. Bocce is a good example. Historian Richard Gambino described the Italian game of bocce this way:

> Played on a long rectangular court, the object of the game is to bowl hard balls closer to a target ball than your opponent or opponents can. The skills of the game include knocking the other side's balls out of position, and the game could be keenly competitive especially when played by teams of two men each. . . . the pleasures [of bocce] were to be enjoyed in a dignified manner. (138)

Although the games could be competitive and were played with intensity, Gambino further stated that "winning a competition that did not have direct bearing on the real life of family [was] regarded with disapproval" (Gambino, 137).

TRANSPORTATION AND VACATION

A Bicycle Not Built for Two

The bicycles that were the rage of the late nineteenth century were unsafe contraptions ridden almost exclusively by men. In the 1890s, a British company's invention of the "safety bicycle" increased the use of the bicycle dramatically for both genders. The safety bicycle consisted of pedals that turned a pair of sprockets connected by a chain to the rear wheel, which was the same size as the front wheel. Other features were a handlebar, contoured seat, and brake. The frame was usually hollowed metal and similar in shape to the models that remained in use throughout the twentieth century. The new transportation choice of the bicycle allowed for easier and quicker movement, and bicycle riding became a rage as a leisure pursuit ("Bicycle," Encarta Encyclopedia [2000], n.p.).

Prior to 1900, bicycling was viewed as strictly a male endeavor. Ellen Gruber Garvey stated that medical research, at that time, claimed that bicycle riding "would be dangerous for women to expend so much of their strength on physical activity" (114). In fact, according to research by Karin Calvert "one of the cardinal rules of child-rearing in the nineteenth century . . . forbade girls to sit straddling any object" (quoted in Garvey, 114). With the popularity of the safety bicycle, straddling a bicycle seat was necessary. The bicycle also allowed a new found freedom of movement by women. Both issues, regarding the bicycle, created both social and moral concerns.

In order for the industry to sell bicycles, mass-market magazines began advertising campaigns to woo consumers. Advertisers avoided the moral and social issues and took an approach to make a clear distinction between male and female bicycles. Some promoted a fictionalized image that for women the bicycle trip "would end in married happiness." Advertisers even began giving bicycles gender-related names such as "Napoleon and Josephine" and "the Victor and Victoria." Manufacturers also changed the basic structural shape of women's bicycles to eliminate the upper crossbar so that women could get on the bicycle while wearing a skirt. This change actually weakened the bicycle's structure. To compensate, other methods that added additional weight to the bicycle, sometimes as much as 10 pounds, were used. Therefore, the so-called weaker sex had to pedal harder on their bicycles (Garvey, 107, 109). By 1900, it was estimated that more than 400 manufacturers produced more than one million bicycles per year. Rich Taylor stated that "[i]t was the 'safety' bicycle, more than the automobile, that first lured Americans outdoors to play" (n.p.). After 1910, however, bicycle use declined dramatically due to the increased availability of the automobile.

The Automobile

In 1901, only about 13,000 automobiles were registered in the nation. For transportation and leisure, America still relied on its 18 million horses, 10 million bicycles, and trolleys, which were in almost every city. Rural and urban areas still contained numerous livery stables and blacksmiths. However, automobile pioneer Henry Ford would change all that.

Ford developed the first car that the average working person could afford, and he had a knack for grabbing the public's attention to sell more cars. In 1909, he perfected the assembly line technique by standardizing and mass-producing one car, the Model T, that sold for about $850. In 1914, he introduced a fully automated assembly line, which reduced the cost of the Model T to less than $500. In 1914 alone, Ford manufactured about 250,000 automobiles, a staggering number that represented almost half of all autos in the entire United States (Tompkins [1996, *American Decades: 1900-1909*], 177). Once cars entered the market, the simple and reliable Model T rapidly began to replace horses.

The initial impact of the automobile was felt in rural areas, as it allowed rural inhabitants easier access to towns and in-town services. The introduction of the tractor saved rural farmers time and labor. The automobile allowed the postal service to create rural free delivery (RFD) of mail. The postal delivery brought mail-order catalogs such as Sears and Roebuck and Montgomery Ward and these catalogs introduced rural inhabitants to a whole new world of conveniences and consumer products that were previously unattainable. The mail service connected them to social activity, amusements, and life away from the farm. The automobile provided for a freedom of movement and could travel distances that were unheard of just a few short years before.

A drive, however, could provide some new and unexpected surprises, and car owners quickly learned that essentials included repair tools, spare tires, and mechanical know-how to overcome the eventual breakdowns. The following excerpt describes a 1907 road trip from New York City to Jamestown, Virginia. The journey lasted three days and went through New York, Pennsylvania, Delaware, Maryland, and Virginia.

On encountering and fixing the inevitable flat tire:

> Down went a tire. . . . Off came the cover . . . and we set to work. . . . The precious tube was soon pushed inside the cover . . . the tire blown up, the wing-bolts tightened and we were ready for the road again.

Of the perils of the country road:

> The roads themselves are mostly bad, the surface heavy with loose sand and worn into deep ruts by the farmers' wagons.

Upon encountering horses:

> [T]he honk of our horn brought folks to their doors and horses and mules resented our approach by backing away and performing other antics . . . with a maximum of caution and a minimum of gasoline, we slowly passed. (www. ibiscom.com)

The automobile continually developed and made dramatic improvements in safety and speed. Up until 1914, however, the railroad, with almost 1 billion passengers per year, was still the main mode of travel for long distances, but mainly for the wealthy (Braden, 297). The automobile would eventually surpass the railroad and make vacations easier and more affordable for middle- and working-class individuals and families.

The Airplane

When Orville and Wilbur Wright made their first successful motorized airplane flight on December 3, 1903, the event was little more than a footnote in most newspapers. Many viewed the airplane as merely an experiment and a toy. As with all new technologies, many were unsure as to the specific purpose of flight. After 1910, as the nation began its fascination with flight, aircraft development came at a quicker rate. Airplanes were still considered a novelty, and in most rural areas, airplanes were virtually unknown. Rural farmers were both anxious and willing to pay an average of 25 cents per person (hard-earned money at the time) to see an aircraft in flight. With a minimum amount of stunting, flights at that time flew for about 15–20 minutes at altitudes not much higher than 3,000 feet. A pilots' pay usually depended on successful flights without any accidents or crashes (Phillips, n.p.). The appeal would spread to the cities' outskirts as people of all ages, genders, and classes wanted to see an air show. The reality of motorized flight would revolutionize the previously insurmountable barriers of time and distance. By 1914, the airplane was a permanent presence in America.

Vacation Resorts, the *Titanic*, and "Gone Fishing"

By 1900, middle-class and wealthy Americans had been vacationing and attending resorts for more than 40 years (Aron, 208). Middle-class Americans who had both the time and money chose either an oceanfront resort such as Ocean Grove or Asbury Park, both in New Jersey, or a chautauqua resort.

The first chautauqua at Lake Mohonk, New York, was a self-improvement summer resort that stressed Victorian middle-class notions of decency and morals with the goals of recreation, reason, and religion. Hundreds more would open as a series of well-established institutions controlled by a Methodist board of directors, located in mountain areas and lakefronts, mainly in the Northeast and Midwest. Curfews were strictly enforced, and gambling, alcohol, and Sunday admittance were not allowed (Aron, 123–126). By the early 1900s, some chautauquas were relaxing their resistance toward vigorous activities and began organizing bike clubs and baseball, football, golf, and tennis games.

The beach resorts at Ocean Grove and Asbury Park were both developed based on similar beliefs as the chautauquas. Historian Glenn Uminowicz noted that both resorts "played a major role in bringing Protestant middle class into the leisure revolution" (34). Both resorts promoted themselves as places where the problems of urban life could be solved by getting away from the pressures and crowds of the city (31).

In 1900, however, some leisure activities that were accepted at Asbury Park but banned at neighboring Ocean Grove included playing cards, dancing, and theater. Ocean Grove stressed plain fashion whereas Asbury Park encouraged "fashion watching" and strolling along the boardwalk to see others who were "putting on style" (that is, dressing fashionably for the time). The boardwalk also contained large pavilions, amusements, arcades, and an annual baby parade. The baby parade in 1912, for example, attracted more than 700 infant contestants and an estimated 150,000 spectators to the weeklong event. Reflecting the morality of the period, however, both resorts were appalled at the bathing suits of "scantily attired females" (Aron, 77). Based on the less restrictive ideas at Asbury Park, other profit-seeking entrepreneurs began to develop a mass leisure resort industry aimed at the middle class.

For the wealthy, luxurious vacations were standard. Some built affluent summer mansions in areas such as Newport, Rhode Island. Fashionable resorts that catered to the upper class and wealthy existed in places such as Atlantic City, New Jersey; Saratoga, New York; and Mackinac Island, Michigan. A popular leisure activity at affluent resorts was to promenade up and down the main thoroughfare. Other popular activities included casino gambling, attending horse races, visiting spas and springs, or bowling (also known as tenpins) (Aron, 87).

Regardless of their wealth, most resorts excluded Jews and Italians, and all excluded African Americans. Therefore, members of these groups began to construct and operate their own resorts. In the latter part of the 1910s, Jews and Italians began building in the Catskills and Adirondack regions of New York. African Americans began construction in the outskirts of Chicago and the Ohio valley, some even based on the chautauqua model.

Some chose ocean travel on luxurious ocean liners to vacation spots such as Miami Beach, Los Angeles, Cuba, Europe, and the Mediterranean. An event that shocked the country was the sinking of the ocean liner HMS *Titanic*, in April 1912. The *Titanic*, publicized as "unsinkable," struck an iceberg and sank within a few hours, taking the lives of more than 1,520 passengers and crew. The reality of the sinking represented a great tragedy and forewarned travelers that not all vacation and travel was without danger.

Also by the 1900s, reformers stressed the idea that women and poor children could absorb important lessons on vacation. Aron pointed out that "[c]amps like Gad's Hill [run by a Chicago settlement house] were not only teaching industrious work habits, they were also imparting a message about leisure and recreation; vacations for working-class people could be used productively rather than simply for relaxation, idleness, or worse." Camps for urban working-class youth were popular and were sponsored in more than 17 major cities, among them Chicago, New York, Washington, Buffalo, Cleveland, and Indianapolis (Aron, 187–188).

Vacations did exist for some working-class women but were not standard for the average working-class man. Two department stores, Bloomingdale's and Siegel & Cooper in New York, began sponsored week-long summer vacation trips for female employees in vacation houses at the New Jersey seashore. After 1910, with pressure mounting from labor organizations, other companies slowly began offering a paid vacation. Many factories, recognizing the need to refresh workers, would close in the summer for a one- or two-week period; however, for almost all of the working class it was a vacation without pay. Those immigrants and working-class employees without extra money chose inexpensive vacations such as visiting relatives, camping, or fishing.

Fishing was a leisure pursuit that existed in the nineteenth century and continued throughout the entire twentieth century. As a leisure activity, it was not limited to participants of any particular age, gender, economic situation, or geographical location. Catalogs and magazines such as *Boy's Life*, *Country Gentlemen*, *St. Nicholas Magazine*, and the *Saturday Evening Post* routinely advertised fishing items such as rods, reels, lures, tackle, and nets (Sheehy, 79). The fishing vacation was mainly a male tradition; camping (which included fishing) served as an inexpensive vacation for the whole family.

Camping with the intent to fish, however, was often a practicality. Historian Cindy Aron said that fishing "served as one way of feeding the family during the time the plant closed 'for vacation' or at least offered the possibility of saving on grocery expenses so that limited funds might be put to the cost of an inexpensive, nearby camping vacation" (Aron, 208).

CONCLUSION

The years 1900 to 1914 represented a struggle by progressives, reformers, and politicians to create a homogenous, although strictly segregated, American society. Due in part to ethnic differences among the population, society itself resisted fitting within the mold, forming new patterns of rest and relaxation. The period marked the beginning of mass consumption of consumer goods fueled by mass-market advertising. Individuals were being coerced into forming their household and leisure habits around what the adman told them. Children were being structured in their play habits, learning gender differentiation between competitive males and submissive females. The competitiveness would serve young American men well as they went "over there" to wage war. The "War to End All Wars" (World War I) would further change the fabric of American society and restrict the freedoms to pursue some of the simple pleasures.

CHAPTER 2

THE WAR TO END ALL WARS: 1914–1918

CHRONOLOGY

1914   The first traffic light is used; World War I begins in Europe.

1915   D. W. Griffith's *The Birth of a Nation* is released; the Ku Klux Klan is refounded; a German U-boat sinks the *Lusitania*; Margaret Sanger begins the National Birth Control League; 26,000 women suffragettes march in New York City; the Victrola becomes available to the mass market.

1916   The first self-service grocery store opens in the United States.

1917   The United States enters World War I; the Selective Service Act (the draft) is enacted; Congress passes the Eighteenth Amendment (Prohibition is ratified by the states in January 1919).

1918   Daylight saving time is introduced; the Boston Marathon is cancelled; influenza epidemic occurs; the armistice to end World War I is signed.

INTRODUCTION

During this period, leisure patterns continued much the same as they had in the early years of the twentieth century. The ability to freely pursue those activities and the choices of activities, however, would be greatly affected by the war and the influenza epidemic.

In August 1914, the "War to End All Wars," as World War I was known, began as Germany invaded France and one month later challenged Paris. The bloody Battle of the Marne slowed the advance. When the Germans were thwarted in their drive north at Antwerp, the war bogged down into a stalemate of horrible trench warfare and senseless slaughter. No one could foresee the mass destruction of the millions who would be killed in battles such as Ypres and the Somme.

The sinking of the *Lusitania* in 1915 and unrestricted submarine warfare in 1917 by Germany enraged the United States and prompted it to enter the conflict. In 1917, American troops were sent to Europe with rousing patriotic enthusiasm, as President Wilson declared a need to "make the world safe for democracy." The effects of the war spread to schools and recreation activities as each promoted themes of patriotism and loyalty, at the same time denouncing all that was German. With the war, no American was unaffected.

PUBLIC INTEREST

The "Leisure Problem"

The labor struggles for an eight-hour workday, with eight hours for sleep and eight hours for recreation, were combined with a need not only for leisure time but also for the individual's right to decide how to spend it. Labor leaders and progressive reformers lobbied for limited workdays and vacations; however, the idea of a paid vacation would not fully materialize until the 1920s. Historian Eric Foner stated that "labor advocates of the eight-hour day" claimed that "rising wages and a reduction in working hours would produce more leisure, more consumption, and more prosperity" (147).

Many legislators and civic leaders, however, still feared that any increase in leisure time would be used unwisely. Temperance societies also claimed that an eight-hour workday would increase drunkenness. According to historian Eric Larrabee,

> When the eight-hour laws were under discussion in 1916 and 1917, the prospect of such accretions of free time led governments and social reformers to talk fearfully of the leisure 'problem.' Temperance societies prepared for increased drunkenness and attention was centered on the real evils of commercialized recreation as it prevailed in most large cities. (Larrabee and Meyerson, 8)

The prevalent idea persisted that idle time would not be put to good use and would actually be a threat to society.

A constant theme of civic leaders, for example, throughout the entire century was that children (especially boys) being left unsupervised to play in the streets of the cities would lead to juvenile delinquency and that play in general was a waste of time. In fact, many cities considered any unsupervised play in urban streets unlawful—even if it was the nation's pastime, baseball. In 1917, Luther Gulick reported that

> [p]laying baseball on the streets of New York City [was] forbidden by a city ordinance. Yet every day during the spring a large proportion of the boys brought before the judge of Children's Court are there for the crime of playing ball. . . . The boys are in the position of lawbreakers, yet most of them are decent, respectable boys, frequently very young and much frightened. (quoted in Kraus [1971], 191)

Progressive educators John Dewey and Maria Montessori, however, introduced the idea that children's creative play was essential to their development. It did not hurt that the new consumerism recognized the profitable toy market for children. At that time, the large majority of all toys sold were sold at Christmas. Ironically, when the government was discussing suspension of Christmas gifts in 1917 to save material for war production, a group of toy manufacturers convinced the government that the toy rifles, tanks, and military figures would make the children "good soldiers." Toy sales figures rose dramatically during the war years.

Mass-produced toys, combined with the introduction of department stores and mail-order catalogs, marked the period's shift in production from capital goods to consumer products. The new consumerism began a changeover from the Victorian-era values of thrift and self-denial toward the avocation of personal fulfillment through the acquisition of material goods (Foner, 148).

Regarding the war, economic conditions were also a factor in America's choice of Great Britain as an ally. During the course of the first two years of the war America's trade with Germany dropped from $169 million to a mere $1 million. At the same time, trade with Great Britain rose from $825 million to more than $3 billion. From a simple economic standpoint it was easy to determine which side America would support to win the war. One newspaper editor, William A. White, summed up the alliance: "[Americans] felt happy because they were busy making money. Naturally as the Allies were our customers, they became our friends" (quoted in Asinof, 24–26).

The increase in production, profits, and demand for labor were such that by 1918 many workers had won the eight-hour workday. The shortage of labor also provided the opportunity for many women and African Americans to enter the industrialized workforce in great numbers. The newfound prosperity allowed the working class purchasing power to obtain material goods and "toys" for their recreational and leisure pleasure.

Committee on Public Information and the "Four-minute Men"

In April 1917, the same month that America declared war on Germany, President Woodrow Wilson formed the Committee on Public Information (CPI) and picked his friend and former journalist George Creel to head the agency. Wilson knew that "making the world safe for democracy" meant launching an advertising campaign to convince the American public to support the war. The CPI enlisted the aid of journalists, illustrators, advertising men, and academic scholars to deliver the message — an intrusion not only into the privacy of Americans' homes but also into their minds. The CPI disrupted and changed the daily lives of all Americans as they used every form of media available to them, including newspapers, magazines, movies, posters, and the spoken word.

The CPI devised a network of volunteer speakers, eventually numbering more than 75,000, who became known as the four-minute men. (Four minutes was considered the average time that an American maintained interest in a subject.) In this time before the widespread use of radio, the idea to create a network of speakers was a brilliant innovation for mass propaganda and advertising. The plan was to deliver a uniform message on a specific weekly topic. Between May 12, 1917, and December 24, 1918, forty-six different "official" topics were presented such as "Food Conservation," "Why We Are Fighting," and "The Meaning of America." Eventually the four-minute men entered all types of public gatherings, including churches, synagogues, lodges, labor unions, social clubs, lumber camps, county fairs, public schools, and Sunday schools. Speakers were known to deliver the message at bridge clubs, garden clubs, amusement parks, public parks, and sometimes in the native languages of their listeners, for example Yiddish or Italian. During this time they also spoke nearly every night in the motion picture theaters (Foner, 169).

To reinforce the message, posters were displayed in all kinds of public facilities, including trolleys, subway stations, schools, and post offices. The posters were extremely effective and inexpensive and were also reprinted in newspapers and magazines. The government, with help from the CPI, was literally continually in the face of all Americans. The most recognizable poster was that of Uncle Sam pointing a finger with the words "I Want You for the U.S. Army." On a trip anywhere out of the house or even a drive in the country one was sure to see a CPI poster on the new roadside billboards or even on the side of a farmer's barn.

An important element of the CPI was the civic and educational division that enlisted the aid of academic scholars, particularly history teachers. This division printed more than 105 publications and distributed more than 75 million total copies of scholarly pamphlets. One example was published in April 1917 and was titled "What Can History Teachers Do Now?" (Mock and Larson, 184, 68). In addition to the indoctrination of students' minds, all schools were encouraged to provide recreation geared to prepare the nation's youth for the fight. Colleges in particular served as "pre-induction centers," and 217 colleges offered, as a required course, the CPI-prepared "War Issues Courses."

No corner of America was left uncovered; in all the CPI had 7,629 branches covering not only every state, but also the territorial possessions of Alaska, Hawaii, Puerto Rico, Guam, Samoa, the Panama Canal Zone, and the Philippines. Rural areas were covered through a CPI division, the Bureau of State Fair Exhibits, that reached an estimated seven million people (Mock and Larson, 70).

Many civic and educational organizations such as the Red Cross, the Young Men's Christian Association (YMCA), settlement houses, churches, the Camp Fire Girls, and the Boy Scouts used their free time to support the CPI and aid the war effort (Mock and Larson, 185). In April of 1917, for example, shortly after the declaration of war, the Boy Scouts and the Women's Suffrage Party placed more than 20,000 recruiting posters throughout New York City. The new "poster armies" appeared in all the major cities (Rickards, 22).

The message that the cause of American involvement was pure, righteous, and blessed by God was continually stressed. In his autobiography, George Creel called the job performed by the CPI "the world's greatest adventure in advertising" (quoted in Uschan, 68) with the main intent being to enlist soldiers in the war effort.

War Leisure and the Invasion of Leisure

In order to meet the demand for soldiers, Congress passed the Selective Service Act of 1917. The new draft law required registration of all male citizens between the ages of 21 and 30. To ensure draft registration and patriotism, the government sanctioned a voluntary organization called the American Protective League (APL). The APL, eventually in every major city and numbering more than 250,000 members, simply amounted to a group of citizen vigilantes who used their leisure time to voluntarily police streets and neighborhoods for draft dodgers, dissidents, and slackers (Asinof, 50). Mainly as a result of fear, more than 24 million men eventually registered, and more than 4 million served in the armed forces.

The draft process, however, moved so quickly that the government enlisted the aid of many outside agencies to support the mobilization. The Playground and Recreation Association, for example, was enlisted to create a system of recreation and leisure in and around the military camps. More than 2,700 full-time workers and 60,000 volunteers provided "wholesome" activities such as sports, social activities, live entertainment, pageants, sing-a-longs, dances, and parties. The volunteer services of the YMCA and the Red Cross also sought ways to keep the soldiers occupied during their idle hours, providing writing paper and postage stamps among other supplies. Volunteers also organized events such as boxing matches, provided Victrolas for music, and arranged to show movies on the home front, on the troop transport ships, and in Europe (Kraus [1971], 201).

The army was also concerned with the lure of sexual vice for its soldiers. The army, aware of what venereal disease (VD) could do to its troops, initiated an awareness campaign distributed through pamphlets that provided many young men with the first-ever method of sex education. To offset sexual temptations, the army provided recreational centers.

The recreational centers had theaters to show motion pictures, stage plays, vaudeville, or concerts. With the aid of the Red Cross, dances were held and sporting events organized. Regarding his social life, one soldier said his trip to Europe was "the most important event in my life" (Kennedy, 206). For many of the recruits, the trip to Europe was usually their first and only opportunity to travel overseas.

On the home front, nativism and "100 percent" Americanism was the accepted law of the land. Those choosing to relax by listening to the new Victrola (an early version of the phonograph that played record albums) usually had a choice only of patriotic and propaganda songs. One example was Irving Berlin's "Let's All Be Americans Now" (1917). As part of the Americanization process, two congressional acts, the Espionage Act of 1917 and the Sedition Act of 1918, had far-reaching implications on the personal lives and leisure pursuits of Americans.

These two laws allowed the postmaster general authority to censor and eliminate any material deemed "unsuitable." Distributing or receiving any periodicals, magazines, or newspapers thought to contain seditious material could result in a prison sentence. Sometimes the mere continuation of previous interests and pursuits had serious implications. Speaking German, for example (or any foreign language, for that matter), was not only suspicious but was against the law in some states. Newspaper editors in Milwaukee and New York were sentenced to prison for publishing antiwar and pro-German stories. Eugene Debs, noted socialist and presidential candidate, for example, was sentenced to ten years in prison for making an antiwar speech.

The "invasion of leisure" extended into individuals' homes and churches. One Reverend Waldron spoke of war as contradicting the Bible and was sentenced to 15 years in prison. A woman in Missouri, Rose Pastor Stokes, wrote a letter to a Kansas City newspaper denouncing the monetary profit made from war; she received a prison sentence of ten years. In all, more than 1,500 people were arrested under such charges (Asinof, 51).

Anti-German sentiment reached a fever pitch. Words such as *hamburger*, *sauerkraut*, and *dachshunds*, were replaced in American English with "liberty sandwich" "liberty cabbage" and "liberty pup." The extremes carried over to the city of Cincinnati, Ohio, where the sale of pretzels was banned. Many orchestras and operas eliminated any German songs and composers, including Beethoven, Bach, and Mozart. Young men whose only apparent crime was to be German or to speak the language were lynched in Butte, Montana; St. Louis, Missouri; and Cincinnati, Ohio, to cite but a few. Historian Eliot Asinof stated,

> The country had gone mad, but the madness became normal. The submission of individual liberties to the dictates of the state was the greatest in [American] history. The government had succeeded in taking away—and the individual in giving up—the rights it had taken centuries to win. . . . With war, or threat of war, people could be led to mass solidarity with cheap slogans from gushing admen and acquiescence from the president [of the United States]. . . . The mystery was the ease with which this was accomplished while the average American continued to believe he was free. (52)

With the continual barrage of propaganda supplied by newspapers, magazines, movies, and the CPI, Americans were convinced that an invasion on U.S. shores was imminent. The only invasion, however, was the invasion on personal liberties and on Americans' leisure time.

LIFESTYLES

Life on the Home Front and Suffragettes

In their leisure time, most immigrants kept to themselves or to towns where others shared their ethnic background. To supply a support network and offer recreation for their communities, they created fraternal organizations. In St. Paul, Minnesota, for example, a Czechoslovakian fraternal organization, The Sokol, operated the yearly Czech Slet, a gymnastics festival that was a carryover from their European heritage. In addition, they sponsored folk dances, plays, and educational programs. Similar fraternal orders that sponsored recreation and leisure activities were the Croatian Fraternal Order in St. Paul, Minnesota; the Polish Knights of St. Casimir in Cleveland, Ohio; and the Italian Society of Victor Emanuel III in Waukesha, Wisconsin. Not all ethnic celebrations were connected to fraternal organizations. Mexican Americans in Mogollon, New Mexico, celebrated with an annual parade in honor of Cinco de Mayo (the Fifth of May, a celebration of Mexican culture to commemorate an 1862 victory over the French [museum text, Ellis Island]).

Many religious holiday celebrations such as Christmas and Easter contained European traditions and were usually observed within the home. The week between Christmas and New Year's Day traditionally was a time for visiting relatives, friends, and neighbors. New Year's Day was a day for family celebration. These holidays, however, were becoming more commercialized and secularized mainly due to the growing consumerism and advertising for the mass-market audience. Halloween became a favorite children's holiday. In 1914, encouraged by advertisers, Congress officially acknowledged the second Sunday in May as Mother's Day, a day of leisure for mothers. Although not officially sanctioned, Father's Day was celebrated on the third Sunday in June (Braden, 75–76).

For the middle class, activities such as gardening and fancy work (see chapter 1) were signs of wealth and cultural refinement. Many middle-class women were becoming more involved in public life by attending college, working for reform, campaigning for suffrage, and participating in other public activities. Supporting the war also became a popular middle-class leisure-time pursuit that eventually spread to all the other classes. Ornamental gardens, also known as victory gardens, extended to the outer portions of a home and created a trend that became more popular and that would continue well after the war.

Within the home, women and children were encouraged to conserve all resources for the war effort. Many leisure pursuits were put aside to allow time to prepare for and support the war effort. For example, families saved countless tons of fruit pits, and deposited them in collection centers to make charcoal filters for gas masks. Free time was used to knit socks and sweaters for the soldiers in arms.

Volunteerism in support of the war took the place of leisure. In 1914, for example, the Red Cross had almost 480,000 members in about 5,000 branches across the country. By 1918, more than 25 percent of the American population (more than 28 million adults and children) volunteered and were actively involved in more than 30,000 branches (www.redcross.org/museum/).

Anti-immigrant feelings were still widespread during this time. In 1917, Congress passed legislation restricting the entrance of immigrants from more than 33 nations, and almost all immigration stopped. Immigrants from these countries had been admitted to the United States prior to the war. In addition, literacy tests were instituted that further restricted immigration (museum text, Ellis Island). Immigrants however, had been a major source of labor, and with the restrictions (and the draft) came labor shortages.

The push to work in the labor shortage market sometimes included 14-to-16-hour days, leaving little time for leisure. Many women, previously not working outside the home, also filled the workplace, replacing the men who left for Europe. Many companies instituted preparedness drills during which businessmen interrupted their day to do exercise and prepare for the "call to arms." Women also drilled and learned how to shoot rifles. Children were encouraged to play a popular new game that included "trench warfare," going "over the top," and attacking the "Hun." Due to additional labor shortages in the north, large numbers of southern African Americans migrated and further changed the way Americans lived.

Prior to 1914, only 10 percent of the nation's African Americans lived outside the former Confederate states. Newspapers such as the *Chicago Defender* told of the opportunities for higher-paying jobs and a better life for African Americans in the industrialized north. As a result, more than 500,000 African Americans moved to northern cities such as St Louis, Cleveland, Detroit, New York, Chicago, and Baltimore. The mass migration brought cultural influences such as the delta blues and New Orleans jazz from the South to Chicago and a renaissance of writers, poets, and artists to New York's Harlem. Not all northerners openly accepted the migration. In July 1917, angry white residents in St. Louis killed more than 40 African Americans and burned many newly arrived migrants' homes. With the racial conflict at home and the call for African Americans to enlist to fight the war in Europe, the NAACP ironically asked President Wilson, "Why not make America safe for democracy?" (Boyer, Clark, 668).

The suffragettes also asked Wilson for democracy at home—for women's right to vote. In 1915, more than 26,000 women suffragettes marched in New York City. The Women's Christian Temperance Movement (WCTU) aided many suffragettes and collectively campaigned not only for the right to vote, but also against vice and alcohol. The WCTU viewed drinking as a male-dominated leisure pursuit and sought the support of the millions of American women who cherished their roles as wives and mothers. Objections to the saloon and the temperance movement also constituted an attack against the leisure pursuits of a vast majority of working-class and immigrant males. As a result, Prohibition became a major issue during the war years.

The temperance movement of the WCTU and the Anti Saloon League (ASL) also added to the growing anti-German sentiment. The most popular saloon drink was beer, and German immigrants or their descendants owned most of the breweries. Drinking had previously been banned in both the military and in areas surrounding military camps. Temperance advocates and supporters of Prohibition, therefore, linked the cause to patriotism, claiming that if the soldiers could go "dry" in support of democracy, the people at home could make the same sacrifice. In response, Congress passed the Eighteenth Amendment on December 18, 1917, which was ratified by the states on January 29, 1919, making Prohibition the law of the land.

Black Death: The Great Flu Epidemic of 1918–1919

By 1918, the war had become an acceptable part of everyday life. The Great Flu Epidemic, however, came without warning and disrupted Americans' lifestyles. The first wave of the flu hit in the spring of 1918 and lasted about three months. Although many were sick nationwide, the sickness was not known to be fatal. The recurrence of the flu in the fall of 1918, however, was devastating beyond compare and continued until the spring of 1919. In a short time span, the flu caused more deaths than all the combined military deaths of World War I. In Europe, more American soldiers (57,000) died from the flu than from the war (54,000). In America, more than 500,000 people died, and more than 20 million became seriously ill. Worldwide estimates cited influenza as the cause of death for an astounding 100 million people (Kolata, 5).

Doctors did not understand why this flu was so deadly. No known cure was available, and the pattern of infection was inconsistent. Those most at risk were children under 5 years of age, older adults aged 70 to 74, and young adults aged 20 to 40. Only one thing was certain—the flu was highly contagious. In a three-month period in the fall of 1918, the flu immobilized the entire nation as it hit equally hard in the cities, rural towns, and even in remote Alaskan Eskimo villages. All sorts of activities, both personal and work related, ceased. The outbreak prevented people from everyday leisure pursuits from taking a simple walk to attending a ball game. Attending a public event put one at risk and could result in death.

In an attempt to slow the spread of the disease, schools, churches, theaters, and other public places were closed. It became common to see people wearing gauze masks in public. In Tucson, Arizona, for example, specific written ordinances were issued stating that all people in public spaces of personal interaction were required to wear gauze masks. People were able to do very little other than stay home and care for the sick and bury the dead (Kolata, 22–23).

The flu epidemic notwithstanding, the war was still active. However, almost every military camp was under quarantine as the army reported over 36 percent of its troops infected (Kolata, 7, 18). The horrible effect of the flu in one of the military camps is illustrated in a letter dated September 29, 1918, by a doctor known only as "Roy," who wrote the following account in Camp Devens, Massachusetts:

> Camp Devens is near Boston, and has about 50,000 men, or did have before this epidemic broke loose. . . . This epidemic started about four weeks ago, and has developed so rapidly that the camp is demoralized and all ordinary work is held up till it has passed. These men start with what appears to be an ordinary attack of LaGrippe or Influenza, and when brought to the [hospital] they very rapidly develop the most viscous type of Pneumonia that has ever been seen. Two hours after admission they have the Mahogany spots over the cheek bones, and a few hours later you can begin to see the Cyanosis extending from their ears and spreading all over the face, until it is hard to distinguish the coloured [sic] men from the white. It is only a matter of a few hours then until death comes, and it is simply a struggle for air until they suffocate. It is horrible. . . . to see these poor devils dropping like flies sort of gets on your nerves. . . . It takes special trains to carry away the dead. For several days there were no coffins and the bodies piled up something fierce, we used to go down to the morgue (which is just back of my ward) and look at the boys laid out in long rows. It beats any sight they ever had in France after a battle. ("Roy's Letter," *British Medical Journal,* 1632-1633)

The complete horror and reality of the flu could not be conveyed into mere words. Many of those who lived during the period and survived refused to talk about the devastation or write about it in memoirs. If mentioned at all, the sheer grief and horror of the awful death was usually not recorded in personal detail. Many individuals lost parents, one or more siblings, and other relatives and friends, sometimes in the course of only a few days. When combined with the destruction and death of friends and loved ones in the war, the total traumatic effect cannot be measured in any analysis or written work. After such a devastating period, many individuals only wanted to try to forget the horror and get on with their lives.

ENTERTAINMENT

Newspapers, Magazines, Advertising, and Books

Leisure reading among Americans continued to increase. In 1914, newspapers introduced photojournalism with special sections devoted to photographs. (Prior to this time newspapers mainly contained drawings and illustrations.) By 1918, more than 2,400 newspapers were in print with an estimated circulation of more than 33 million (Uschan, 44). In late 1913, the *New York Sunday World* published the first crossword puzzle, which quickly became a popular feature. After the war, the crossword puzzle would be picked up by most publications. Newspapers carried advertisements for new popular children's toys such as Erector Sets and Lincoln Logs. Consumers could also search the pages for the increasing number of advertisements for automobiles, vacations, and ocean travel.

In this age before widespread radio use, television, and mass communication, the written word of newspapers was far-reaching. Oftentimes in newspapers and in the general dissemination of information, rumors were rampant and facts were few. The idea of "yellow journalism" (a term applied to newspapers and periodicals that distort and sensationalize the news to attract readers) was prominent, aided mostly by patriotic fever. President Wilson also enforced the Comstock Law that allowed for indiscriminate moralistic censorship of any written material. Propaganda filled the newspapers, and many people did not notice that the news and facts were fed to the newspapers directly from the CPI. In addition, the British navy cut Germany's transatlantic cable; therefore, all news concerning the war came via England and was heavily censored in England's favor. As a result, according to Eliot Asinof, America was "perhaps the most ill-informed nation on earth" (60).

Apart from increased newspaper circulation, magazines were still the most popular choice for readers. Magazines also served as an instrumental support network of the CPI. Almost every popular magazine of the time contained numerous pages of artwork, illustrations, and slogans supplied by the CPI to support the war effort.

Despite the popularity of leisure reading, many reformers still considered reading of anything besides the Bible to be immoral—along with alcohol, contraception, pool halls, and motion pictures. With the support of many ministers, parents, and the Comstock Law, reformers were successful in attacking and eliminating many forms of written material, including many of the dime novels and romance literature that were popular among the youth.

The most popular book among young readers was *Seventeen* by Booth Tarkington (1916). Popular adventure series books were mainly geared toward specific genders and ages. For girls, popular series included the *Bobbsey Twins*, the *Ruth Fielding* series, *Motor Girls*, and *Girl Aviator*. Boys enjoyed the adventures of the *Rover Boys* and *Tom Swift* (Rollin, 27). Among adults, best-sellers with the war as a central theme were popular, including Alan Seeger's poems in *Letters and Diary*, Robert W. Service's *Rhymes of a Red Cross Man*, and Arthur Guy Empey's *Over the Top*. Empey was an American who went to England to serve and fight in World War I. The book contains tales of the front, very positive in nature; it sold more than 350,000 copies in the first year and further helped the war effort (Kennedy, 182–183).

Amusement Parks

Amusement parks were still in vogue during this time; however, the war did have a direct bearing on the nature of the attractions contained in them. By 1917, with the continued threat of submarine activity and fear of invasion, the seaside

Atlantic City, New Jersey, 1915: Beach, boardwalk, and vaudeville theater—all forms of inexpensive entertainment that attracted all classes of people. Courtesy of Library of Congress.

amusement parks such as Atlantic City and Coney Island, which were so famous for their nightly displays of millions of lights, were forced into nightly blackouts. The reality of war and death also helped to phase out most of the public fascination with the "disaster attractions" that were so trendy in the previous decade.

MUSIC AND THEATER

Broadway and Vaudeville

During this time, Broadway was considered to be the premier entertainment site of the world. It continued to grow as a favored leisure pursuit of the wealthy and middle class. Lighthearted fare and musicals that featured contemporary, romanticized American settings dominated Broadway. *Ziegfeld's Follies* were one example that contained extravagant song, dance, and sketches. Other favorites included musicals by Jerome Kern, Irving Berlin, and George Gershwin, the dancing of Vernon and Irene Castle, and humorists Eddie Cantor and Will Rogers. In 1917 and 1918, with the war at hand, many shows used the war and patriotism as their themes.

The traditional fare of Vaudeville stage productions, however, was most adversely affected by the tremendous popularity of motion pictures. In a short period, from 1914 to 1918, many cities converted their large Vaudeville theaters into movie houses. In order to survive, Vaudeville compromised, offering a balance between movies and stage acts.

Music and Ragtime

Ragtime remained popular as did patriotic songs. Upon the American declaration of war in April 1917, George M. Cohan wrote the patriotic hit "Over There." Other songwriters and singers were quickly caught up in the patriotic fever. George Gershwin, for one, responded with a comedic tune of army life, "Oh, How I Hate to Get Up in the Morning." Singers such as Enrico Caruso and Al Jolson staged shows to raise money for the war effort.

No longer did Americans require access to Broadway or the big cities to hear the music and vocal talents of entertainers. Thomas Edison's talking machine, the Victrola, enabled the American public to hear these entertainers in the comforts of a family living room. The middle class especially began buying the Victrolas and the recordings of popular artists.

The Motion Picture

Sound had yet to become part of the movies, but as film companies began moving to the warmer climate of Hollywood, California, the public's fondness of movies continued to increase. The main attraction was the feature film that ran between one and a half to two hours long. A *New York Times* article dated July 30, 1916, estimated movie attendance at 25 million people per week and further stated that "[a]ccording to statistics compiled by the National Board of Review of Motion Pictures . . . boys and girls constitute only 17 per cent of the average audience. The evening audiences are made up almost entirely of adults" (8).

Most middle-class and wealthy individuals still viewed the movies as the domain of working-class people and immigrants and not a respectable entertainment environment. To attract the middle-class and wealthy audiences, movie producers sought to eliminate negative aspects of their productions. Moviemakers and reformers voluntarily joined together to establish the National Board of Censorship (NBC). The board mainly censored and regulated depictions of sexual and social relationships between the genders. Beginning in 1914, the NBC reviewed almost all of the Hollywood films as producers sought to make films with acceptable themes.

Short movies called "serials" achieved wide popularity during this time. One example of a movie serial was *The Perils of Pauline* (1914), a continuing serial that first introduced movie audiences to the cliff-hanger ending. These serial shorts usually lasted about 15 to 20 minutes and ended with Pauline the "hapless heroine" dangling in a dangerous scene. The anticipation of how Pauline would be rescued caused the audience to come back week after week. Hollywood also gained respectability by producing many feature films with acceptable wartime themes.

The popularity of the feature film *Battle Cry of Peace* (1915) represented a new development in which the feature film served as both entertainment and propaganda. Other movies of a similar nature followed including *The Yanks Are Coming*, *To Hell with the Kaiser*, and *The Kaiser, the Beast of Berlin*. One film, *Our Colored*

Fighters, was produced as an attempt to specifically encourage enlistment of African Americans (Mock and Larson, 139).

However, the most notorious film of the period, D. W. Griffith's *The Birth of a Nation* (1915), was not about World War I but about America's Civil War. The movie was the first of the grand Hollywood spectacles, incorporating many innovative camera angles. From a social point of view, it not only stereotyped and caricatured African Americans, but it also gave credibility and rebirth to the Ku Klux Klan (KKK). A *Variety* review stated that the film "knew just what kind of a picture would please all white classes" (Nasaw, 202). *Birth of a Nation* was a major financial success, and crowds lined the streets to see the film. Even President Wilson and members of his cabinet viewed the film favorably (Kennedy, 281). The acceptance of the racial stereotypes and the rebirth of the KKK would drastically affect the everyday pursuits of African Americans and other minorities for many decades to follow.

With the war at hand, movie audiences were particularly fond of comedies. Favorites included movies featuring Charlie Chaplin and comedies by Mack Sennett with the Keystone Kops. Sennett wrote of the intricacies of making a comedic movie and the difficulty of making an audience laugh:

> [T]he time is past and almost forgotten when you could be sure of a laugh by merely making one of your characters walk up behind another and suddenly push him down or trip him, or do any one of the scores of stunts the old slapstick comedian was able to get away with. To put a comedy over now you have got to have a story—a real story, filled with human interest. . . . I have tried my hand at acting in all kinds of film plays and later at directing them, and I am quite frank to say that comedies are the hardest of all to act and to produce. ("The Comedy 'Fillum' Man," *New York Times*, 30 July 1916: 7)

All of the theaters—Vaudeville, Broadway, and the movies—joined in the patriotic effort. The theaters proudly decorated both their interiors and exteriors with banners, bunting, and flags patriotic red, white, and blue. Movie theaters gladly put up recruiting posters, served as sites for patriotic rallies, sold Liberty Bonds, and provided a forum for the four-minute men. At the same time, Hollywood was able to eliminate the notion that the movies themselves were not respectable.

The popularity of the feature film and the association of patriotism with the movies changed the mindset of many Americans so that they began choosing to spend their leisure time at the movies. Prior to 1914, those of the so-called respectable classes would not entertain the thought of entering a movie theater. However, by 1918, millions of individuals from all walks of life flocked to the movies.

SPORTS AND GAMES

Amateur and Professional

Americans increasingly embraced sports as both spectators and participants and wanted a relief from the constant bombardment of war propaganda. The sports pages of newspapers carried equal amounts of sports results for both amateur and professional sports. Baseball continued to become more popular and was the most popular spectator sport. In 1916, under the corporate sponsorship of Wanamaker's department store, the Professional Golfers Association (PGA) was formed and held its first tournament. On the amateur level, golf remained well established among the wealthy and at private country clubs. By 1917, with the construction of more than 470 public golf courses, the game was becoming more accessible and was gaining appeal among the middle class (Braden, 174). Women continued to become more interested in golf, but discrimination and restrictions against them at public and private clubs continued.

The first Stanley Cup in hockey was played in 1917. At the same time, attendance at horse racing tracks continued to increase. Bookmaking, or taking bets, was still illegal in most states. Among the popular amateur sports were yachting, polo, tennis, soccer, and track and field. Tennis expanded beyond the East Coast as the construction of clay courts within the cities increased the sport's appeal to the middle and working classes. Most of these events were held in preparation for Olympic competition. As the war in Europe intensified, the Olympic Games scheduled for 1916 in Berlin were canceled.

America's involvement in World War I directly affected sports on the home front. Civilians were asked to support the war effort and the War Industries Board (WIB) tried to convince both industry and civilians to conserve material (Zieger, 70). In response to conserve both gasoline and steel, the popular Indianapolis 500 auto race was suspended in both 1917 and 1918. In order to promote patriotic support of the troops, PGA golf tournaments were suspended in 1917 and 1918. The April 1918 Boston Marathon was also cancelled. In its place was a relay competition of ten-man military teams from neighboring camps, each running about two and a half miles (Tompkins [1996, *American Decades: 1910–1919*], 535–550). Recreational events for the almost two million stateside soldiers were also organized in sports such as football, basketball, boxing, wrestling, baseball, golf, shooting, soccer, swimming, and tennis.

TRANSPORTATION AND VACATION

Traveling to the "outdoors" became more popular, mostly among the wealthy classes in the eastern and midwestern cities, who viewed it as a civilized pursuit. The most popular of the destinations was the Adirondack Mountains. With a vast network of lakes, rivers, and streams, the mountains offered opportunities for hunting, fishing, boating, and camping. The western portion of the United States was still considered by many to be untamed and hazardous.

The Automobile

In 1914, Henry Ford shocked the business world by reducing his workers' shifts to an eight-hour day/forty-hour week and by doubling their salaries. His fellow millionaires labeled him "a traitor to his class." Ford's theory on increased wages and more free time for his workers was that these changes would reduce labor cost, increase production, and therefore increase profits. Ford ardently opposed laziness and did not support leisure time. His motto was "life is work." He spoke out publicly against the moral decay of the working class citing alcohol,

Detroit, Michigan, 1917: The new automobile also created the traffic jam. Courtesy of Library of Congress.

gambling, jazz music, dancing, city life, and art as working-class vices (Time-Life Books [1969, *This Fabulous Century: 1910–1920*, Vol. 2], 99). The shorter work-day and additional pay, however, did in fact allow the workers to seek out new leisure pursuits—especially those involving the automobile.

In 1914, the new production techniques of the automated Ford assembly line produced cars at an astounding rate. The company standardized auto parts, produced only the Model T, and lowered the price to $440, which made the automobiles accessible to almost any individual. Yearly production increased from 460,000 cars in 1914 to 1.8 million in 1917. During this period, 126 other companies also manufactured automobiles. Some companies, such as Oldsmobile and Cadillac, sought the high-end market with cars costing in excess of $2,000. By 1914, most of the high-end cars eliminated the dangerous hand-crank starter and included a self-starter, thereby making the car more marketable to women. Some companies also introduced payment installment plans to make purchase easier (Bruccoli and Layman [1996, *American Decades: 1910–1919*], 177).

Auto-Touring and Auto-Camping

With the advent of the automobile, Americans discovered a new type of inexpensive vacation—"auto-camping." Even Henry Ford, despite his objection to idle time, endorsed this newfound leisure trend. Photographs of the period showed Ford and others "camping" with their automobiles. Some have speculated that

A family stops by the side of the road for an impromptu "auto-camping" picnic, around 1914. A Ford Model T is in the background. Courtesy of Brown Bros.

Ford did this for publicity to sell more cars. In either case, Americans seemed to enjoy taking Sunday drives or extended auto-camping trips. For most, the automobile provided a family with an easy and affordable escape from the city or the farm. More adventurous travelers packed the car with essentials such as food and clothing, and the family or group drove to an out-of-the-way place and camped for a few days. The roadside site chosen was usually used free of charge. The vacation schedule was left up to the individuals, and the secluded spots chosen for auto-camping offered a relaxation different than that found at the organized resorts or in the crowded cities. According to a Public Broadcast Service (PBS) documentary, auto-camping was becoming increasingly popular during this time and the "life of leisure" could be had "for the next day, week, or even month" (PBS Online, "Car Camping," n.p.).

Automobile travel offered new experiences and new scenery to Americans. In response to automobile travel, many ancillary businesses arose, such as roadside camping areas, hotels, restaurants, and service stations. Local towns and chambers of commerce also joined forces with car dealers and formed "trail associations," which provided, among other things, road signs, maps, and route markers.

Popular routes and travel destinations were published in newspapers and magazines. The following excerpt is from an advertisement by the Automobile Club of America that outlined a round-trip route from Boston, Massachusetts, through the White Mountains in New Hampshire:

> [O]ur round trip through New Hampshire is laid out with the Massachusetts capital as the starting point. . . . Dixville Notch is 235 miles from Boston, at the northern extremity of the White Mountains. It is situated in a region of unique beauty and the country round is famous for its fishing and hunting. . . . winding amid lofty hills, . . . The Percy Peaks, over 3,000 feet high, rise conspicuously in the east. . . . The last lap of the trip follows the valley of the Merrimack, the largest city in New Hampshire. . . . the road runs through Billerica and Burlington to Boston . . . and rounding off a total distance of the whole tour of 495 miles. (*New York Times*, 30 July 1916, XX: 2)

Whether it was in a $440 Model T or a $1,450 Stearns-Knight Four, auto-camping and auto-touring were trends that became more and more popular and appealed to all classes. The automobile offered a newfound freedom for Americans—mainly privacy.

The Airplane and Dogfights

Although aviation did not play a significant military role in World War I, the tales of fighter pilots captured the imagination of the nation. During the course of the war, development in aircraft speed and altitude increased dramatically. In 1914, the maximum altitude for the 80 horsepower (hp) rotary engines used in airplanes was about 6,000–8,000 feet, with airspeeds around 60 miles per hour (mph). By 1918, some planes with 130 hp stationary engines could achieve altitudes close to 20,000 feet and fly at over 120 mph. Development and production of wartime aircraft would slow after the war; however, the public was hooked on aviation.

U.S. newspapers were quick to seize upon the popular tales of airmen, especially those of a French unit of American volunteers called the Lafayette Escadrille. Americans on the home front followed the accumulating aerial victories and the tales of chivalry in the air and dogfights (the term was applied to the machine-gun battle between opposing aircraft).

In the 1920s, attending air shows performed by barnstorming (see Chapter 3) pilots would become a favorite pastime for many Americans. The appeal of the flying aces would intertwine with American leisure pursuits as the image of the chivalrous lone aviator would be popularized in movies, novels, magazines, and hobbies throughout the century. In the 1990s, the aviation terms *dogfights* and *joystick* entered the language of popular leisure pursuits in reference to video games and computers.

Ocean Travel and the *Lusitania*

During the first quarter of the twentieth century, the grand ocean liners were becoming faster and offered luxurious travel and vacation opportunities. The Ocean Steamship Company, for example, advertised in the *New York Times* an

Cruise ships were a desired form of luxury vacation travel. The *Lusitania*, pictured here, embarks on her final voyage in 1915. She was torpedoed off the coast of England by German U-boats during World War I, which hastened America's entry into the European conflict. Courtesy of Library of Congress.

opportunity for leisure and relaxation asking Americans to "try an ocean trip" as an answer to "clear your brain, put vigor in your step, give you an appetite, and make you sleep like a top." One famous ocean liner, however, would drastically alter oceangoing vacation plans.

Tragedy occurred in May 1915 when the *Lusitania* (a British luxury ocean liner) sailed into a known war zone off the coast of Ireland and was torpedoed and sunk by a German U-boat. More than 1,100 passengers died, including 128 Americans. American newspapers picked up British propaganda that said the ship was sunk without warning. Historian John M. Taylor said, however, that on May 1, 1915, a day of sailing for the *Lusitania,* "the German embassy had inserted advertisements in a number of American newspapers warning of dangers in the waters around the British Isles" (155). The tragic fate of the *Lusitania* was that it was the first major ocean liner to be sunk by torpedo, and this angered Americans to the point of eventually declaring war on Germany in 1917.

As a result of the tragedy, ocean liner passenger lists declined. Companies sought ways to alleviate the fears and increase the number of travelers. During 1915 and 1916, newspaper advertisements carried specific wording in response to the submarine threat. The Scandinavian-American, a line to Norway, Sweden, and Denmark, claimed "Neutral Flag—Outside war zone—No contraband carried."

Many others simply stayed away from the war zones. The S.S. *Bermudian*, for example, advertised "a delightful sail of 1,140 miles" to Bermuda. Others simply chose to sail along the East Coast of the United States, with ports of call including Providence, Rhode Island; Boston, Plymouth, and Cape Cod, Massachusetts; New York; and Philadelphia. For those seeking vacations of a more exotic nature, other ports of call included Africa and South and Central America.

Vacation Resorts and Sharks in the Water

With many still fearful of ocean travel, resorts and hotels both on the seashore and in the mountains sought to fill the void. One New Jersey resort, the Diamond Spring Inn, advertised "a comfortable quiet and refined Hotel located in Morris County one of the healthiest spots in the country." One Cape Cod hotel, the Prospect House, advertised "golf, tennis, yachting, bathing garage, dance and concert daily" (*New York Times*, 18 July 1916: 16). Vacation resorts such as these still mainly were patronized by the wealthy and middle class.

Vacations were not fully available to the working classes; however, some forward-looking companies began to realize that work quality would improve for businesses that offered their workers time off. The National Cash Register Company (NCR), for example, had a regular two-week vacation in place by 1914. In an employee newsletter, the NCR encouraged workers to forget about work and enjoy the vacation summer period so that upon return to work employees would "be physically and mentally stronger, and [the] vacation [would] have been a profitable one" (Aron, 197).

Many NCR employees, as well as many other working- and middle-class employees, enjoyed oceanfront resorts such as Asbury Park, Ocean Grove, Atlantic City, and Coney Island for either an extended stay or a one-day excursion. During the height of the submarine scare, attractions and resorts by the water had to contend with another terror—the shark.

In July 1916, the New Jersey area was in the midst of a summer heat wave while some cities (mainly New York City) suffered through a polio epidemic (see chapter 6). Many were looking to escape the epidemic and to find relief from the heat, so they traveled to the beachfront resorts. In a span of two weeks, however, sharks in the waters off the New Jersey shore killed four swimmers and seriously injured a fifth. The unexplained attacks received national newspaper attention. Panic was widespread, and some blamed the Germans; even Congress became involved and authorized funds to eliminate the shark problem. Officials overreacted by hunting and killing any fish that looked like a shark. The biggest victims of the shark terror were the resorts and beaches. The negative publicity kept many from the oceanside resorts and out of the water causing business to suffer.

CONCLUSION

In making the world safe for democracy, the war to end all wars left many with doubts as to whether life would even continue. Worldwide war casualties of both dead and wounded amounted to more than 50 million, and the flu epidemic added another 100 million dead. Between the war and the flu, many Americans were affected. After such death and destruction, Americans, especially the returning war veterans, were ready to put the awful past behind them. The time was ripe for Americans to have fun and live recklessly—as the ensuing period of the Roaring Twenties would prove.

CHAPTER 3

BLACK DEATH TO BLACK TUESDAY: 1919–1929

CHRONOLOGY

1919   The second phase of the worldwide influenza epidemic hits; the gambling fix of baseball's World Series occurs.

1920   Prohibition officially begins; the first commercial radio broadcast is sent from KDKA in Pittsburgh; the U.S. urban population exceeds rural population; the Nineteenth Amendment guaranteeing women's right to vote is passed; the Jazz Age begins; flappers offend older adults.

1921   The 25th Boston Marathon is held.

1922   *Reader's Digest* is first published.

1923   The Charleston dance becomes popular; *Time* magazine is founded.

1924   More than four million Americans belong to the Ku Klux Klan.

1925   F. Scott Fitzgerald publishes *The Great Gatsby*.

1926   American Gertrude Caroline Ederle becomes the first woman to swim the English Channel.

1927   The first "talking" movie, *The Jazz Singer*, premieres; Lindbergh flies solo across the Atlantic; the Lindy hop dance craze begins.

1928   Bubble gum is invented; the first Mickey Mouse cartoon appears; the first *Oxford English Dictionary* is published; penicillin is discovered.

1929   The first Academy Awards are held; the New York stock market crash occurs.

INTRODUCTION

Sometimes known as the Roaring Twenties or the Jazz Age, this era was considered one of prosperity; as President Calvin Coolidge said, "the business of America is business." Business was in fact good, but mainly in the urban areas.

The progressives and moral reformers who for years had been attempting to control individuals' private lives made significant gains during this time, especially with Prohibition. In 1920, by virtue of the Nineteenth Amendment to the Constitution, the United States became the 27th nation in the world to give women the right to vote. Insulin was discovered in 1921, making it possible to treat the major health problem of diabetes and allowing millions of Americans with diabetes to regularly pursue the same leisure activities as others.

Many individuals were tired of the destruction and death of the war, labor strife, and influenza and simply wanted to put it all behind them, get on with their lives, and hopefully have a little fun. American leisure patterns would be greatly influenced by three major developments that became the most popular leisure pursuits: the movies, radio, and the automobile.

Between 1925 and 1927, Robert and Helen Lynd studied the lifestyles and leisure habits of the inhabitants of Muncie, Indiana (pop. 50,000 people). The published report *Middletown: A Study in Contemporary American Culture* (1929) became the classic portrait of small-city life in Middle America for the period. For this reason, numerous references to this study are included in this chapter.

PUBLIC INTEREST

The period began with an average 6-day, 60-hour workweek in 1919 that dropped to a 5-day, 48-hour workweek by 1929. Workers had additional time at the end of the workday, and both Saturday and Sunday became available for leisure. It was during this time that the concept of the weekend was born.

For many workers the reduction in work hours came as a result of bitter labor disputes and violent strikes. In the steel industry, for example, workers during the war had won an 8-hour workday, higher wages, and safer working conditions. After the war, with decreased production and demand, the United States Steel Corporation reinstituted a 12-hour, 7-day workweek at reduced wages (Asinof, 180). The corporations called for an "open shop" (nonunion) and insisted on a signed agreement that employees could not join a union. Federal support of the large corporations fueled paranoia against the supposed radical element of unionism and linked the cause of the unions and strikers to Bolsheviks. (The Bolsheviks were Russian workers who overthrew the Russian government in the Russian Revolution of 1917.) Newspapers distorted the images of striking workers, and a "Red Scare" swept the country. The Red Scare reflected fears that Bolshevism and communism would spread to the United States. To try to prevent this, the government sought to suppress any radicalism within the country.

In response, in 1919 the Department of Justice arrested and deported thousands of suspected Bolsheviks and radicals. Many of those deported were union organizers and immigrants. The union organizers were not Bolsheviks; they simply sought better working conditions, a shorter workday, decent wages, and as Mary Harris "Mother" Jones, an outspoken union supporter, stated, "What we need is a little leisure, time for music, playgrounds, a decent home, books and the things that make life worth living" (Asinof, 182).

However, the extra time off for leisure was not going to be left to the discretion of immigrants and urban workers. Nationwide anti-immigrant sentiment and disdain for the cities continued, as did the wartime obsession of demanding unwavering loyalty and 100 percent Americanism. The Johnson Quota Act of 1924 severely restricted immigration from southern Europe, eastern Europe, and Asia. The prewar average of more than one million immigrants was severely reduced. Of the 4.1 million immigrants who entered the country between 1919 and 1929, most were white Europeans from northern Europe, the British Isles, and Scandinavia. In 1927, for example, only 150,000 were allowed entry; of those 65,700 were Irish, and only 5,000 were Italian (museum text, Ellis Island). Immigrants as a whole also began an assimilation process into American culture formulated by religious affiliations, fraternal organizations, congressional laws, and government-supported recreational associations.

Fraternal Organizations and Youth Leadership

Many fraternal organizations that began initially as opportunities for business people to socialize, such as the Rotary Club, Kiwanis Club, and Lions Club, expanded into community service organizations and grew in membership almost tenfold. (Fraternal orders were voluntary nonprofit associations established for the mutual aid and sociability of the community.) By 1929, total membership in fraternal societies stood at more than 20 million. The Kiwanis Club, founded in 1915 in Detroit, Michigan, by "business and professional men" with the intent to "sponsor projects to benefit disadvantaged children," expanded from 205 chapters nationwide to more than 1,800 chapters and more than 100,000 members (Kiwanis.org, "About Kiwanis," n.p.). Other fraternal organizations, mostly founded in the previous decade, included trade unions, labor groups, motor clubs, ethnic societies, religious affiliations, and college fraternities and sororities developed as leisure-time associations. During the 1920s, these organizations became firmly established American institutions as they sought to improve civic and social conditions and to promote hobbies and sporting activities.

Some organizations, such as the American Legion, which began in 1919, were formed "to foster and perpetuate 100 percent Americanism" (Asinof, 149). Many such nativist groups flourished during this time. One such fraternal organization was the order of the Ku Klux Klan (KKK), which in 1920 had an estimated 4,000 members, which rose to more than four million members (all white, Protestant, native born) by mid-decade. Traditionally a southern-based organization, the KKK spread nationwide. At this time, the KKK was an acceptable fraternal organization embraced by the white general public and had some support in the U.S. Congress. In 1924, for example, huge rallies of more than 40,000 KKK supporters marched in Washington, D.C., and on July 4, 1924, more than 15,000 supporters gathered in Long Branch, New Jersey. During the 1920s, the KKK was the single largest private fraternal organization in America (Foner, 188).

In addition to fraternal organizations, clubs also sprang up for a wide array of activities including hunting, fishing, yachting, golf, tennis, baseball, music, art, drama, nature, reading, and bridge (Steiner [1933], 125). Organized youth programs with adult leaders grew at an accelerated pace. By 1926, the Boy Scouts claimed 625,000 members, the Girl Scouts 167,000, the Camp Fire Girls more than 150,000, the Young Men's Christian Association (YMCA) 961,000, and the Young Women's Christian Association (YWCA) 600,000. The Boy Scouts alone claimed more than 189,000 adult leaders (Kraus [1971], 198).

The Playground Movement and National Parks

At this time, urban streets still served as a playground for many young children, usually playing simple games including jumprope, hopscotch, leapfrog, and baseball. The streets, however, caused increased concern due to the increased amount of automobiles (see "the Automobile" later in this chapter) competing for street space with people and the unsupervised play of young adults and children. The federal government, concerned about the wholesome use of leisure time, placed emphasis on recreation development in parks and community centers. In connection with the Playground and Recreation Association of America, the government advocated planned activities with supervised leadership, which became known as the Playground Movement. The association published *The Playground*, a monthly magazine that sought to help organize community recreation, professionalize recreational work, and provide leadership direction for Americans of all ages. At the time, more than 140 colleges joined the movement and began offering courses for recreational leaders (Steiner [1933], 20–21).

In 1928, 128 national organizations attended the National Conference on Outdoor Recreation in Washington, D.C. As a result L. H. Weir wrote a *Manual on Parks* with recommendations that were immediately implemented by park and recreation administrators throughout the country. A typical playground included spaces for field hockey, volleyball, handball, shuffleboard, horse shoes, bowling, tennis, and clock golf. Clock golf is a simplified playground form of golf in which a hole is at the center of a larger circle in varying diameters from 6 to 18 feet. A player putts a golf ball from different positions around the circumference of the circle towards the center hole. Larger play areas included fields for baseball, football, and soccer. Community areas included recreation centers and swimming pools. Planned activities included handicrafts, artwork, nature study, and folk and social dancing. Almost all of these parks and recreation centers intended to employ supervised recreation leaders (Kraus [1971], 202).

Segregation was still prevalent, and most communities attempted to segregate the races in recreation and leisure. In Lexington, Kentucky, for example, the Lexington Civic League operated separate boards to plan and operate recreation and leisure programs for the white and African American communities. Parallel activities for each included music weeks, community days, community singing, holiday celebrations, community drama, pageantry, and talent programs. In Lexington in the 1920s and 1930s, both communities also enjoyed an annual pet day and talent events, however, in segregated parks (The Daily Aesthetic, "Leisure and recreation in a southern city's segregated park system," n.p.).

In March 1926, *The Playground* printed two articles titled "Recreation for Colored Citizens" and "Recreation in Colored Communities." The association recognized that recreation had "been sadly neglected" therefore "special emphasis" was put on specific activities within the "colored communities." Studies of playgrounds and parks showed that although both white and African American children, teens, and adults pursued the same recreational and leisure activities, they were mostly kept segregated.

In a 1928 study of public playgrounds sponsored by the National Urban League, Charles S. Johnson surveyed nine area playgrounds in Fort Wayne, Indiana. The playgrounds typically included a merry-go-round, slides, seesaws,

Children play leapfrog on a city street around 1920. Street games were common in all urban areas among the children of working-class individuals. Courtesy of Library of Congress.

swings, teeters, sandboxes, horse shoe pits, a swimming pool, and tennis courts. He also observed pavilions where band concerts were given in the evenings. The games played in the playgrounds included volleyball, baseball, tennis, and checkers. Johnson noted that two of the playgrounds were used exclusively by white children, three exclusively by African American children, and four were mixed. Johnson also observed both white and African American children playing together in baseball, checkers, swings, and, in one playground, a swimming pool. At one park, he observed that "[t]here was no supervisor in attendance and the white and Negro boys and men were swimming together with no suggestion of segregation" (72–73).

Public playgrounds did not exist in rural communities. Only 73 of the more than 13,000 towns nationwide with populations of less than 2,500 people reported having an organized playground. These small towns, however, did have vast amounts of open space for athletic fields and outdoor events. Most towns simply relied on a community building that served as a site for many different event and activities including fairs, exhibits, lectures, a chautauqua, and social dancing (Steiner [1933], 163).

National parks and forests existed in 26 states and became popular destinations for camping, hunting, and fishing. These parks included more than 1,750 campgrounds and 1,200 hotels. Total visitation rose from 920,000 in 1920 to 31.7 million in 1929; the most popular destinations were Yosemite, Yellowstone, Mt. Rainier, Platt, and the Rocky Mountains. The dramatic increase in visitors was due mainly to the construction of roads for automobile access. In 1929, 6.9 million hunting licenses and 5.3 million fishing licenses were issued (Steiner [1933], 41–47).

Hiking was also a popular year-round activity in the national parks. The Municipal Hiking Club of Minneapolis, for example, was founded in 1920, and by 1928, it sponsored 88 separate hikes with a total of 4,187 participants. Other such clubs operated in San Francisco; Portland, Oregon; Seattle, Washington; Denver, Colorado; and portions of the Northeast (Steiner [1933], 51). Recreational fishing organizations and clubs also sprang up all over the country. Some, such as the Izaak Walton League, the Sierra Club, and the Audubon Society, lobbied Congress to preserve wilderness areas from development.

Prohibition: The Law of the Land

With a congressional override of President Wilson's veto and ratification by the states, the Eighteenth Amendment (or the Volstead Act, as Prohibition was officially known) took effect on January 16, 1920. Prohibition made it illegal for "the manufacture, sale, or transportation of intoxicating liquors" and most importantly to the American public, made consumption of alcohol illegal. Enforcement of the law proved to be very difficult. Many individuals, especially those in the cities, continued to drink.

Prohibition led to the proliferation of gangland warfare and bootlegging. (Bootlegging was the term applied to the illegal business of manufacturing and selling alcohol.) Alcohol smuggling could not be prevented on a large scale, and the illicit manufacture of liquor sprang up with such rapidity that authorities were unable to suppress it. A replacement for the saloon called the speakeasy came into being. Some smaller neighborhood speakeasies replaced the saloon as the center of male leisure and social activity; in large urban areas the function of the speakeasy broadened to become a fashionable nightspot not only for drinking but also for music, dancing, and entertainment.

Although no accurate records of the speakeasies were kept, because their operation was illegal, historian Eliot Asinof noted that in Detroit alone it was estimated that "the illegal importation of alcohol was a new business that escalated to $215 million a year, second only to the manufacturing of automobiles" (263). Graft (offering money to persuade a municipal official to allow an illegal activity to continue without interference by authorities) and violence accompanying this industry became so intolerable that eventually these were important factors in the final repeal of Prohibition in 1933.

LIFESTYLES

Youth Culture and Flappers

In Robert and Helen Lynd's study of leisure activities in Middle America, more than 30 percent of school-age children and high school students were actively involved in music or music lessons. Sewing was mentioned as a leisure activity by more than 25 percent of high school girls, and listening to the radio was mentioned by more than 20 percent of both boys and girls. The automobile was most mentioned among young adults, and a youth subculture was developing away from parental supervision (Lynd and Lynd [1929], 243).

With the automobile's addition into American culture, a new form of privacy was afforded individuals in a "mobile room" that was free from chaperones. As a result, an informal method of dating developed among all classes. The youth culture promoted a new form of sexual freedom with open talk of sexual relations. Birth control was a major topic as women sought to separate sexual activity from procreation through the use of contraceptives. Moral concerns arose about the new manner of kissing and petting occurring during dates. Moral reformers created new nicknames for the automobile such as "sin wagon" or "devil wagon."

In the 1920s, college campuses became synonymous with freedom for the new youth culture, and pledging fraternities and sororities became the rage. Using slang terms inspired by the Rudolph Valentino movie *The Sheik* (1921), young men began referring to themselves as "sheiks" and to young women as "shebas." In defiance of Prohibition, young men sported hip flasks to hold their "hooch" (alcohol). Also popular on campuses was the cut-in dance.

The idea at a cut-in dance was that more men than women would be invited to a dance. The men were expected to cut-in during the course of a dance as many times a possible during the evening with different women. Young women dressed in the style of the flapper (the term *flapper* first appeared in a 1920 collection of short stories by F. Scott Fitzgerald). Flappers, unlike their Gibson girl mothers (see chapter 1), were smoking, drinking, and speaking openly in public on subjects such as sexual relations—in general offending the adult generation.

One young woman, Ellen Welles Page described the flapper in her article "A Flapper's Appeal to Parents" that appeared in *Outlook* magazine on December 6, 1922:

Two flappers do the Charleston dance on a railing in Washington, D.C., around 1925. Courtesy of Library of Congress.

If one [judges] by appearances, I suppose I am a flapper. I am within the age limit. I wear bobbed hair, the badge of flapperhood. (And, oh, what a comfort it is!), I powder my nose. I wear fringed skirts and bright-colored sweaters, and scarfs, and waists with Peter Pan collars, and low- heeled "finale hopper" shoes. I adore to dance. I spend a large amount of time in automobiles. I attend hops, and proms, and ball-games, and crew races, and other affairs at men's colleges. (Page, "A Flapper's Appeal to Parents," n.p.)

Louise Brooks, a popular Hollywood film star of the time, further personified the flapper image in the film *A Social Celebrity* (1926). The excess, fun, frivolity, and carefree attitudes were characteristic of the period's youth culture, but they were limited mainly to the youth of the middle and wealthy classes and were mostly confined to urban areas.

Family Leisure

Recreation and leisure needs for the family were continually stressed. In a December 1926 article for *Playground Magazine*, A. H. Reeve indicated that the National Education Association had issued a list of seven suggestions to revise the curriculum of public schools to relate closely to life. According to Mrs. Reeve, "[n]ear the top of the list [stood] the wise use of leisure. . . . Children need to be taught *how* to play, but parents must [also] be taught to *play*. . . . Leisure is a habit of mind; like rest, it should be a change of occupation" (Vol. 20, No. 9: 494).

Unlike previous periods when leisure was centered around a special event, in their *Middletown* study the Lynds discovered that the reduction in the hourly workday allowed leisure to become "a more generally expected part of every day rather than a more sporadic, semi-occasional event" among Middle American families. Overall, the three most popular activities among adults were the "passive" enjoyments of the automobile, movies, and radio, and "the leisure of virtually all women and of most of the men over thirty is mainly spent sitting down." Other popular leisure activities among the adult middle class were reading and gardening (226).

In 1928, the National Urban League sponsored Charles S. Johnson to provide a sociological survey of areas with large African American populations in the South and Midwest. Among African Americans, life in both the towns and cities still remained segregated; the lifestyles and leisure pursuits remained similar but parallel (not integrated) to those of whites. Venturing out into white communities for recreation or entertainment was still not an option.

In one Kentucky community, Johnson asked the adults, "Where do you spend your leisure time?" A large majority simply stated "at home" (75). Young African American males often reported spending many hours in the poolroom. The Kentucky community studied had only one recreation center, and this center did attempt to provide organized activities such as clubs and camping. Regardless of race, all of the community's clergy (white or African American) had objections to young people dancing. Johnson discovered that a popular social dancing program for young people was eliminated "by the public protestations of the Negro ministry" (74–76).

Similar to African Americans, most immigrants still sought leisure among their own groups and at the same time attempted to maintain their traditional heritage. Immigrants brought many typical leisure activities with them from their native countries. Paul Sturman, a Czechoslovakian immigrant, described the leisure time enjoyed aboard ship as he traveled to America in 1920: "In the evening there was usually dancing and music. Some immigrants would always come out with a harmonica or some musical instrument and the dance would follow" (museum text, Ellis Island).

Typically, old-world entertainment trends and activities would continue if a community had a significant immigrant population to continue the old-world traditions. One such example was the 1925 Norwegian centennial celebration in Minnesota, which drew more than 100,000 people (mostly Norwegian), including President Calvin Coolidge (museum text, Ellis Island). However, traditions would be hard to maintain. The United States began looking inward as the nativist movement led the call for 100 percent Americanization of all existing inhabitants. Aided by consumerism and mass marketing, immigrants began assimilating into American culture.

Americanization and Consumerism

The woman's role was still considered to be that of the traditional housewife (only about 20 percent of women worked in full-time jobs outside the home). Although housewives spent an average of 50–60 hours a week on household chores, technology was reducing the workload for women within the home. New electrical appliances such as the clothes iron, washing machine, and the vacuum cleaner eased the burden and time required for daily chores. During the course of the day, and usually while they were performing household duties, housewives were drawn to the radio and the new soap operas. The soap operas were sponsored by commercial product advertisers whose ads were targeted specifically toward housewives (Baughman, 276–277). The combination of media and marketing through radio, magazines, and newspapers led to a new consumerism for products advertised as time-savers that would allow for more leisure time.

With department stores accessible by automobile, consumers relied less on mail-order catalogs. In 1925, Sears and Roebuck, which had been functioning as a mail-order company since 1895 offering products mainly for rural America, began the first in a series of chain stores that grew to number 324 in cities nationwide by 1929. (A chain store had the same name and sold the same products in all its stores.) F. W. Woolworth's was another example of a chain store that spread across the country during this period. Woolworth's was noted for expanding into working-class neighborhoods, and it advertised itself as a "five-and-dime store."

Department stores in many cities sponsored Christmas parades. Specially decorated Christmas windows in the stores featured mechanical toys and marionettes and ushered in the leisure activity of a family stroll to see the new window displays. In 1924, the first Macy's Thanksgiving Day parade was held, mainly as an advertising campaign to herald the Christmas shopping season. The parade was an immediate success that paralleled the growth in the toy industry as toys became year-round items in department stores.

Rural Lifestyles

Unlike urban dwellers, many rural inhabitants had never drunk alcohol, heard jazz, or entered a speakeasy. Old-fashioned conservative views on idleness and leisure still held fast in rural areas. Lifestyles and leisure pursuits were still hampered by the amount of time required working in the fields. In addition, the economic condition of many rural residents did not allow them to share in the same expenditures for commercial leisure and recreation as urban residents.

The automobile eased the isolation factor of rural living, but the introduction of tractors and other labor-saving devices reduced the need for communal labor. For those living in rural areas, the development of the fractional horsepower motor, for example, saved time in labor but actually decreased the opportunities for social leisure. An electrical motor of even one horsepower was both too large and too powerful to operate small machinery. The development of the fractional horsepower motor made it possible for smaller motors with less power to operate small appliances such as power tools, refrigerators, vacuums, sewing machines, and factory conveyor belts. Prior to the implementation of small labor-saving devices, when additional labor was needed members of the community usually supplied it. Gathering for community labor usually resulted in a social gathering that included recreation and dancing (see chapter 1). The reduced need for communal labor decreased the opportunity for communal gatherings. In many areas the communal gathering of labor that led to socialization and recreation simply disappeared (Steiner [1933], 152).

However, all community recreation did not stop. Edwin Jewell reported that Omaha, Nebraska, began having "organized play for adults." The Omaha Walking Club, organized in 1919, maintained an active membership of 250 individuals and a yearly attendance of more than 4,800 people. In addition to weekly walks that averaged four miles, play activities included volleyball, tennis, and horse shoes. There was swimming and canoeing in the summer and ice-skating in the winter. Many other similar clubs existed throughout the country (*The Playground*, March 1926, Vol. 19, No. 12: 668).

In 1926, in Cokesbury, South Carolina, Blanche Torrent wrote, "Farm women . . . realized the value of recreation in their community life." These women actively read books and magazines in search of new games to try that would include women, men, and children. In addition to relay races and singing games, dancing continued to be a popular activity (*The Playground*, March 1926, Vol. 19, No. 12: 669).

For many rural inhabitants, it was the church that provided recreation. For those who had an automobile driving to Sunday services served as a form of recreation and socialization. Large tent revivals and traveling chautauquas (see chapter 1) filled the idle time of many. Some of the large revival meetings by evangelists Billy Sunday and Aimee Semple gained nationwide media attention. The increase in automobiles and radios continued to link the cities and the rural areas. The introduction of radio and mass-marketing magazines were slowly diminishing the barriers between urban and rural residents.

ENTERTAINMENT

Radio, Radio, Radio

In 1920, Pittsburgh radio station KDKA transmitted the first commercial radio broadcast. The radio quickly became popular across the nation as an entertainment source, eventually influencing most of the population. By the mid-1920s, telephone lines made it possible for simultaneous live broadcasting (known as networking) from a baseball game, concert, or commercial program to most of the nation. The radio was an inexpensive entertainment choice (the cost was for the initial purchase of the radio and a few cents for electricity), and listeners had an almost unlimited choice of programs including news, sporting events, musical concerts, comedies, drama programs, and religious sermons. Radio reached into the rural heartland as well as the cities as networking proved to be an easy way to communicate information to a widespread audience. For the first time, those who could not get to a ball game or a vaudeville theater could listen on the radio, and all listeners shared in the same experience, including hearing advertisements for the same commercial products.

Radio further spread the idea of mass marketing for new commercial products directly to the consumer. Advertisers were able to quickly spread information on their products by providing commercial sponsorship of popular programs. Daytime shows such as *The Smith Family* were geared specifically to women and became known as soap operas. (So named because early advertisers for the daytime dramas would advertise soap and detergent products.)

The radio became family entertainment. In the evenings, families gathered around the radio for the nightly broadcasts. According to Elliott West, "[a]s a popular program began, the family sat around the set, all ears turned in common to the speaker. The antics and crises of radio characters were discussed around the dinner table by the whole family" (91). By 1929, more than 600 stations regularly broadcast commercial programs to more than 12 million households, over 40 percent of all American homes (Steiner [1933], 119).

Newspapers, Magazines, and Books

With radio, movies, magazines (with the addition of color printing for ads), and newspaper chains, it became possible to advertise the same products nationally to all areas of America. At this time, advertising firms began associating products with an image or a celebrity that created consumer demand rather than filling a basic need of the buyer. Publishing as a whole became commercialized and concerned with mass-market circulation and advertising.

In 1919, newspaper tabloids began to appear. The first of the tabloids, the *New York Daily News*, founded in 1919, emphasized "sex, scandal, and sports" and quickly became popular among readers who had not regularly read newspapers in the past. Circulation of the *Daily News* went from 400,000 in 1922 to over 1.3 million in 1929, and the paper became the most circulated newspaper in the world. In response, William Randolph Hearst countered with a competing tabloid publication, the *Daily Mirror* (began in 1924), as did Bernarr Macfadden with the *New York Evening Graphic* in the same year. According to historian Eliot Asinof, the tabloids were "so loaded with distortion that the news was regulated to what could be told in glaring headlines" (347). The tabloid, however, was popular with the public, especially among the working class, and newspapers in many other cities copied the format. The national circulation of newspapers increased from 20 million in 1919 to 40 million by 1929.

Publisher Bernarr Macfadden, who began his publishing career in 1899 with the physical fitness magazine *Physical Culture*, which remained popular during the 1920s, applied the tabloid idea to mass-market magazines. Magazines such as *True Story* and *True Detective* told of "true confessions" and provided titillating stories of love, lust, and intrigue that appealed to readers. During the 1920s and 1930s Macfadden's magazine publications totaled as many as 15 million copies a month

(*Smithsonian*, December 1997, n.p.). Macfadden also sought to capitalize on both titillating stories and the automobile in one publication titled *Your Car*. The premier issue in May 1925 was advertised as "A Magazine of Romance, Fact and Fiction." In his editorial, Macfadden said,

> It is our intention that this magazine shall enter into the intimate personal details of the life of every car owner. Most publications devoted to the automobile are dry as dust. They are full of technical details. But in our search for material we intend to look for romance in its association with the automobile. . . . Stories of business successes that seethe and throb with human interest, details of love and romance that enthrall the senses, together with many other interesting features, will fill our pages. (5)

Within the issue were fictional stories such as "Her Handsome Chauffer," "Romance and a Red Runabout" and factual stories titled "Stars and Their Cars," and "Spring Styles for Women Motorists" (*Your Car*, May 1925, Vol. 1, No. 1: 5).

Magazines were extremely popular among all classes and catered to a wide variety of preferences and tastes. Middle-class readers continued to favor traditional publications such as *The Saturday Evening Post*, *Collier's*, and *National Geographic*. Publications first introduced during this period that remained popular for the entire twentieth century include *Reader's Digest* (1921), *Time* (1923), and the *New Yorker* (1925), a publication catering to the social elite. The *American Mercury*, a radical magazine published by H. L. Mencken, was viewed by the "lost generation" as an instrument of rebellion that promoted new fads and heralded writer F. Scott Fitzgerald and painter Pablo Picasso. The cynical magazine was also noted for attacking religious establishments and the middle-class notion of values. Mencken claimed religious people lived "in mortal fear that somewhere, somehow, someone might be enjoying himself" (Baughman, 383).

The 1920s proved to be a time of great advancement in American literature and increased readership among Americans. Book publishers began marketing books in department stores and by mail order. In 1926, the Book-of-the-Month Club and the Literary Guild introduced the concept of selling books at reduced prices by mail.

Two of the most prominent authors of the period were F. Scott Fitzgerald and Ernest Hemmingway. Both wrote of disillusionment and disenchantment with American values. Hemingway's works included *The Sun Also Rises* (1926) and *A Farewell to Arms* (1929). Fitzgerald's novels captured the contemporary feeling of the period and told stories of flappers and the glamorous times had by returning war veterans. His first novel *This Side of Paradise* (1920) was widely read; however, his novel *The Great Gatsby* (1925) was the definitive work of the period. *The Great Gatsby* depicted the lavish lifestyles of the idle rich, which included luxurious mansions, expensive automobiles, gambling, dancing, drinking, and partying among young people between the ages of 20 and 30.

Book publishers and readers of the time had to contend with two agencies that banned books within the United States. The New York Society for the Suppression of Vice and the New England Watch and Ward Society were successful in banning more than 60 books including James Joyce's *Ulysses* (1922), Sinclair Lewis's *Elmer Gantry* (1927), and Sherwood Anderson's *Dark Laughter*. In addition, various magazine issues were banned including issues of *The American Mercury* and one issue of *Scribner's* (Baughman, 33).

Commercial Dance Halls and the Charleston

Dancing continued to be popular among people of all ages. Many preferred old standard dances such as the Foxtrot and the Waltz. Social dancing was available at community centers, social clubs, fraternal lodges, public parks, private country clubs, and homes using a phonograph or radio for music. Public dancing was also available at resorts, hotels, and commercial dance halls. Arthur Murray began teaching standard ballroom dances and started a chain of dance studios (see chapters 4 and 6). Many adults took ballroom classes and also sent their children to tap and ballet classes (Steiner [1933], 114).

The dominant dance craze of the period, however, was the Charleston, danced to jazz music. The dance premiered in 1923 in an all–African American Harlem show called *Running Wild* and quickly became popular among those between the ages of 16 and 35. The Charleston was a fast-paced, bouncy dance featuring torso movement and many synchronized arm and leg movements. In order to perform the dance, the women's restrictive corsets were discarded, and dress hemlines were shortened. The fast-paced dance and jazz music raised morality questions among ministers and members of the older generation. An Oregon evangelist said, "[D]ancing is the first step and easiest step toward hell. The [Charleston] cheapens womanhood. The first time a girl allows a man to swing her around the dance floor her instinct tells her she has lost something she should have treasured" (Time-Life Books, *This Fabulous Century: 1920–1930*, 41). The *Ladies Home Journal* published an article by J.R. MacMahon in December 1921 titled "Unspeakable Jazz Must Go!" stating that "[j]azz dancing is degrading. It lowers all moral standards" (Time-Life Books, *This Fabulous Century: 1920–1930*, 41). Many of these reactions were also due in part to the fact that the dance was closely associated with illegal drinking.

With Prohibition making it illegal to sell alcohol, dance halls sought new ways to stay in business. Two popular kinds of dance hall were the taxi-dance hall and the public dance hall. The taxi-dance hall (or closed dance hall) had paid admittance for male patrons only. These dance halls in turn employed female "hostesses" to serve as dance partners. Once inside, male patrons purchased individual tickets at a cost of five or ten cents, which they presented to a female hostess in exchange for a dance. Typically these halls held about 500 to 600 people. Taxi-dance halls were quite popular. In 1925, in New York City alone more than 8,000 dance hostesses were legally employed (Baughman [1996, *American Decades: 1920–1929*], 273).

The main attraction for public dancing, however, was the commercial public dance hall. Overall, the number of smaller commercial dance halls actually declined, but due to the opening of large dance halls, each capable of accommodating 3,000 to 5,000 dancers at any one time, the total capacity of public dance halls increased dramatically. The large halls employed popular orchestras (sometimes two at a time to provide continuous music) to attract dancers and charged an admission fee. One such dance hall, New York's legendary Savoy Ballroom (opened in 1926) covered an entire city block in Harlem and could accommodate

A honky-tonk on the outskirts of San Antonio, Texas. Honky-tonks and juke joints were inexpensive places of entertainment usually featuring dancing and alcohol. Most were located in rural areas outside of city limits. Courtesy of Thelma Lynn Olsen.

more than 5,000 dancers. The Savoy was also believed to be the first integrated dance hall and is credited with originating the Lindy hop dance that became popular during the depression. The Lindy hop developed from the Charleston and used a combination of six and eight count steps. The "Lindy," as it was simply known, incorporated fast paced dancing with acrobatic lifts, jumps, and turns. The origin dates to 1927 in New York's Harlem and was named after Charles Lindbergh's "hop" across the Atlantic (see The Airplane, Barnstormers, and "Lucky Lindy" later this chapter). It was also the forerunner of swing and the jitterbug (see chapter 3).

Dance halls throughout the country were mostly segregated. Those that did allow African Americans to enter were careful to keep African American couples separate from white couples in "unofficial" segregated areas. Most dance halls adopted a policy of admitting African Americans on special "colored only" nights such as Mondays or Thursdays. In southern California, for example, the segregation would further be defined with an addition of a "Mexican only" night (see chapter 5). Many African Americans simply chose to dance in small speakeasies, social clubs, jook joints, honky-tonks, and private house parties that catered to African Americans (Trotter, 424).

Nevertheless the large dance halls such as New York's Roseland, Cleveland's

Crystal Slipper, Detroit's Greystone, Chicago's Trianon, Boston's Raymor, Hollywood's Palladium, and Los Angeles's Palomar were popular and lucrative. Every major city had one or more large dance halls, and many towns had smaller versions (Steiner [1933], 113). Both New York and Chicago each had more than six million dance hall admissions in 1924 (Baughman, 273).

Fads, Board Games, and Mah-jongg

Encouraged by newspapers, magazines, and radio, many fads swept the nation during this decade. Dance marathons, mah-jongg, crossword puzzles, and miniature golf were immensely popular, as were yo-yos, roller-skating, and parlor games.

Dance marathons were popular attractions and drew thousands of spectators. In 1923, the *New York World* reported that "[o]f all the crazy competitions ever invented the dancing marathon wins by a considerable margin of lunacy" (quoted in Time-Life Books, *This Fabulous Century: 1920–1930*, 248). In the dance marathons, dancers competed for prizes, mostly money, in hourly increments of about 45 to 50 minutes of dance with 10 minutes of rest. In order to encourage spectators to attend, sponsors devised all sorts of antics to be performed during the marathons such as speeding up the music, relay races, and elimination games. As the days passed and contestants tired, arguments would break out, and some participants would physically fight with each other (Baughman [1996, *American Decades: 1920–1929*], 275).

A popular parlor game of the time called Personality Typing was influenced by the work of psychologist Sigmund Freud. (Many Americans did not actually read Freud, only excerpts and interpretations by others.) The game consisted of 40 questions people used to determine the personality types of their playmates. Words such as *sublimation*, *repression*, and *complex*, were commonly used in the game (http://angelfire.com/co/pscst/freud.html). Another parlor game enjoyed by family members was a Parker Brothers card game called Touring. In this automobile-influenced game, the players went on a simulated road trip, encountering obstacles such as a flat tire, a collision, a countryside tour, and running out of gas (Braden, 326).

Model electric trains fascinated both adults and children during this time. Joshua Lionel first marketed electric trains in 1903, but it was not until after the war that interest in electric trains peaked. By 1921, more than one million electric train sets were purchased for American homes, mainly as a father-son endeavor. The peak of the fad occurred during the 1924 Christmas season (Panati, 129).

The game of mah-jongg (sometimes spelled "mahjong") took the country by storm. In 1922, Joseph Babcock simplified the rules of the ancient Chinese game, and it became an instant success, in one year selling more than 1.5 million sets. The game used a combination of dominoes and dice, came in a carrying case that held 144 tile pieces, and could be played almost anywhere. Mah-jongg clubs sprang up among middle-class women and among businessmen, and the game was very popular on college campuses and in the parlors of many American homes (Baughman, 274).

Another fad that could be found just about anywhere in the country was the crossword puzzle. Although crossword puzzles had been carried in a few newspapers, it was not until 1924 that Simon and Schuster published a collection of crossword puzzles bound in a book with the novelty of an attached pencil. Within one year the book sold one million copies, and Americans took part in the fad at home, on the train, in college dormitories—just about anywhere.

Amusement Parks and Traveling Chautauquas

Amusement parks in small towns began to close; however, the parks continued to flourish in the bigger cities and summer resort areas. A National Organization of Amusement Parks was established, and amusement parks continued to expand in cities throughout the country. More than 1,500 parks were reported to be in operation in 1919 (Braden, 174). Popular amusements at these parks included Ferris wheels, merry-go-rounds, roller-skating, dancing, shooting galleries, arcades, and sideshows. White City was an amusement park at Lake Quinsigamond in Worcester, Massachusetts. White City had attractions similar to those at Coney Island, and daily attendance averaged over 30,000 people. A separate area near the lake offered "dancing, canoeing, fishing, merry-go-rounds, skating, arcades, bowling" (Rosenzweig, 180). Coney Island continued to thrive and remained New York City's most popular resort. The Cyclone roller-coaster was added in 1927, and daily attendance at the park was estimated at 800,000 (Steiner [1933], 116).

Around this time, many municipalities began training and supplying lifeguards for the public beaches adjacent to the amusement areas. In 1924 at Coney Island, for example, New York City took over responsibility for lifeguards. As a result, drowning incidents were reduced from an average of more than 50 per year to less than six (Stanton, n.p.).

In smaller towns, the traveling chautauqua offered commercial recreation in areas that did not have the population to support an amusement park. Although different from amusement parks in that they did not offer thrill rides, chautauquas offered speakers, musicians, and other entertainers who traveled from town to town, sometimes staying in one place for a few days or a week. The Chautauqua Bureau sponsored these shows and provided the necessary equipment, personnel, and transportation for them. Many rural inhabitants would travel for many miles to attend a chatauqua and would stay by camping or pitching a tent. In 1920, it was estimated that more than 12,000 towns hosted a traveling chautauqua with a total annual attendance of more than 20 million people. However, during the course of ten years chatauquas suffered a steady decline to less than 10 percent of their previous numbers by 1929 (Steiner [1933], 116-117).

Traveling circuses, another popular form of rural entertainment, began to decline in popularity. In order to continue operation, Ringling Brothers circus merged with Barnum and Bailey in 1919 to become the largest circus of its time and continued to perform at outdoor sports stadiums and county fairs, as did some other independent, smaller circuses (Braden, 173). The decline of both the circus and the chautauqua was due mainly to the rising popularity of movies, radio, and the automobile (Steiner [1933], 116–118).

MUSIC AND THEATER

Broadway and Theater

Broadway theater continued as an influential form of entertainment and did not have to compete with the movie audiences. Tickets remained expensive, and audiences were made up mainly of the wealthy class. Musicals such as *Ziegfeld's Follies* developed elaborate productions of song, dance, and gaudily dressed showgirls. Broadway broached previously taboo subjects such as segregation and slavery in dramatic plays such as Eugene O'Neil's *All God's Chillun' Got Wings* (1924) and the musical production by Jerome Kern and Oscar Hammerstein, *Showboat* (1927).

Comedies and lighthearted musicals were the most popular Broadway productions. Critics panned one such production, *Abie's Irish Rose* (1922 to 1927), but audiences loved it, and it ran for (a then record) 2,327 performances over a five-and-a-half-year period. Harlem productions with all-African American casts extended Broadway's appeal. Productions in Harlem became the rage as numerous stage productions, speakeasies, and nightclubs catered to white audiences. *Shuffle Along* (1921) was the first of many fashionable Harlem reviews that drew large wealthy white audiences in search of "Negro entertainment" (Horsham, 84).

This period saw the development of community theater. In 1921, the Cleveland Playhouse became the country's first resident professional theater outside of New York. Many amateur theaters providing inexpensive entertainment to small towns and rural areas also flourished. Most of the actors were local residents who had "regular" jobs and who studied and performed during their leisure hours. Community theater spread across the country and provided an inexpensive opportunity for residents outside of New York to enjoy Broadway-style shows.

Popular Music and All That Jazz

There was a trend in American homes of purchasing mechanical player pianos, thereby eliminating the need for either sheet music or actual piano playing. It was estimated that between the years 1900 and 1930 more than two and a half million homes had player pianos (Braden, 115). The introduction of better recording techniques, phonographs, and radios caused a slow decline in player-piano purchases by the end of the decade. Popular music included songs by entertainer Al Jolson, operatic songs, and "sweet bands" such as those headed by Gene Austin and Guy Lombardo. In 1929, Lombardo began a tradition that lasted more than 50 years when his band played "Auld Lang Syne" on New Year's Eve at New York's Waldorf Astoria hotel.

Jazz music would become synonymous with the era and would also be closely associated with bootlegging, dancing, and questionable moral behavior. Jazz was fast-paced, combining elements of ragtime and blues that encouraged improvisation and spontaneity. When speeded up, the music was known as "hot jazz." For many young listeners, the music captured a joy and sense of adventure that was an exciting and radical departure from the other music of that time. The music promoted close, fast-paced dancing such as the Charleston and was viewed by some as scandalous. Popular jazz musicians included "King" Oliver, "Jelly Roll" Morton, Bix Beiderbecke, and Louis Armstrong.

With recording improvements and the increase in commercial radio, jazz spread quickly. The most popular commercial success and best-known jazz musician in the country were Paul Whiteman and his orchestra. Known as the "king of jazz," Whiteman was credited with making jazz "respectable," and his orchestra received major support from commercial advertisers and a significant amount of radio airplay (Erenberg, 12). One of Whiteman's most popular recordings was the song "Charleston," which was written for the stage show *Runnin' Wild* (1923).

Speakeasies and nightclubs were quick to feature the new jazz bands. One such club, the famed Cotton Club, (owned by gangster Owney Madden) opened in 1923 in Harlem, New York, with a white clientele and African American entertainers. Venues such as the Cotton Club offered food and alcohol at high prices and offered music and cabaret-style entertainment and musical revues geared toward wealthy audiences. The small-town equivalent of the speakeasy was the roadhouse. Roadhouses were usually on the outskirts of town or outside the city limits (easily accessible by automobile) and therefore farther from law enforcement.

"All Talking" Movies and Rudolph Valentino

Without question, the movies became the most popular entertainment choice outside of the home. During the period, movie studios produced more than 700 full-length (one and a half hours duration or more) films per year. A growing number of nationwide movie theater chains opened including Loews, MGM, and United Artists. The movie theaters became luxurious and elegant environments, creating an exotic setting of fantasy and escape similar to the movie-viewing experience itself. One such theater was Grauman's in Los Angeles. Grauman's opened in 1918 and could seat 2,200 moviegoers. Many other large theaters soon followed—housing in excess of 3,000 patrons each. The Roxy Theater opened in New York in 1927 and could seat 6,200 people. Many theaters continued to combine live vaudeville acts with newsreels, shorts, and feature films; usually the feature was changed weekly (Braden, 185).

By the middle of the decade, the country had more than 20,000 movie theaters (Nasaw, 224). Almost every town, no matter how small, had at least one. The city of Muncie, Indiana, for example, with a population of about 50,000, had nine movie theaters open seven days a week, all year long, from one o'clock in the afternoon until eleven o'clock at night. The nine theaters offered over 22 different features and programs each week. Theater attendance fluctuated with the seasons; in July, estimated weekly attendance was just over 26,000, and in December that number rose to over 42,000 weekly. Of the Muncie teenagers surveyed by Robert and Helen Lynd, over 75 percent indicated they attended the movie theater regularly, and 25 percent indicated they attended with their parents. Approximately 10 percent of the total population attended as an entire family once a week (Lynd and Lynd [1929], 263–266).

The movies quickly became part of Americans' lives and provided an escape to a fantasy world. Publications such as the *Saturday Evening Post* praised the entertainment value of the movies: "Before you know it you are living the story—laughing, loving, hating, struggling, winning! All the adventure, all the romance,

Movie theater marquee advertising *The Jazz Singer*, the first "talkie," in 1927.
Courtesy of Picture Desk.

all the excitement you lack in your daily life are in the Pictures. They take you completely out of yourself into a wonderful new world" (Braden, 186).

Although movie theaters were everywhere, so was segregation. In 1928, Charles S. Johnson of the National Urban League indicated that "Negro patronage" was discouraged within movie theaters, and African Americans were expected to use the balconies. Johnson further stated that "[t]he Negro population is too small to sustain a Negro moving picture house"; therefore, they preferred to simply "stay away" (Johnson, Charles S., 74).

The movies were able to use real scenery and locations that Broadway could not match. *Wings* (1927), for example, the first film to win an Academy Award for Best Picture, featured actual surplus airplanes from World War I that were crashed and burned to add authenticity to the movie. (The first Academy Awards, held in 1929, acknowledged the best films from both 1927 and 1928.) The characters in *Keystone Kops*, a popular comedy series, rode in real automobiles in real cities. The first sound film *The Jazz Singer* (1927) created a national stir, and by 1929 "all-talking" films were the mainstay of the industry. The advent of sound and talkies caused weekly movie attendance to almost double, and by 1929 weekly attendance would approach 100 million. The movies provided spectacles that Broadway, vaudeville, or any other entertainment venue could not match. With sound, musicals became popular film features that in effect ended vaudeville, and Broadway shows were no longer the entertainment leaders.

The movie industry began to run promotional advertisements for feature films in numerous newspapers and mass-market magazines and chronicled both the on-screen and off-screen lives of the movie stars; thus the concept of the Hollywood celebrity was born. It was no longer Broadway performers but movie stars who set the standards for parties, cars, and fashion. As a result, more than with any other form of entertainment, movie fans could fantasize about the life of leisure they saw portrayed on the screen. The movies became responsible for the way average Americans dressed, talked, and acted in their daily lives.

The Sheik (1921) established Rudolph Valentino as a major Hollywood star. His on-screen style, mannerisms, and fashion provided romantic fantasies for women that men sought to emulate. The tango dance caught on once again mainly due to Valentino's tango scene in *The Four Horsemen of the Apocalypse* (1921). When Valentino died at age 31 in 1926 from complications of a perforated ulcer, he was the most popular film star of the time (at least among women). At his funeral, more than 15,000 women attempted to view his body (Horsham, 37).

Due to the sex appeal of screen idols such as Valentino, some people disapproved of the moral content of movies, especially for young moviegoers. *Playground* magazine estimated that over 90 percent of school-age children attended the movies regularly but blamed the movies as the main source of delinquency (*Playground*, July 1925, Vol. XIX, No. 4: 172). In 1929, in order to monitor and control the content of the movies, producers formed the Motion Picture Producers and Distributors of America (MPPDA) association that listed specific items that could and could not be portrayed in film.

SPORTS AND GAMES

Professional Sports and the Sports Celebrity

In 1919, baseball had to contend with a scandal involving the legitimacy of the game itself. Newspapers reported that eight players for the Chicago White Sox were in consort with gamblers to put a fix on the 1919 World Series. Chicago lost the series, and the eight players were indicted by a grand jury. After a highly publicized trial they were found innocent. The day after the verdict, however, newly appointed baseball commissioner Kenesaw Mountain Landis banned the eight ballplayers from ever playing baseball again in an attempt to maintain the credibility of the league and its owners.

In 1920, at this time of uncertainty about baseball's future, George Herman

"Babe" Ruth was traded by the Boston Red Sox to the New York Yankees and almost single-handedly erased all memory of the 1919 scandal. Ruth set a new standard for the game, had corporate sponsors seeking to use his image to endorse products, and became the first professional athlete to have a press agent. Newspapers carried accounts of his carefree attitude and mounting home run totals and increased their sports coverage. Fans who could not attend games could now not only follow Ruth's progress, but also that of their hometown heroes. More than any other celebrity or sport of the period, Ruth and baseball were on top for the entire decade; baseball attendance figures were just over 8 million in 1919 and remained steady, increasing to a little over 10 million by 1929 (Steiner [1933], 84). Historian Eliot Asinof might have summed up the American attachment to the game best by saying that "[b]aseball was a reliable key to the way Americans liked to see themselves. It reflected the pride, the honesty, the skills of American men. The national pastime transcended ethnic, class, and social lines" (341).

Baseball was so popular that a separate National Negro Baseball League was formed in 1920 with teams in Kansas City, Indianapolis, Dayton, Chicago, Detroit, and St. Louis. In 1923, a rival Eastern Colored League was established with teams in cities such as Philadelphia, Brooklyn, Baltimore, and Atlantic City. The 1923 season drew a combined attendance of more than 400,000 fans to Negro National League and Eastern Colored League games. A world series was held between the two leagues from 1924 to 1927 (Trotter, 400). The leagues faced financial difficulty and folded. A new Negro National League was formed in 1933 and the Negro American League was formed in 1937, they continued play until 1948 when Jackie Robinson (see chapter 6) broke the "color line" in baseball (BlackBaseball.com, "History of the Negro Baseball Leagues—The Big Years," n.p.).

It was during this period that sports figures first became celebrities. Sportswriters of the period such as Paul Callico, Damon Runyon, and Grantland Rice wrote exciting accounts of the games and colorful descriptions of sports figures. Football player Harold "Red" Grange and University of Notre Dame coach Knute Rockne became two of the most well-known American public figures. Other popular sports celebrities included swimmer Johnny Weismuller, professional golfer Walter Hagen, and tennis stars Bill Tilden and Helen Wills Moody. Boxer Jack Dempsey also enjoyed celebrity status. One heavyweight championship fight between Dempsey and Gene Tunney in Philadelphia had more than 120,000 spectators in attendance, and millions more tuned in on the radio. A rematch between the two the following year in Chicago drew more than 145,000 spectators (Steiner [1933], 101).

Amateur Sports and Active Participation

Amateur sports grew more popular, and more Americans were participating in amateur sports. Many municipalities and colleges expanded their playing facilities and recreation areas to accommodate the growing public need for sports facilities. At the time, participation in amateur sports for sheer enjoyment was regarded as a worthwhile pastime. The quintessential athlete who characterized the true spirit of amateurism was golfer Bobby Jones. Jones became a national idol and a well-known celebrity of his time. His charismatic appeal sparked an interest in golf, both in amateur participation in the sport and in the construction of new courses.

In 1923, there were 1,903 golf courses nationwide, of which only 72 were public courses. By 1929, the number increased to 5,856 with 543 public courses in 46 states. Most of the golf courses were near urban areas. Sociologist Jesse Steiner found that despite the tremendous increase in the number of courses there was still great demand to play golf. He claimed that it was "not infrequent for [golf courses] to have a continuous stream of players from dawn to dusk during the weekends of summer months." Accurate statistics of the number of players were not kept for the period; however, it is known that in the year 1929 alone, more than 3.1 million golf clubs and 8 million golf balls were purchased (Steiner [1933], 63, 71).

The public's growing desire to participate in sports spread to many other activities, and many municipalities began to provide free activity programs in parks and playgrounds that most people could not normally afford. In 1926, the city of Dallas, Texas, for example, provided 43 public tennis courts, 30 baseball fields, 4 football fields, 4 golf courses, and 16 outdoor basketball courts to its citizens" (Attwell [1926], 657).

Baseball was popular among many age groups in both organized amateur leagues and sandlot games. The National Recreation Association reported that by 1929 amateur baseball leagues had 241,766 players. The American Legion claimed another 300,000 participants. Many cities provided baseball diamonds for youth to play in nonleague sandlot games. However, many cities such as Chicago, Brooklyn, and San Francisco reported that they did not have nearly enough fields for those who wanted to play. Colleges reported that over 10 percent of their total enrollment played either intercollegiate or intramural baseball. The numbers themselves are quite high, but baseball was ranked fourth among collegiate sport participation as more students took part in basketball, football, and tennis (Steiner [1933], 71).

One sporting equipment statistic is startling and provides a small sense of how many individuals were participating in sports. The United States Census of Manufacturers reported that in 1929 alone more than 1.8 million baseball bats, 8.5 million baseballs, 1.3 million basketballs, 3.2 million pairs of roller skates and ice skates, half a million footballs, and 628,000 tennis rackets were produced and sold to the American public. Other popular forms of sports and recreation included bowling, horse shoes (sometimes called "quoits"), archery, and swimming (Steiner [1933], 62–63).

American Gertrude Caroline Ederle became the first woman to swim the English Channel in 1926. Ederle had been a gold medal winner at the 1924 summer Olympics in Paris. However, it was her 1926 accomplishment that made her a celebrity in the United States and further popularized women's swimming.

Many high school and collegiate sports drew large crowds of spectators. For example, the small town of Mitchell, South Dakota, hosted the state high school basketball tournament in 1923, which drew more than 5,000 spectators. College football games routinely filled huge stadiums. The University of Michigan played to capacity crowds in a stadium seating more than 100,000 people. Other colleges that built stadiums in the 1920s with capacities of more than 65,000 included the University of Alabama, University of Illinois, University of Nebraska, Ohio State

Mitchell, South Dakota, 1923. Five thousand spectators witness the state high school basketball tournament. Courtesy of Library of Congress.

University, Purdue University, Stanford University, and Texas A & M. The total amount of spectators at college football games of over 100 colleges rose from 4 million in 1921 to an estimated total of over 10 million in 1929 (Steiner [1933], 88).

The popularity of sports led to the reintroduction of daylight saving time. The plan (first instituted by Congress as a war measure during the summers of 1918 and 1919) asked Americans to set their clocks ahead one hour during the summer months, thereby providing an extra hour of sunlight at the end of the day. Many states adopted the plan, and it eventually led to the National Daylight Saving Association, which provided a federal standard. Most people enjoyed the extra hour of daylight for recreation and leisure activities.

Ice Carnivals, Ice-Skating, and the National Ski Association

Ice festivals and ice carnivals were still popular during the decade and were slowly spreading across the Northeast and Midwest. At the time, many towns simply flooded park areas or used frozen lakes for ice-skating or hockey. Municipalities recognized the inconsistencies of the weather and the danger of frozen lakes and began constructing permanent skating facilities in addition to toboggan trails, ski trails, and ski jumps.

In November of 1925, Oak Park, Illinois, was one of many towns that began adapting the popular idea of the ice carnival. Oak Park converted a newly erected athletic stadium capable of seating 6,000 persons into an ice arena. Organizers planned a two-day program of fun and competition to coincide with New Year's of 1926. Events included dashes, backward skating, three-legged races, and obstacle races. Lighting was installed for evening exhibitions by world-renowned speed skaters, and according to Oak Park administrators, bands were to play "lively dance tunes" (*Playground*, March 1926, Vol. 19, No. 12: 662–663).

Ice-skating remained the most popular winter activity. In St. Paul, Minnesota, 18 skating rinks reported that the 7-week 1928 season attracted more than 387,000 skaters. More than 60 amateur teams used 10 hockey rinks for a total of over 200 games. Skating meets and exhibitions drew 46,000 spectators (Steiner [1933], 78). Snow skiing also began to become more popular.

In Michigan in 1920, the National Ski Association (founded in 1904) had 25 clubs and about 800 members. During the following 10 years, the number increased to 110 clubs and more than 7,000 members. More importantly, during the same time span, the association sponsored tournaments that grew from 15 per season to 125 per season. The number of spectators at the tournaments increased from 8,000 to over 400,000 (Steiner [1933], 77). Similar ski clubs developed in the Northeast and in the western Rocky Cascade and Sierra Nevada mountains.

In 1924, the Intercollegiate Winter Sports Union was formed, organizing competitive meets in ski jumping, downhill racing, cross-country skiing, and various ice-skating events. Facilities were expanded at two major centers: Lake Placid in northern New York State in the East and Minneapolis, Minnesota in the West. Each of these centers maintained an elaborate winter program including figure skating, ice circuses, ice yacht races, snow modeling contests, and ice carnivals (Steiner [1933], 78).

TRANSPORTATION AND VACATION

The Automobile and the Auto-Vacation

The automobile was the single most important catalyst of the period that changed Americans' social behavior and leisure pursuits. By this time, more than 110 companies offered auto financing, and almost anyone could afford to purchase an automobile on an installment plan. In 1924, to offset the high cost of new cars, the auto industry increased its involvement in the used car market, making cars available in many price ranges (Fink, 147).

The Federal Highway Act of 1921 dramatically increased road construction to more than ten thousand miles of road per year and instituted a national highway numbering system. The federal highway program was expanded in 1925 to include local road and directional signs. Also in 1925, the famed Route 66 was opened. On Route 66, a motorist could leave Chicago, Illinois, travel southwest through Missouri and Oklahoma, head west through Texas, New Mexico, Arizona, and into Los Angeles, California, all on a continuous paved highway of almost two thousand miles. For those wishing to travel cross-country, U.S. Highway 20 extended more than 3,200 miles from Boston, Massachusetts, to Newport, Oregon.

In addition to the construction of numerous bridges, the first automobile tunnel, the Holland Tunnel, opened in 1927 connecting Manhattan and New Jersey.

The vast number of paved roads provided average Americans with new freedom to leave the home, neighborhood, town, city, or state where they lived whenever they chose. Some used the car to make the Sunday trip to church more convenient, others to venture outside their communities. Some drove for pleasure or for an extended vacation. The ability to get away from the regular daily routine of work, school, or housework created a new form of leisure—sightseeing. It was popular to simply go out and drive and just about any destination would do—a few miles or even hundreds miles from the home. The road literally became an open highway to connect the individual with all the sights and enjoyments of America.

Sightseeing sometimes led to an extended auto-vacation. The growing number of automobiles on the open road venturing farther away from home, for days or even weeks at a time, created the need for many support services and businesses. More than 120,000 service stations, 1,400 roadside camps, and countless diners and other attractions and accommodations opened nationwide. Isolation in rural areas diminished as easier access to towns and cities became available. Suburban populations increased, sometimes tenfold. Supermarket chains such as A & P expanded to more than 14,000 stores nationwide, many in suburban areas. Roadside "burger joints" and drive-in restaurants such as A & W appeared. By 1929, billboards advertising all the new amenities were permanent fixtures on American highways (Steiner [1933], 46).

The automobile was not only a focus of enjoyment, but also a family's main recreation expenditure. In response to the amount of money spent on leisure and recreation, an adult resident of Muncie, Indiana, provided a typical response: "We don't spend anything on recreation except for the car." As a result of the presence of the automobile in Muncie, Robert and Helen Lynd observed that "walking for pleasure [became] practically extinct" (Lynd and Lynd, 257, 260). At the same time, the automobile slowly pulled apart traditional family togetherness as young adults increasingly sought the privacy and escape from their parents that the automobile provided.

During this period, the number of registered automobiles grew from 8 million in 1919 to more than 24 million by 1929. Technological improvements such as hydraulic brakes, safety glass, and balloon tires were developed. Engines became more powerful and automobile speeds increased. With increased speed came more traffic accidents. Historian James Fink noted that during the period "automobile accidents accounted for 23,600 deaths [and] over 700,000 injuries" (165). The introduction of antifreeze for car radiators in 1926 provided for increased winter use of cars. Enclosed vehicles with heaters and air-conditioning became the preferred style. Charles Kettering developed a fast-drying paint in 1923 that allowed the introduction of paint colors (besides black) on inexpensive cars (Baughman [1996, *American Decades: 1920–1929*], 172). Styling and aesthetics became important features for new automobiles. Americans developed a greater dependency on the automobile and grew increasingly passionate about the freedom it provided. Americans of all classes crossed over from previously viewing the automobile as a novelty to having an outright "love affair" with their cars.

The automobile allowed vacationers to get to areas that were previously inaccessible such as camping areas, mountain resorts, and national parks. By the end of the decade over 80 percent of all vacation trips were taken by automobile. The previous style of impromptu free roadside auto-camping (see chapter 2) quickly gave way to the use of privately owned roadside camping sites and hotels (Braden, 323, 326). Entrepreneurs purchased much of the roadside land; roadside camps and small hotels sought to attract the auto-vacationer, as did restaurants and permanent rental cottages with modern sanitary features. Within a very short time, the opportunity for an inexpensive auto vacation existed from coast to coast, in areas such as Coronado Beach, California, and Oceanside Camp, Maine, and just about everywhere else in-between.

The Airplane, Barnstormers, and "Lucky Lindy"

In 1919, a U.S. Navy flying-boat, *NC-4*, piloted by Captain John Alcock and Lt. Arthur W. Brown made the first successful transatlantic trip, crossing from the United States to Europe. Newspapers heralded these two aviators and all others who continued to set altitude, distance, and speed records. The airplane itself and the daredevils who pushed their machines to the limits were given extensive media coverage. The popularity of air shows increased, and unlike in the years before the war, the public now wanted to see stunts and aerobatics. Aviators known as barnstormers traveled around the country performing stunts such as wing-walking and other aerial acrobatics. Wing-walking was a daring attraction involving one or more barnstormers who climbed out of the cockpit and walked on the airplanes wings, as the airplane was actually in flight.

Airplanes of the time could not compete with railroads in either speed or in the luxury accommodations of the Pullman sleeping cars. Most of the airplanes were two-seat biplanes constructed of wood and fabric that were limited in the speed and distance they could achieve. Few aircraft could fly at speeds in excess of 150 miles per hour (mph), and their endurance was limited to about 3 hours of flight time. Commercial support and government interest in the airplane did not begin until after the Air Commerce Act of 1926 was passed. The main requirements of the bill were that pilots become licensed and that aircraft meet minimum maintenance standards. Many of the former barnstorming pilots and airplanes could not meet the requirements and therefore ceased to operate (Taneja, 6). Other barnstormers such as Clyde Cessna and William Piper pursued private enterprise in civilian aviation.

Cessna, an early barnstormer, was unlike the many other pilots in exhibition and stunt flying. Cessna wanted to build and sell airplanes in addition to providing instruction to civilian pilots for personal use and pleasure flying. Piper introduced the J3 Piper Cub, a single-engine, high-winged, fabric-covered monoplane that offered a fully enclosed cockpit. The Piper Cub became a popular aircraft both for training pilots and leisure flying (Taneja, 10). The names Cessna and Piper became synonymous with civilian aircraft and leisure flying throughout the twentieth century.

Interest in aviation reached an incredible frenzy in 1927 with the first solo transatlantic flight by Charles Lindbergh. Lindbergh's impact on aviation and popular public opinion cannot be understated. All across the nation, newspapers, magazines, and radio honored him, and there was a ticker-tape parade in New York attended by hundreds of thousands of people in his honor. The solo flight by

"Lucky Lindy" dramatically increased public attention to aviation both as a recreational pursuit and means of travel. According to the Federal Aviation Administration (FAA), prior to Lindbergh's flight only 28 commercial aircraft existed in the entire country with a total of only 112 total passengers in flight at any one time (Newark Airport Museum text). After Lindbergh's flight, commercial aviation and air transportation increased dramatically. In 1926, it was estimated that only 5,800 passengers flew in airplanes. By 1929, more than 3.5 million flew as airplane passengers—most for sightseeing or for short trips, others for weekend or hunting trips. At this time, Pan-American also began international service by providing air travel from Key West, Florida, to Havana, Cuba (Steiner [1933], 58).

The Railroad and Third-Class Accommodations

The railroad continued to be the most popular mode of public travel. Railroad travel peaked in 1920 with 1.2 billion total passengers. On any given night, it was estimated that more than 100,000 people slept in Pullman sleeping cars as the railway trains sped across the country. Reflective of the period, new designs introduced luxurious dining and sleeping accommodations to lure wealthy travelers, and first-class was considered the best way to travel. In 1927, Pullman introduced the ultimate in first-class travel with the single room car. This feature provided the traveler with an individual private compartment containing a bed, toilet, washstand, and storage area (Halberstadt, 55–63).

Around the same time, railroads began offering accommodations to the less wealthy middle-class passengers. Sleeping accommodations were provided in upright chair cars. To entice additional travelers, some railroads began offering better dining services. One advertisement for the Burlington, Ohio, route advertised "free pillows for overnight coach and chair car passengers" (Halberstadt, 112).

In southern states, segregation was strictly enforced, and African Americans and some immigrants were relegated to undesirable sections of the train in what could be described as third-class accommodations. A train traveling interstate from the north would require African Americans to move into separate railroad cars upon entering a southern state. Contrary to the notion of "moving to the back of the bus," on these trains African Americans were asked to move to the undesirable front of the train, directly behind the engine and coal cars, which meant increased heat, noxious smells, and increased noise and dirt.

During the entire period, the number of those traveling by railroad decreased by almost 20 percent. The decline was attributed to the rapid increase in automobile production (Duke University, n.p.). Nevertheless, railroad travel remained a popular mode of travel well into the mid-1940s.

Ocean Travel and Vacation Resorts

For the wealthy and elite, ocean travel was still quite popular. It became fashionable to cross the Atlantic in ultra-extravagant first-class accommodations. The ocean liners became so luxurious and grandiose that they were nicknamed "floating palaces." For the wealthy, it also became fashionable to travel the Atlantic on a Blue Riband ship. Ocean liners from European nations and America vied for the coveted Blue Riband, the award to the ocean liner that crossed the Atlantic in the quickest time. The British grand luxury liner the *Mauretania* held the record from 1920 to 1927. In 1928 and 1929, Germany held the fastest ships with the *Bremen* and the *Europa* (Horsham, 100). Water travel was not restricted to the ocean liners. During the period, there was an increase in pleasure boats of all kinds with more than 450 yacht clubs nationwide (Steiner [1933], 55).

Luxury resorts were still popular among the wealthy (and with Prohibition, drinking and gambling became fashionable). Unlike in previous years, it became acceptable (and popular) for an unchaperoned female to attend a resort. In 1927, the *Woman's Home Companion* stated that it was "now quite the usual thing for a party of girls to go unchaperoned to a summer resort." The article also provided advice on tipping and selecting the proper clothes for these resort vacations (Aron, 228). One such area was Santa Catalina Island off the coast of southern California, which was popular for a day at the beach, a night of ballroom dancing, or an extended stay. Most guests arrived by one of the two steamships that provided roundtrip service from Wilmington, California to Avalon on Santa Catalina Island while others arrived by private yacht. Judy Wade said Santa Catalina Island featured "[e]legant seaside hotels like the St. Catherine." The favorite spot on the island was the Casino Ballroom, which drew crowds of more than 5,000 to dance and listen to popular bands (Wade, n.p.).

Some unions recognized the continued need for a regular yearly vacation for the working class, and in order to provide suitable vacation options, unions began to purchase resorts for their members. The International Ladies Garment Workers Union (ILGWU), for example, purchased the Forest Park Hotel (a resort formerly frequented by the wealthy) in the Pocono Mountain region of Pennsylvania. Indoor facilities included a library, reading room, and a recreation area for dances. Outdoor facilities included tennis courts, hiking trails, and a lake for boating, fishing, and swimming (Aron, 219–220).

The idea of a regular scheduled vacation was beginning to take hold across the country, and by 1929, the idea of a two-week summer vacation was considered the norm. Not all Americans had vacation opportunities, but commercialization and advertising brought the idea into the mainstream. It would not be until the end of the 1930s that most of the working class was afforded a two-week vacation (Aron, 184).

CONCLUSION

By the end of the Roaring Twenties, more Americans lived in urban areas, and the city became the center of cultural influence on America's leisure patterns. Thanks to the automobile and mass media, a homogenized version of American trends, fashion, and games expanded into all areas of the country. With Americans spending money on commercial recreation, the old Puritan edict against idleness began to disappear as recreation and leisure came to be regarded as healthy and fruitful uses of time.

On October 29, 1929, however, the stock market collapsed. The jazz era was over, and Americans' leisure pursuits would once again change. With very little money available and much more time available than ever before, leisure and recreation during the Great Depression would achieve a newfound importance.

CHAPTER 4

THE GREAT DEPRESSION AND THE NEW DEAL: 1929–1939

CHRONOLOGY

1930   CBS and NBC begin live radio broadcasts of classical music.

1931   The first long-playing (LP) record is released.

1932   Air conditioning introduced to the market; Amelia Earhart becomes the first woman to fly solo across the Atlantic; unemployment reaches more than 13 million; Franklin D. Roosevelt (FDR) is elected president.

1933   FDR launches the New Deal; Prohibition ends in the United States; the first baseball all-star game is played; American Softball Association (ASA) is formed.

1934   The dust bowl hits the U.S. plains states; Parker Brothers introduces the game Monopoly.

1935   Alcoholics Anonymous is founded; Social Security is enacted in United States.

1936   Hoover Dam is completed; *Life* magazine is founded.

1937   The *Hindenburg* disaster occurs.

1938   U.S. Route 1 opens; the radio broadcast of *The War of the Worlds* causes panic.

1939   The first commercial passenger flight over the Atlantic takes place; World War II begins in Europe.

INTRODUCTION

The stock market crash of 1929 was an economic catastrophe that drastically altered the lifestyles and leisure patterns of all Americans. Millions were unemployed, and more than 40 million of the nation's 122 million people were living in poverty. Those who had jobs saw work hours and wages decreased. Marriage rates and birthrates declined. Population growth almost came to a standstill with a minimal growth rate of 7 percent in the ten-year period (the previous decades had birthrates that approached 20 percent). The low birth rate was a direct result of the severe economic conditions. Individuals could not support or feed either themselves or their current family so they put off marriage and having children. The economic hardships created an unprecedented amount of leisure time for all classes of people.

Recreation and leisure assumed a new importance in Americans' lives. Leisure would serve as a relief from worry and a way to pass time until people could work again. The irony was that even though most individuals had more time to enjoy leisure, they did not have money to spend. In search of inexpensive entertainment, people spent more time at home and listened to the radio. With what little money they had, they escaped to the movies. The depression also marked the first time that the federal government showed a serious interest in public recreation and leisure-time programs. In an attempt not only to spur the economy, but also to provide for recreation and entertainment, Franklin D. Roosevelt and the New Deal assumed a key role in the daily lives, both public and private, of all Americans.

There are two important studies on American lifestyles and leisure habits that serve as valuable references to the study of individual leisure habits during the depression. Robert and Helen Lynd returned to Muncie, Indiana, and performed a comparative study between the years 1935 and 1937, which they published in *Middletown in Transition: A Study in Cultural Conflicts*. George Lundberg and colleagues performed a thorough study of early 1930s Westchester County, New York, in *Leisure: A Suburban Study*. Lundberg's study examined a geographical area that contained more than 500,000 individuals. A significant number of references to each of these studies is included in this chapter.

PUBLIC INTEREST

The Great Depression

The effects of the 1929 stock market crash were staggering and triggered a worldwide depression. Nationwide, production of goods plummeted, and unemployment stood at 25 percent. Some areas such as Ohio and western Pennsylvania had unemployment rates of over 80 percent. As a result, those who had jobs saw their hours and wages drastically reduced (wages would not return to 1929 levels until 1940). Families could not pay mortgages and lost their homes and farms. Breadlines and food relief programs had a constant presence in most cities. Millions were homeless, and some simply packed up their families and moved in search of work to support and feed family members. In general, money was not available for entertainment and recreation.

The 1932 election of President Franklin D. Roosevelt and the establishment of the New Deal would actively change the government's involvement in the lifestyles of all Americans. In 1933, Roosevelt established the first of many federally funded programs to help the economy. The National Recovery Administration (NRA), for example, set a 40-hour workweek (for those still working) as a general guideline, a reduction of more than 20 percent from the previous minimum of a 48-hour workweek. The idea behind mandating fewer work hours was to balance

Depression breadline in 1932. People line up adjacent to a newspaper/magazine stand waiting to be fed in New York City. Courtesy of FDR Library, New Hyde Park, New York.

production with demand. In 1937, the Fair Labor Standards Act made the 40-hour workweek accepted practice (Aron, 250). The reduction in work hours and massive unemployment actually forced a significant amount of leisure time on the middle and working classes at a time when people could least likely afford to enjoy it. Because of this, the federal government saw the need not only to sponsor leisure and recreational programs, but also to increase and expand them. One of the first acts by the administration regarding leisure was to repeal Prohibition.

Prohibition and the Numbers

Prohibition (see chapter 3) ended on December 5, 1933, with the ratification of the Twenty-first Amendment to the U.S. Constitution. When drinking once again became legal, the speakeasies disappeared, and nightclubs flourished. The Cotton Club in New York's Harlem was widely known for its lavish entertainment and wealthy clientele. Among the middle and working classes, the saloons, road-houses, and jook joints prospered. With alcohol once again legal, they advertised themselves as a "new" place for social gatherings involving eating, drinking, and dancing. Sociologist Jesse Steiner's research of federal tax receipts between 1933 and 1935 noted a "growing popularity of forms of entertainment associated with the sale and consumption of liquor" ([1972], 102).

Many other new kinds of eating and drinking establishments that offered an opportunity to socialize without alcohol came into being. For example, the soda fountain became popular, especially among young people. Usually located in a drugstore or general convenience store, the soda fountain was a service counter that served up food, ice cream, and soda. Some businesses enlarged the soda fountain areas to include tables and chairs. Other public places that offered the opportunity for groups of adults to gather included diners and restaurants. These public establishments catered to the middle and working classes and did not charge admission fees. Many also offered recreational features such as pinball, Ping-Pong, billiards, or even miniature golf; this encouraged patrons to linger long enough to purchase food and drink. Most of these places provided music by either a radio or a jukebox, and some allowed dancing. For a small amount of money some people could congregate, socialize, and have fun for an entire evening. Many others, however, could not even afford the least inexpensive entertainment, and some of them turned to criminal activities.

A popular illegal urban activity that became popular, especially in working-class urban areas such as New York's Harlem and South Side Chicago, were policy games simply known as "the numbers." Policy games involved illegal betting. The numbers involved placing a bet with a bookie on a three-digit number. In order to win, the number had to match the last three numbers of the pari-mutuel betting at a predetermined local horse racing track. (Pari-mutuel was the total gross receipts from a day's betting at a horse racing track. The bookies developed a system of betting against the random pari-mutuel numbers.)

For example, if the gross receipts for the day were $1,345,013, anyone who had placed a bet on "013" would win. A typical payoff was 100 to 1, or $10, in return for a ten-cent bet. Various combinations of numbers could be bet on for lesser odds. Millions played the numbers every day, but very few were winners. The numbers was extremely lucrative for gangsters since they controlled the bookies and the profits from the illegal betting, and for the economically deprived, it served as both a leisure activity and a chance to win some easy money. During this time, in any given year in Chicago, it was reported that more than 7,000 people were "employed" running numbers. Many businesses such as taverns, grocery stores, and other small enterprises stayed afloat by taking bets (Trotter, 455).

The WPA and CCC

Free public recreation and leisure-time programs were desperately needed to offset idle time and social disorder. However, most state and local municipalities did not have the economic resources to maintain public recreation programs. In 1934, Roosevelt responded by creating the Federal Emergency Relief Administration (FERA), which established the Works Progress Administration (WPA) and the Civilian Conservation Corp (CCC), which in turn created jobs and provided public recreation and leisure-time programs. According to Steiner, the federal government's involvement at this time stood out "as a landmark in the history of the public recreation movement" ([1972], 59).

Between 1935 and 1943, the WPA provided jobs for more than 8.5 million previously unemployed workers. WPA projects built more than 650,000 miles of road, hundreds of bridges, 8,000 parks, and more than 125,000 public buildings (Gillon, 987). More than 20,000 projects built public recreation facilities including swimming pools, campsites, parks, band shells, and 15,000 community centers. The WPA not only built and renovated recreation facilities, but it also sponsored a recreation section employing more than 50,000 people nationwide to conduct and administer leisure-time programs. It also trained an estimated 250,000 volunteer leaders in 7,000 different communities to supervise more than five million weekly participants. Nearly 85 percent of the sponsored programs took place in communities that previously did not have a source for organized public recreation, and 70 percent of the programs were in rural areas. Community activities included carnivals, social games, and pet shows. There were dance lessons of all sorts including ballroom, tap, folk, and square dancing. Group instruction was provided in drama, choral singing, music, and hobby activities such as drawing, crafts, and photography (Wrenn and Harley, 224–227).

The WPA was also responsible for constructing and improving numerous roads, hiking trails, lakes, and campsites in the national parks and forests through the CCC. Many of the CCC projects created campsites within easy access of the large cities. In July of 1935, the *New York Times* reported "over 1,800 shelters and cabins existed in New York State free of charge in the State Forests. Of that number over 600 were recently constructed by the CCC." The CCC employees both worked and lived on the campsites. A typical campsite included a recreation building for indoor activities such as music, Ping-Pong, or board games. Outdoor activities at one North Dakota camp, for example, included baseball, basketball, volleyball, horse shoes, tennis, swimming, and track and field. The camps also sponsored teams that played in an intercamp league (Rollin, 84).

The WPA and the CCC also constructed or improved numerous national historic sites, seashores, and recreation areas. Included among them were the Mount Rushmore memorial in South Dakota; Jones Beach in Long Island, New York; and the Hoover Dam at Boulder City, Nevada.

The Hoover Dam, on the Colorado River, was initially constructed to provide electricity and water for a major portion of the Southwest. Behind the dam was the largest man-made lake in the United States, Lake Mead. At its deepest point, Lake Mead measured over 500 feet deep and the shoreline stretched for 550 miles. Almost immediately, campgrounds and small hotels were constructed, and the area quickly developed into a major recreation facility that included swimming, boating, and hiking. The lake itself offered some of the best recreational fishing in the United States with an abundance of catfish, bluegill, trout, and striped bass (Gorp.com, "Lake Mead National Recreation Area—Activities," n.p.). A significant amount of WPA resources were also used to develop recreational facilities in municipal parks and playgrounds.

Parks, Playgrounds, and Open Space

Municipalities and government agencies wanted to get the most out of their recreation dollar and therefore sought to provide leisure and recreation that would reach as many people as possible for a limited cost. Public parks and playgrounds represented the most economical use of space to provide a maximum amount of recreation and leisure and offered a variety of recreational opportunities for the American public. Between 1935 and 1939, the WPA either renovated or built 40,000 parks and playgrounds. Facilities included baseball fields, basketball courts, gymnasiums, swimming pools, ice-skating rinks, golf courses, and tennis courts.

Outdoor park activities included volleyball, tennis tournaments, horseshoe meets, pet shows, doll shows, community singing, public dancing, and band concerts. A new outdoor recreational pursuit, popular among young men and boys, was the building and flying of model airplanes. In Westchester County, for example, it was noted that no less than ten boys' model airplane clubs existed in the county parks and playgrounds, and there was an annual model airplane tournament (Lundberg et al., 64).

Planned Communities: Radburn, New Jersey

Many municipalities continued to search for an ideal community that could provide both housing and recreation. Unlike in previous planned communities such as Pullman City, Illinois, the new urban problem was finding a way to accommodate the automobile. Prior to the mass production of the automobile, city streets served as playgrounds and areas of socialization for urban residents. Automobiles competed for limited space, which resulted in traffic jams and many pedestrian fatalities. In an attempt to alleviate traffic congestion, many WPA public works projects built countless roads and bridges, many connecting the cities with the growing suburban areas.

In 1929, Clarence Stein and Henry Wright planned a middle-class community in Fair Lawn, New Jersey; a suburb 12 miles from New York City. The plan called for a self-contained "walkable" community of 25,000 residents living in detached homes. There was to be a full separation of pedestrians from automobiles with clusters of houses facing inward toward 23 acres of "passive parks." Recreation facilities were to include two swimming pools, four tennis courts, four baseball fields, five basketball courts, an archery range, three playgrounds, and a community center containing a library and a performance theater. Unfortunately, the corporation was hit hard by the 1929 stock market crash, and only a small portion of the community accommodating 3,000 residents was built by 1930. Planned communities would continue to be built both during and after World War II (Maguire, n.p.).

LIFESTYLES

Rural Areas and the Dust Bowl

Farms and rural areas had begun to feel the effects of economic deprivation in the early 1920s. Between 1932 and 1934, for many farmers in the plains states such as the Dakotas, Nebraska, Kansas, New Mexico, Oklahoma, and Texas the American dream of economic recovery became a total nightmare. Due to unusual and unexplained weather conditions of excessive heat and drought, the topsoil dried up, and the farms literally blew away in the wind; this phenomenon became known as the dust bowl. More than two and a half million people simply packed up their families and belongings and headed west to California and the Pacific Northwest in search of jobs and a better lifestyle.

The WPA attempted to alleviate the dust bowl problem with projects such as the Tennessee Valley Authority and the Hoover Dam. These two projects sought to provide jobs, water, and electricity to the impoverished areas. The introduction of electricity to rural areas by the Rural Electrification Administration (REA) had a profound impact on rural life.

Up until 1935, it was estimated that only 10 percent of rural areas had electrical power. By 1940, electrical power lines had been delivered to over 40 percent of rural homes and farms and to over 90 percent by 1950 (Moss, 170). With electricity, rural homes could enjoy the newfound electrical appliances and conveniences such as the vacuum cleaner, refrigerator, and radio. The radio would eventually serve as a means of connecting rural and urban areas through the common experience of syndicated news and music programs and commercial advertising, especially for rural farm women who did not venture far from home.

In 1938, Lucile Winifred Reynolds performed a study of the leisure-time activities of more than 1,000 adult midwestern farm women. She discovered that the most common leisure-time activities were centered within the home and included reading, writing letters, listening to phonograph records, and listening to the radio. Although reading (combined with studying and writing) was mentioned by almost 99 percent of the women, Reynolds discovered that it was not reading but a recent development that most contributed to the decline of needlework. Reynolds pointed out that needlework or fancy work (see chapter 1) had been extremely popular thirty years earlier. However, "much of the lingerie, table and bed linen that was formerly made at home [was now] purchased ready made," mostly from mail-order catalogs. Some other popular indoor pursuits included collecting glassware (such as pitchers and water jugs) and making scrapbooks (such as for postcard collecting and genealogy). Some of the glassware was handed down from family members while some was made or purchased through mail-order catalogs (5–10).

Among outdoor leisure pursuits, gardening was the most popular choice for over 90 percent of farm women. Other popular outdoor activities included growing strawberries and nature study. Although walking was mentioned by over 25 percent of the women, it was not one of the more popular choices. Reynolds stated that unlike urban dwellers, "[farm] women had no tradition of walking just for the fun it afforded. Many of them were settled on the farm before the days of automobiles and when they wished to get away for the afternoon to visit a neighbor they frequently had no alterative but to walk" (9). Outside of the home, voluntary membership in church societies and community organizations that met year-round was mentioned by over 50 percent of the women. For rural areas in general, recreation and leisure activities on the social or community level tended to be centered around either church membership or fraternal agricultural associations.

The most popular fraternal organization in rural communities was the National Grange. The Grange provided community leadership to enrich social life through plays, drama, music, dancing, and athletics. Most branches maintained a community hall to be used for community entertainment, of which, by 1935 at least 3,600 existed in rural areas nationwide. Another popular agricultural organization, the American Farm Bureau Federation, encouraged families to join as a single unit. In 1935, the bureau had 1.2 million members. Recreation and leisure activities provided by the bureau included family functions such as picnics, camping, hiking, community pageants, and singing (Wrenn and Harley, 148–151).

At the same time, 4-H clubs were located in all 48 continental states with more than 78,000 individual clubs that engaged more than 1.4 million youth in various agricultural activities. The 4-H clubs were supervised by almost 150,000 adult volunteer leaders under the administration of more than 6,500 full time U.S. Department of Agriculture employees (Wrenn and Harley, 148). Another youth organization, the Future Farmers of America (FFA) was composed of mostly high-school-age boys; the organization had more than 225,000 members in 6,300 local chapters. The FFA not only encouraged the improvement of rural life, but it also organized recreational activities for members. In rural areas, most organizations such as the FFA were strictly segregated and reserved for whites only. A similar farm group for African American youths was called New Farmers of America (Wrenn and Harley, 148–151).

An intensive study of African American life during the depression by Swedish sociologist Gunnar Myrdal found that for the most part, African Americans continued to have inferior facilities in comparison with whites. In southern states in particular, almost no funds were directed to African American communities for recreation facilities or leadership programs. As a result, African Americans continued to remain segregated within their own social clubs, churches, athletic clubs, and fraternal organizations (Kraus [1971], 301).

Urban and Suburban Leisure and Church Sponsored Recreation

Within the home, there was a trend toward simple entertaining and visiting relatives and friends. Comparative studies in Muncie, Indiana; Westchester County, New York; and among midwestern farm women found that listening to the radio was mentioned as the most popular form of home entertainment. In many instances the radio was usually on while housework chores were being done or while other leisure activities were taking place such as eating, reading, working on hobbies, entertaining friends, playing bridge, or dancing (Lundberg et al., 104).

Extravagant spending and recreational pursuits continued among some of the wealthy. In 1935, Robert and Helen Lynd returned to Muncie, Indiana, and observed that the wealthy class had adapted new leisure interests "as a symbol of status." Golf and tennis that had previously been exclusive recreations of private country clubs had lost some of their appeal. This loss of interest was attributed to the fact that the increased number of public golf courses and tennis courts made them "everyman's game." New interests in expensive pursuits such as horses and private aviation developed. In 1930, two private riding clubs were established in Muncie. In 1932, the first of an annual horse show was staged that drew entries from all over the Midwest. In that same year, a group of wealthy Muncie businessmen opened a private airport (Lynd and Lynd [1937], 247). The depression did in fact affect the wealthy, and those who did not lose their fortunes had to economize. Sociologist Jesse Steiner said that it "meant the sale of expensive yachts, the closing of one or more of their summer or winter estates, the giving up of extended foreign tours or planning for less expensive vacations" ([1972], 40).

Both the wealthy and middle class reported that almost 25 percent of their time outside the home was spent "eating out." Visiting, which was inexpensive, occupied a large portion of working-class leisure time. One working-class woman said, "I have to stay home with the children and there's not much to do except sew and read" (Lundberg et al., 178–179).

Lundberg and his colleagues asked people about the amount of leisure time families spent together. For the most part, the family ate at least one meal (dinner) together. At breakfast the father usually ate earlier than the children in order to go to work. The father ate lunches in the vicinity of the workplace. Over 70 percent of families spent significant holidays such as Thanksgiving and Christmas together. While spending time together, most families listened to the radio. Both adults and children played games, with bridge and jigsaw puzzles leading the list (184–186).

Equal among all classes was the amount of time spent outside the home in automobiles and at the movies. Over 70 percent of people in the Lundberg study traveled as a family in the automobile, and over 40 percent regularly went to the movies as a family. Most of children's weekday time was spent at home with listening to the radio occupying more than half their weekday time. Children played outdoors during the weekends. Boys tended to play baseball, football, marbles, or just about any sport. Girls spent time socializing with each other and going to the movies. Movies were popular for both genders (Lundberg et al., 181–182).

The time required for traveling to and from work among the middle class, combined with rising early and arriving home late, caused many commuting men to adjust their leisure time schedules. Weekday nights usually consisted of quiet recreation hours spent reading or sleeping, and the weekend was reserved for outdoor or family activities. Lundberg and his colleagues observed that the middle class spent more time reading and gardening, whereas the working class centered their time around the family meal and listening to the radio. Many middle-class and wealthy homes contained a recently introduced space—the playroom. Lundberg and his colleagues observed that the playroom was usually "furnished with ping-pong tables, billiards, backgammon, or a bar" (Lundberg et al., 175–177).

Women's leisure habits within the home were similar to those of their husbands in time devoted to eating, reading, and listening to the radio. A wealthy suburban home was more likely than an urban home to contain a yard and a garden. Wealthy homes were also more likely to contain a bar for the private consumption of alcohol. Flower gardening was a popular hobby among all classes. Women in particular joined clubs such as the Garden Club of America that encouraged "vegetable gardens as a source of food supply" and flower gardening as a leisure pursuit (Lundberg et al., 61-62).

Membership in clubs and fraternal organizations continued to increase. By 1939, fraternal organizations, women's clubs, and cultural and civic organizations nationwide numbered more than 20 million members in more than 250,000 lodges (Wrenn and Harley, 140). One Indiana resident, in response to the number of clubs in comparison to the 1920s exclaimed, "Goodness! We have more than ever" (Lynd and Lynd [1937], 280). Churches typically sponsored a majority of fraternal organizations and clubs.

The role of the church in recreation was drastically changing. One minister acknowledged that the chief competitors to Sunday worship were "the automobile, golf habit, and the weekend excursion" (Lundberg et al., 194). Early in the 1920s, churches began joining forces with recreational leaders in recognizing the need for organized leisure. Churches took an active role in social and recreational activities in both women's and men's clubs and also in sponsoring youth groups such as the Boy Scouts, Girl Scouts, and Campfire Girls. A large percentage of those who took part in church functions were not regular churchgoers or were not even of the same religious denomination. The Catholic Youth Organization (CYO) was an example of a church-sponsored social and recreational organization that served the community (see "Sports and Games" later in this chapter).

Despite the marked increase in social recreation, churches and clubs still remained segregated. E. Franklin Frazier, author of *Black Bourgeoisie*, criticized the negative effects segregation had on depression-era African Americans. Without the same access as whites to public entertainment and recreation, Frazier said that many poorer and middle-class African Americans had very few choices, and they became obsessed with sports, the numbers rackets and a "preoccupation with gambling, especially poker" (Frazier, 208–211). Poker especially was noted as a popular activity among many middle-class African Americans.

African Americans remained segregated throughout the entire country. In Westchester County, for example, Lundberg and his colleagues observed segregated "Negro settlements" and noted African Americans' absence from any public recreation activities or places of entertainment (132). In the south, both rural and urban African Americans remained segregated by law. They continued to congregate in jook joints or honky-tonks (see chapter 1) located in "undesirable" areas or on the outskirts of towns. A unique entertainment form that first developed among urban African Americans was the rent party.

Rent parties began in the 1920s when African Americans first migrated to northern urban areas, but they became common during the depression. The idea was to provide entertainment at a house party and charge a small admission fee that in turn would be used to pay the host's rent. Entertainment included alcohol, gambling, food, music, and dancing. Rent parties became a regular source for urban social entertainment (Trotter, 455).

The National Youth Administration and Cellar Clubs

A 1938 study sponsored by the American Council on Education charted some of the leisure habits of American teens. Responses to the study included "I play cards, loaf, eat, and sleep" and "Nothing to do, just do nothin' [*sic*]." In the segregated South, "[t]he majority of both races find nothing to do but to sit idly around, tramp off to their neighbors, or while away the time at the store." One positive result of this was that youths tended to stay in school longer. High school attendance rose to almost 75 percent of those eligible to attend in 1940 as opposed to less than 50 percent in 1930 (Bondi, 328).

For those not in school, the formation of the National Youth Administration (NYA) provided both full- and part-time employment. More than two million of those who were not in school found jobs through the NYA, and more than two million still in school were employed part-time (Moss, 170). In 1939, for example, more than 275,000 youths were employed by the NYA to work with the CCC in distant national parks and forests where they also lived in one of more than 1,500 camps. Their evenings and weekends were free, and recreation and leisure

Oakland, California, 1940. "Hanging out" on a street corner was a common leisure activity for young adults and teenagers around this time. Courtesy of U.S. National Archive & Records Administration (NARA).

activities were provided. Most camps had an education building that contained a library, reading room, and some classrooms. A typical recreation building provided tables for playing cards or board games, Ping-Pong, and pool. All of the camps were able to show movies (Wrenn and Harley, 216).

For many of the urban youth, gathering on the sidewalks or forming their own social clubs became a way of passing time. A distinctive street culture developed in the formation of cellar clubs. The cellar clubs were organized by youths between the ages of 16 and 25 to provide themselves with social and recreation programs including sports and dancing. The size of a club numbered from 6 to 100 members, and membership was usually limited within a neighborhood or similar ethnic group. Youths made use of abandoned storefronts, vacant buildings, or the cellar areas of local tenement buildings in almost all cities. In New York City alone, it was estimated that by 1940 more than 6,000 cellar clubs existed (Kraus [1971], 204–205).

ENTERTAINMENT

Radio, the *Hindenburg*, and *War of the Worlds*

Radio was one of the few forms of commercial entertainment that did not suffer drastically during the depression. Between 1930 and 1932, radio ownership increased by four million sets, and an additional six million sets were sold between 1932 and 1935. By the end of 1939, it was estimated that 90 percent of the nation's homes had at least one radio (Steiner [1972], 95). Radio's popularity could be attributed to the fact that it allowed an escape into a fantasy world of fun and entertainment and allowed people to forget the realities of the depression, all with little or no cost.

Radio offered a wide array of programs including news, religious sermons, music, sports, adventure shows, and comedies. The popular adventure shows included the *Green Hornet*, *Lone Ranger*, *Jack Armstrong*, *Little Orphan Annie*, and the *Shadow*. Families remained riveted to their radios and continued to tune in week after week. Popular comedies included *Jack Benny*, *The Goldbergs*, and *Fibber McGee and Molly*, but it was the comedy *Amos 'n' Andy* that became the most popular of all radio programs.

Amos 'n' Andy focused on depression-era humor and the trials and tribulations of two southern African Americans. It was estimated that 42 million people (in a nation of 125 million) regularly tuned in to *Amos 'n' Andy*. The show first aired in 1929, just a few weeks before the stock market crash. It continued to air six nights a week, Monday through Saturday from 7:00 to 7:15 P.M., well into the 1940s and eventually became a television program (Panati, 180–181).

Radio captured two of the twentieth century's most powerful media events. One was the May 6, 1937, explosion of the German airship *Hindenburg* that burst into flames during a landing attempt at Lakewood, New Jersey. The event was carried live by radio and stunned the listening audience (see "Airplanes and Airships" later in this chapter). The other was the October 30, 1938, broadcast of *War of the Worlds*. The fictional story of an alien spaceship invasion from Mars sent millions of listeners who mistook the performance for a news broadcast into a nationwide panic. The following day the *New York Times* reported that "the broadcast disrupted households, interrupted religious services, created traffic jams and clogged communication systems" (*New York Times*, October 31, 1938, 1:4).

Newspapers, Magazines, Books, and the Pinup

Although book production decreased by almost 50 percent from 1929 to 1933, reading remained a popular leisure activity among all classes. George Lundberg's 1934 study of Westchester County revealed that at least 75 percent of the population read with some regularity and "reading of some kind [was] one of the most common leisure pursuits" (Lundberg et al., 323). Americans yearned to read, and with less money to spend, they turned to libraries. Across the nation, libraries reported a significant increase in book circulation, especially among adults. The libraries would not have been able to respond to the demand for books without the support of federally funded projects administered by the WPA.

WPA projects renovated existing libraries, added more than 4,000 new reading rooms and 1,150 traveling libraries, and built more than 3,500 new branch libraries. The WPA also provided staff assistance in cataloging more than 20 million library books. In addition, 34 million books were cleaned, repaired, and reconditioned, which kept them in circulation (Wrenn and Harley, 230). Independent studies in Muncie, Indiana; Westchester, New York; and by the CCC agree that the average yearly circulation in books borrowed per person increased from about 6 in 1929 to about 11 or 12 by 1937.

One of the most popular books of the period that also became a popular movie was Margaret Mitchell's *Gone with the Wind* (1936), a best-seller for almost two years with sales in excess of two million copies. Another popular book was Dale Carnegie's *How to Win Friends and Influence People* (1937), which also sold more than two million copies (Panati, 175). The *Hardy Boys* and *Nancy Drew* mystery series both began in 1930 and were targeted primarily to teenage boys and girls, respectively. During the period, 16 individual books in the *Nancy Drew* series were published, and the series continued to be popular among girls for the remainder of the century (Rollin, 98).

Studies in the new suburban areas such as Westchester County, New York, revealed that almost half of all commuters read on their way to work, the overwhelming majority preferring a newspaper or a magazine rather than a book. Syndicated tabloids still dominated the newspaper market and provided advice columns, how-to and self-help articles (such as guides for painting or renovating a home), sports scores, crossword puzzles, gossip columns, entertainment, and just about anything containing scandal or exploitation. Newspapers also increased their use of color cartoon strips and photographs to accompany stories (Lundberg et al., 46, 318). Popular cartoon strips included *Blondie*, *Dick Tracy*, and *Little Orphan Annie*.

In 1939, the first of the superhero comics appeared with the introductions of *Superman* and *Batman*. Among young teens, interest in the new "pulp" comics grew. Pulps resembled magazines in appearance. They usually had color covers and featured fantasy stories of adventure and science fiction such as *Buck Rogers*, *Flash Gordon*, and *G-8 and His Battle Aces*.

In the beginning of the decade, subscriptions and newsstand purchases of magazines dropped. Most of the decline was among those magazines that were regularly purchased by individuals with medium to low incomes. By 1935, magazine circulation began to rise once again. Among adults, the *Saturday Evening Post*, *Time*, the *New Yorker*, *National Geographic*, and *Reader's Digest* (which, for example, had a circulation of more than 7 million) were popular. Women continued to purchase *Good Housekeeping* and *Ladies Home Journal*. Despite the depression new magazines continued to appear. *Esquire* (1933), for example, was a specialty magazine marketed as a guidebook to leisure for middle-class men. *Esquire* was expensive and contained articles on fashion and food, cartoons, and photographs of female movie stars, which came to be known as the pinups. By 1938 the magazine had a circulation of more than 700,000. In addition to fashion and food tips, many magazines also featured articles on popular music and dancing.

Dancing and the Jitterbug

Dancing continued to be popular and took place at resorts, hotels, and commercial dance halls. The new dance couple that many sought to emulate was Fred Astaire and Ginger Rogers, who gracefully danced their way through a series of Hollywood films. During the 1930s, they made nine films that featured dancing including *Flying Down to Rio* (1933), *Swing Time* (1936), *Shall We Dance?* (1937), and *The Story of Vernon and Irene Castle* (1939). As a result of the couple's popularity, dance studios such as Arthur Murray continued to attract students, and it was estimated that more than two million attended Arthur Murray's nationwide chains (Braden, 180). Latin dances such as the Samba and Rumba were popular, as were a few fad dances. Two popular fad dances were the Lambeth Walk and the Big Apple. In the Big Apple, popular in 1937, dancers "paraded in a circle, hands joined, and a caller indicated which pair was to move to the center and 'Shine!' or 'Peel!' . . . with hands waving above their heads." The Lambeth Walk was a short-lived fad dance in 1938. The couples strutted forward and back and "jerked their thumbs in the air to the exclamation 'Oy!' " (Panati, 167–168). The most popular dance of the period was the Jitterbug.

The Jitterbug was an adaptation of the Lindy hop that allowed the dancers to keep up with the faster music of swing. Unlike the Lindy hop, which was an eight-count syncopated dance rhythm, the Jitterbug was a fast-moving six-count, single-step beat. It encouraged improvisation in the "breakaway" position and incorporated lifts, jumps, and aerials. The Jitterbug was most closely associated with swing music, and for many, both the dance and the music became synonymous. Swing dancing was immensely popular, especially among those between aged 16 to 25, and quickly became a national craze.

Fads, Hobbies, and Games

With little money, many Americans sought inexpensive entertainment to fill their leisure hours. Miniature golf is one example of a dominant fad and popular activity that was an inexpensive way to spend part of an afternoon or weekend. Construction of a miniature golf course required very little land and a minimal amount of money. By 1932–1933, the country had more than 40,000 miniature golf courses. They were constructed in every part of the country in parks and hotels, adjacent to highways, and just about anywhere else. Mainly due to the overabundance of courses, the fad began to fade by the end of 1931 (Panati, 151–152).

Pinball was another example of an inexpensive entertainment fad. Pinball machines had been in existence for a few decades and were found mainly in arcades and amusement parks. Electric circuitry was added to pinball machines in 1933; this meant the game now featured illuminated lights, buzzers and bells, automatic ringing up of the score, and free game offerings, all of which created a new interest in the game. Pinball was viewed as a harmless fad and many soda shops, roadhouses, and bars installed the game (Panati, 152).

Hobbies first became popular after World War I, but they were mainly pursued by children and by the very old. During the depression, hobbies became popular among all age groups. Most hobbies centered around inexpensive or no-cost pursuits. President Roosevelt, for example, encouraged stamp collecting as a popular hobby. Magazines and newspapers encouraged many of the hobbies by encouraging readers to either "do-it-yourself" or begin a how-to project within the home (Braden, 106). Bird-watching was also an inexpensive hobby that became very popular. Bird-watchers were aided by the publication of Roger Tory Peterson's *A Field Guide to Birds* (1934), which sold more than three million copies.

Board games and jigsaw puzzles became popular among those in search of inexpensive leisure within the home. Jigsaw puzzles consisted of numerous odd-shaped cardboard pieces that interlocked to form a picture. The puzzles ranged in size from one square foot to sometimes as large as three feet by four feet but usually were not larger than a kitchen tabletop. The number of pieces could be as few as twelve for children's puzzles or as many as one thousand for adults or for the whole family to do together.

The trendy card game of bridge was another inexpensive way to entertain and have fun within the home. The game was so popular, especially among the suburban, white middle class, that it was considered "an obligatory social skill." Bridge was played by four people with a deck of 52 cards with two players as partners competing against another pair of players. The game was also played among high-school and grade-school children. Other popular card games were pinochle, pedro, knock-rummy, and poker (Lynd and Lynd [1937], 269–270).

New board games that sold well included the *Lindy Flying Game* and *Voyage Around the World*, both inspired by Lindberg's epic flight. Milton Bradley also introduced *Go to the Head of the Class*, an educational children's board game that remained a favorite throughout the century. The board game that was all the rage of not only the era but also the entire century was Monopoly.

Charles Darrow first introduced and copyrighted the depression-inspired game of Monopoly in 1933, and it became an instant sensation. Parker Brothers bought the rights to Monopoly in 1935 and began mass production of the game. Unlike other board games that were usually quick to play, Monopoly could go on for hours. The game could be played by people of all ages and genders and encouraged family participation (Bruce Johnson, n.p.).

Another favorite board game, played both inside and outside the home, was bingo. In this game, numbers were placed in a rotating drum and were then selected and called out one at a time. The object was to match a series of thirty-six random numbers that had been preprinted on a square board so that the player ended up with six numbers arranged vertically or horizontally on the card. By the mid-1930s bingo became a permanent fixture in Roman Catholic parishes as a way to raise money. The game's main appeal, however, was that it was a legal way to gamble because the winner would claim a cash prize, and in hard economic times a cash prize was an attractive reason to participate. By 1935, more than 10,000 parishes across the country operated weekly bingo games (Panati, 164).

Amusement Parks and the Parachute Jump

As with all forms of commercial entertainment, amusement parks suffered a decline in attendance and profits during this time. Many were reluctant to invest in building new rides and attractions, mainly because they did not have the money from profits and because banks were not in a position to make loans. In addition, many parks fell into disrepair due to the limited amount of money they were bringing in did not allow for proper maintenance.

One successful amusement park was Playland in Westchester County, New York. The park was undertaken as a community project with the goal that not only would it be self-supporting, but that it would also provide funds for the county park system. In the 1931 season, the park recorded 3.8 million visitors, most coming from within a 65-mile radius of the park (Lundberg et al., 78).

Annual county fairs continued and usually catered to local interests. Rural fairs included rodeos, agricultural displays, sporting contests, competitions, carnival rides, and sometimes airplane displays and acrobatics. The World's Fairs of the decade in Chicago, Illinois; San Diego, California; and New York were highly publicized as catering to a wider array of interests, and they drew spectators in the tens of millions. The consistent theme of all of the World's Fairs of the period was a fantasy escape from the realities of the depression featuring exhibits, rides, and amusements. Overall, the World's Fairs were not financial successes, but they left an indelible impression on American life.

The Chicago World's Fair (1933–1934) sold more than 39 million tickets and featured a giant-screen movie theater and burlesque dancer Sally Rand. Rand introduced the provocative fan dance to the public. Her suggestion of a nude body covered only by hand-held fans got her arrested for public indecency. The highlight at the San Diego World's Fair (1935–1936), which drew 17 million visitors, was a replica of Shakespeare's Globe Theater. When the fair was over, the theater was left intact and eventually became one of the country's most important regional theaters.

The New York World's Fair of 1939 was the most publicized fair of the decade and promoted a hope for a "better tomorrow." In its first season, 25 million visitors went to the fair. The most notable item at the fair was the introduction of the television. One of the most popular rides was the parachute jump. The official fair guidebook claimed that the parachute jump was "the largest and highest amusement ride in the world" and described it as a "rise skyward 250 feet for an elevated view of the Fair, and in less time than it takes to think about it you glide to earth [suspended by one of the eleven parachutes]. You bounce a bit when the 'chute lands but shock absorbers soften the process." The complete ride took less than a minute. In 1939, 551,621 visitors took the jump. In 1940, the jump was moved to Steeplechase in Coney Island (see chapter 5) (Bondi, 326–328).

MUSIC AND THEATER

Broadway and the Federal Theater Project

Vaudeville continued its rapid decline. Many former vaudeville theater owners eliminated costly live performances and converted to movie theaters showing new talkies in hopes of attracting paying customers. By the end of 1930, only one large vaudeville theater remained in operation—the Palace Theater in New York. In an attempt to find work, many of the more popular vaudeville performers took their acts to radio and Hollywood.

Popular Broadway productions such as the *Ziegfeld's Follies* were also affected. Live theater was expensive for both producers and ticket buyers. As with many other industries, theater owners and producers could no longer afford the high cost of production, and many simply ceased production and closed their theaters. At a time when it appeared that live theater productions would cease to exist, the federal government made a unique decision.

Many in the theater suffered the same levels of unemployment as the rest of the nation. The government realized that unemployed theater workers not only required assistance, but that they could also provide entertainment on a large scale. As a result, in 1935 the WPA created the Federal Theater Project (FTP). The FTP would extend beyond Broadway-style theaters and aid many other cultural programs.

The FTP eventually employed more than 30,000 actors, directors, musicians, dancers, and artists and maintained more than one hundred theater companies throughout the nation. The theater companies staged an average of 2,800 performances per month, presented to audiences numbering more than one million per month. The FTP also sponsored more than one hundred symphony orchestras and thousands of dramatic and musical performances and enrolled more than 160,000 in music classes (Kraus [1971], 204). Unlike previous theater performances that were confined to elaborate indoor theaters, the FTP brought shows to CCC camps, hospitals, schools, and rural areas. Many of the traveling performances were either free or presented at a minimal cost. Many millions of Americans who previously could not afford to attend a Broadway-style production were able to see quality theater productions for the first time.

The Fantasy World of the Movies

Even the movies were not immune from the depression. Attendance declined by almost 40 percent from 1929 to 1932. During that period, over 30 percent of the nation's 22,700 movie theaters were not in use, and no new theaters were constructed. Although attendance was in steady decline, theater managers saw the potential for profit with the changeover to sound and continued to install the new technology. In 1929 alone, more than nine thousand theaters were equipped for sound, and by 1932, the total number was 14,800 (Steiner [1972], 94). In further attempts to increase attendance, theater owners introduced the double feature in

1931 (two different full-length movies for the price of one admission) and the outdoor automobile drive-in movie theater in 1933 (see chapter 6). By 1935, it became profitable for the movie theaters to add live musical performances by swing bands.

Theater owners also began providing special features to attract a younger audience. Short cartoons featuring characters such as Mickey Mouse were shown before the feature film. By 1935, the Saturday movie matinee was a regular part of Americans' weekly schedules, and children accounted for approximately 35 percent of the total movie audience. One theater owner reported that each child would stay between three and six hours and that "the children's matinee [attracted] more than 1,000 children every Saturday even on the coldest of winter days, and the summer attendance [was] by far larger" (Lynd and Lynd [1937], 262).

For most cities, suburbs, and small towns, movies played seven days a week, from early afternoon to late evening. Of all the different types of entertainment available outside of the home, the movies were still the most affordable. Audiences sought the fantasy world of movies with escapist themes such as gangster movies, westerns, comedies, and musicals. The idea was to be entertained and forget the harsh realities of life and the depression. In Westchester County, it was estimated that adults went to the movies about three times per month and that teens and children between the ages of 8 and 19 attended at least once a week (Lundberg et al., 291). By 1939, it was estimated that over 65 percent of the American population attended the movies on a regular basis.

Music and the King of Swing

During the early years of the depression commercial radio sponsors continued to promote predominantly white "sweet" jazz bands such as Paul Whiteman, Guy Lombardo, and Fred Warring and crooners such as Bing Crosby. (To croon a song was to sing it in a soft or sentimental manner.) Jazz, however, was not the only popular music format.

Hillbilly music (sometimes know as country and western music) was popular in the southern part of the United States. The radio transmission of the Grand Ole Opry from Nashville, Tennessee, did much to promote the music, as did artists such as Jimmie Rodgers and Bob Wills and the Texas Playboys. In 1930, both CBS and NBC began broadcasting classical music in addition to their regular programming. Orchestral, choral, and opera music also were becoming more popular, especially as a result of the increase in free concerts in municipal parks.

In 1930, the recording industry attempted to increase sales with the introduction of a single home unit that combined a record player and a radio. In 1931, the industry introduced the long-playing (LP), 78 revolutions per minute (rpm) record capable of storing four minutes of music on each side of the record. In 1935, Decca Records lowered the price of records from 75 cents to 35 cents, and sales increased. As a result, the record industry was once again a viable commercial venture. However, the main supply of records was not for in-home use, but for use in jukeboxes.

Music played in jukeboxes would account for more than 30 million record sales a year, and jukeboxes did much to promote dance bands and popular artists of the era (Horsham, 42). Many commercial establishments such as soda shops, diners, roadhouses, social clubs, jook joints, and honky-tonks installed jukeboxes to solicit business. These places became popular, especially among teens who wanted to listen or dance to the music. The term *juke joint* became a slang term among whites for any commercial establishment that had a jukebox. Among African Americans the term *juke joint* became interchangeable as slang with *jook joint* (see chapter 1). In the early 1930s, the preferred jukebox music was jazz. It was an offshoot of jazz, however, that both defined the entire era and became the most popular jukebox and radio music—it was known simply as Swing.

Swing differed from jazz in that it was accentuated by resounding drum beats, and featured more brass instruments—horns, trombones, and saxophones (swing

New York, 1939. Swing musicians jam in a studio. Courtesy of NARA.

bands had as many as five of each of instrument)—resulting in the subsequent name of the "big band" sound. Some of the music had a "jump" that appealed to the jitterbug dancers, and there was also a fair mix of slow ballads to keep dancers on the floor. Bands such as Duke Ellington, Count Basie, Fletcher Henderson, and Benny Goodman were ethnically diverse, mostly made up of African Americans and descendants of Italian and Jewish immigrants. Duke Ellington was credited with naming the musical style in the title of a popular 1932 song, "It Don't Mean a Thing if It Ain't Got that Swing." However, many date the beginning of the swing craze to 1935.

In 1935, Benny Goodman and his swing orchestra had toured the country with limited success, and he planned to disband the orchestra at the end of the tour at the Palomar Ballroom in Los Angeles, California. At the Palomar Ballroom, however, he was met by a crowd of more than 2,500 people and a nationwide radio audience. The response from the dancers and the listening audience was overwhelming. Upon arriving back in New York more than three thousand fans showed up for a performance at the Paramount Theater. Goodman's resounding success quickly earned him the nickname "the King of Swing." The boost provided by Goodman, combined with the outlet of jukeboxes and radio, made swing big business. It was estimated that over 70 percent of all musical recordings during the period featured swing (Braden, 177).

It was also Goodman who brought swing to the mainstream public attention with a concert at New York's Carnegie Hall on January 16, 1938. At Carnegie Hall, Goodman presented an ethnically diverse all-star orchestra including Harry James, Fletcher Henderson, Teddy Wilson, and Gene Krupa. Goodman and his orchestra presented a portion of American culture that was racially and ethnically mixed, something that existed in some small segments of society but not as part of mainstream America. Historian Lewis Erenberg called the concert "a cultural phenomenon that bridged the significant gap between races and classes" (67).

Some Americans were in a panic over the moral implications of the music. One Catholic archbishop, for example, claimed that swing and the jitterbug dancers represented "cannibalistic rhythmic orgies . . . wooing our youth along the primrose path to hell" (Stowe, 24).

Although some swing bands were integrated, the reality of life during that time was that segregation laws existed in the South, and although the north was not legally segregated, evidence of the Jim Crow mentality was prevalent everywhere in the United States. One noted example involved African American singer Marian Anderson.

Anderson was a widely acclaimed singer who had toured Europe to rave reviews. In 1935, the *New York Times* called her "one of the great singers of our time." In 1939, Anderson was scheduled to perform in Washington, D.C., at Constitution Hall. The Daughters of the American Revolution, who owned Constitution Hall, intervened and refused to let her sing there because of the color of her skin. Anderson chose to perform outdoors on the steps of the Lincoln Memorial instead. The concert was held on a cold April day and drew an audience of more than 75,000, both African American and white, and it was estimated that millions more tuned in by radio (Trotter, 485–486). Sadly, equal opportunities for all Americans, either as performers, participants, fans, or vacationers, would still be 25 years in the future when federal legislation would begin to prevent such incidents.

SPORTS AND GAMES

Professional Sports and Spectators

During the bleakest years of the depression from 1929 to 1932, attendance at professional sporting events declined. In 1932, the Associated Press reported a 40 percent decline in college football attendance. Major league baseball showed a similar decrease from 10 million in 1930, to 8 million in 1932, to 6.3 million the following year. By 1935, with the introduction of night games, radio broadcasts, and special promotions such as an annual all-star game (began in 1933), baseball attendance began to rise back to predepression numbers. Special matches between highly publicized celebrities and championship games such as the World Series maintained capacity crowds throughout the worst times (Bondi, 508).

During the 1930s and well into the 1940s, boxing continued to be the second most popular sport in America (behind baseball). Boxing was an international sport that became intertwined with politics and world events. In June 1936, African American boxer Joe Louis lost a heavyweight fight in twelve rounds to German Max Schmeling. Adolf Hitler later claimed the victory as a symbol of Aryan superiority. A highly publicized rematch in 1938 was billed as a bout between Hitler's master Aryan race and American democracy. More than 80,000 fans filled New York's Yankee Stadium, and millions more tuned in on the radio to witness Louis's one-round knock out of Schmeling. However, much of boxing's appeal waned throughout the period as stories of gambling and fixed fights continued to permeate the sport.

Gambling was the main appeal to spectators attending horse racing events. In addition to spectators looking to make some money by betting on horse races, many states looked to horse racing for an additional source of revenue. During the depression, 15 states legalized betting at horse tracks in addition to the six states that had previously legalized it, bringing the total to 21 (Steiner [1972], 103).

Amateur Participation, the CYO, and Bowling

By 1932 the sporting goods industry reported a decline in sales by almost half of its 1929 figures (Steiner [1972], 45). Individuals did not necessarily give up on popular recreational activities; they either continued to use their equipment longer or searched for less expensive sports and recreation. In golf, for example, it was estimated that more than two million people continued to play each year during the depression even though 90 percent of all golf courses in the country were private, and many were forced to give up their memberships. Players turned to municipal courses, which as a result became overcrowded. Others sought inexpensive recreational activities such as visiting beaches and swimming. Swimming at both public beaches and municipal swimming pools ranked as the most popular sporting activity. In cities that were hard-pressed to maintain budgets and per-

New Jersey Lake, 1934. Unemployed workers learn to swim at a WPA-constructed swimming area. Courtesy of FDR Library, New Hyde Park, New York.

sonnel, almost all retained lifeguards at bathing beaches and swimming pools (Steiner [1972], 43–44).

The Catholic Church responded to the need for inexpensive activities with free recreation programs through the Catholic Youth Organization (CYO). The CYO made considerable use of community buildings, parks, and playgrounds. The organization's most popular program was boxing, which engaged thousands of participants. CYO-sponsored boxing tournaments attracted hundreds of thousands in cities nationwide (Kirsch, 93–94).

A truly American tradition that began during the depression was the soap box derby. In the soapbox derby, entrants made a homemade, nonmotorized, wheeled car and would roll or coast down a hill. In 1933, the first of the annual soap box derbies was held in Dayton, Ohio. In 1936, with the services of the WPA, a permanent paved raceway was built in Akron, Ohio. During the course of the century, the soap box derby became a nationwide event that attracted thousands of participants and hundreds of thousands of spectators in events leading to the annual finals held in Ohio (Braden, 267).

The sport of bowling was highly influenced by female bowler Floretta Doty McCutcheon and gained newfound popularity among the middle and working classes. McCutcheon was 39 years old in 1927 when she first gained national attention (she bowled her very first game in 1923 at the age of 35). She toured the country from 1930 to 1938 putting on exhibitions and providing free bowling lessons. She was especially partial to teaching high school and college students. She publicized and promoted the fact that women of any age could begin to bowl, and bowling was one sport where women could compete on an equal basis with men (Bondi, 511–512).

Winter Sports and Ski Lifts

The 1932 Olympic Games at Lake Placid, New York, the first to be broadcast by radio, renewed an interest in winter sports, especially ice-skating and skiing. The increase in skiing in northern areas stretched from Vermont to Wyoming and Idaho. In response to the growing interest in winter sports, 18 of the 24 national parks kept the roads for automobiles open year-round. One-day excursions and weekend trips to mountain areas for skiing increased (Steiner [1972], 44). Many winter resorts began to upgrade their ski facilities.

At Sun Valley, Idaho, for example, four electric mechanical lifts were installed to serve four separate skiing areas, allowing skiers easier and quicker access to the top of the hill as opposed to the long uphill climb by foot. Regarding winter

Haverhill, Massachusetts, 1938. WPA winter recreation and fun at Winnikinni Park. Courtesy of NARA.

sports in general, one vacation guide stated that in a few short years Americans progressed "[f]rom a nation that very nearly hibernated from November until April . . . to a participation in outdoor winter sports activities that, for extent and popularity, rivals that of summer" (Benjamin, 214–229).

TRANSPORTATION AND VACATION

The Automobile and the Auto-Vacation

The depression caused severe economic hardships that forced many families to sacrifice and do without items they had previously taken for granted. However, they were not willing to give up their automobiles. The national sentiment was that the automobile ranked as one of the essentials of life along with food and clothing. Although new car sales dropped, car ownership remained steady. Rather than purchasing a new car, many Americans began to maintain and repair their cars as they got older. For some, home auto repair served as a hobby. Winter driving was made less hazardous because of the introduction of better roads and tire chains. Tire chains were designed to easily fasten to the tires to provide better traction in snow and icy road conditions.

To accommodate the increasing automobile traffic, the WPA built an expanded network of federal highways that included bridges, tunnels, and cloverleaf inter-sections. In 1938, the first completed federal highway was U.S. Route 1, a continuous road of more than 2,500 miles. The highway extended along the eastern seaboard through 14 states from Kent, Maine, to Key West, Florida, and quickly became a popular route for vacation trips (Kostof, 194).

Many Americans chose to take short day trips, sometimes to a ballgame, an evening's entertainment, or just a ride to get away. In Westchester County, Lundberg and his colleagues noted that "on almost any holiday or weekend all highways near the city [were] crowded with cars filled with people going nowhere in particular but apparently traveling just for the sake of traveling" (62). Whatever the destination, the ability to travel by automobile offered many options. The most important was that an auto-vacation could fit within any budget or amount of time. An Automobile Association of America (AAA) travel guide offered the following advice:

> [T]he cost can be only as much as you're willing to pay. You may want to stop at the finest hotels and inns or, on the other hand, you may stay overnight at clean and comfortable cabins and pay a minimum rate. Meals, too, can be had in expensive restaurants along the way or at clean roadside stands. Or you can even take along your own supplies and picnic in some shaded spot at the side of the highways. (Benjamin, 13)

In 1934, the AAA also reported that lower gasoline prices contributed to an increase in extended road trips as an estimated 45 million people took to the roads for auto-vacations (Steiner [1972], 96). The most popular vacation destinations included New England, the national parks, Florida, California, the Southwest, New York, and the Wisconsin and Minnesota lakes. By 1939, it was estimated that over 80 percent of all vacation trips were by automobile (Benjamin, 13).

The introduction of motor vans and trailers further increased the affordability of an auto vacation. A trailer could be towed behind a regular automobile, and the motor van was a specialty vehicle on an automobile chassis, the forerunner of a motor home. Each provided lodging and could carry food and provide the basic living essentials. Trips could be taken without the added cost of a hotel room or a roadside cabin. By 1939, more than 300,000 trailers had been sold in the United States (Braden, 334).

Bicycles and Buses

In the 1920s, the automobile served as a replacement for the bicycle. However, in 1935, bicycle sales showed a significant increase. Some considered the increased sales to be a growing fad on college campuses as most models were sold to individuals under the age of 21. The Census of Manufactures noted that in 1935 the national production of bicycles exceeded 630,000—the first time since 1899 that yearly production exceeded one-half million (Steiner [1972], 5).

Buses also became a more popular transportation choice. By the mid-1920s, many small independent bus lines were in operation. Most served a very limited area and did not offer much interstate service. By the late 1920s, two larger carriers, Greyhound and Trailways, began nationwide operation. During the early 1930s, travel by bus provided an inexpensive alternative to the automobile. By 1936, Greyhound had bus routes that covered the entire country. The number of riders further increased when the bus companies began an intensive advertising campaign highlighting affordable trips to many of the scenic national parks and sites.

Airplanes and Airships

Aviation grabbed a fair share of newspaper headlines and magazine stories during this decade. A popular event of the period was the Cleveland Air Races held every August from 1929 to 1949 in Cleveland, Ohio. Participating pilots such as Roscoe Turner, Wylie Post, Amelia Earhart, and Jacqueline Cochran became household names. The event not only drew hundreds of thousands of spectators, but it also created interest in aviation and air travel. In 1930, the airport at Cleveland was the site of the first radio-equipped air traffic control tower in the United States (Taneja, 10).

It was the federal government, however, that was most responsible for the growth in civilian passenger aviation. The Air Mail Act of 1925 permitted the U.S. Postal Service to transport mail by air instead of by railroad. Many airlines combined passenger service with mail service in their cargo holds, thereby greatly reducing the cost per passenger. The Air Mail Act of 1934 revised the regulations to ensure fair and competitive airmail rates among the airlines. In addition, it established the Civil Aviation Authority to maintain control over airports, maintenance, and radio communications in an effort to promote air safety. However, it was not until the early 1930s that technological improvements in aircraft design made it both practical and profitable to carry only passengers.

In 1933, the Douglas Aircraft Corporation introduced the DC-3, which would revolutionize air travel and transport. With a 24 passenger-capacity and flight speeds of more than 200 mph, the DC-3 allowed airlines to operate at a profit by carrying only passengers, so they no longer had to rely on carrying mail. Dozens of airlines purchased the DC-3 and offered competitive commercial airline service including American Airways, Delta, Eastern, Northwest, and United Airlines. More than 10,000 DC-3 aircraft were built in a period of ten years, and they would become the most dependable passenger and transport aircraft of the twentieth century (Taneja, 6–9). The airplane, however, only had a nonstop range of 1,100 miles and therefore could not compete with the ocean liner for transatlantic service.

Two methods of air travel that could compete with the ocean liner were flying boats and airships. The Rigid Airship, or Zeppelin (first used in World War I as a military weapon), was reintroduced in 1924 for transatlantic luxury travel. The airship could cross the Atlantic nonstop in about 30 hours (less than half the time that it took the fastest cruise ship). By 1930, airship travel captured the public's fantasy and imagination, and many magazines proclaimed it to be the future of travel. By 1934, airships offered regularly scheduled transatlantic and South American flights. Airship travel came to an abrupt end in 1937, however, with the *Hindenburg* disaster in Lakewood, New Jersey. During its landing approach, the *Hindenburg* unexpectedly burst into flames. The event was captured live on the radio and was heard by millions of horrified listeners. Pictures of the flaming airship were also widely circulated through newsreels and newspaper coverage. The horror of the disaster caused the public to lose faith in the safety of airships (Panati, 159).

By the mid-1930s, the flying boat also made its appearance as an alternative to ocean liners. The flying boat was an airplane that had the ability to land on water due to the reconfiguration of the lower portion of its fuselage to resemble a boat's hull. The flying boats offered sleeping accommodations for 20 to 30 passengers. (Some flying boats could accommodate up to 74 seated passengers.) In all other aspects, the flying boats did not offer much in comparative comfort to the ocean liners. The flying boat's main attraction was that travel time was cut by almost two-thirds. Pan American Airlines began regular Atlantic flights in June 1939, but they were short-lived due to the outbreak of war in Europe later that same year. Most flying boat travel in the Pacific to distant areas such as the Philippines was also curtailed and was virtually nonexistent by the time of the Japanese attack on Pearl Harbor in December 1941 (Horsham, 107).

The Railroad and the Diesel Zephyr

Railroad passengers numbered almost one billion in 1929. However, during the course of the depression the numbers steadily declined. In 1934, railroads introduced the new technology of aerodynamically designed, streamlined passenger cars and diesel powered locomotives. Diesel engines were not only more efficient than the contemporary steam engines, but they were also much faster. The first of the streamlined diesel locomotives was the Burlington, Chicago, and Quincy's Zephyr. The Zephyr ran a regular intercity route from Chicago, Illinois, to Denver, Colorado, in 13 hours, almost half the time it took with conventional engines. The streamlined passenger cars featured air-conditioning, fluorescent

A streamlined train of the Burlington Line pulls into a railroad station in Chicago, Illinois. Courtesy of Library of Congress.

lighting, roomier sleeping accommodations, and an observation deck with a lounge.

Railroads were once again able to advertise an advantage with the new comforts and affordability of the passenger train. A December 1937 *Time* magazine advertisement by the Great Northern Railroad "offered an air-conditioned ride that traveled . . . through the scenic Rockies." With the new features, passenger rail travel gradually increased from 1934 to 1939 to the predepression numbers (Duke University, n.p.).

Ocean Travel and River Cruises

Despite the depression, it was still fashionable for the wealthy to cross the Atlantic in ultra-extravagant first-class accommodations. For example, the Cunard Line advertised vacation options not only to Europe, but also to warm and exotic locations such as Cuba and the South Pacific. One advertisement offered the possibility of swimming "at world-famous beaches, [or] fishing, sailing, golf, tennis, polo–cooling rum swizzles on the terrace of a fine hotel" (*Time*, December 20, 1937: 33). The cruise ships eventually felt the effects of the depression and saw the need to offer economical vacations. As early as 1930 and 1931, in order to offset the high cost of transatlantic travel, ocean liners began offering short cruises for the less wealthy vacationer.

The short cruises offered all of the appeal and amenities of the long ocean voyages to Europe without the expense and extended travel time. For people on the West Coast, Hawaii became a fashionable vacation spot. On the East Coast, regular cruises left for Bermuda and the Caribbean.

Ocean voyages were not the only offerings for vacation by ship. Cruises were available on many of the main U.S. rivers. On the Mississippi River, although the river steamboats were almost nonexistent and the number of showboats was decreasing, other ships were available for cruises of various lengths from a few hours to 21 days. One 21-day cruise from Cincinnati, Ohio, to New Orleans was described as:

> floating down the winding Ohio to the Mississippi. . . . view the old colonial plantations of the South, the little river landings where cotton once started to sea, the old sugar mills, and the rich rice fields of the Creoles and the Acadians. . . . If you cannot make the Mississippi trip, then be consoled by the knowledge that you can cruise the Ohio, the Tennessee, and the Illinois [rivers] all through the summer [with a choice of] a grand tour of inland rivers, and several shorter trips. (quoted in Benjamin, 246–247)

Some short trips could also be taken aboard new streamlined ferryboats such as the one-of-a-kind *Kalakala*. This boat traveled across Puget Sound in Washington State and offered a ride for either a few hours or an evening's entertainment of a moonlight cruise with dinner and dancing.

Vacation Resorts and the Two-week Vacation

During the bleakest years of the depression from 1929 to 1932, popular vacation spots experienced both a decline in the total number of visitors and an increase in the number of vacationers seeking less expensive accommodations. Niagara Falls and the national parks such as Yellowstone and the Grand Canyon each reported a 50 percent decrease in visitors. Of those that continued to visit vacation resorts, most opted for less expensive accommodations. Despite the economic hardships, vacations were viewed as not only desirable, but also essential. In August of 1930, the *Ladies Home Journal* advised readers to "save nickels and dimes from food and clothing; get your vacations, and never, never, say they are not important" (Aron, 238, 252).

Although cost and affordability were usually the most important factors, no matter where in the United States an individual lived vacation options were available. One vacation advertisement said, "No matter what the condition of your family budget, there's a fine vacation waiting if you learn how to take advantage of Uncle Sam's national parks." George Copeland, travel editor for the *New York Times* wrote:

> Think of our national and state parks. Think of Jones Beach, on Long Island, where, for a little [money], you can spend a summer day on a perfect beach and an evening watching a ballet or light opera under the stars. Think of that log cabin in the Great Smokies [along the border of Tennessee and North

Carolina] or in Alabama; of that campsite near a lake in the Adirondack pine-woods; of that guest plantation in the deep South or that gringo hacienda on the Mexican border. Consider the incredible beauty of Arizona's Painted Desert, the magnificence of Montana's Glacier Park, [and] the brilliant sun and clear air of Florida's coast. (Benjamin, v-vi)

By 1935, it was reported that more than 17 million people (many of them families) visited national parks and forests, a substantial increase from previous years (Benjamin, 69).

At the same time, a paid two-week vacation became increasingly available to most working-class Americans. A 1937 Bureau of Labor Statistics survey of 90,000 companies reported that the number of companies offering paid vacations had tripled since 1934. In addition, over 70 percent of all companies that had paid vacations first offered them after 1930 (Aron, 247).

Luxury resorts remained fashionable among the wealthy, and those who could afford it continued to vacation in grand and luxurious style. Resorts such as the Bath and Tennis Club in Palm Beach, Florida offered guests a pampered stay. The Roney Plaza and Miami Biltmore, two Miami Beach resorts, claimed that the vacationer could "live luxuriously in America's favorite winter playground [and enjoy] exceptional facilities for golf, fishing, and surf bathing" (*Time*, December 20, 1937: 32).

The middle class also continued to attend vacation resorts. Western vacations were popular for the middle class beginning in the 1890s. Dude ranches were the preferred choice for entire families as they combined affordability with a fantasy of living in the Old West. Although dude ranches could be found in some eastern states and in California, the most common destinations were in Oregon, Montana, Wyoming, New Mexico, and Arizona (Benjamin, 100). Western vacations were not limited to just horseback riding and ranching. One 1937 magazine advertisement for Phoenix, Arizona, said, "[I]f you find rest in recreation, there's literally every outdoor sport under the sun . . . Phoenix and the surrounding towns offer all types of modern accommodations—hotels, apartments, bungalows, dude ranches and desert inns" (*Time*, December 20, 1937: 28).

Other types of vacations included fishing, hunting, hiking, canoeing, and cultural vacations. Unlike the outdoor vacations that offered a trip away from urban areas, cultural vacations promoted visits to cities. The cultural vacation touted drama, art, opera, and folk festivals such as the Mozart festival in Asheville, North Carolina; summer symphonies in San Diego, California; Shakespearian plays in Ashland, Oregon; or the Bach festival in Bethlehem, Pennsylvania (Benjamin, 258).

Many popular magazines provided economical vacation advice. The *Ladies Home Journal* told readers how to "Match Yourself to a Vacation" (June 1931) and "Pack Up Your Family and Go" on an auto-vacation (July 1932). In June 1931, *Better Homes and Gardens* offered "Tips for the Two-Week Vacationists." The President's wife, Eleanor Roosevelt, even told how a pleasurable, inexpensive vacation could be had "By Car and Tent" for the *Woman's Home Companion* (August 1934), encouraging the use of the "nearest state park" for fishing, swimming, hiking, reading, or writing, among many other forms of relaxation including simply sleeping (Aron, 253). Despite the severe economic hardships of the time,

Americans continued to promote, endorse, and take vacations and the vacation became an established American institution.

CONCLUSION

The economic effects of the depression were most certainly devastating. However, the previously held national view that leisure and recreation was reserved for the wealthy and elite few had changed. As opposed to the prevailing opinion in previous decades, the idea that leisure for the working class should be put to use to make better workers slipped away. The view among all classes was that recreation, leisure, and even a vacation could be enjoyed by any individual.

Despite the overwhelming amount of government support through WPA recreation and leisure programs, it was estimated that at its peak the WPA's programs were able to meet the needs of only about 40 percent of the actual nationwide demand. Critics of Roosevelt's New Deal programs indicated that the relief measures, such as those administered by the WPA and CCC, were only meant to provide temporary relief for unemployed workers and not a permanent source of employment. The subsequent Congressional 1939 Relief Act required that any individual who had more than 18 months of continuous employment on federal relief programs be dismissed. The Recreation Section of the WPA, for example, had to eliminate over half of its 40,000 workers and the Federal Theater Project was totally eliminated. By 1939, the reality of war in Europe forced the issue of American involvement into the forefront of the nation's consciousness, and the issue of recreation and leisure was no longer a priority.

CHAPTER 5

THE GOOD WAR AND THE AFTERMATH: 1940–1946

CHRONOLOGY

1940   The Selective Service Act goes into effect and the peacetime draft begins; nylons go on the market.

1941   The Japanese attack Pearl Harbor; the United States enters World War II; the jeep is invented; "Rosie the Riveter" joins the military; Mount Rushmore is completed.

1942   Japanese Americans are sent to internment camps; the T-shirt is introduced.

1943   Racial conflicts erupt in more than 50 U.S. cities.

1944   Ballpoint pens go on sale; the D-Day invasion occurs.

1945   Franklin D. Roosevelt dies; the microwave oven is invented; the United States drops atomic bombs on Japan; World War II ends; television is first licensed for commercial use.

1946   The bikini bathing suit is introduced; Dr. Spock publishes *The Common Book of Baby and Child Care*; ENIAC, the first computer, is invented.

INTRODUCTION

At the beginning of 1940, Americans were slowly emerging from the devastating effects of the Great Depression. In Europe, war was raging throughout the continent, but most Americans were too preoccupied with the economic troubles at home to worry about involvement in another European war. However, the 1941 surprise attack by the Japanese government on the American military base at Pearl Harbor in Hawaii outraged the American public. Within days of the attack, the United States was involved in war with both Japan and Germany.

World War II instantly became the dominant force of this period. No portion of the country or, for that matter, the entire world was unaffected. The government's total effort shifted to support the war and convince Americans to contribute and sacrifice. The war also proved to be the economic stimulus that took the country out of the depression. Millions who were previously unemployed were suddenly in high demand—many as workers in the new war material production factories. By 1942, the American economy was in full production mode, and workers found themselves with a newfound prosperity that had a profound impact on their lifestyles and leisure habits. Author and radio personality Studs Terkel called it "the good war," and for many considering their newfound prosperity, it was.

However, the new economic prosperity was not used for the purchase of material goods because rationing and shortages were a way of life. Many used their additional income for entertainment. Record numbers went bowling or went to the movies. To some, with the war at hand, recreation and entertainment were viewed with a sense of urgency as splurges at nightclubs and gambling became commonplace because many felt that they might not live to see the next day.

PUBLIC INTEREST

The Selective Service Act and Volunteer Organizations

As early as 1939, the U.S. government foresaw the threat of war and sought to increase the size of the military which at that time consisted of just over 160,000 soldiers. In 1940, Congress passed the Selective Service Act, the first peacetime draft in American history, and quickly increased the numbers of the armed forces to more than one and a half million. The soldiers were quickly dubbed GIs after the phrase *government issue*. The men were G.I. Joes and the women were G.I. Janes. In the fall of 1941, more than 350,000 of the new citizen soldiers took part in military maneuvers in Louisiana.

When the United States entered the war, the need for soldiers was drastically increased. There would eventually be 34 million men registered with the selective service between the ages of 18 and 45. Between 1940 and 1946, more than 16 million served in active duty; more than two million witnessed actual combat; almost one million were wounded, and more than 500,000 were killed. Registering for selective service was not an option; it was mandatory. Those who did not register received prison sentences, including more than 5,500 conscientious objectors who refused to serve based on religious beliefs.

The necessity of manpower for all facets of the war effort caused the nation to come to a single-minded purpose. For many Hungarian, Polish, and Italian immigrants, and others, the war marked a period of cultural intermixing where they were all considered Americans. Members of ethnic and minority groups were readily drafted, although the military still practiced strictly enforced segregation.

More than 500,000 African Americans served in the strictly segregated military. Most of them were assigned to menial noncombative roles such as cooks, laborers, and truck drivers. The extent of segregation was so severe that the American Red Cross (by military mandate) carefully separated blood units for wounded soldiers between the white and African American soldiers (Foner, 243). When given the chance to fight, African American units proved to be equal or, in some cases, better than white units. For example, the 332nd Fighter Group, known as the

Tuskegee Airmen, had the unmatched distinction of never losing a bomber to enemy action during escort duty.

Native American Indians also served with valor and distinction during the war. Pima-born Indian Ira Hayes was one of the U.S. Marines who raised an American flag on Mount Suribachi on Iwo Jima, a Pacific island off the coast of Japan. The battle for Iwo Jima was one of the costliest of the war with over 6,000 U.S. soldiers killed in action. Joe Rosenthal's photograph of this event (one of the most famous of the war) was printed in *Life* magazine on March 26, 1945. It was also reprinted on millions of Office of War Information (OWI) posters and on the cover of countless magazines and newspapers.

The Indian Reorganization Act of 1934 had granted some social status and rights to Native American Indians (citizenship was granted by Congress in 1924), but for the most part discrimination continued. New Mexico did not allow Native American Indians the right to vote. In a 1943 article in *New Mexico Magazine* Margretta Dietrich asked, "If [Indians] are good enough to fight, why aren't we good enough to vote?" (June 1943: 30). Full voting rights for Native American Indians in New Mexico and throughout the United States were not secured until the 1948 Supreme Court decision of *Trujillo v. Garley* (Nash, 143–144).

With the war at hand, however, Americans did not have time to think of their internal discriminatory problems. It was the military and the war that received priority. Regarding public recreation for civilians during this time, historian Richard Kraus wrote that "many programs had to be curtailed [due to] manpower shortage and travel restrictions" ([1971], 207).

As early as 1941, during peacetime, it was noted that military training needed to be supplemented with recreation. The National Recreation Association (see chapter 2) joined with the Special Services division of the army to increase the recreation programs and entertainment facilities near military bases. More than 13,500 officers of all branches of the service and thousands of volunteers were engaged in providing recreation for military personnel. The most widely recognized military entertainment unit of the war was the USO.

The United Service Organization (USO), formed in 1941, represented a joint effort of the Young Men's Christian Association (YMCA), the Young Women's Christian Association (YWCA), the Salvation Army, the Jewish Welfare Board, Catholic Community Services, and the National Travelers Aid. The USO provided canteen services (stores to supply servicemen with candy, newspapers, and other items), showed movies, sponsored dances, and put on camp shows both on the home front and abroad (Kraus, 207). In April 1944, the *New York Times* magazine described a camp show as follows:

> In the simplest terms, [the] Camp Shows' job is to bring Hollywood and Broadway to the servicemen. . . . The talent falls into two classifications. First there are the paid USO Camp Show performers, hired from theaters, vaudeville companies, nightclubs, and shows, as permanent troupers. They form the backbone of the entertainment for our soldiers and sailors. In the second class are Broadway, Hollywood, and radio volunteers who offer their services for a minimum of six weeks. (*Annals of America*, Vol. 16: 221)

Camp shows played to an estimated 37 million servicemen and civilians on the home front and to similar numbers overseas.

Volunteerism to support the war effort was continuously stressed. In January 1942, immediately after the Pearl Harbor attack, 5.6 million Americans volunteered for civil defense training (see "Lifestyles" later in this chapter). Civil defense included coast watchers and air raid wardens. By mid-1943 more than seven million volunteers were actively involved with another five million registered and waiting to serve (Lingeman, 59).

The volunteer services of the YMCA and the Red Cross also mobilized immediately after the Pearl Harbor attack. More than 3,740 combined local chapters engaged thousands of volunteers to roll bandages and prepare to care for the wounded. The American Red Cross alone engaged more than 5,500 leaders who supervised more than 100,000 volunteers. Overseas the Red Cross created more than 250 mobile entertainment units and more than 750 clubs in addition to providing hospital services (Kraus [1971], 207). The Red Cross was also active in setting up blood centers for citizens to donate blood. During the course of the war, more than 6.6 million individuals donated more than 13.3 million units of blood (Time-Life Books, *This Fabulous Century: 1940–1950*, 158). The only rewards were small service ribbons. Silver ribbons indicated five hundred hours of volunteer service and gold indicated one thousand hours; a small group of volunteers earned an upper-level ribbon indicating more than 14,000 hours of volunteer work, or an average of ten hours each day for the entire war (Time-Life Books, *This Fabulous Century: 1940–1950*, 158).

The Four Freedoms and the Office of War Information

As early as January 6, 1941, in his message to Congress, President Roosevelt sought to define America's role in the European war and outlined his concept of the four freedoms that winning the war would preserve. Roosevelt stated:

> We look forward to a world founded upon four essential freedoms. The first is freedom of speech and expression everywhere in the world. The second is freedom of every person to worship God in his own way. . . . The third is freedom from want. . . . The fourth is freedom from fear. (Record of 77th Congress, January 6, 1941: 44–45)

Roosevelt spoke on the four freedoms on numerous occasions throughout the war and continuously stressed the fact that the world could not "exist half slave and half free." Supporters applauded the pluralistic approach to an acceptance of cultural diversity.

Wendell Wilkie (who lost to Roosevelt in the 1940 presidential election) supported the four freedoms idea. At the time, Wilkie's influence on American public opinion was considered by most to be second only to that of Roosevelt. In his publication *One World* (1943), Wilkie wrote, "If we want to talk about freedom, we must mean freedom for others as well as ourselves, and we must mean freedom for everyone inside our frontiers" (quoted in Foner, 246).

Inspired by both Wilkie and Roosevelt, the *Pittsburgh Courier*, an African American newspaper, coined the phrase *double-V*, which meant victory over fascism abroad and victory over segregation at home (Foner, 243). Preserving the four freedoms meant once again launching an advertising campaign to convince the

American public to support the war. In June of 1942, Roosevelt officially created the Office of War Information (OWI). The OWI was just one of no less than three dozen "alphabet agencies" created to oversee almost all aspects of American life. (Alphabet agencies were so named because of the acronyms used to refer to them.) Some of the agencies included the WPB (War Production Board), which coordinated the overall wartime economy; the WLB (War Labor Board), which monitored labor disputes; the OPA (Office of Price Administration), which monitored consumer pricing and rationing; and the ODT (Office of Defense Transportation), which monitored transportation (Lingeman, 104–106).

The OWI employed more than four thousand writers, artists, and advertising people to deliver the message to Americans. Similar to the Committee on Public Information (CPI) during World War I (see chapter 2), the OWI used every form of media available including newspapers, magazines, pamphlets, book jackets, radio, movies, and posters.

The posters once again proved to be extremely effective and inexpensive and were also reprinted in newspapers and magazines. They relied on simple phrases such as "Loose Lips Sink Ships" and "We Can Do It." The OWI also reissued the Uncle Sam "I Want You for the U.S. Army" poster from World War I. To distribute the posters, the OWI enlisted the aid of volunteers such as the one and a half million members of the Boy and Girl Scouts. Posters were placed everywhere including subways, schools, post offices, places of business, neighborhood saloons, and war plants (Time-Life Books, *This Fabulous Century: 1940–1950*, 163).

Unlike the CPI, according to historian Eric Foner, the OWI sought "to impart a coherent ideological meaning to the war, while seeking to avoid the nationalist hysteria of World War I" (227). The prevailing ideology was that of Roosevelt's four freedoms. The freedoms were reiterated in books, magazines, posters, and on the radio. The most well-known examples of this were illustrations by Norman Rockwell that appeared in four successive issues of the *Saturday Evening Post* in February and March of 1943. The OWI reproduced all four illustrations on a single poster under the title "Ours to fight for" (Foner, 226).

Roosevelt's opponents felt that the promises of the four freedoms would upset the balance of segregation and big business. Using the money they had gained through war production that had not been available to them during the depression, big business and manufacturers began counteradvertising campaigns attributing the power of production and rising wages to free enterprise and not to the power of labor. In late 1943, Congress (becoming increasingly anti-Roosevelt and supportive of big business) severely cut the OWI's budget, effectively nullifying its power. In late 1944, with the end of the war in sight, the OWI was disbanded by Congressional action (Foner, 229–230).

Executive Order 9066 and Japanese Internment

Segregation and severe racism was still a fact of life for many Americans. In 1930, the U.S. Census Bureau reclassified Mexican Americans as "nonwhite." In response to claims that Mexican illegal aliens were in jobs in the Southwest that could be better served by whites, the United States forced more than 400,000 assumed illegal aliens to leave the country and return to Mexico (later estimates revealed that at least half were American born). In 1943, as a result of labor shortages in the same southwestern farm areas, thousands of Mexicans were allowed reentry status. According to Foner, the pattern "lasted into the 1960's and stimulated a far broader movement of Mexican men, women, and children into the United States" (240).

The U.S. government also continued to restrict Asians from immigrating. (In 1943, restrictions on Chinese immigration were eased, but only a paltry 105 Chinese immigrants were allowed in.) The December 7, 1941, attack on the Hawaiian Islands caused hysteria along the entire west coast of the country and fueled anti-Japanese sentiment to a fever pitch. Many, including the military, feared an invasion upon American shores. Anyone of Japanese ancestry was immediately suspected as a spy or potential saboteur.

In early 1942, Roosevelt signed Executive Order 9066, which required the immediate relocation of all Japanese Americans from the West Coast. More than 120,000 Japanese Americans (the entire Japanese American population) were removed from their homes and businesses and moved inland to internment camps. The majority were from four major West Coast cities—60,000 from Los Angeles, 20,000 from San Francisco, 10,000 from Portland, Oregon, and 10,000 from Seattle, Washington. Those who owned businesses or homes were forced to sell

Children playing the board game Monopoly at a Japanese-American internment camp in 1942. Courtesy of Corbis.

rather quickly, sometimes only in a matter of days (Nash, 149). Military personnel guarded the internment camps and kept the people within barbed wire fences and forced them to live in barracks. Most of the Japanese Americans were kept in the camps until late 1944, and upon returning to the coast, almost all found their homes and businesses no longer available.

Planned Communities for War Workers

The nationwide unemployment that had remained high until 1939 was virtually nonexistent by the peak war production years of 1942 and 1943. Unlike during the depression when jobs were few, American industry was operating at production levels unlike any in previous history, and labor could not meet the demand. The dramatic increase in the number of war workers migrating to urban areas created a severe housing shortage.

In 1940, San Diego, California, had a population of 202,000. By 1944, mainly because of the influx of war workers and military personnel, the city population swelled to more than 500,000 (Nash, 59). In response, many cities hastily converted garages or warehouses as housing units; some even erected tents as temporary housing. In Chicago, Illinois, more than 250 used trolley cars were used as homes (Halberstam, 134). Many cities quickly began erecting federally funded planned housing communities.

The Farm Security Administration (FSA), first established in 1937, served as the lead government agency to administer and issue guidelines for housing projects for defense workers. By 1940, the FSA (later designated as the Federal Housing Administration [FHA]) had designed and built a planned community in Yuba City, California, for eight thousand displaced depression-era farm workers. With the increasing war production need, Yuba was quickly expanded to well over 25,000 housing units by the end of 1943. In the haste to build more housing, compromises were made regarding safety, comfort, and community recreation facilities (Albrecht, 101–105). Despite the increased number of housing units, not enough housing was available to satisfy the demand.

In reality there was a home-front battle for wartime housing throughout the country. In 1943, in Detroit, Michigan (the site of largest defense producers and employers because of the converted automobile factories), the FHA built the Sojourner Truth housing project (named after the abolitionist leader) intended to house mostly African American war workers in a white neighborhood in northeast Detroit. In February 1942, a mob of angry whites attacked the first African Americans to move in. In June 1943, full-scale violence erupted; 34 people were killed and more than 675 injured in two days of rioting that required military intervention (Albrecht, 110–114).

Twenty miles outside of Detroit, in Willow Run, Michigan, another defense housing project was hastily erected. This housing project was fully segregated; most of the units were nothing more than converted trailers and conditions were less than desirable. One critic observed that the absence of any substantial community recreation facilities only "encouraged heavy drinking, wild parties, and extremely high rates of venereal disease." One resident spoke of the lack of facilities for children, indicating that the camp had only one swing for more than thirty children. The remainder of the children "amused themselves by playing in the mud" (Albrecht, 117).

With the tremendous number of female war workers and displaced families, child care was a necessity. In 1943, Congress authorized funds under the Lanham Act for federally funded child care centers for war workers. One community that successfully incorporated such a child care facility was at Vanport, Oregon.

In 1944, Vanport was completed as a planned community for more than 42,000 residents (the largest single wartime housing project). The community included 5 social buildings, 16 playgrounds, a library, a theater, and a childcare center for working parents. According to architectural historian Donald Albrecht, the childcare center at Vanport contained "fifteen playrooms [that] surrounded an outdoor play area with a wading pool" (122–125).

In all 2,892 federally funded child care facilities were scattered throughout the country, benefiting more than 107,000 children. By 1946, Lanham Act funds were diverted to support the G.I. Bill of Rights (see chapter 6), and child care centers for more than 100,000 children were disbanded. Much of the political response of diverting funds was an attempt to subjugate women to return to the home and provide care for their own children. By 1948, the last of the wartime child care centers had exhausted its funds and closed. In the same year, the community of Vanport, Oregon, was completely destroyed by a flood (Albrecht, 134).

LIFESTYLES

Life on the Home Front—Rationing, Shortages, and Scrap Drives

In January 1941, Roosevelt said that the national policy would be "[t]o change a whole nation from a basis of peacetime production of implements of peace to a basis of wartime production of implements of war [and would be] no small task" (Record of 77th Congress, January 6, 1941: 44–45). In the change to wartime production, it was estimated that almost 25 million Americans moved, most to find wartime jobs (Foner, 219). In the first two months of 1942 alone, more than one million Americans moved to the West Coast—a large majority from Texas, Oklahoma, Arkansas, and Louisiana—most to the shipbuilding yards in either California, Oregon, or Washington (Nash, 176). Famed war correspondent Ernie Pyle wrote, "We had to go through that transition period of letting loose of life as it was, and then live the new war life so long that it finally became the normal life to us" (*Annals of America*, 182).

The threat of invasion on either coast was perceived as real, and the sound of an air-raid siren became part of the American lifestyle. Under the supervision of civilian defense volunteers, Americans actively took part in air-raid drills. Upon hearing a siren, all were required to go into a total blackout. All streetlights were shut off, and homes and businesses had to either shut off the lights or have blackout curtains on the windows to prevent light from showing on their exteriors. By June 1942, government-mandated blackouts took effect along both coasts. The blackout became an accepted part of life.

House and Garden magazine offered helpful blackout advice. For bathroom windows, it advised the reader to "[a]bandon your pastel window and shower curtains for the duration and put up, instead a completely opaque black shower curtain" and "if your color scheme permits . . . make a blackout shade by seaming together two pieces of fabric, one black and one to match your curtain" (Lingeman, 49). Americans continued to sacrifice during the remaining war years to support the common cause, and rationing and shortages became a way of life.

In the home there were shortages of appliances such as toasters, coffeemakers, clothes irons, batteries, cooking utensils, vacuum cleaners, and razor blades as production of all home appliances ceased. Rationing was extended to include gasoline, rubber, coffee, tea, sugar, butter, meat, and almost all food products.

In January 1942, the Office of Price Administration (OPA) oversaw more than 600,000 retail stores and began ration coupon book distribution to the American public. Food items were assigned both a dollar and a point value. For example, one pound of hamburger meat was assigned a value of seven points. Butter was 16 points, margarine 4 points, a 14-ounce bottle of ketchup 15 points, and baby food 1 point. To purchase food, an individual had to provide both the coupons with appropriate point value, and the price of the item as set by the OPA. The OPA periodically issued directives such as the following:

> All red and blue stamps in War Ration Book 4 are worth 10 points each. Red and blue tokens are worth 1 point each. Red and blue tokens are used to make change for red and blue stamps only when purchase is made. Important! Point values of brown and green stamps are not changed. (Time-Life Books, *This Fabulous Century: 1940–1950*, 164)

It sounds confusing, and it was. It was also cumbersome. In order to replenish the public stock of ration stamps, grocers were required to turn in the stamps at local banks. Grocers handled more than 14 billion points per month, or about 3.5 billion stamps (Time-Life Books, *This Fabulous Century: 1940–1950*, 166). With rationing also came the black market for the illegal purchase of rationed goods and additional ration coupons.

Rationing even extended to fresh fruits and vegetables as produce farms were commandeered to feed the army. In order to obtain fresh vegetables, and also to support the war, Americans were encouraged to grow their own "Victory Gardens." Government agencies and newspapers and magazines provided the uninitiated with seeds and even advice for the proper planting seasons. As a result, gardens sprang up everywhere including rural areas, suburban backyards, and city streets. By 1943, it was estimated that more than 20.5 million Victory Gardens produced over 30 percent of all vegetables grown during the war (Time-Life Books, *This Fabulous Century: 1940–1950*, 158). The gardens were intended to be in full public view, and the vast number of gardens stimulated an interest in gardening that continued long after the war.

Americans were also asked to conserve and lend a hand by providing items to recycle through scrap drives. Just about anything that Americans had within their homes was salvaged. Among the items collected in scrap drives were tin cans, bronze padlocks, old car tires, and even discarded stockings and toothpaste tubes. Homemakers collected bacon grease, which was turned in at local meat markets and used to make ammunition. Women's stockings were turned in to make gunpowder storage bags. A common OWI poster read, "Uncle Sam needs your dis-

A woman and her daughter tend to a "Victory Garden" in the backyard of their home in Brooklyn, New York, in June 1942. Author's archives.

carded silk and nylon stockings for gun powder bags. Please launder and leave here" (Time-Life Books, *This Fabulous Century: 1940–1950*, 162–163). By 1945, the scrap drives provided more than half of the needed steel, tin, and paper that industry required.

Women in Wartime and "Rosie the Riveter"

Life on the home front took on a decidedly different trend for women, especially in the workplace. In 1941, Roosevelt established the Fair Employment Practices Committee (FEPC) saying, "In some communities employers dislike to employ women. In others they are reluctant to hire Negroes. . . . We can no longer afford to indulge such prejudices" (quoted in Gillon, 1036). During the course of the war, the FEPC monitored the hiring practices of industries involved in defense contracts thereby seeking to provide a fair opportunity for many women and African Americans to enter the industrialized workforce.

A large percentage of American women remained homemakers during the war. Some received public attention as a "gold star" mother. If a family member was killed in action, the U.S. government provided a small flag with an embroidered gold star to be displayed in the window of the family's home. Multiple gold stars indicated that more than one child (or spouse) had been killed. With the loss or separation from loved ones, in addition to repairmen or service shop owners being away in the war, homemakers had to learn how to "do-it-yourself." Many magazines and advertisers provided articles and home repair advice for women on subjects such as carpentry and plumbing. With the war, the traditional roles of women were rapidly changing, and they were acclimating to roles that traditionally had been reserved for men.

A significant number of women enlisted in the military. During the war, more than 350,000 women had volunteered, most designated as either WACS (Women's Army Corps) or WAVES (Women Accepted for Voluntary Emergency Service). Most were placed in noncombative roles such as clerical and typing positions. A small number, led by famed aviator Jacqueline Cochran served as Women Air Service Pilots (WASP) ferrying military aircraft to battle zones. During the war, more than 1,000 women flew, and 38 were killed. More than 70,000 registered nurses (RNs) enlisted and earned the respect of wounded military personnel, both on the home front and in battle zones (Faragher et al., 811–812). As with the rest of the military, female branches of the services remained segregated. For example, African American female nurses were recruited because white nurses were not allowed (and in some cases refused) to care for African American soldiers.

On the home front, women filled the workplace in large numbers. In 1940, working women numbered 11.9 million. By 1944, more than 18.6 million women were working and made up over 36 percent of the workforce (Bondi, *American Decades: 1940–1949*, 334). One OWI poster, "We Can Do It," became a nationwide rallying cry as the name "Rosie the Riveter" became synonymous with the female American war worker.

The image of Rosie was that of a shorthaired, kerchief-clad woman in a work shirt with rolled up sleeves. Newsreels and newspapers popularized the Rosies who welded, riveted, and operated heavy machinery. A significant number of these women had children, and those who were not fortunate enough to be in an area

Recycling silk stockings for the war effort at a local store in 1943. Scrap drives and recycling were an integral part of the daily lives of all Americans during World War II. Courtesy of FDR Library, Hyde Park, New York.

with a government-funded child care center either left children with relatives or sometimes left children to fend for themselves. With their newfound economic prosperity, others were able to afford a baby-sitter, which became a popular new part-time job trend among teenage girls.

Rosie the Riveter became the symbol of the working American woman during the war. After the war, Rosie did not keep her job, and women in general did not receive the same accolades that men enjoyed in wartime. The Veterans of Foreign Wars (VFW) rewrote their bylaws and banned women from membership. In addition, the postwar GI Bill of Rights did not provide complete benefits for female veterans.

Youth, the Box Social, and the Zoot Suit Riots

The need for wartime labor was so great that many teenagers left school to enter the workforce. In 1944, the U.S. Census Bureau revealed that 35 percent of all teenagers between the ages of 14 and 18 had left school. Twenty percent of boys between 14 and 15 years of age and 40 percent aged 16 and 17 were employed full-time. Over 30 percent of all girls aged 16 to 18 had at least a part-time job. Most of the jobs for both genders were in war industry and manufacturing plants. Teenagers being in the workforce and having economic independence from their parents loosened the grip of family control, which became a cause for concern. In 1942, in a pamphlet titled "Guidance Problems in Wartime," the U.S. Department of Education stated that it was "obvious that there was an unfortunate effect of young people's sudden prosperity: their op-

A corner jukebox in the student union at the University of Nebraska, 1944. Relaxing at an eatery and listening to music from a jukebox was common across the United States from the late 1930s through the late 1950s. Courtesy of Library of Congress.

portunity to have a good time; to enjoy elaborate food, clothing, [and] automobiles" (quoted in Bondi, *American Decades: 1940–1949*, 340).

A teen gathering considered acceptable by adults of the time was the box social. The social, usually sponsored by a church or school, served as an adult-chaperoned community gathering between the genders. The female attendee was required to bring a food item in an unmarked covered box. The box was auctioned off to the highest-bidding male attendee, and he shared the food with the female who made it. During the war, box socials also served as a way of raising money for war bonds (Braden, 29).

Promiscuity was an unacceptable teen behavior. Concerns also arose over the supposed increased promiscuity among the newly enlisted soldiers going off to war. *V girls* became a term applied to young women who hung around USO dances looking to engage in activities (both social and sexual) with soldiers. Disorderly conduct also became a common charge against youths who simply hung around, whether it was at a dance, on a street corner, or at a record shop or juke joint. Many adults were concerned about an increase in juvenile delinquency.

Instead of attending chaperoned box socials, many urban youths preferred forming their own social clubs or simply gathering on the sidewalks to hang out as a way of passing time. As a result, a distinctive street culture developed among teens, who for the most part remained self-segregated within their own ethnic groups.

In East Los Angeles, an economically depressed Mexican American neighborhood was known as the barrio. As an offshoot of the swing culture, they developed a flamboyant style of dress. For women, the style was short, tight skirts and styled hairdos. For Mexican American men, known as *pachucos*, it was the Zoot suit, characterized by colorful long draped jackets, baggy pants, and flamboyant feathered *tando* hats. This style of dress was evident in all major cities and among all ethnic groups across the United States. Many Americans, however, viewed the excess material of the zoot suits as unpatriotic.

At the height of World War II, the preferred men's clothing style was a "Victory Suit" with either slim jacket lapels or none at all, narrow pant legs, and no cuffs at the ankles to preserve clothing material for the war effort. Newspapers and radio added to the "unpatriotic" fervor and falsely called the *pachucos* violent war protestors, draft dodgers, and likened the Mexican Americans as having inherited the "naturally violent tendencies from the bloodthirsty Aztec's" (Jimenez, 159). It was mainly this view that caused military personnel to indiscriminately attack zoot-suiters in the summer of 1943.

On a June night in 1943, a group of eleven sailors on shore leave claimed that a gang of *pachucos* attacked them. The following night, and for two weeks thereafter, the sailors, joined by hundreds of other military personnel and escorted by local police, roamed the streets of Los Angeles attacking at random anyone dressed in a zoot suit. This incident of racial attacks was not isolated. Similar riots occurred in more than 50 cities throughout the United States. Only a decree by navy officials, who feared an all-out mutiny, ended the riots.

ENTERTAINMENT

In 1943, the labor supply had been exhausted. In response to this, Roosevelt decreed it patriotic duty to support the war effort by working and mandated a

48-hour, six-day workweek in munitions factories and a 45-hour workweek for all other factories (Lingeman, 136). With production in full swing, leisure time was at a premium. However as historian Eric Foner points out, "the war witnessed a significant redistribution of income in favor of ordinary workers" (229). Because they were not able to purchase material goods, due to shortages and rationing, people spent their money on entertainment and enjoyed the movies, dancing, music, and nightclubs. *Downbeat* magazine noted that "[w]orking people newly burdened with war production pressure at home, and with casualty reports from abroad, are seeking the gayer atmosphere of clubs for entertainment and relief" and that "[e]ntertainment and sports are the greatest antidote against hysteria, and we need them to win the war" (quoted in Erenberg, 146).

Radio and "We Interrupt this Broadcast"

Radio remained popular and was the main form of shared family entertainment. The format of dramas and adventure and music shows was basically the same as it had been in the depression era. Unlike in the depression era, news began to occupy more and more airtime.

In 1939, it was estimated that only four percent of the total radio airtime was devoted to news stories. By 1944, the networks devoted over 25 percent of on-air time to news (Lingeman, 223). At any given time, a newscaster might interrupt the regular broadcast with a special war bulletin. It was radio that provided the American public with the first news of the Japanese attack on Pearl Harbor. The following day, an estimated 80 percent of the nation listened as Roosevelt told them "Yesterday, December 7, 1941—a date which will live in infamy—the United States of America was suddenly and deliberately attacked by naval and air forces of the Empire of Japan" and asked Congress and the American people for a declaration of war against Japan.

Radio brought the war directly into the American home. The voices of newscasters such as Edward R. Murrow and William Shirer became familiar and comforting presences in the family living room. Even with the war news broadcasts, radio was still the most popular form of entertainment used to forget the war from time to time. *Your Hit Parade*, a radio music program that rated songs in a top-ten format, was one of the most popular of the period. One *Saturday Evening Post* advertisement proclaimed, "Radio entertainment is a vital part of America's morale-building program" (June 12, 1943, Vol. 215, No. 50: 4).

Newspapers, Magazines, Paperbacks, Comic Books, and the Pinup

American newspapers sent more than five hundred correspondents overseas to cover the war (more than five times the number sent during World War I). The correspondents maintained a steady flow of war stories and information that kept those on the home front actively reading the morning newspapers. One of the most widely read war correspondents was Ernie Pyle. His column was carried six times per week in 310 newspapers that reached more than 12 million readers nationwide (Lingeman, 302). The military also published many newspapers to keep the military personnel informed; the most noted of these was *Stars and*

Stripes. However, newspaper comic strips proved to be even more popular than war coverage.

By 1942, more than 70 million people read the daily comics (out of a total population of 130 million). The favorites, in ranked order, were *Joe Palooka, Blondie, Li'l Abner*, and *Little Orphan Annie* (Lingeman, 304). Newspapers and magazines regularly supplemented the old favorites with war-related cartoons such as Bill Mauldin's portrayal of two regular GIs named Willie and Joe.

The American public relied on newspapers for their information, but magazines remained influential in shaping America's views and opinions. Publications ranged from the "sophisticated" magazines such as *Harper's* and *National Geographic* to magazines popular with much of the general public such as *Reader's Digest, Life, Look, Saturday Evening Post*, and *Time*. A notable new magazine called *Seventeen* premiered in 1944 and found an untapped audience in teenage girls. The magazine featured articles on fashion, makeup, and dating.

Reading books was encouraged. The *Saturday Evening Post* said, "The best tonic for a weary soldier is a letter from home. Ranking a close second is a good book. . . . Between the covers of a good book, a fighting man may find a brief yet welcome furlough" (June 12, 1943, Vol. 215, No. 50: 60).

Mail-order book clubs prospered during this time; membership exceeded 3 million and distribution was more than 11.5 million books per year. During the war, at least fifty mail-order book clubs existed such as the Negro Book Club and clubs specializing in religion, aircraft, history, and science. Estimates at the end of the war indicated that at least 49 million people read at least one book a month (Panati, 231).

Books about the war or the world situation dominated the best-seller list including Eugene Lyons's *Stalin: Czar of All the Russians* (1940), Joseph E. Davies's *Mission to Moscow* (1940, of which a film version was released in 1943), William Shirer's *Berlin Diary* (1941), and Quentin Reynolds's *Only the Stars Are Neutral* (1942). Wendell Wilkie's publication of *One World* (1943) quickly sold more than two million copies. One successful war novel, Marion Hargrove's *See Here, Private Hargrove* (1943) related the whimsical adventures of an average American in the military service and sold more than two and a half million copies.

War correspondent Ernie Pyle, who often shared foxholes with the GIs and was often on the front line in the thick of battle, published three best-sellers, *Ernie Pyle in England* (1941), *Here is Your War* (1943), and *Brave Men* (1944), that each sold more than two million copies (Foner, 245). In *Here Is Your War*, which was also excerpted in more than three hundred newspapers, Pyle described the war to the average American:

> It is hard for you at home to realize what an immense, complicated, sprawling institution a theater of war actually is. As it appears to you in the newspapers, war is a clear-cut matter of landing so many men overseas, moving them from the port to the battlefield, advancing them against the enemy with guns firing, and they win or lose. . . . I only know what we see from our worm's-eye view, and our segment of the picture consists only of tired and dirty soldiers who are alive and don't want to die; of long darkened convoys in the middle of the night; of shocked silent men wandering back down the hill from battle; of chow lines . . . and blown bridges and dead mules and hospital tents and shirt

collars greasy-black from months of wearing; and of laughter too, and anger and wine and lovely flowers and constant cussing. All these it is composed of; and of graves and graves and graves. That is our war, and we will carry it with us as we go on from one battleground to another until it is all over, leaving some of us behind on every beach, [and] in every field. (*Annals of America*, Vol. 16: 181–186)

Pyle himself was a casualty of the war. He was killed while covering the U.S. Marine landing at Iwo Jima in 1945.

For the most part, the dramatic rise in reading rates during the period was the direct result of the comic book and the paperback. In 1940, comics targeted specifically for teens became popular with more than 150 titles in print. Superhero comics *Superman* and *Batman* remained the most popular choices. In 1941, *Archie* comics first appeared and quickly became the most popular of the nonsuperhero comics. Comic book themes carefully supported the war effort. One 1942 issue of *Superman* devoted the entire cover to feature the superhero proclaiming "The American Red Cross needs your support! Give generously" (Time-Life Books, *This Fabulous Century: 1940–1950*, 370).

In 1939, Robert de Graff introduced the idea of the paperback in America and formed the Pocket Book Company. Pocket Books published familiar titles written by well-known authors at an inexpensive cost and incorporated new distribution techniques. The books were sold in outlets such as drugstores, bus stations, grocery stores, candy stores, and train stations. Paperback outlet estimates ranged as high as 40 outlets for every one traditional hardcover book outlet. In its first year, Pocket Books sold 1.5 million copies and in its first ten years printed more than 600 popular titles and sold more than 260 million books. Other competitors, including Avon, Dell, Popular Library, and Bantam Books, quickly began to produce paperbacks as well (Braden, 81).

During the war, the Armed Services Edition Program adopted the policy of printing inexpensive paperbacks that were a little wider and shorter to fit in a serviceman's pocket. Some of the favorites were westerns by Max Brand and Ernest Haycox and mysteries. The program issued on average 40 different titles each month and eventually distributed more than 350 million free copies to servicemen, both overseas and on the home front (Lingeman, 278). The U.S. government, however, did not distribute the most sought-after printed material of the war—the pinup.

The pinup, first introduced by *Esquire* magazine in the 1930s (see chapter 4), became incredibly popular among the millions of young servicemen cooped up in training camps and war zones. Two of the enduring favorites were of Betty Grable in a bathing suit and Rita Hayworth in a nightgown. During the course of the war, pinups could be found in barracks, submarines, tanks, airplanes, and dorm rooms. There was some moral outrage against the pinups, which lead the postmaster general to ban them from the mail in 1944. The demand by the soldiers overseas was too great and the postmaster general removed the ban.

Nightclubs and Dancing

Nightclubs were favorite sources of wartime entertainment, and almost every city had more than one. In 1942, nightclubs reported a 40 percent increase in business from the preceding year (Lingeman, 282). Nightclubs billed top-name entertainers such as singers Frank Sinatra and Dick Haymes, comedians Joe E. Lewis and Jimmy Durante, and bandleaders Benny Goodman and Duke Ellington. Popular nightspots in New York City included the Copacabana, Leon and Eddie's, and the Stork Club. *Variety* magazine reported that the trend in nightclub entertainment was "flashy, elaborate floor shows, and hooked-up gaiety" (Lingeman, 282). If a nightclub did not have a floorshow, the patrons would dance. Nightclubs were noted for having patrons waiting in line to get in, and many were overcrowded.

On November 28, 1942, an overcrowded nightclub in Boston, Massachusetts, became the scene of a tragedy. At the famed Coconut Grove, more than eight hundred patrons crowded into the nightclub. During the course of the evening, there was a fire in the club; in the ensuing panic, 484 people died (Lingeman, 308). Dominick Dattilo of New Jersey recalled that he heard of the fire because his boyhood film hero, cowboy star Charles "Buck" Jones, died while trying to save victims. At the time of his death in the Coconut Grove fire, Jones was on tour selling war bonds and promoting his latest film. Jones's career stretched back to an early silent film titled *Riders of the Purple Sage* (1918). Throughout the following twenty-five years Jones filmed dozens of movies and serials with his white stallion, Silver, and was one of the biggest western stars of his time.

The Coconut Grove fire caused concern (mainly criticism against the drinking and dancing that occurred in the clubs), and many cities instituted curfews and restrictions. Nightclubs, however, were a welcome relief for servicemen on leave and for war workers seeking relief from the mounting pressures of the war. By January, 1943, New York's Mayor Fiorella LaGuardia was the first to ease nightclub restrictions, and other cities followed.

The dance most associated with the period was swing (see chapter 4). In 1943, *Life* magazine called swing dancing "America's national dance." At the same time, dance schools such as Arthur Murray and the New York Society of Dance Teachers began teaching a ballroom version of swing. Most of the dance schools flourished in the cities. In Chicago in 1940, there were more than 180 dancing schools for adults listed in the telephone directory (Chicago Recreation Survey, 139). Ballroom standards were still popular, and the most popular dance among older adults was the foxtrot.

Dancing was so popular that more than two thousand war production plants had facilities for dancing during lunch or breaks. In addition, many of the plants were located near roadhouses, juke joints, and dancehalls that were frequented by the workers. Towns and cities near the war plants and army bases regularly sponsored dances, many supported by the USO, in churches, community centers, and YMCAs (Lingeman, 280).

Fads, Hobbies, and Games

The popularity of hobbies that began in the depression continued throughout the war even though full employment allowed limited spare time. A 1941 issue of *Popular Science* magazine ranked the five most popular hobbies as photography, stamp collecting, music, model making, and home workshops. Large hobby shows were sponsored across the country. In New York City in 1941, the New York

Stock Exchange sponsored the first annual large hobby show that would continue until 1954. The U.S. armed forces supported hobbies and crafts as rehabilitation for wounded servicemen. Model airplane building was popular as a father-son activity (Gelber, 49–52).

A 1942 survey reported that over 87 percent of Americans played card games in the home, the most popular being bridge. Other popular games included chess, checkers, finch, rook, and Chinese checkers. The increase in the number of people playing cards and board games was due in part to the availability of material to produce these items, which was mainly wood. Board games that required metal, rubber, or petroleum products had to search for alternative materials and as a result could not meet demand (Lingeman, 272).

Simple activities such as slumber parties were popular among white middle-class teenage and college-aged girls. A group of 4 to 12 girls would congregate at one person's house and try to stay up all night playing records and talking about dating, fashion, and makeup (Rollin, 128).

Amusement Parks

New York was a major military port during the war, and seaside amusement parks such as Coney Island, although they were becoming less popular, were encouraged to remain open to serve soldiers on leave. With wartime shortages, prizes in the game arcades at almost all of the parks nationwide were replaced with food ration coupons. A 1940 published report titled *The Youth of New York City* indicated that "segregation" and "social prejudice" still prevented African Americans from gaining access to the same recreation and amusement parks that were readily available to whites (quoted in Kraus [1971], 299).

In 1944, Luna Park at Coney Island was completely destroyed by a fire and was not rebuilt. Steeplechase remained as the only survivor of the famed Coney Island amusement park area (see chapter 1). The public fascination with all things military made the parachute jump at Steeplechase popular during the war years (see chapter 4). The parachute jump also served as a prominent landmark for those soldiers either entering or leaving New York harbor. After the war, interest in the ride waned. It remained opened as a ride until 1964 and remained standing for the rest of the twentieth century (Vita, n. p.).

MUSIC AND THEATER

Broadway

At the outbreak of war, approximately two hundred Broadway-style theaters existed nationwide. The large majority (more than 100) was in New York; Chicago was a distant second with nine theaters with varied seasons lasting from 13 to 50 weeks. By late 1940 summer theater was a regular feature in New England resort areas (Chicago Recreation Survey, 41). Broadway remained strong, but it was not immune from the effects of war.

In early 1942, with the first mandatory war blackout, the lights of Times Square and Broadway went dim, causing confusion and disorientation. On June 13, 1942 the *New York Herald Tribune* reported that theatergoers were "[c]ompletely baffled by the lack of familiar West Side landmarks and feeling their way from Sardi's [restaurant] to the Shubert Theater and back by an elaborate system of navigation based on the Braille system and dead reckoning. . . . [Some] found themselves for a time in the right seats but in the [wrong] theater" (Lingeman, 46).

Broadway would quickly adapt to the war and join in supporting it. In 1942 and 1943, Broadway offered more than 40 new productions with war themes. Leading the way was Irving Berlin's *This is the Army*. In 1942, James Cagney appeared in an Uncle Sam costume performing the patriotic song and dance number "Yankee Doodle Dandy" in the Broadway musical of the same name. After 1943, many of the productions were comedies and musicals with escapist themes. The musical *Oklahoma* (1943) set a new standard for Broadway. It ran for 2,212 performances, and the sound track was released on a collection of 78-rpm records and sold more than one million copies (Panati, 226). It would later be eclipsed by the comedy/drama *Life with Father*, which ran from 1939 to 1947 for 3,242 performances.

Theater attendance increased, and for the first time in many years, a new audience was exposed to Broadway. War workers could afford ticket prices and sought out the theater. The USO also distributed free tickets to servicemen on leave, and a new sight filled the theater as military uniforms and work clothes became common among audience members (Lingeman, 290–291). For many of the servicemen, it was their first and only visit to Broadway.

The Movies and Newsreels

The movies remained the most popular from of entertainment outside the home. By 1940, more than 18,800 movie theaters existed nationwide. The city of Chicago, Illinois, with only 190 theaters reported more than 20 million moviegoers per year, and one survey revealed that over 85 percent of all theaters regularly played double features (Chicago Recreation Survey, 28–29).

With the war, the movies would once again find themselves serving a patriotic cause. The Selective Service Act declared movie production to be an "essential" industry and therefore exempted all its employees from the draft. Despite the exemption, more than 2,700 cameramen, directors, stagehands, and actors enlisted (almost 15 percent of the industry workers). Film stars who enlisted included Henry Fonda, Jimmy Stewart, and Clark Gable (Lingeman, 170). One film, *Buck Privates* (1941), featured the comedy team of Bud Abbott and Lou Costello and the uniformed Andrews Sisters singing their hit song "Boogie Woogie Bugle Boy." Both the song and movie encouraged the public to accept selective service. The movie was voluntarily made just prior to America's entry in the war, and the government sought to ensure that all films followed the same theme of wartime unity.

Only ten days after Roosevelt asked Congress for a declaration of war against Japan, he officially designated the Bureau of Motion Pictures (BMP) as a division of the OWI to monitor the content of every Hollywood film produced during World War II. Roosevelt declared, "The American motion picture is one of our most effective mediums in informing and entertaining our citizens." Many films that sought to both entertain Americans and strengthen public support for the war were quickly produced. Between 1942 and 1944, more than 1,300 Hollywood films were produced, of which over 30 percent contained war themes (Lingeman, 205).

At the peak of the war and with the economy thriving, the U.S. Department of Commerce estimated that over 80 percent of all dollars spent on "spectator amusements" (including theater, concerts, and sports) was spent on going to the movies. Weekly audiences remained steady at more than 90 million people. The movies as entertainment included feature films, occasional double features, cartoons, serial shorts, and previews of coming attractions.

Hollywood also recognized that almost 15 million moviegoers were African Americans and attempted to capitalize on the segregated market. Film historian Thomas Doherty said, "With this emergent audience in mind, and with hopes of crossing over to a white audience that had long accepted blacks as performers, 20th Century-Fox and MGM each produced moderately budgeted all-black musicals in 1943, *Stormy Weather* and *Cabin in the Sky*, respectively (208–209).

Unlike radio and newspapers, the movies were able to provide Americans with gripping visual accounts of the war through the increased use of newsreels. Newsreels were approximately eight minutes long and were issued twice a week. According to film historian Thomas Doherty, newsreel content included "headlines, human interest stories, cheesecake [starlets in bathing suits], and sports highlights" (229). It was estimated that at least 70 percent of the theaters regularly showed at least one newsreel as a part of their daily features.

A film crew was at Pearl Harbor on the day of the attack (by coincidence filming for a movie) and shot footage of the Japanese attack. The scenes, although heavily censored, were seen on the newsreels in late February 1942. Audiences were spellbound, and in the remaining war years more than six hundred newsreels were released each year (most within ten days of the event they covered). The war occupied over 80 percent of newsreel content. All the newsreels were carefully monitored and heavily censored. Images of fierce fighting or any American soldier killed in action were not allowed into any from of visual media until late 1943 when the first such photograph appeared in *Life* magazine (Doherty, 231, 239).

The newsreels were careful to omit any reference to minorities. It was estimated, that in 1,200 newsreels in two years, only 3 in 1943 and 18 in 1944 contained any evidence of African American soldiers. Censors in the South completely eliminated all images of African Americans (Doherty, 221). Little was even said of the U.S. Army 442nd Infantry Regiment, made up entirely of Americans of Japanese ancestry, which was the most decorated regiment of any branch of the armed services.

In 1942, the OWI estimated that over 85 percent of urban African Americans received their news information through newsreels and therefore created a separate "All-American Newsreel" to distribute information specifically for African American audiences. The newsreels, viewed by more than four million African Americans on a weekly basis, were regularly shown in the estimated 365 all–African American movie theaters nationwide and were carefully distributed by the Army Motion Picture Service to 70 segregated military bases. Doherty cited "an OWI survey reporting that 85 percent of Negroes in five large cities got most of their news not from the Negro press but from the All-American News" (221). As a result, African Americans themselves were very much aware of the exploits of the Tuskegee Airmen and African American infantry divisions such as the 92nd and

93rd, but the American public was mostly ignorant of these groups until the 1980s.

In the Mood for Swing and Sinatra

In the prewar years, Saturday night became a popular evening for going out. Teenagers and young adults might go to a soda fountain, roller-skating rink, or an open-house party. Roller-skating at indoor rinks featured a jukebox with music to appeal to servicemen and younger adults. Jukeboxes were still a dominant entertainment force; more than 400,000 existed and played more than 5 billion songs per year (Panati, 198).

Music was a big attraction, and the inexpensive 78-rpm record allowed Americans to recapture the sounds of radio, advertisements, and Hollywood within their own homes. Record shops provided glass-enclosed, soundproof listening booths for buyers to sample and listen to the music. By 1946, more than two hundred million 78-rpm records were being sold each year.

Most popular song lyrics of the period supported the war. "Don't Sit Under the Apple Tree" encouraged the girl at home to be faithful to the fighting soldier away at war. Country singer Ernest Tubb sang "A Rainbow at Midnight," which promised a better future beyond war. The enduring classic of the era was "White Christmas," in which Bing Crosby sang of nostalgia for celebrations with family and friends. Swing, however, was the music that was most closely associated with World War II. The music itself was enlisted to aid in the war effort, and nowhere was that more evident than in the music of Glenn Miller.

Miller first achieved prominence with his orchestra in 1939. His song hits included "Little Brown Jug," "Moonlight Serenade," "In the Mood," and "Chattanooga Choo Choo," which was the first record to individually sell more than one million copies. By 1940, Miller's nationally syndicated radio show drew millions of listeners. On the road, his tours broke all contemporary attendance records. In St. Louis, Missouri, for example, his band drew more than 5,400 people and in Kansas City more than 7,800 people (Erenberg, 169). Miller, however, felt that his services would be better put to use if he enlisted.

In September 1942, Miller was commissioned as a captain and placed in charge of the 418th Army Air Forces Band (AAF). Within the AAF, he organized a 42-man marching band, a 19-piece dance big band, a small jazz combo, and a radio show. Instead of the preferred marches by John Philip Sousa, Miller convinced the military to let him play swing music, the popular music that most of the young enlisted men preferred. He also added a unique twist to the marching band, incorporating two drummers playing from jeeps (Erenberg, 182). Unfortunately, in December of 1944, Miller was lost in an airplane accident over the English Channel. Nevertheless, Glenn Miller's army band was credited as being just as instrumental to the war effort as any other American industry of that time.

Ironically, it was the war that was most responsible for the end of swing music. The Selective Service declared musicians to be "nonessential"; as a result, many were drafted causing most bands to break up. Touring bands had to curtail their lucrative engagements because of gasoline rationing and travel restrictions. The final problem was a strike by swing musicians from mid-1942 until late 1944 (a lifetime in popular music) that prevented any new commercial recordings. (Many

Eleanor Roosevelt and Frank Sinatra hold a statue of President Franklin D. Roosevelt at a banquet in Los Angeles, California, in 1946. Courtesy of FDR Library, New Hyde Park, New York.

bands did record previously released tunes—however, only on government-issued "V" discs intended for servicemen.) As a result of the strike, individual singers (who were not part of the musician's union and therefore not on strike) replaced bands in popular recordings and performances. The most well-known of these singers was a young, thin Italian-American from Hoboken, New Jersey, named Frank Sinatra.

Before Sinatra's entrance on the music scene, the band was the star attraction and the vocalist was a featured attraction. In 1939, Sinatra himself started as a vocalist with the Tommy Dorsey Orchestra. In 1942, however, the blue-eyed singer set out on his own and created a never-before-seen sensation that was called "Sinatra-mania." Screaming young female teenage fans called bobby-soxers (because of their fashion style of knee length dresses, white scrunched-up socks, and two-toned saddle shoes) were known to faint as Sinatra crooned. Sinatra was besieged with more than five thousand fan letters a week and more than two thousand fan clubs for him were started nationwide. In one concert in October 1944, more than 3,600 bobby-soxers packed the Paramount Theater in New York City. Crowds outside, which could not get into the theater, were estimated at more than 20,000. The scene could only be described as fan hysteria. Phyllis Giordano, a Brooklyn resident, recalled her attendance at the show:

> When I heard that Frank Sinatra was going to appear at the New York Paramount, I wanted to go and camp out at midnight with the other girls. But my father wouldn't let me. I asked if I could get up at 5:00 A.M., and again he said, "No!" However, the next morning, he woke me up at five (the time he usually got up to go to work) and said I could go. Before I left, my father said "I don't want you screaming like a maniac like all the other girls." . . . By the time we got to the theater, the line was already long and around the block. Also, we were playing hooky from school, but we weren't afraid of the truant officer since we knew he wouldn't arrest over 10,000 other girls who were doing the same thing. . . . When Sinatra came onstage and all the other girls screamed, I was afraid to scream. I thought my father would find out and not let me see another Sinatra show. . . . But he was worth all the effort to see him. (Giordano interview)

Giordano would remain a fan for more than 50 years and witness more than 150 Sinatra shows and concerts.

SPORTS AND GAMES

The Professionals Go to War

Professional athletes were not exempt from the Selective Service Act. Of the 5,700 professional baseball players, in both the major and minor leagues, more than 4,000 either enlisted or were drafted. In the minor leagues, because of travel restrictions combined with the high loss of players, only 9 out of 41 leagues were able to continue play throughout the war years. In both leagues, game times were adjusted to accommodate war workers. Some games were scheduled to start as early as 10:30 A.M. and some as late as 9:30 P.M. (Lingeman, 311). Baseball was still a popular spectator sport, and with the large number of players away in the armed forces, an alternative was provided. In the Midwest the All-American Girls Professional Baseball League (AAGPBL) was formed.

In 1943, the AAGPBL began with four teams located in Rockford, Illinois; South Bend, Indiana; and Racine and Kenosha, Wisconsin. Throughout its history, the league's teams played in communities with populations between 50,000 and 150,000 people. Attendance at games rose from 150,000 in the initial year to more than 450,000 in 1945. The single-game attendance record was 7,800 in a 1946 contest in Indiana between the South Bend Blue Sox and the Racine Belles. The league's attendance peaked in 1948 with more than 910,000 fans and ten teams, but the league was disbanded after the 1954 season. The league's decline in the 1950s was attributed mainly to increased television coverage of men's baseball and alternative forms of entertainment that became increasingly available in the postwar years (All-American Girls Professional Baseball League, "League History," n.p.).

Almost all of the other professional spectator sports suffered a fate similar to baseball's. Boxing suspended all official championship fights because all of the titleholders were in the armed services. Famed heavyweight Joe Louis was drafted in 1942 and promoted the sale of liberty bonds and performed other duties to aid the war effort. Many boxing promoters tried to continue the sport and staged fights for just about anyone who was willing to step into the ring. A resulting development was an increase in the number of African American fighters. Many African Americans suffered discrimination when attempting to enlist for the army and were declared 4F (unfit for duty), so many were available as professional fighters. During the war approximately 75 percent of professional fighters were African American.

Amateur Participation

Because of the war, the Olympic Games of 1940 and 1944 were cancelled. The strict rationing on gasoline and tires also caused suspension of auto racing for the duration of the war; the Indianapolis 500 did not run from 1942 to 1945.

College attendance also suffered during the war. Colleges did not receive the selective service exemption that they would receive during the 1960s. As a result, almost all college football teams suspended play. However, the military service academies and army base teams were overflowing with former college players and continued to play to large crowds. The two main military teams playing at this time were the U.S. Military Academy team at West Point and the Great Lakes Naval Training Station team in Ohio. Every military unit had some sort of team including baseball, boxing, and football. Many of the teams were made up of professional athletes who put on exhibitions to entertain the troops. Other sports teams provided recreation activities for servicemen. The U.S. Army Special Services Division dedicated more than 12,000 officers and 50,000 enlisted personnel to supervise recreation facilities and programs on military bases both at home and abroad that included basketball, volleyball, baseball, and softball.

Interest in softball as a participation sport increased dramatically during the war years. The National Recreation Association had been encouraging adults to play the game as early as the late 1920s. In 1933, the Amateur Softball Association of America was formed, and by 1938, more than eight thousand softball diamonds, many with lights for night play, had been built, many aided by federal works projects. Also in 1938, the city of Chicago reported that there were more than 2,500 softball teams in that city alone. By 1940, more than three million adults participated in one of 300,000 softball clubs. The teams were sponsored by churches, companies, fraternal organizations, and intramural organizations on college campuses (Braden, 273).

Bowling also continued its rise in popularity. At the beginning of 1940, the nation had more than 10,000 bowling establishments with more than 11 million participants. Amateur bowling competitions were becoming more and more popular. One event in New York City in 1938 attracted 4,017 five-person teams, 5,883 two-person teams, and 11,755 individual entrants (Chicago Recreation Survey, 58).

By 1940, there were more than 60,000 basketball teams nationwide that were either college, high school, fraternal, church, or company-sponsored teams. In addition to the players, in 1937 more than 80 million people attended basketball games (Chicago Recreation Survey, 68).

Horse racing tracks and gambling continued to be popular. During the war years, attendance at horseracing tracks steadily increased from the prewar high of 15 million per year to 17 million by 1944. However, during the first five months of 1945, the Office of War Mobilization (OWM) closed all horse racing tracks, claiming that material that could be better used for the war effort was being wasted on horseracing (Lingeman, 266). States complained of lost revenue from the betting pari-mutuels, and the tracks were reopened in late 1945. After the tracks were reopened, attendance reached a new all-time high of 17.2 million in that shortened season.

In 1940, the *Recreation Yearbook* estimated that 11 million Americans played tennis and another 8 million played golf. Between 1942 and 1945, all major professional tennis and golf tournaments were suspended. Golfers were restricted by the closing of over 25 percent of the nation's courses. Some of the closed courses were converted to Victory Gardens. The famed Augusta National Golf Course in Georgia, home of the Master's championship, closed in 1943 to graze cattle for the war effort. Golfers were also encouraged to recycle their metal clubs and the material used for golf balls, which were in short supply. One golf course in Atlanta, Georgia (as did many other courses), drained a lake to discover more than 16,000 golf balls, which were reconditioned for play (Bondi, *American Decades: 1940–1949*, 554–555).

TRANSPORTATION AND VACATIONS

Gasoline Rationing and the Auto Vacation

In 1940, it was estimated that over 20 percent of Americans owned an automobile. In 1942, the War Production Board (WPB) halted all commercial auto production. Auto factories were quickly converted to producing jeeps, trucks, tanks, airplanes, and other war-related vehicles. The jeep (initially given the military designation GPV for general purpose vehicle) would be adapted for civilian use after the war and became a popular recreation vehicle (Bondi, *American Decades*, 189).

In early 1942, the OPA lowered the national speed limit to 35 miles per hour and instituted full gasoline, rubber, and metal rationing as national policy. Automobile owners were issued windshield stickers labeled either A, B, or C. Class A stickers were assigned to nonessential vehicles used for shopping, church, or a personal medical emergency and were limited to three gallons of gasoline per week. The other two labels were classified as essential and were given to vehicles used for military personnel, war workers, and emergency vehicles, and these vehicles received higher gasoline allotments. Tires were not available due to strict rubber rationing caused by the fact that over 97 percent of the country's rubber supply had been previously imported from Far East territories that had been overtaken by the Japanese. In 1943, the OPA prohibited all automobile pleasure travel. By early 1944, the OPA rescinded the ban but limited gasoline purchases for A sticker vehicles to only two gallons of gasoline per week (Lingeman, 240). The severe restrictions almost completely stopped auto-vacations, and vacation resorts reached by auto routes suffered a sharp decline in visitors.

The Bicycle and the Bus

Prior to the war, bicycle riding was promoted as a healthy endeavor and was also a favorite pursuit of many Hollywood film stars. One 1937 survey revealed that more than 700,000 people in Chicago had actively taken up bicycling (Chicago Recreation Survey, 96). However, by 1942 the endeavor came to a quick halt. Bicycles were rationed, and in order to buy a new one an individual had to obtain a certificate of necessity from the local rationing board. In addition, even if an individual's old bicycle was still in working order, tires and inner tubes were in short supply (Lingeman, 243). As a result of the limited availability of automobiles and bicycles, bus ridership increased dramatically during the war. Later in the war, however, buses would also be affected by gasoline and tire shortages.

The Airplane

By 1940, individuals were using airplanes increasingly for vacation travel as airlines continued to add vacation destinations and provide service to resort areas. In 1941, more than 350 passenger planes were in service by various airlines. The Pennsylvania Central Airlines offered service originating in Pittsburgh to resort areas in the South and in the Great Lakes regions of Minnesota, Michigan, and Illinois. Pan American Airlines offered tourists international vacation trips to Latin America, Mexico, and the Pacific. Eastern Airlines provided commercial service to more than 40 cities nationwide (Benjamin, 255–256). In June 1941, six months before the Pearl Harbor attack, TWA Airlines advertised the use of the four-engine Boeing Stratoliner, claiming greater speed and comfort than the DC-3 (see chapter 4). One advertisement proclaimed, "[O]f course you can find time for a vacation this year! Just take to the air with TWA. You'll return feeling fit and eager to tackle the problems ahead" (*Time*, June 16, 1941).

Immediately after the Pearl Harbor attack all pleasure air travel ceased, and all other civilian planes and pilots were grounded. The civilian pilots, numbering more than 100,000, were quickly enlisted to aid in military pilot training or in the newly formed Civilian Air Patrol (CAP). The CAP was trained to patrol both coastlines, the east for German U-boats and the west for an anticipated Japanese invasion. In addition to pilots, the CAP enlisted the aid of 80,000 adult volunteers and more than 20,000 boys and girls between the ages of 15 and 18 (Lingeman, 45).

The government also commandeered almost all operational aircraft, both civilian and commercial, for military use. The remainder were put to use by the airlines carrying cargo and a limited number of passengers. In order to obtain a seat on an airplane, a priority designation from the government was required (Lingeman, 240).

The war did provide a distinct advantage to the advancement of civilian aviation. Just before December 7, 1941, only 72 airfields nationwide were capable of handling large passenger airplanes. With the dramatic increase in aircraft production (in 1941 the number of aircraft produced numbered in the hundreds, between 1942 and 1945 the number averaged more than 68,000 per year), the size and capacity of quality airfields increased to more than 650. These included new passenger terminals containing waiting rooms, rest rooms, and restaurants. Technological advances made during the war included the jet engine, helicopters, and cabin pressurization (Jakle, 182).

With the end of the war, many military airplanes became surplus and formed the basis for commercial airlines and civilian pilots. Hundreds of the military airfields, both large and small, were turned over for both civilian and commercial use and were easily converted to airports. With the increased availability of aircraft and airports, hundreds of flight training schools emerged, and thousands of Americans learned to fly for recreation (Taneja, 16).

The Railroads: Standing Room Only

Railroads that had experienced declines in passenger travel since 1920 saw a sharp increase in passenger travel during these years, mainly because of the war. With gasoline rationing and the ban on pleasure driving, Americans relied on the train for travel and vacation. The wealthy traveled by rail from Los Angeles to Chicago on the Santa Fe Super Chief and from Chicago to New York on the Broadway Limited or the Twentieth Century Limited. Both of these lines were favored by the wealthy, especially by film celebrities. For those who traveled in coach or regular seating, accommodations on passenger trains were crowded (Stover, 203).

During the war, the military made wide use of the railroad, and it received top priority. Over 95 percent of all troop movements and 90 percent of civilian movements within the 48 states were by passenger train. The number of military personnel aboard trains was estimated to be at least one million per month (Stover, 203). In 1944, the total number of passengers (nonmilitary) topped 910 million, and that year was the last great year for passenger numbers (Stover, 205). For the duration "standing room only" was commonly advertised as the only availability on passenger trains.

Passengers were usually inconvenienced as the war took priority. The catchphrase advertised by the OWI was "think before you travel." In 1943, the *Saturday Evening Post* explained:

> the railroads must move individual servicemen or smaller groups traveling under orders—soldiers, sailors, marines, and coast guards on furlough—families visiting servicemen in camps—businessmen and other workers on war business—those who can no longer use their automobile—and every other sort of traveler by rail. . . . understand why travelers sometimes have to wait at ticket windows or why they cannot always get accommodations when they want them. Whether you travel this summer—and where—and when, are questions which you alone can answer—but answer them with your eyes fixed on the fighting fronts and with the needs of the armed forces in your mind. (June 12, 1943, Vol. 215, No. 50: 41)

During the course of the war all locomotive and rail cars were pressed into service as the railroads provided vital shipments within the nation to try and offset the U-boat menace that closed almost all shipping lanes (Stover, 204).

Ocean Travel, U-boats, and Vacation Resorts

The nation's vulnerability on both the Pacific and Atlantic coasts became evident shortly after the attack on Pearl Harbor located on the Hawaiian island of Oahu. With a declaration of war and threat of a possible invasion upon the Hawaiian islands or the West coast of the United States all cruise ship travel and vacation to Hawaii abruptly ended. Many of the resort hotels such as the Royal Hawaiian on Waikiki Beach were leased by the United States Navy Recreation and Morale Office for use by navy personnel.

In early 1942, German U-boat attacks disrupted Atlantic shipping and cruise ship travel lanes. During the first months of the year, dozens of ships were torpedoed just off the east coast of America, some in plain sight of beachgoers. The U-boats not only scared away passenger ships, they also contributed to shortages of gasoline and other products as supply tankers were sunk and threatened along the eastern seaboard. Because of the submarine threat, all transatlantic pleasure travel ceased, and the cruise ships were converted into troop carriers. In 1942, the British-owned Cunard Line converted the *Queen Mary*, *Queen Elizabeth*, the *Mauretania*, and *Normandie* to carry troops. Prior to the war, each ship comfortably handled 2,500 passengers. As troop transports, they accommodated 8,500 to 10,000 troops (and in some cases as many as 15,000). The accommodations could in no way be described as even comfortable. In 1945, the ships were used to transport millions of troops home and in 1946 were refitted for cruise ship service.

Travel restrictions hurt the entire tourist industry. Because of coastal blackouts, many resorts closed their beaches at sundown, and some even closed for the duration of the war. In Florida, a popular prewar destination, only a limited amount of hotels were available because many had been commandeered by the government either for administrative use or for rest and relaxation centers for servicemen. Later in the war, the tourist trade slowly returned. With railroad access available, Florida promoted itself as a vacation getaway for hard-working, and now highly paid, civilian workers. The Daytona Chamber of Commerce advised, "Like a soldier YOU need a civilian furlough" (Florida Memory Project, "Florida During World War II," n.p.).

CONCLUSION

The atomic bombs dropped on Hiroshima and Nagasaki in August 1945 brought an end to a long and destructive war. Americans who had grown so accustomed to war suddenly had to adjust to a new postwar life. A short time after the war ended, gasoline limitations, rationing, and other wartime restrictions were eliminated. Both the country and the returning war veterans wanted to put the war behind them and get on with their lives. The war economy put more money in the hands of individuals as Americans dreamed of a postwar world of peace and prosperity. The war workers, who had sacrificed and supported the fighting forces, would have to move aside and revert to their prewar roles; roles that required the reintroduction of more than 12 million American servicemen into civilian life. The year 1946 presented Americans with a new challenge. In 1946, with the immediate end of the war, more than 3 million women left the work force, and birthrates increased by more than 20 percent. Unlike the Great Depression when Americans had the time but not the money, and unlike World War II when Americans had the money but not necessarily the time, the postwar period would present Americans with both the time and money to pursue recreation and leisure.

CHAPTER 6

TELEVISION, TEENAGERS, AND ROCK AND ROLL: 1947–1964

CHRONOLOGY

1947 Jackie Robinson breaks the "color line" in baseball; the National Association of Stock Car Auto Racing (NASCAR) is formed.

1948 Selective service is reinstated; the Frisbee is invented; Alfred Kinsey publishes *Sexual Behavior in the Human Male*; Leo Fender introduces the solid-body electric guitar.

1949 Silly Putty is introduced.

1950 The first modern credit card is introduced.

1951 The color television is introduced.

1952 Mr. Potato Head is the first toy advertised on television.

1953 Kinsey's *Sexual Behavior in the Human Female* is published.

1954 The Supreme Court rules that segregation is illegal in *Brown v. Board of Education*.

1955 Disneyland opens in California; James Dean dies in a car accident; the polio vaccine is announced; Rosa Parks refuses to give up her seat on a bus; the movie *Blackboard Jungle* premiers that has teenagers dancing in the theater aisles to the rock and roll song *Rock Around the Clock*.

1956 Elvis Presley appears on the *Ed Sullivan Show*; television remote control is invented; the Interstate Highway Act is passed.

1957 The Soviet satellite *Sputnik* launches the Space Age; the television show *American Bandstand* first airs.

1958 Hula hoops become popular.

1959 The first NASCAR super speedway is opened in Daytona Beach, Florida; Alaska becomes the 49th state, and Hawaii becomes the 50th.

1960   The first televised presidential debates air; the birth control pill goes on the market.

1961   Freedom rides begin throughout the South.

1962   The Cuban missile crisis occurs; Chubby Checker debuts the twist.

1963   Betty Friedan publishes *The Feminine Mystique*; Martin Luther King, Jr. delivers his "I Have a Dream" speech; President John F. Kennedy is assassinated.

INTRODUCTION

At the end of the war, the United States was in the midst of its greatest economic growth of the twentieth century. It had survived virtually intact while the rest of the world lay in ruins. In the new economically powerful America, conformity was considered the norm, goods were plentiful, and most Americans could afford to buy them. New industries, consumer products, and neighborhoods began to appear. One result was the "baby boom," during which more than 76 million babies were born. This time period was defined by the development of interstate highways, the GI Bill of Rights, and the suburban transformation, the television, the automobile, vacations, and the purchase of a new home.

For many women and minorities, the newfound freedoms that the war provided would create conflicts in the following years. A clash of cultures began between those who were trying to conform to a new American idea of consumption and prosperity and those who would desperately fight for civil rights and equality in a country that had just fought a world war to preserve the supposed ideals of freedom that did not actually exist for some on the home front. Although segregation laws did not exist in the north, mainstream attitudes toward African Americans and other minorities were such that society remained segregated. During this time the social consciousness of America was being aroused by events such as school desegregation, Rosa Parks, Emmett Till, and Elvis Presley. Americans were also worried about the spread of Communism and the threat of a nuclear attack.

PUBLIC INTEREST

The GI Bill of Rights

With the end of the war in sight and concern rising over the reintroduction of more than 12 million active servicemen into civilian life, Congress proposed the Servicemen's Readjustment Act of 1944, signed into law by President Roosevelt. More commonly known as the GI Bill of Rights, the act made benefits available for an honorably discharged veteran who had served at least 90 days after September 16, 1940. Administered by the Veterans Administration (VA), the bill provided benefits including job-finding assistance, loan guarantee for the purchase of a home or farm, and education funds.

In 1947 alone, more than one million veterans enrolled in college on the GI Bill (the VA paid substantial amounts for tuition, books, and housing allowances).

When the program officially ended in July 1956, more than 7.8 million veterans had received educational and vocational training (2.2 million in college, 3.5 million in other schools, 1.4 million in on-the-job training, and 690,000 in agricultural training). In 1952, the GI Bill was adjusted to include Korean War veterans, benefiting an additional 2.4 million individuals ("GI Bill of Rights"). In addition to servicemen's being better prepared for the civilian workforce, because of time spent receiving education their transition into the workforce occurred over a ten-year period, thereby avoiding flooding the job market.

During this period over 60 percent of the nation's citizens were classified as wage earners or as being solidly in the middle class. Union organizers such as American Federation of Labor and Congress of Industrial Organizations (AFL-CIO) president George Meany stressed the importance of "not only more money but more leisure and a richer cultural life" (Kaplan, 14). For many returning veterans, that meant applying for a VA mortgage to purchase their own home in the newly developing suburbia.

Planned Communities: Levittown and the New Suburban Ideal

In 1940, less than 10 percent of Americans lived in suburbs. During the postwar period, spurred by Federal Housing Administration (FHA) and VA-supported loans, more than 40 million Americans moved to the suburbs. Between 1946 and 1949, more than five million new homes were built. Another eight million were added by 1964. Over 85 percent of the new homes were single-family, detached homes in suburban developments. The most significant was Levittown, Long Island, which constructed more than 17,500 homes and had a total population of more than 82,000. A second Levittown of 16,000 homes was also built in Pennsylvania (Albrecht, xiv).

Part of the unique significance of the newly constructed suburban homes was that specific areas within the home were set aside for leisure. Rooms not previously available in rental units included the recreation room, family room, outdoor patio, and backyard, all serving as areas of shared family leisure activities. Within the suburban home, for the first time many children and teens had their own rooms to which they could retreat and where they could have their own choice of entertainment and leisure. Parents had the home workshop, the kitchen, and the lawn. The lawn, the symbol of the new suburbia, was a well-kept area of green grass, especially in the front of the house. Mowing the lawn and keeping an immaculate garden became symbols of civic pride.

By 1964, the country's population was almost evenly divided in thirds among the suburbs, cities, and rural areas. More significant was that for the first time, more Americans owned homes than rented them. The planned suburban communities such as Levittown came to represent the "American dream." However, these communities did not include African Americans in that dream.

Desegregation and Civil Rights

Because of carefully enforced segregation, African Americans, ethnic minorities, and women had limited access to the new suburbia. The FHA and VA refused to provide loans for African Americans and female veterans. They also redlined communities. Redlining was the practice of not allowing loans for homes in designated areas within inner cities. Although the Supreme Court in 1948 declared the loan discrimination to be illegal, developers and financial institutions continued the practice.

African Americans continued to maintain social, recreational, and leisure activities within their own communities. The most important social center was the community church. The two predominant African American denominations were Methodist, with more than 2 million members in 12,000 congregations nationwide, and Baptist, with more than 7 million members nationwide in 35,000 churches. Other forms of social life were maintained as part of segregated fraternal organizations. For example, by 1947, membership in the African American Order of the Elks (1898) stood at more than 500,000 in 1,000 lodges (Frazier, 88, 91–92).

The African American churches and fraternal orders maintained a social life similar to, but parallel to, that of the white population. Events such as debutante balls, the "Pink Cotillion" in Philadelphia, Pennsylvania, and the Black Miss America Pageant were but a few examples. The Mississippi State Fair in Jackson traditionally held a "whites only" event for the first week and after that let in African Americans for three days (Williams, 218). Diane Nash, who grew up in Chicago, recalled a leisure trip to attend the Tennessee state fair: "I had a date with a young man, and I started to go to the ladies' room. And it said 'white' and 'colored,' and I really resented that" (Williams, 218, 130). E. Franklin Frazier concluded that the ability to enjoy a "social life became identified with the condition of freedom" (203). The first step was to approach the Supreme Court.

The GI Bill did allow African American veterans to enroll in higher education. Many took advantage of the benefit but found themselves limited to predominantly African American universities. At that time, 17 states and Washington, D.C., legally required segregated school systems, and most other states had segregated systems in practice. In 1954, the case of *Brown v. Board of Education* was brought before the Supreme Court. In a unanimous decision the Court ruled that school segregation was illegal (overturning the 1898 *Plessy v. Ferguson* ruling; see chapter 1). The ruling was also the benchmark that paved the way for desegregation of public accommodations such as movie theaters, amusement parks, and motels.

Few schools voluntarily desegregated. In fact, as a response to the decision, more than 100 U.S. congressmen signed the Southern Manifesto in *opposition* to the Supreme Court ruling. Many southern states formed White Citizens' Councils to stop any attempts to integrate the schools (Halberstam, 43). In 1957, an attempt by nine African American students to enter Central High School in Little Rock, Arkansas, was met by a violent mob of angry whites. President Eisenhower was forced to send in military troops to protect the students.

In August 1963, the long struggle for equality made dramatic headway when more than 350,000 Americans marched on Washington, D.C., in support of civil rights. At the rally, Martin Luther King delivered his famous "I Have a Dream" speech on the same Lincoln Memorial steps where the Marian Anderson concert of 1939 was performed (see chapter 4). The march made it apparent that many

Americans were concerned enough about civil rights that they would forego leisure activities and devote their free time to the chance for a future of equal opportunity.

Antibiotics and the Polio Vaccine

During this period, the introduction of antibiotics effectively eliminated the threat of deadly bacterial diseases such as tuberculosis and diphtheria. In the decade from 1945 to 1955, along with the baby boom, there was a steady and visible rise in the number of polio cases. Polio was a crippling disease that had no known cure, no identified causes, and could strike any healthy individual, especially children. (Franklin D. Roosevelt was polio's most famous victim.)

Unlike the great flu epidemic (see chapter 2) when most victims died, most polio victims survived, but with lasting effects. Similar to during the earlier flu epidemic, during the polio epidemic public places were closed, and people were cut off from contact with one another. In 1952, the worst epidemic year, three thousand people died from polio. Death, however, was not the main concern; it was the hundreds of thousands that were crippled by the disease and became disabled. Hospitals were reluctant to accept polio patients because they could do very little for the patient, and as a result, many patients were forced to receive treatment within their homes in a device known as an iron lung (a machine that cleared patients' lungs of mucus and helped them breathe), which immobilized the patients and permanently confined them indoors. For those not confined indoors, the wheelchairs, braces, and crutches that existed at the time were expensive, heavy, and quite often painful to use; they were also not available in sufficient quantities.

In 1954, Jonas Salk discovered a cure for polio and described his polio vaccine in a televised interview with Edward Murrow on the CBS television show *See It Now*. The show made millions of viewers aware of the available vaccine. Inoculation for children began almost immediately. In 1956, Albert Sabin developed a polio vaccine that could be administered orally, thereby eliminating the need for an injection. The vaccine was so successful that polio was effectively eliminated.

President's Council on Physical Fitness and Outdoor Recreation

In 1956, the President's Council on Physical Fitness was started under President Eisenhower to challenge Americans (especially the youth) in both schools and public recreation programs to develop physical fitness programs. Outdoor exercise including cycling, jogging, swimming, and brisk walking was promoted to maintain total physical fitness. Eisenhower, often accused of spending too much time on his golf game, portrayed an image that according to historian Donald Albrecht, demonstrated "the conversion of the ethics of work and struggle into the project of recreation and leisure" (239).

The 1960 transition to President John F. Kennedy's administration featured the same devotion to outdoor recreation. Kennedy and his family routinely skied, sailed boats, and played touch football on the White House lawn. The Kennedy administration was particularly noted for extending recreation and physical fitness opportunities to disabled children and adults. Spurred by the interests of two active presidents, the federal government increased availability of outdoor recreation for the public.

The 1961 *Recreation and Park Yearbook* listed 13 federal agencies involved in administering recreation services (by 1966 the number would increase to 72 federal agencies). The National Park Service responsibilities included maintaining and protecting all national parks, monuments, and memorials and preventing hunting or commercial fishing at these sites. Hunting was pursued on private land and in state parks. The Park Service oversaw 214 areas and 231 million acres, which provided and maintained camping sites, park hotels, horse and hiking trails, boat docks, picnic areas, and recreational fishing areas. By 1955, national park attendance was more than 50 million people per year. By 1964, the number topped 121 million (Kraus [1971], 27).

American rivers and other waterways were under the direction of the U.S. Army Corp of Engineers, which made improvements and instituted programs for fish and wildlife development. The corps oversaw beaches, harbors, intercoastal waterways, and more than 350 reservoirs in 44 states. All of the facilities under corps control had access for public recreation including boating, fishing, and hunting. In 1955, there were 63 million visitors, and this increased to 128 million by 1964. The Bureau of Reclamation, in conjunction with the Army Corp of Engineers, administered water areas in 17 western states including the Hoover Dam (see chapter 4) for operation as recreation areas. Active use of bureau-controlled areas increased from 6 million visitors in 1950 to more than 49 million by 1964 (Kraus [1971], 29–30).

In the Southeast, the Tennessee Valley Authority (TVA) converted areas for recreation, mainly on the shores of lakes and reservoirs. By 1964, more than 10,000 miles of shoreline and 600,000 acres of water were available for use, which greatly benefited inhabitants of Kentucky, North Carolina, Tennessee, and other Tennessee border states. TVA area attendance estimates increased from 14 million in 1950 to more than 40 million in 1964 (Kraus [1971], 30).

In 1952, the U.S. Army Corp of Engineers began operation of the John H. Kerr dam and reservoir along the North Carolina–Virginia border. Designed as a flood-control reservoir and to provide hydroelectric power to the surrounding areas, the area was a boon for recreation. Known locally as Buggs Island Lake, the 50,000-acre lake extended 39 miles above the Roanoke River with an accompanying 800 miles of wooded shoreline and 30 recreation areas. Recreation activities included fishing, boating, camping, swimming, and even two seaplane-landing areas.

Almost every state acquired additional land for recreational use during this period. By 1960, the recreational acreage had increased from 4.6 to 5.6 million, and the number of individual state parks increased from 1,531 to 2,664. Campsites accounted for over 60 percent of the new areas. Attendance figures rose from 92.5 million per year in 1946 to more than 259 million by 1960—an increase five times faster than the population growth (Madow, 95–96).

The federal government and states acquired a large portion of the funds to maintain these programs through entrance fees to sites, fees for hunting and fishing licenses, and tax on ammunition, guns, and fishing tackle. Almost all state parks offered camping, fishing, hunting, and boating. Some states differed in their approach to state park use. Beginning in 1956, California began to acquire and develop oceanfront areas, a boon for surfers and beachgoers (Madow, 96).

LIFESTYLES

McCarthy, the Red Scare, and the Fallout Shelter

At the end of World War II, many Americans thought they would enter a period of prosperous peaceful isolation. After all, the United States had the most destructive weapon in the history of humankind in the atomic bomb and therefore could dictate world policy and live in peace. To the American public, however, the Soviet Union and Communism appeared to be gaining a foothold in much of the recently liberated free world. In 1948, to combat the threat, peacetime selective service was reinstated. In 1949, the Soviet Union exploded its own atomic bomb, and the United States was faced with the threat of a nuclear attack. It was in this unpredictable environment that the HUAC and Wisconsin Senator Joseph McCarthy rose to prominence.

The House Committee on Un-American Activities (HUAC) attempted to root out alleged communists and Soviet spies that might be subverting American activities, businesses, and entertainment. The most notorious occurred in 1947 as a group of ten movie directors, writers and producers known as the "Hollywood Ten" were imprisoned, and in 1949 Alger Hiss, a former high official in the U.S. state department, was convicted of perjury. By 1950, McCarthy seized the headlines with his warnings of a new "Red Scare," warning that Americans were endangered by Communist infiltration in Hollywood and government. From 1951 to 1954, McCarthyism was in full gear, and fear of the HUAC was so widespread that the federal government, state agencies, and most businesses required employees to take an oath of loyalty to the United States of America. The question, "Are you now, or have you ever been, a member of the Communist Party?" was as routine as questions of name and address on an employment application. Any individual who refused to answer was routinely fired and unofficially blacklisted. Historian Stephen Whitfield recalled that the requirement was so ridiculous that "[a] loyalty oath was imposed on [New York state] applicants who wanted to fish in municipal reservoirs" (45).

The Soviet hydrogen bomb (about one hundred times more powerful than the atomic bomb) was enough to scare Americans into adjusting their lifestyles so that they could seek shelter in the event of a nuclear attack. Civil defense air-raid sirens became a common sound in cities as most tested the siren at noon each day. In 1954, a massive air-raid drill was held in all 48 states and the territorial possessions of Alaska, Hawaii, and Puerto Rico. The yellow and black symbol of a civil defense air-raid shelter and the sound of the siren remained in the memory of those who lived during the period. Phyllis Giordano of Brooklyn recalled, "When we were outside playing we used to know when to go home for lunch by the sound of the air-raid sirens at 12 [noon]" (Giordano interview).

How real was the Red Scare? A Gallup poll revealed that over 53 percent of Americans believed that a nuclear war with the Soviets was imminent. The new Red Scare was so pervasive that for the first time, the distinction between politics, culture, and leisure lifestyles was almost completely obliterated. In the mid-1950s, the fear reached professional baseball, and the Cincinnati Reds baseball team changed their nickname to the "Redlegs." Hollywood movies and popular culture of the period supported the HUAC and the political brainwashing of the American public.

The fear of Communism caused a rise in patriotic support and religious affiliations. In 1954, as an affirmation against the atheistic beliefs of the Soviets, Congress added the words "one nation under God" to the pledge of allegiance. Membership in patriotic fraternal organizations increased. In 1954, the American Legion had more than 3 million members, and the Knights of Columbus membership stood at 920,000 members. The Catholic War Veterans claimed more than 200,000 members (Whitfield, 92).

In 1957, the census bureau indicated that over 96 percent of the nation's citizens cited a specific religious affiliation. Of that number, 66 percent were Protestant, 26 percent Catholic, 3 percent Jewish, and 1 percent "other." During the period, church membership of all denominations reached an all-time high. Religious leaders such as Catholic Bishop Fulton Sheen, Protestant minister Norman Vincent Peale, and evangelist Billy Graham rose to national prominence. Each had syndicated newspaper columns, best-selling books, and television programs (Whitfield, 83). In 1952, Graham's column was carried in more than 125 newspapers, his weekly television show was viewed by an estimated 50 million people, and he was receiving more than 10,000 letters per week. Graham promoted regular church attendance and preached a message that applied to daily leisure habits, saying that sins included "[d]rinking, smoking, card playing, dancing, swearing, [and] reading salacious magazines" (Whitfield, 77–79).

Magazines and comic books of the time also warned of the Soviet threat. Some examples included *Look* magazine's "How to Spot a Communist" (March 4, 1947) and "We Are in a Life and Death Atomic Race" (July 14, 1953), *Life* magazine's "What We Must Do to Stop Communism" (November 10, 1961), and thousands of other articles. In 1962, Marvel Comics introduced two new superheroes: *Spiderman* and *The Amazing Hulk*. According to the comic stories, both superheroes were created as a result of genetic mutations caused from radioactive fallout.

The national paranoia was also fueled either directly or indirectly by Hollywood. Movies featured titles such as *The Red Menace* (1949), *I Married a Communist* (1949), *Spy in the Sky* (1958), and *War of the Satellites* (1958).

For in-home entertainment, a family board game was introduced in 1952, Victory over Communism—which was advertised as an "educational all-American game." A children's card game called Satellite Space Race (1958) awarded points for a "friendly satellite" card and deducted points for a Soviet "sputnik" card" (Barson and Heller, 13, 120–122).

In 1957, the Red Scare was launched into a new era when the Soviets placed the satellite *Sputnik* into space. Although *Sputnik*, a 22-inch diameter sphere, did not have any military capabilities, it was the threat that the Soviets had control of outer space that deeply scared Americans. In response, America launched its own satellite into orbit, and a space race ensued. Words such as *rocket* and *missile* became part of the everyday American vocabulary. The period of uncertainty of a war with the Soviet Union was called the "Cold War."

The 1962 Cuban missile crisis held the nation at a standstill for 12 tense days

A set of standard playing cards and a children's card game called Satellite Space Race (1958) created in response to the Soviet "Red Scare."

in October after it was discovered that the Soviets had placed missiles in Cuba—aimed directly at the United States. The crisis heightened American fears that nuclear war would become a reality. All schools provided fallout shelters, as did many suburban homes.

Many civil defense posters and magazine advertisements recommended that homeowners construct home fallout shelters. In its October 21, 1961, issue *Life* magazine devoted its cover story to the subject. Included among recommendations for a fallout shelter, the article stated, "[I]f war never comes, children can claim it for a hideaway, father can use it for poker games, and mother can count on it as a guest room." Historian Kenneth Rose reported that by 1964 "sixty thousand family fallout shelters had been built." He did estimate, that since the idea was to keep the shelters a secret, as many as 200,000 might have actually existed (202).

In 1992, *Washington Post* reporter Ted Gup revealed the existence of a massive underground fallout shelter in Greenbrier, West Virginia. The shelter, constructed between 1956 and 1962, was intended to house 1,100 members of Congress and government staff members. Other facilities were built at Mount Weather, Virginia; Denton, Texas; Culpepper, Virginia; and in at least 26 other states (Rose, 115–116). By 1964, the United States government itself had conducted well over 100 tests of exploding atmospheric nuclear devices in Nevada, New Mexico, Utah, and the South Pacific Bikini Islands. Most of the explosions were widely covered by newspapers and newscasters and were most certainly a part of Americans' daily lives.

Suburbia, Barbecues, and Do-it-yourself Projects

More than any other development, the expansion and evolution of suburbia was the most visible example of postwar social changes. As previously mentioned, this time period became known as the baby boom as a total of 76 million babies were born. Between 1947 and 1952 alone, more babies were born than in the previous 30 years combined. By 1950, the workweek had been reduced to 40 hours and was further decreased by 1964 to 37.5 hours. Americans had more leisure time, and many of them turned to home improvement and backyard projects. Don and Susan Sanders of Texas recalled similar suburban upbringing:

> Each morning our fathers left in the family car to go to work. We went to school and our mothers stayed home in order to plan and cook that night's dinner, to attend PTA Meetings and Tupperware parties. . . . Our lives had a predictable rhythm to them; scouting on Monday nights, piano and ballet lessons on Tuesdays, church on Wednesday evenings, bowling leagues and shopping on Saturdays, and church again on Sunday. Every afternoon after school we would play outside with the other neighborhood children—throwing the football, riding bikes, playing Red Rover, and Hide and Seek. (Sanders and Sanders, 6)

Another common suburban leisure pursuit was spending time in the backyard, sometimes tending to the lawn, gardening, relaxing in a hammock, or simply putting some charcoal on the grill and firing up a barbecue.

For many, the thought of owning a suburban home and being able to buy items that were either in short supply or nonexistent during the war became a new craze called consumerism. Consumer values and the pressure from advertising to buy and keep up with their neighbors led many to buy on credit.

In 1950, Diners Club introduced the first credit card, initially with the idea to pay for restaurant dinners. Many other businesses such as gasoline companies, hotels, and department stores copied the idea. (A credit card allowed the consumer to pay back a third-party creditor for charges made in monthly payments with interest added.) American Express marketed a credit card in 1958 and issued more than 250,000 cards within the first year. By 1960, Sears and Roebuck claimed ten million charge account customers. Television supported the idea of consumerism and also continued to support the idea that a woman's place was in the home.

Most television and magazine images glorified the happiness of middle class motherhood and marriage. The definition of what was feminine changed from Rosie the Riveter in a factory to a woman who devoted herself to staying at home and raising a family in complete marital bliss. Even high school education courses steered boys toward vocational and professional courses while girls were encouraged to take cooking and secretarial classes. Girls were encouraged to engage in home leisure pursuits such as home decorating, sewing, quilting, and embroidery.

In 1952, *Business Week* magazine declared the 1950s the age of do-it-yourself. The suburban man was encouraged to care for the lawn, spend time in the home workshop, or paint the house. In 1954 alone, homeowners purchased more than 150 million gallons of paint and 8 million paint rollers. Between 1946 and 1954, Americans purchased more than 15 million power drills. The U.S. Department of Commerce estimated that more than 12 million suburban workshops existed, a number that represented half of all homeowners (Gelber, 271–278).

For the suburban man, converted garages or basements served as a substitute for the urban saloon as a meeting place. Men had little choice other than a home workshop or a backyard barbecue for male bonding because saloons and fraternal clubs had not yet made their way to the suburbs. The do-it-yourself craze of the mid-1950s fostered this bonding. Magazines and television advertisements illustrated home workshops and backyard barbecues as almost exclusive male environments.

The Teenage Juvenile Delinquent

The trend in the new economically powerful America was conformity. Most adults were afraid of change, nonconformity, heightened sexuality, and rebellion, but they were mainly afraid of the weakening of segregation. In the meantime, teenagers began to look at themselves as real people with real problems who need not conform to the suburban ideal.

By 1956, estimates placed the number of American teenagers at more than 13 million with each having a total disposable income equal to that of an entire American family in 1940 (Halberstam, 473). More so than in any other preceding period, teenagers constituted a defined demographic with powerful purchasing force. Many teenagers—rural, urban, and suburban—continued a simple leisure pursuit from World War II, which was "messing around" or "hanging out." These terms simply implied that teenagers passed time by hanging around a soda shop, record store, or even a street corner. The idea of simply doing nothing was viewed by many older adults as inviting trouble and likened the idle teenagers to juvenile delinquents.

The image was portrayed by actor Marlon Brando in the movie *The Wild One* (1954). In the movie, Brando wore a black leather jacket over a white T-shirt with denim jeans and rode a motorcycle. These clothes would become a rebellious fashion statement for teenagers, as did the motorcycle. As did so many other consumer products, the motorcycle came into wide use during this period. In a June 1950 advertisement in *Collier's* magazine, the Harley-Davidson motorcycle company claimed that motorcycles were "the way to fun . . . after hours, on weekends, during vacation, anytime! . . . Merely 'riding around' is wonderful sport! Your age is no bar" (Braden, 281).

Many teenagers had access to automobiles. In many small towns and cities, the concept of "cruising" in an automobile developed. Mainly a Saturday night pleasure among teenagers, cruising was simply driving up and down a main thoroughfare with no particular purpose. Fixing up jalopies, which developed as a necessity during the war (see chapter 5), became a prominent hobby among teenagers. Many of the jalopies were combined with the powerful new V-8 engines and were nicknamed *hot rods*. New magazines such as *Rod and Custom* catered to the growing hobby. Much of the fad was in response to the growing appeal of race car driving and speeding.

Speeding was cause for another worrisome image—that of actor James Dean in the movie *Rebel Without a Cause* (1955). Most adults viewed Dean's image both on- and offscreen as that of a rebellious leader of juvenile delinquency. In fact, in September 1955, one month before *Rebel* opened, Dean was killed in a car crash and quickly became a legendary icon among teenage youth, which gave adults more reasons to worry. Many adults also blamed teenage rebellion on rock and roll music. *The Blackboard Jungle* (1955), a serious movie about troubled high school teens, featured the first rock and roll soundtrack. During the opening credits, the song "Rock around the Clock" by Bill Haley and the Comets had teens dancing in the movie theater aisles and ended up with record sales of more than 2.5 million.

ENTERTAINMENT

Television and "Whatever Happened to Radio?"

At the end of the war, the nation still relied on more than 31 million radios for entertainment and news. With the advent of television (TV), radio did not so much disappear as it went through a transition into a music market dominated by rock and roll (see "Music and Theater" later in this chapter). A new development in radio transistors, which allowed them to become smaller and portable, provided for more radios in automobiles and also in the hands of many teenagers.

It was television, more than any other technological development of the twen-

A man in Brooklyn, New York, with his new television set in June 1953. Author's archives.

tieth century, that drastically changed American social and leisure habits. In 1947, only nine thousand or so television sets existed nationwide. By 1950, the number quickly jumped such that televisions were in 3.9 million households (9 percent of the total population), and by 1960 more than 45.8 million households had at least one television set. Almost immediately, studies revealed that the average individual (with access to a television) was watching more than five hours of TV a day. Television's immense popularity resulted in an immediate decline in other forms of out-of-the-home entertainment such as going to restaurants and the movies (Panati, 240).

The *Texaco Star Theater* (1948–1956), an early weekly program starring Milton Berle, was seen by 4.4 million viewers each week. In the early 1950s, quiz shows were favorites. In 1955, the *$64,000 Question* had an estimated viewing audience of more than 55 million. Similar quiz shows such as *Tic Tac Dough*, *Twenty-One*, and *The Big Surprise* averaged more than 25 million viewers per week during that same year (Halberstam, 647).

However, the dominant television format was the family comedy. The most notable was *I Love Lucy* (1951–1957), the top-rated television show of the period with an average viewing audience of more than 70 million each week. According to Charles Panati, the show was so popular that "President Eisenhower [once] delayed an address to the nation rather than run against the show, and department stores installed TV sets to keep shoppers from staying home on Monday nights" (302–303).

Other popular sitcoms of the 1950s portrayed homogenous white suburban families, reflecting the social conformity of the period, in which the mother did not work and the father came home for dinner. The most notable included *The Adventures of Ozzie and Harriet* (1952–1957), *Father Knows Best* (1954–1960), and *Leave it to Beaver* (1957–1963).

Television changed Americans' leisure pursuits in the same manner that the automobile did—only now they were staying home instead of going out. Studies reported that the moment the television was turned on family conversations stopped and that television also interfered with the traditional family dinner hour. Many families began placing a "TV dinner" on a snack tray and ate and watched television at the same time. Introduced in 1951, the TV dinner was a preprepared frozen meal that could be heated up and served in a fraction of the time it took to prepare a traditional dinner.

In 1960, more than 75 million people (the single largest audience to date) witnessed the televised presidential election debate between Vice-President Richard Nixon and Senator John F. Kennedy. Nixon appeared to be sweating under the hot camera lights. Kennedy, however, appeared calm and comfortable. According to broadcast historians Robert Hilliard and Michael Keith "politics would never again be the same: image would replace issues in reaching the public through television, and most of the public would thereafter vote on the basis of personality rather than policy" (164).

Newspapers, Magazines, Paperbacks, and Comic Books

By 1950, many newspapers saw a decline in circulation (the nationwide total dipped to 1,763 newspapers); in part because of television and the automobile.

Many commuters, who had in the past read newspapers on the train, increasingly chose the automobile rather than mass-transportation to commute to work.

Magazine circulation was also affected by television. In 1963, despite having a circulation of 6.3 million, the *Saturday Evening Post*, ceased publication because of advertising revenue lost to television. With the advent of televisions, the weekly publication *TV Guide* quickly became the magazine with the largest circulation. In its first year (1952), circulation was a modest 2.2 million copies but quickly grew to well over 25 million (Kammen, 182).

After an initial downturn during the early years of television—1947 to 1953—reading took an upturn and grew steadily for the rest of the period. In 1951-1952 *Reader's Digest* magazine introduced a condensed book program (providing abridged versions of popular books and novels) with a mail-order subscription of more than 500,000. By 1962, circulation of *Reader's Digest* magazine had increased to 13.3 million (Kammen, 181).

The period was noted for an increase in specialty magazines aimed at the growing interest in sports, recreation, and leisure (almost seven thousand were published, and 45 magazines circulations of at least one million per year). *Sports Illustrated* magazine was first published in 1954 as a weekly magazine centered on baseball, football, basketball, boxing, horse racing, auto racing, and golf. Its audience was mostly middle-class men (Olson, *Historical Dictionary of the 1960s*, 269).

In January 1960, an 82-page magazine titled *Leisure* debuted, featuring articles on gambling, hunting, travel, music, movies, cooking, spelunking, and flying; also included was a fishing guide and 16 pages on chess. Most of these publications offered advice for men. Most women's interests were still centered on bringing up children, so many women turned to Dr. Spock.

Dr. Benjamin Spock's *The Common Sense Book of Baby and Child Care* (1946) stressed nurturing, caring, and affection in child rearing as opposed to strict punishment and alienation of affection. From 1946 to 1952, the book, published as an inexpensive paperback, sold more than four million copies. By 1960 more than 30 million copies were in print, and it continued to sell at a steady rate of more than 1 million per year until 1970 (West, 234). The book remained controversial throughout the century, as did a 1948 publication on human sexuality.

In 1948, Alfred Kinsey published *Sexual Behavior in the Human Male*. The report documented the sexual habits of the American male such as premarital intercourse, adultery, and masturbation. The book was met with criticism, but not as much criticism as was generated by his follow-up report, *Sexual Behavior in the Human Female* (1953).

The easing of tensions over sexual attitudes was reflected in a controversial work by author Mickey Spillane. Spillane's hardcover book *I, the Jury* (1947) sold about 15,000 copies. Once published in paperback, the book, which featured coarse language, action, sexual innuendos, and titillating covers with images of seductive females, sold more than two and a half million copies. Spillane's next six books, all on the same theme, averaged sales of almost three million each. By 1956, his seven books were among the ten best-selling fiction titles in American publishing history (Halberstam, 60).

In 1960, Americans purchased 813 million books, a figure that doubled that of 1955. By 1964, the number was more than 1.3 billion, of which a significant number were paperbacks (Madow, 148). The best-selling book of the period was the Bible with more than 26.5 million copies sold (Whitfield, 84). Comic books offered more than 650 titles with total sales averaging more than 60 million per month (Kaplan, 14).

Library book circulation increased 40 percent, mainly due to federal sponsorship of the Library Services Act of 1956, which established libraries in 169 towns and cities that previously did not have library services. The act also added two hundred bookmobiles to rural routes, which provided more than four million individuals access to books and made improvements at facilities that served an additional 32 million people (Madow, 153).

Dancing and the Twist

A 1959 Gallup poll reported more than 32 million Americans participated in some form of recreational dancing. Many people danced either within the home, at family gatherings, or in small nightclubs. Many of the large ballrooms had closed and were converted to supermarkets or demolished to make room for drive-in movie theaters.

Dance instructors Arthur and Kathryn Murray (see chapter 4) achieved national

A gathering at a New York nightclub, 1952. Nightclubs, very popular during World War II, continued to be popular as Saturday night destinations for adults. Author's archives.

prominence through their television dance show, the *Arthur Murray Dance Party* (1950–1961). The TV exposure increased the amount of people enrolling for dance classes in their franchised chain of nationwide dance studios (see chapter 4). By 1970, more than 500 Arthur Murray studios were in operation.

Organized dance events for young people took the form of cotillions and "sock-hops." The cotillion was a formal dance where young debutantes still held a dance card (see chapter 1). Sock-hops received their name from teenagers who went to school- or church-sponsored dances held in gymnasiums. In order not to damage the gym floor, teens were encouraged to remove their shoes and dance in their stocking feet. The dances were heavily chaperoned, and the dance music was carefully selected by adults.

By the mid-1950s, teenagers were dancing to rock and roll music, inspired by the song "Rock around the Clock" by Bill Haley and the Comets (see "Music and Theater" later in this chapter). Of the song, music legend Dick Clark said, "[I]ts initial impact was incredible. Kids hadn't been dancing since the end of the swing era. Suddenly, this spirited tune with a bouncy, rhythmic beat had the kids clapping and dancing" (Uslan and Solomon, 17).

In 1956, television, rock and roll music, and dancing would come together in a show hosted by Clark called *American Bandstand*. The show was first broadcast regionally in Philadelphia and went national in 1957. The large majority of its 20 million viewers were teenagers who rushed home from school to watch the late-afternoon show.

In 1960, Chubby Checker introduced a song and a dance of the same name, *The Twist*, on *American Bandstand*. The dance was done by each individual separated from their dance partners raised up on the balls of their feet and used their arms to perform a twisting motion with the body in unison to a rock and roll beat. The twist was an instant sensation and remained the most dominant dance craze of the entire century. Of the twist Clark said, "Adults could dance and publicly show that we weren't afraid to like this music. . . . That's why the twist was so terribly important. It didn't have so much to do with the dance itself as much as the fact that everybody was dancing it" (Uslan and Solomon, 77). The twist would also lead to a host of other fad dances such as the stroll, calypso, limbo, bunny hop, pony, and mashed potato.

Fads, Hobbies, and Games

In 1952, the Topps Bubble Gum Company introduced its first baseball card series, two sets of 52 cards. The cards came packaged five to a pack with one stick of gum included. Most young boys quickly put the gum in their mouths and proceeded to thumb through the cards. Many games were associated with the baseball cards such as trading and flipping. Trading involved one or more boys making a deal to swap one or more of their baseball cards for a card or cards of a particular player that they wanted. Flipping cards involved one player flipping a baseball card to the ground. If it landed either "heads" (the side with the player's picture) or "tails" (the side with the statistics), the other player had to match the heads or tails otherwise they would lose their baseball card to the other player.

Young girls were drawn to the Barbie doll. First introduced in 1959 by Mattel, it would become the doll that all others were judged against for the remainder of the century. The doll stood at 11.5 inches tall and was advertised as "the only anatomically similar" doll manufactured to date. The doll itself not only sold millions, but Mattel also sold millions of clothes and accessories and spawned fan clubs and a *Barbie* magazine (Whitfield, 71).

In 1954, the *Davy Crockett* show, with a television audience of more than 40 million viewers (many under 15 years of age), produced a consumer fad of purchasing products associated with a show's title character. Davy Crockett toys included the desirable coonskin hat, wristwatches, books, games, tents, and cap guns. The theme song alone, *The Ballad of Davy Crockett*, sold more than four million copies. Due in part to the Davy Crockett craze, Lincoln Logs toys also sold in great numbers (Panati, 88).

One of America's most recognizable toys was the Slinky, a lightweight steel coil. After its debut in 1945, at least one million Slinkys were sold each year for the remainder of the century. Another such toy was Silly Putty. First manufactured in 1949, it was a synthetic product that when rolled on newspaper comics could pick up the color comic images. Silly Putty was packaged in brightly colored plastic eggs (to prevent the putty from drying out). Between 1950 and 1955, more than 32 million Silly Putty eggs were sold. The most enduring toy of the period was the yo-yo. (The yo-yo is probably the oldest known toy dating back to 500 B.C.) Popular among children and adults, in 1962 alone, more than 45 million were sold and manufacturers could not keep up with the demand. The yo-yo continued to sell in similar yearly quantities for the rest of the twentieth century (Crosby, "The Yo-Yo: Its Rise and Fall," 53).

In 1958, the Wham-O Company created what amounted to the biggest fad of the century—the hula hoop. The device, a circular lightweight plastic hoop about 42 inches in diameter, was intended to be spun around a person's waist in a fashion similar to a Hawaiian hula dance. In two short months, more than 25 million hula hoops were sold, and within a few years more than 100 million, mostly for children and teenagers. Although the hula hoop remained a popular toy for the rest of the twentieth century it certainly never approached its initial sales (Panati, 264).

New board games were marketed for all ages from the preschool game Candyland, school-age game Chutes and Ladders, and teenage and adult games Clue and Scrabble. Old favorites remained popular such as chess, checkers, parcheesi, and Monopoly. In 1954, Scrabble (first developed in the 1930s as a table-top version of the crossword puzzle with movable letter blocks) experienced a resurgence as Americans bought more than 4.5 million sets; by comparison, only 58,000 sets were sold in 1952 (Panati, 265). Most of the board games of the time encouraged family togetherness.

In 1950, a national survey revealed that over 56 percent of adults played cards at least once a week and that 83 percent of American families played cards. Playing card sales averaged 50 million decks per year, with a high of 80 million decks in 1950 that was mainly attributed to the fad of playing canasta. Canasta was played by either 2 or 4 players with two 52-card decks and 4 joker cards (Rosenberg and White, 419).

A new development during this period was the opening of hobby and crafts stores specifically for the purpose of selling unassembled model kits and craft accessories. Tandy Leather Corporation specialized in leather products for hobbyists

Plastic model airplane kits, circa 1958–1960. Hobby and crafts stores sold unassembled model kits and craft accessories. The kits included precut pieces that required assembly by gluing, painting, and finishing. Author's archives.

to use in assembling belts, wallets, and moccasins (Gelber, 53, 54, 263). The model kits sold in hobby and craft stores included precut pieces that required assembly by gluing, painting, and sometimes sanding. The postwar development in injection molded plastic made it possible to produce plastic scale-model kits. Companies such as Lindbergh, Revell, Airfix, and Aurora produced kits with models patterned after automobiles, airplanes, trains, warships, and military vehicles.

Palisades Amusement Park, Disneyland, and Las Vegas

Many of the urban amusement parks experienced a steady decline from a high of over 2,500 parks prior to World War I (see chapter 1) to a low of 245 by the end of World War II. One such park was Palisades Amusement Park (first opened in 1908) located in Fort Lee, New Jersey. In the early 1950s the park was known for live rock and roll music, and it attracted as many as 150,000 teenagers in a single day (and also broadcast concerts on local television affiliates). In 1962, singer Freddy Cannon immortalized the park with his song "Palisades Park," which sold more than two million copies. Between 1947 and 1971 (when it closed), Palisades Park averaged more than six million visitors per year, with an all-time high of ten million visitors in 1969. The park was criticized for attracting teenagers and not providing a wholesome family atmosphere (Gargiulo, 101,

142). The trend was shifting from the urban amusement parks to the suburban theme parks.

In 1955, Disneyland redefined the amusement park as a theme park. Located on a 160-acre tract of land in suburban Anaheim, California, it provided a clean family atmosphere free of the social, political, or economical conflicts of the time. Unlike the earlier amusement parks that were easily accessible by public transportation, the park was far from the inner urban areas and only accessible by automobile or excursion bus. Disneyland was an immediate success, attracting more than one million customers in its first six months. By 1992, total visitation exceeded 300 million.

The opening of Las Vegas gambling casinos provided a different form of amusement. During World War II, Las Vegas, Nevada (pop. 2,000), experienced an influx of war workers who were drawn to some smaller hotels such as the Golden Nugget, the Pioneer, and the Mint, which offered gambling and top-name entertainers. (In 1931, Nevada had become the first state to legalize gambling.) In 1946, the Flamingo Hotel opened as the first legalized gambling casino in the United States offering a lavish, opulent environment of lights and glitter and booked even more popular entertainers and Hollywood celebrities than the smaller hotels.

Other hotels and casinos quickly followed the Flamingo style, and millions of people visited the new casinos for entertainment and gambling. In 1955, gambling of all kinds totaled $20 billion, a number that provided staggering evidence that gambling consumed a large amount of American leisure time (Kaplan, 157).

MUSIC AND THEATER

Broadway and Community Theater

Broadway maintained its status as "legitimate theater" although prominent theaters existed in other cities around the country. The National in Washington, D.C. opened in 1835 and carried the title "America's first theater." The National sometimes served for preview productions prior to their opening on Broadway, but it mostly showcased the road productions of proven successful Broadway hits. In January 1955, playwright Arthur Miller wrote in *Holiday* magazine,

> little theater people in New York, Texas, California and elsewhere . . . claim that Broadway is not the United States and that much theatrical production is going on in other places. I agree . . . [however] the *new* American plays originate on Broadway. . . . In the audience itself, though the bulk of it is of the middle class. . . . There is a vast group of people for whom the theater means nothing but amusement, and amusement means a musical or light comedy; and there are others who reserve their greatest enthusiasm for heavy dramas. (quoted in *Annals of America*, Vol. 17: 332–333)

During this period, Broadway offered a diverse fare. Long-running musicals that also produced successful soundtrack cast albums included *South Pacific* (1949) with 1,925 performances and more than one million albums sold and *My Fair Lady* (1956–1963) with 2,717 performances and more than five million albums sold (Panati, 284). The *Threepenny Opera* had a seven-year run of more than 2,600 performances from 1954 to 1961. One song from the play *Mack the Knife* sold more than ten million copies for singer Bobby Darin. Other favorite musicals included *Guys and Dolls* (1950) and *West Side Story* (1957); each would be made into Hollywood movies. New stage dramas included Arthur Miller's *Death of a Salesman* (1949) and Tennessee Williams's *A Streetcar Named Desire* (1951).

The Broadway classics influenced theater groups throughout the nation and became standards performed by community theater groups for the remainder of the century. In the postwar years, community theater experienced significant growth. By 1952 more than 1,400 community theater groups existed nationwide with more than 70,000 stage participants (Kaplan, 11). Other cultural institutions also fared well.

By 1954, museum attendance nationwide rose to an impressive 55 million. Advertising certainly helped, and museum visits began to appeal to the middle class. In 1963, during a tour of the *Mona Lisa* (on loan from the Louvre in France) at the Metropolitan Museum of Art in New York City and the National Gallery in Washington, D.C., the lines stretched around the block outside the museums, and the number of visitors broke all previous attendance records (Kammen, 117).

CinemaScope, 3-D Movies, and the Drive-in

For a short time from 1947 to 1950, movie attendance remained steady at 90 million per week. However, beginning in 1951 attendance quickly dropped to 50 million per week (and to less than 24 million per week by 1960) as television quickly became the dominant entertainment choice. As a result, by 1953, over 25 percent of the nation's movie theaters closed. In southern California 134 theaters closed, and 55 closed in New York City (Whitfield, 153). In response, Hollywood sought to counter the decline with new features such as CinemaScope, 3-D movies, and the drive-in theater.

Three-dimensional (3-D) movies were a feature that television could not match. In 3-D movies, a unique projection technique was used that made the movie appear to be three-dimensional. Moviegoers had to wear special glasses, developed by Polaroid, to experience the three-dimensional effect. The first 3-D movie, *Bwana Devil* (1952), featured lions that appeared to be leaping toward the audience. However, the 3-D movie was a short-lived fad because many viewers complained about headaches caused by watching the movies. The wide-screen technique known as CinemaScope fared better.

Prior to CinemaScope, movie screens were basically square (a ratio of 1.3 times width to height), as were television screens. CinemaScope screens were long and rectangular at a ratio of 2.5 times width to height. The new wide-screen feature of CinemaScope allowed for massive, extravagant epics with thousands of extras such as *The Robe* (1953), *The Ten Commandments* (1956), and *Ben-Hur* (1959). The wide-screen epics of CinemaScope were something television could not match, as another movie innovation—the drive-in.

The drive-in was a paved, open-air movie theater that allowed a car and its occupants to drive up to a designated parking spot located in sight of a large movie screen. A speaker, wired to a pole at each parking spot, was placed on the car window so that viewers could hear the movie. Some drive-ins also provided seats for people who walked in and playgrounds for families with children.

By 1949, the nation had 1,100 drive-ins. In one year, that number doubled, and by 1960 more than five thousand existed, most located in suburbs and rural areas. Texas had the most drive-ins with 475 locations. Most theaters were capable of accommodating two hundred to seven hundred cars. The largest drive-in was in Copiague, New York, and it covered 28 acres, had capacity for 2,500 cars, indoor seating for 1,200 people, a restaurant, cafeteria, and an outdoor playground (Sanders and Sanders, 36). Special attractions featured at some drive-ins included fireworks at night, cartoon festivals, kids under 12 admitted free, and special rates for an entire carload of viewers. Many moviegoers enjoyed a particular thrill by trying to sneak in without paying an admission fee. Some cars attempted to back in through exits, others hid additional people in car trunks, and some would climb over fences to join their car mates.

Drive-ins were usually advertised as providers of family entertainment. However, teenagers were attracted to drive-ins because the privacy of a car allowed for making out and petting on dates, thereby earning drive-ins the nickname *passion pits*. Sally Blanton of Dallas, Texas, recalled:

> We were teens needing a place to call our own, which was what the new drive-in offered. . . . [It] was the place many girls were first kissed or asked to go steady. A very big deal! Dating couples were harassed by random flashing headlights. There was lots of socializing between cars. There was usually static on the speakers, so I wonder if anyone really saw or heard a movie in its entirety. (Sanders and Sanders, 82)

The drive-in's popularity with teenagers caused Hollywood to respond with a series of movies with teen themes centered on science fiction, horror movies, rock and roll, and other subjects popular with teenagers.

Rock and Roll and Elvis Presley

Between 1947 and 1955, music was in a state of flux. The big bands were out; mellow pop standards and bebop jazz were in. Bebop was created to be purposely off the dance beat so that people would sit and listen to the music instead of dancing. At that time nightclubs also remained popular, but their popularity would decrease with the advent of television that kept many inside.

In the postwar years, Saturday night continued to be a popular evening for going out. Teenagers and young adults, especially in suburbia, continued to congregate at soda fountains, roller-skating rinks, diners, and drive-in burger joints. Jukeboxes were still a dominant presence, and more than 400,000 existed nationwide with a steady annual play of more than five billion songs with the addition of a "wall box." The wall box was a compact tableside selection device that allowed individuals sitting at tables away from the main jukebox to select songs—usually rock and roll songs—for the jukebox to play.

The decline of radio programming that came with the advent of television created a market for rock and roll music. Unlike swing and jazz, which assigned drums and bass to play rhythm, rock and roll used those instruments to play a heavy beat that drove the sound of the music. The most prominent instrument in rock and roll was the solid-body guitar.

In 1948, Leo Fender introduced the solid-body Broadcaster electric guitar (renamed the Telecaster in 1950). In 1954, he introduced a revised version the Stratocaster incorporating a string-bending unit known as a "tremolo." Prior to the solid-body, guitars were deep bodied with a hole under the strings to allow the music to resonate. The solid body enabled the music to be picked up electronically and transferred to an amplifier, thereby allowing a heavier downbeat and louder sound. The solid-body guitar would become the trademark of all rock and roll bands.

The arbiters of the new music were the radio disc jockeys who became folk heroes to teenagers. The most notable of these disc jockeys was Alan Freed. In 1951, Freed began airing the late night Moondog Show on WJW-AM, a 50,000-watt Cleveland radio station. He played mainly black rhythm and blues artists, which Freed called *rock and roll*. He drew a faithful audience of teenage listeners, both black and white. He also began sponsoring live rock and roll shows that brought together many of the same acts he played on the radio.

The first show on March 21, 1952, held in the Cleveland Arena drew an integrated sold-out crowd of more than ten thousand teenagers. Thousands of others who were trying to get in were turned away, causing a near riot. In 1954, Freed moved to the WINS radio station in New York City. His popularity soared, and he appeared in Hollywood movies such as *Rock, Rock, Rock* (1956) and *Don't Knock the Rock* (1957).

In 1959, Dick Clark organized a touring version of a rock and roll show called the *Caravan of Stars*. The nature of a segregated society was apparent during the tour; Clark recalled, "In the southeast we had to play before divided audiences—sometimes blacks upstairs and whites downstairs, sometimes split right down the middle with whites on one side and blacks on the other" (Uslan and Solomon, 61). Municipalities tried to enforce segregation, but the reality was that for the first time both black and white teenagers were sharing the same experiences through a common music.

Teenagers not only listened to rock and roll music, they also bought records of it. In the postwar period, more than four hundred new record labels produced records at an amazing rate. In 1950, Americans purchased 190 million records, and by 1960 the number was more than 600 million per year, of which over 70 percent were purchased by teenagers (Kammen, 180). The introductions of the long-playing (LP) 33 1/3 album, 45-rpm (revolutions per minute) record, and portable record players allowed young people the privacy of listening to the music of their choice. In 1956 alone, more than 10 million portable record players were sold (Halberstam, 474). In his first breakthrough year in 1956, one artist alone sold almost 4 million recordings, and he sold 28 million over the course of the next two years—his name was Elvis Presley.

More than any other artist, Elvis Presley defined the image of rock and roll. Elvis was a musical pioneer—a young white man whose music crossed the cultural barrier between black and white. According to early blues singer Ruth Brown, "where Elvis was concerned there was no color line, because everybody liked his music" (Time-Life Video). By 1956, Elvis was a nationwide celebrity and the subject of much controversy. Presley's September 9, 1956, performance on the *Ed*

The introduction of 45-rpm records and portable record players allowed individuals the privacy of listening to their own choice of music. For teenagers it was usually rock and roll. Author's archives.

Sullivan Show (viewed by an estimated 42 million people) showed Presley only from the waist up. Sullivan thought Presley's hip gyrations were vulgar and refused to allow his wiggling hips to be broadcast to a national audience.

Presley also made a series of successful movies, beginning with *Love Me Tender* (1956), *Loving You* (1957), and *Jailhouse Rock* (1957). Many other Elvis movies had vacation and leisure themes such as *Blue Hawaii* (1961), *Fun in Acapulco* (1963), and *Viva Las Vegas* (1964).

SPORTS AND GAMES

Not all Americans embraced sports with the same enthusiasm during this time. An American-born daughter of one Hungarian refugee family claimed,

> The fact that my parents were raised in a European country has had a great effect on how they spend their leisure time. Americans place great emphasis on sports, football, and baseball (to watch) and golf and fishing. My parents were never raised with this kind of sports enthusiasm and have never learned to like them. (Kaplan, 72)

However, in both participation and spectatorship, sports were a major part of many Americans' leisure time enjoyment.

Professional Sports and Television Spectators

Between 1947 and 1953, with the introduction of television, more people stayed home and actually decreased the amount of spectators attending sporting events (Kammen, 183-185). However, television would eventually become the major catalyst for increased number of spectators at professional sports events. Early sporting events covered by television included wrestling, boxing, and roller derby. Television cameras were in their infancy, and multiple angles were not yet perfected, so a single, fixed-position camera would cover these sports.

Baseball was the most popular spectator sport and drew an average of more than 28 million spectators per year. Television drastically affected attendance at minor league baseball games. People living in small cities and towns could now see major league teams on television and stopped going to minor league games. In 1949, minor league baseball games drew more than 42 million fans; by 1957, that number had dropped to 15 million overall (Olson, *Historical Dictionary of the 1950s*, 286).

By 1958, major league baseball was also broadcast to large portions of the nation and set the stage for a major breakthrough in American society. In 1947, segregation in professional baseball came to an end when the Brooklyn Dodgers fielded Jackie Robinson. Robinson became the first African American to play major league baseball in the twentieth century. He faced staunch resistance from many other players and fans. His exemplary play and perseverance to remain un-challenging to racial taunts provided a role model for all young African American men who wished to pursue a career in professional baseball. Prior to Robinson's playing for the Dodgers, young African American men who played baseball for fun did not have the opportunity of turning this leisure pursuit into a professional baseball career.

In 1956, the Dodgers relocated to Los Angeles (followed by the New York Giants to San Francisco in 1959), firmly entrenching professional sports on the West Coast. (In 1946, three football franchises—two in Los Angeles and one San Francisco—were the first professional teams on the West Coast.)

Television broadcasts of professional football would also mark that sport's transition into a major spectator sport. The turning point for football came with the 1958 National Football League (NFL) championship game between the Baltimore Colts and New York Giants. The game, the first NFL championship broadcast on national television, was also the first to go into overtime (the game was tied at the end of regulation play necessitating a continuation of play until one team scored). The exciting ending, called the "greatest game ever played," captivated the national television audience and set the stage for increased interest in the sport. By 1960, attendance at professional football games numbered more than 3 million per year; the sport's television audience numbered more than 30 million (www. nfl.com).

Amateur Sports, Active Participation, and NASCAR

A 1959 survey revealed that with more than 33 million participants, swimming was the most popular recreational activity. Fishing and dancing were a close second with 32 million participants each. Other activities with more than ten million participants each included hunting (16 million) and baseball and softball (11 million combined).

Bowling also continued its rise in popularity. In 1947, more than 18.5 million people actively participated in more than 33,000 bowling leagues throughout the nation. Millions more bowled for fraternal lodges, clubs, and as individuals. In 1952, the first mechanized pinsetters were introduced (prior to that time the pins were set by hand), and new bowling alleys were constructed that offered improved lighting, food service, babysitting services, and other amenities that further enhanced bowling's appeal to women and married couples. By 1964, it was estimated that more than 30 million individuals bowled on a regular basis (Braden, 273).

Horse racing tracks and gambling remained popular, and horse racing attendance figures remained high. In 1955, horse racing was legal in 24 states (an increase from 19 states in 1952), and more than $2 billion were bet on horse racing (Kaplan, 157). Attendance averaged 18 million per year, which is even more notable considering that the tracks were open only on a seasonal basis. For example, Garden State Park in New Jersey offered 25 racing days in the spring and 25 racing days in the fall averaging attendance of 16,000 fans on weekdays and 35,000 fans on Saturdays (*New York Times*, April 29, 2002: NJ10).

In 1947, the National Association of Stock Car Auto Racing (NASCAR) was formed in Daytona Beach, Florida. Stock car racing first began in the early 1930s on small dirt tracks in the Southeast with cars that came "stock" right out of the showroom. The 1950 season featured the first NASCAR event on the newly constructed Darlington International Speedway in South Carolina. Seventy-five cars participated in the 500-mile event on Darlington's banked, paved speedway. In 1959, the first of the "super speedways," a 2.5-mile circular paved course with banked turns, opened in Daytona Beach, Florida. In the next few years, similar speedways opened in Hanford, California; Hampton, Georgia; and Concord, Charlotte, and Raleigh, North Carolina ("Know Your NASCAR—History," www.nascar.com).

The thrills of speed and racing carried over to the American streets. In 1957, *Life* magazine claimed that there were more than 100,000 hot rods and street-racing cars in the United States. The popular activity known as drag racing grew mainly among male teenagers and took place on urban streets and in rural hide-aways. Street racing was not only illegal, but it was dangerous. Excessive speeds caused accidents and even deaths. The popularity of the activity and the resulting concern for safety spurred the development of the National Hot Rod Association (NHRA). By 1956, the NHRA organized more than 130 legal drag strips in more than 40 states, attracting more than 2.5 million fans (Time-Life, *Our America Century: Rock & Roll Generation*, 142). Other motorized spectator sports included demolition derbies, motorcycle racing, speedboat racing, and air races. (Demolition derbies involved drivers crashing old cars into each other until only one car was still able to move, and that was the winner.) In 1959, attendance at all motorized race events totaled more than nine million.

Winter Sports

The Americans' success at the 1952 Winter Olympics in Saint Moritz, Switzerland (the U.S. for the first time earned gold medals in snow skiing and figure skating), encouraged many Americans to participate in winter sports. A 1959 poll reported that more than six million Americans actively ice-skated as a recreational pursuit. Snow skiing had more than three million active participants. An increase in the number of spectators at skiing events was noted. For example, a 1953 international competition of more than 100 athletes at Iron Mountain, Michigan, drew more than 30,000 spectators to witness a ski jump competition. Spectators watched skiers leap off a long slide (in excess of 550 feet high) and soar in the air for almost 300 feet at speeds in excess of 60 miles per hour (*Time*, March 16, 1953: 87).

TRANSPORTATION AND VACATION

This period represented a time when vacationing became a permanent way of life for Americans. A 1954 Department of Commerce survey indicated that over 83 percent of the middle class and the wealthy took regular vacation trips, as did 47 percent of the working class. Over 62 percent of all Americans took at least two vacations with a combined stay of 18 days (Jakle, 186). The vacations were not confined to a particular season. Summer was favored by 40 percent of vacationers, but 25 percent took trips in the fall, 18 percent in the spring, and 17 percent in the winter months. Ocean travel amounted to 1.8 percent of the trips, and 5.5 percent of vacationers traveled by bus, 8.2 percent by airplane, and 13.6 percent by railroad. An astounding 80 percent of all pleasure trips were taken by automobile (Kaplan, 212).

Automobiles Everywhere and the Interstate Highway Act

In 1945, the country had 25 million registered automobiles (most of those over ten years old). By 1950, that number increased to 49 million and to 75 million by 1964. Sixty-eight million of the automobiles were new purchases, and more than 4.5 million were scrapped annually (Halberstam, 487). More than 12 million families, mostly suburban, owned at least two cars. Many of the second cars were recreational vehicles and station wagons (Kaplan, 10).

Advertisers continually stressed the idea of trading in a car every couple of years to buy a new and improved model that included such features as automatic transmission, power steering, and seat belts. Automatic transmission eliminated the clutch pedal and did not require manual shifting. The most prominent automotive developments were in the power of engines and increased speed.

In 1954, the V-8 engine was capable of 250 horse power (hp) (an increase from the 160-hp military models and 100 hp of prewar models). The extra power provided for the addition of power windows, power brakes, and air-conditioning. Auto manufacturers sought to capitalize on speed capabilities and advertised new engines with increases to 300 and 400 hp. Oldsmobile provided a catchy name for its "Rocket V-8," and Ford countered with its "tunnel port" 427-cubic-inch engine. The increased speed that cars were capable of would be put to good use on the nation's new highways (Halberstam, 495).

A major boon to the auto industry was the passage of the Federal Interstate Highway Act of 1956. More than 41,000 miles of highway created by the act provided an endless open road that allowed Americans to travel at their own leisure with amenities never before dreamed of. The interstates were wider (averaging two and three lanes in each direction) and straighter than old roads, and better road material allowed the motorist to travel faster over longer distances.

The Auto-vacation, Holiday Inn, and Howard Johnson's

The U.S. Bureau of Public Roads estimated that over 93 percent of all trips for outdoor recreation were by automobile (Jakle, 186). A 1952 survey by the Michigan Travel Bureau of automobile travelers in the state indicated that 55 percent fished, 40 percent went to the beaches and lakes, and 13 percent camped. Over 70 percent of the combined respondents went sightseeing. A 1953 survey in Colorado indicated similar results. The beaches still did well; Coney Island, for example, on any given hot summer day attracted between 500,000 and one million beachgoers in a single day (Jakle, 187).

Unlike the early adventures in automobiles (see chapter 1), the auto-vacation during this period contained very few surprises. The interstate highway system with interchanges many miles apart decreased the number of roadside encampments and encouraged the proliferation of standardized motels, restaurants, and service stations. Two such early standardized establishments were the Holiday Inn and Howard Johnson's.

In 1951, more than 26,000 motels existed across the country; however, no two were alike, and conditions varied greatly between hotels, as did room prices and extra charges for children. In 1952, Kemmons Wilson opened the first Holiday Inn outside Memphis, Tennessee, and sought to standardize services and create a friendly environment for the traveler and family. The Holiday Inn sign came to represent a clean room, an available restaurant, no surprises, and children always staying free of charge. Wilson eventually franchised the idea, and by 1970 more than 1,500 Holiday Inns were in operation along the nation's highways (Halberstam, 179).

Prior to World War II, Howard Johnson's was a small chain of restaurants offering inexpensive meals and ice cream flavors. By 1954, there were more than 400 Howard Johnson's restaurants in 32 states. In 1959, Howard Johnson's followed the Holiday Inn lead and opened its first motor lodge—a combined motel and restaurant. By 1979, the chain would expand to more than 1,000 restaurants, 520 motor lodges, and would average 15 million overnight stays per year. Howard Johnson's trademark orange roof became instantly recognizable to most American travelers, and motoring families knew immediately what to expect (www.howardjohnson.com).

Along the vast interstates, at the cloverleaf intersections, arose similar corporate chains of restaurants, service stations, and by 1961, more than 62,000 motels. In less than a decade, the roadside commercial strip was almost standard nationwide. Almost all the hotels, motels, and restaurants catered to the automobile traveler.

Marya Annette McQuirter said, "The automobile literally changed the lives of African Americans, allowing us to travel without hassle. With an auto, African Americans could avoid discriminatory acts experienced on trains and buses." The standardized restaurants and motels did not necessarily mean that African Americans were always a welcome guest especially in the southern states. An indispensable booklet for African American travelers was the *Travelguide* (it was first published in 1946 and there were also three similar guides: *The Negro Motorist Green Book; The Greenbook Vacation Guide,* and the *Travel Guide of Negro Hotels and Guest Houses*). The guide was arranged by state and then by city and offered important information on segregation and civil rights laws. Also included were the names and addresses of restaurants, guest houses, golf courses, amusements, and other points of interest that allowed admission to African Americans. Andy Razaf said of the guide, "It shows us where to eat and stay/where to while the time away/Without humiliation!" The guides were invaluable, for without one, an African American traveler attempting to enter a "whites only" establishment, especially in southern states, could end up being much more than humiliated. Going to the wrong establishment could be severe, resulting in violence or even death (see Emmett Till's Summer Vacation) (McQuirter, "A Love Affair with Cars," n.p.).

The Railroad in Decline, Everybody Move to the Front of the Bus

Immediately after World War II, railroads were still the preferred choice for overland travel. The California Zephyr offered a scenic route through the Rocky Mountains on its San Francisco to Chicago run. The Southern Pacific Railroad offered service from Chicago and Los Angeles and advertised "it's fun to go to California on the Golden State via southern Arizona, where you can bask in warm sunshine at famous resorts" (*Time*, March 16, 1953: 55). However, by 1955 the number of railroad passengers rapidly began to decrease because of the increased use of automobiles on the interstate highway system and the quickness of jet travel.

Intercity bus travel remained a popular and preferred choice for many minorities and members of the working class. Many bus riders traveling either for pleasure or vacation were subjected to individual state laws on segregation. Within the South, interstate bus terminals had "white only" and "colored only" signs designating separate waiting areas.

In December 1955, in Montgomery, Alabama, Rosa Parks's refusal to give up her seat on a local bus sparked a significant bus boycott by African Americans that culminated in a Supreme Court decision making segregation illegal on local buses, interstate bus transportation, and in railroad stations. However, that decision did not stop the white southern segregationists. According to Juan Williams, "Since the bus boycott, racial tension had intensified in Montgomery. The city had recently closed all its public parks and its zoo rather than allow blacks to visit them" (157).

In May 1961, two groups of "freedom riders" attempted an interracial group bus ride through the South. However, when the buses stopped in Anniston and Birmingham, Alabama, they were met with violence and were attacked by an angry white mob. Alabama Governor John Paterson displayed little sympathy saying, "When you go somewhere looking for trouble, you usually find it." Upon hearing the news, an outraged President John Kennedy phoned Paterson but was told that the governor had "gone fishing" (Williams, 148–149).

Air Transportation and Jet Lag

With air travel, Americans were exposed to faraway places. In 1956 alone, more than 1.2 million Americans flew to areas outside the United States. More than half traveled to Mexico and the Caribbean and 42 percent to Europe. In 1957, there were 1.4 million air travelers logging an average of more than 6,500 miles per trip. Estimates of the percentage of international air travelers who traveled for pleasure and vacation ranged as high as 65 percent. In 1958, with the addition of the economical Boeing 707 and Douglas DC-8 (each capable of traveling at least twice as fast as their propeller driven predecessors), almost all airlines switched to jet aircraft. The lower operating cost, combined with faster speed, allowed airlines to offer lower passenger rates, which increased the number of passengers traveling for leisure and vacation (Kaplan, 212–213).

With jet aircraft, passengers discovered a new traveling discomfort that became known as jet lag. Jet lag occurred as travelers quickly crossed into different time zones. The disorientation of arriving at a different time disrupted the individual's regular daily routine causing symptoms that included malaise, lightheadedness, and insomnia. There was generally no medical cure other than allowing a few days for the body to adjust to the new time zone.

With the increase in air travel also came greater concern for safety. Mid-air collisions of aircraft had occurred in 1956 over the Grand Canyon and in 1960 over New York City, killing more than 500 onboard passengers. The Federal Aviation Act of 1958 replaced previous airline legislation and established the Federal Aviation Agency (FAA) to regulate airspace and establish air traffic control and other safety measures.

The airports left over from the war that handled propeller-driven aircraft were not large enough to handle the new jets, which required longer takeoff and landing runways, so new airports had to be constructed. The complaints from citizens about increased noise, coupled with the need for vast amounts of land, caused new airports constructed in Chicago, Illinois; Detroit, Michigan; and Long Island, New York to be located as far as 20 miles from the cities.

The increased distance of the airports from the cities provided a boost for the rental car business. Hertz Rental Car developed the idea of the "fly-drive" car rental system and located franchises at airports in Atlanta, Georgia, and Milwaukee, Wisconsin. Hertz's major competition arose from Avis Rent a Car, and the two companies dominated the car rental business during the period. In the latter part of the twentieth century, many other car rental companies offered competitive services and remained closely linked to the airline industry.

Ocean Travel and Pleasure Boats

By 1947, many of the ocean liners were reconverted from troop carriers back to passenger liners. Before the end of 1947, air travel was becoming increasingly available for the islands once reserved strictly for cruise ship travel. The Bermuda Tourist Agency acknowledged the alternatives and advertised "you can go quickly by plane or leisurely by ocean liner [with] days bursting with fun—swimming, picnicking, cycling, shopping, sightseeing [and] filled with sunshine for golf, tennis, sailing, fishing" (*Time*, March 16, 1953: 83).

In 1958, the first nonstop jet flight to Europe marked the end of the monopoly for transatlantic travel by ocean liners. The cruise lines sought to counter the jet competition. The United States Lines, for example, advertised "Europe's less than 5 days away—just a long weekend . . . [we will] wine you and dine you in faultless style, entertain you with 3 Meyer Davis orchestras, and get you to Europe so fast you'll regret leaving [the boat]" (*Time*, March 16, 1953: 4).

In 1959, Hawaii and Alaska became the forty-ninth and fiftieth states. Alaska, sometimes called the last frontier, offered Americans new recreation and leisure opportunities such as dogsledding and "Aurora viewing" (viewing the natural wonder of the northern lights of the Aurora Borealis). After World War II, many of the Waikiki, Hawaii, resorts, such as the Royal Hawaiian underwent refurbishing and by 1947 reopened for tourists. Waikiki Beach was featured as an exotic getaway for vacationing, relaxing, and surfing. The introduction of the jet airlines offering competitive rates reduced the number of cruise ships to Hawaii.

In 1950, Bill Tritt introduced the Glasspar fiberglass runabout, which changed the nature of pleasure boating. Fiberglass boats were inexpensive, easy to maintain, lightweight, and smaller than earlier boats and therefore could be kept on a trailer in a suburban driveway (instead of at an expensive yacht club). In 1953, the boats became increasingly popular with the addition of outboard motors fastened to the back such as the Kiekhaefer Corporation's Mercury Mark 5 and Mercury Mark 15. The motors could easily be replaced and stored in a garage during the winter months. The outboard motor and the fiberglass boat were a perfect match and added to the increase in smaller craft use.

In 1953, *Life* magazine reported that there were more than eight million recreational boats in America, a number that represented a dramatic increase from the less than 300,000 pleasure boats that existed prior to 1947. With increased recreational boat use there was also an increase in fishing, water skiing, snorkeling, and scuba diving. The smaller boats also renewed interest in inexpensive canoeing, rowing, and sailing.

Inexpensive vacations were not limited to boating and camping. In 1951, *Liberty Travel* began operation in New York City and introduced the package plan vacation for middle- and working-class travelers. A package plan vacation offered travelers a total cost rate that was less than the sum would be if each portion (such as transportation, food, and lodging) were purchased individually. Package plans varied from long weekends to a city destination, to an airplane trip to a Caribbean island, to even a luxury cruise. The package plan's wide appeal caused other travel agencies to quickly copy the idea and offer competitive rates. However, not all individuals or families could freely vacation to wherever they pleased.

Emmett Till's Summer Vacation

In August 1955, Emmett Till from Chicago, Illinois, was sent to Mississippi by his mother to spend a summer vacation with relatives. Supposedly, upon leaving a store after purchasing some candy, Till, who was unaware of the strict Mississippi segregation laws said "bye, baby" to a white woman, thereby "insulting her honor." Three days later two white residents kidnapped Till. In his book *Eyes on the Prize*, Juan Williams described how "Till's body was found three days later. The barbed wire holding the cotton-gin fan around his neck had become snagged on a tangled river root. There was a bullet in the boy's skull, one eye was gouged out, and his forehead was crushed on one side" (43). In a published response carried in hundreds of newspapers across the country, Till's mother awakened the consciousness of the nation asking, "Have you ever sent a loved son on vacation and had him returned to you in a pine box, so horribly battered and water-logged that someone needs to tell you that sickening sight is your son—lynched?" (44).

The Till story was not an isolated incident. The reality for the entire century to date was that segregation was an ugly monster that interfered with taking a simple vacation and the daily leisure pursuits of many Americans.

CONCLUSION

The lines were rigidly divided, and the struggle for equality would be a major factor shaping the lifestyles of the period to follow. In January 1963, Alabama's new governor, George Wallace, declared "Segregation now! Segregation tomorrow! Segregation forever!" On June 12, 1963, President Kennedy spoke to a national television audience regarding the civil rights tensions stating, "We face, therefore, a moral crisis as a country and as a people. I am therefore asking the Congress to enact legislation giving all Americans the right to be served in facilities which are open to the public—hotels, restaurants, theaters, retail stores and similar establishments. This seems to me to be an elementary right" (Williams, 195). On that same day, civil rights leader Medgar Evers was assassinated in Jackson, Mississippi.

On November 22, 1963, the assassination President John F. Kennedy left an optimistic nation stunned. The entire nation stopped all other leisure activity and mourned the event; over 96 percent of American homes witnessed the funeral on television. Lee Harvey Oswald, Kennedy's accused assassin, was murdered two days after Kennedy's assassination while being transferred to county jail. Oswald's murder was captured on film and broadcast on national television; the footage of the incident was replayed over and over and became the forerunner of instant replay, a technique that would become popular for televised sporting events.

The sudden assassinations signified the sudden changes that would soon explode in America, such as the Vietnam War, equal rights, disco, free sex, and drugs, and would shake the roots of American conformity and the comfort levels of the baby boom generation. The sudden changes would break many of the barriers of segregation and gender discrimination that previously prevented a large majority of Americans from pursuing leisure activities by free choice.

CHAPTER 7

THE JET AGE AND
TURBULENCE: 1964–1979

CHRONOLOGY

1965   Medicare and Medicaid are established; the United States sends troops to Vietnam.

1966   The National Organization for Women (NOW) is founded.

1967   Kathrine Switzer runs in the Boston Marathon; the first Super Bowl game is played.

1968   Martin Luther King, Jr. and Robert F. Kennedy are assassinated.

1969   The *Apollo 11* spacecraft lands on the moon; the Stonewall riot occurs in New York City; the Woodstock concert is held.

1970   The Beatles break up; students at Kent State are shot by National Guardsmen.

1971   Disney World opens in Florida.

1972   The modern skateboard is invented.

1973   Selective service ends.

1974   VCRs go on the market.

1976   The nation celebrates its bicentennial.

1977   Elvis is found dead; the miniseries *Roots* airs on television; *Saturday Night Fever* and *Star Wars* movies are released.

1978   In response to the *Animal House* movie, toga parties begin.

1979   Sony introduces the Walkman.

INTRODUCTION

Whereas the period following World War II preached conformity, the succeeding years were characterized by nonconformity as a counterculture calling for sexual freedom and an end to the Vietnam War developed. Significant gains in civil rights were achieved as a result of the women's liberation movement, gay liberation, and the American Indian movement. Gains made largely because of these and other civil rights movements gave many Americans access to leisure activities that they previously could not freely pursue. Civil rights issues dominated American society during this period and would be the cause of culture clashes during these turbulent years that challenged American conformity in ways never before seen.

Television was still the overwhelming choice as a way to spend leisure hours. During this period, retirement among individuals over the age of 55 increased, as did shorter workweeks, a travel industry business, recreation as an opportunity for professional employment, and leisure activities as firmly established institutions.

PUBLIC INTEREST

The Civil Rights Act of 1964 and the Great Society

Just days after President John F. Kennedy's assassination, newly sworn-in President Lyndon B. Johnson said that "no memorial or eulogy could more eloquently honor President Kennedy's memory than the earliest possible passage of the civil rights bill" (Williams, 226). On July 2, 1964, Johnson officially signed the Civil Rights Act, declaring racial discrimination in restaurants, hotels, movie theaters, and other places of public accommodation to be illegal. However, many southerners and southern states refused to acknowledge the federal legislation. On July 4, 1964, in Selma, Alabama a few African American students decided to exercise their federal right to attend an all-white drive-in movie theater. In the process, they were attacked by angry whites and arrested for trespassing (Williams, 254).

Johnson also announced plans for the implementation of the Great Society program in which "leisure is a welcome chance to build and reflect"; the program declared a "war on poverty" and an extension of certain New Deal programs (for New Deal see chapter 4) (quoted in Unger, 18–20). As part of the Great Society program, the Appalachian Regional Development Act provided more than $1 billion in economic aid to more than 17 million poverty stricken individuals in the Appalachian mountain region extending from Alabama to Pennsylvania. In 1965, Congress also enacted the Medicare and Medicaid programs to be administered under Social Security. Medicare provided health services for people over the age of 65, and Medicaid provided health care assistance for low-income individuals.

Part of the war on poverty was the implementation of federally funded Community Action Programs (CAP). The CAP recognized that recreation and leisure-time activities were "essential to individual and community well-being, to be planned for and made available to everyone irrespective of their ability to pay" (Kraus [1971], 39). For the most part, however, inner-city recreation needs were ignored. These inner-city recreation needs were cited as a major grievance during the 1967 racial riots, which many have cited as the worst case of urban violence during the entire twentieth century.

In Detroit, Michigan, the riots reportedly started after a routine police raid on an after-hours drinking establishment in an all-African American neighborhood.

A few nights later, the police also raided a local motel, the Algiers, in response to reports of white women socializing with African American men. In both cases, violence ensued. At the Algiers motel, three African Americans were killed, and all of the motel occupants, including the women, were severely beaten. Protests followed, coupled with looting, riots, and more violence. Police made many arrests, 43 individuals died, and more than 700 were injured. Similar situations erupted in cities all over America.

According to a report by the National Advisory Commission on Civil Disorders, "[a]mong the 20 cities that accounted for the most serious disorders in the summer of 1967, recreation grievances were found in 15 cities" (Young, 289). In New Brunswick, New Jersey, for example, researcher Lynn Young discovered that "the recreation grievances were largely focused on the lack of swimming pools." Many of them had been closed down rather than allow integration (291).

Tensions continued the following year as both civil rights leader Martin Luther King, Jr. and Robert F. Kennedy (the brother of former President John F. Kennedy) were assassinated. Kennedy, who opposed the Vietnam War and supported civil rights, was assassinated on June 5, 1968 during a campaign for the presidential primary elections. In addition, the war in Vietnam escalated, and student protests reached massive proportions.

Vietnam and Antiwar Demonstrations

Selective service had been an active part of young American men's lives since World War II. A significant number of soldiers continued to be drafted and deployed in Europe and other parts of the globe during the continuing Soviet threat (see chapter 6).

In 1965, American military involvement in Vietnam caused an upheaval within American society. American military advisement in Vietnam had extended back to 1954 during French occupation of that country. However, in 1965 the United States increased its troop strength in Vietnam to more than 16,000 soldiers, and intense fighting ensued. As the war escalated, so did the draft. According to the U.S. Census Bureau, between August 1964 and January 1973 more than 75.7 million Americans were registered by selective service, 8.6 million were examined for military duty, and 1.8 million were inducted, or drafted. A significant number would serve in Vietnam, and more than 58,000 were killed there.

Selective service did have its loopholes; for example, those actively registered in college were exempt. Other American men not attending college who chose to avoid the draft either served a prison sentence or left the country, thereby forfeiting American citizenship. A culture clash ensued because many older adults perceived the college deferments and draft dodgers as unpatriotic and subversive. The growing disenchantment of the youth toward Vietnam and the draft triggered massive antiwar demonstrations. For example, in 1967 more than 350,000 war protesters marched on the United Nations building in New York City.

By 1968, the United States committed itself to an all-out war in Vietnam and increased U.S. military strength there to more than 543,000 troops. During that same year, the Tet Offensive by the North Vietnamese troops turned the course of the war against the Americans. The United States responded with unprece-

174 FUN AND GAMES IN TWENTIETH-CENTURY AMERICA

dented bombing raids extending beyond Vietnam into Laos and Cambodia. The massive bombings triggered further protests and demonstrations at home.

Student protest and unrest on college campuses extended nationwide. In incidents in 1969, students took over university administration buildings at many colleges and universities including Harvard, Cornell, Columbia, and Berkley. The protesters were usually met by National Guard or local police forces and forcibly removed by tear gas and beatings. Many thousands were also jailed. On May 4, 1970, the situation was taken to the extreme as National Guardsmen fired into a crowd at Kent State University in Ohio, killing four protestors. In response, five days later more than 100,000 protesters marched on Washington, D.C., and thousands more protested at more than five hundred college campuses. During a protest on May 14, 1970, National Guardsmen also killed two protesters and wounded thirty at Jackson State University in Mississippi (Foner, 304).

Many in Washington came to view the war as fruitless and one that the United States would not win. As a result, President Nixon announced a steady decrease in the number of soldiers being sent to Vietnam, with a complete withdrawal by 1973. In that same year, the country decided to institute an all-volunteer army and eliminated the selective service draft.

In 1977, President Jimmy Carter announced an unconditional pardon to all Vietnam draft evaders. Citizens' faith in the country and in the government was at an all-time low and would require a slow healing process. A unifying event that helped begin the healing process was the nation's 200th birthday.

The Bicentennial Celebration and the Three-day Weekend

With the onset of the bicentennial (the 200th anniversary of the ratification of the Declaration of Independence), the nation prepared for the biggest celebration in its history. Hundreds of thousands of special events and celebrations were planned. All across the nation, millions of people began displaying American flags and literally painting almost everything red, white, and blue, including postal mailboxes, fire hydrants, and the sides of barns. Television also prepared a countdown a full year in advance with short, informative segments on American history titled "Bicentennial Minutes."

On July 4th, 1976, more than six million people gathered in New York and three million in Philadelphia for massive Independence Day celebrations. Operation Sail, a special celebration of the bicentennial, attracted more than two hundred tall ships and military ships from around the world to New York Harbor. Thousands of small pleasure boats also filled the harbor and joined in the celebration.

Interest in the bicentennial also sparked interest in all things American. Historic American sites recorded record numbers of visitors. Monticello, Thomas Jefferson's home, recorded an all-time high of 671,486 visitors and continued to attract more than 500,000 visitors every year through 2000 (Monticello Newsletter, Vol. 13, No. 1: 3). Trips to historic sites became ideal for family minivacations and were usually planned as part of a three-day weekend.

In 1968, Congress authorized the creation of four permanent three-day weekends by assigning specific Mondays as the official day for the celebrations of George Washington's birthday in mid-February, Memorial Day at the end of May,

Labor Day in early September, and Columbus Day in mid-October. Many other industries began providing the Friday after Thanksgiving as a holiday, thereby creating a four-day weekend, and extended time off for workers during the Christmas and New Year holidays.

Overall the average workweek had dropped to less than 40 hours, as many companies instituted the Monday-to-Friday, nine-to-five job, with one hour per day for lunch. By the mid 1960s, employees who had been employed for a certain amount of time by some industries obtained a four-week vacation. In the automobile industry, for example, four-week vacations were granted after 15 years of continuous service. Some other industries extended five-week vacations after 20 years of service (Kraus [1971], 310).

For most of the century, leisure time had always been secondary to work hours. By 1970, the trend had reversed, and leisure evolved as a full-fledged lifestyle. Leisure time was also a preference, and many adults sought shorter workdays, longer weekends, increased vacation time, and earlier retirement.

Planned Retirement Communities and Leisure as a Professional Occupation

On January 1, 1960, Sun City, Arizona, opened as a planned retirement community designed specifically for people 55 and older. Unlike suburban developments, which built houses first, Sun City built a golf course, recreation center, and shopping center prior to offering homes for sale. By 1970, a lake and private park were added to include boating activities, fishing, and picnicking. By 1980, Sun City's population exceeded 45,000 people, and it became the prototype for all other retirement communities. Sun City would eventually encompass more than 80,000 homes made up of nine other planned communities: two each in Arizona and California and one each in Nevada, South Carolina, Texas, Florida, and Illinois By 1976, California alone would have almost 700 new retirement communities with populations numbering more than 350,000 people (Findlay, 169).

In the early 1960s, California was also the site for the first Leisure World retirement village. Amenities included tennis courts, biking paths, an 18-hole golf course, indoor swimming, a health spa, a ballroom, an auditorium, a theater, and activity rooms. Leisure World, which eventually opened villages on both coasts including in Maryland and New Jersey, advertised a "world of indoor recreation, [and] cultural and social activities . . . [all] within a gated community." A gated community provided a 24-hour security force, and usually a wall or a gate literally surrounded the entire property. The idea was a self-contained community that also included stores, beauty salons, banking services, a post office, restaurants, a tavern, and even a hospital center. Most important was the secure knowledge that outsiders could not enter.

Some communities were built for the very wealthy. One example was the Village of Oak Brook near Chicago, Illinois. The village was built around an 800-acre sports complex that included 12 polo fields, a riding academy with a stable for 300 horses, an airstrip, a golf course, and skeet shooting. Within an adjoining 1,800-acre forest preserve was a riding trail, a foxhunting preserve, and a lake for canoeing and sailing (Kraus [1971], 297). During this period, more than eight million Americans migrated in search of retirement villages and gated communities.

In 1965, Merrill Lynch, a leading brokerage house, charted annual leisure spending at over $150 billion, and according to financial columnist Sylvia Porter, the "surge in travel, sports, vacations, etc., has become a major creator of jobs—going far beyond the familiar categories of camp counselors, lifeguard, park ranger, and the like" (quoted in Kraus [1971], 103). In 1965, the U.S. Department of Labor documented employment in leisure-related fields such as radio and television (more than 200,000 employees), travel and hotels (500,000 employees), and manufacturing of games and sporting goods (90,000 employees). In addition, more than 35,000 recreation workers were employed full-time by various organizations and the national parks. In all, more than sixty different fields of employment were listed with the total number of full- and part-time workers at more than 1.4 million (Kraus [1971], 103–105).

In 1966, the National Recreation and Parks Association was formed, and within one year the organization claimed more than 14,000 members and issued a monthly magazine, *Parks and Recreation*, with more than 25,000 subscribers. The association's mission statement was to develop "a more adequate national philosophy of leisure in which we are no longer dependent on work for meaning in life" (Kraus, 113–115).

State Parks, the National Parks, and Fishing Rights

Individual states including Alabama, California, Michigan, New York, and Pennsylvania continued programs of acquiring additional land for outdoor recreation. Total attendance in state parks alone increased from 263 million in 1960 to 391 million in 1967. The most frequently enjoyed activities included picnicking, sightseeing, camping, fishing, and hunting.

The U.S. Fish and Wildlife Service reported that in 1975 more than 35 million fishing licenses and 26 million hunting licenses were issued. More than 40 million people spent at least one night camping outdoors, and more than half of these chose to camp at a lakefront or campsite by a reservoir. More than 40 percent of all campers also owned a recreational boat.

The U.S. Census Bureau reported an increase in the number of recreational boats in the United States to more than 11 million by 1979. Of that number, 6.8 million were outboards, 1.3 million were canoes, and 1 million were sailboats. The total number of participants in boating activities totaled 41.7 million people. In addition, powered motorboats introduced water skiing as a new sport that quickly attracted more than ten million participants per year.

In 1968, national park attendance was more than 150 million and continued to increase throughout the period. The U.S. government also increased its participation in administering and monitoring recreation services with 72 federal agencies, including 3 presidential committees, 9 cabinet-level departments, 49 separate agencies, and 11 independent agencies (Kraus [1971], 27).

The publication of *Silent Spring* (1962) by Rachel Carson forced the U.S. government to make changes in the nation's environmental policies. In her book, Carson revealed that the aerial spraying of DDT was harmful to both humans and wildlife. (DDT was an insecticide used to control insects.) Within a short time

A public park, such as Clove Lakes Park in Staten Island, New York, pictured here, offered many middle- and working-class families an inexpensive opportunity for social gatherings, relaxation, and recreation. Author's archives.

after the book's publication, a U.S. Public Health Service report documented that insecticide runoff along the Mississippi River had killed more than ten million fish. A substantial additional number of fish were infected by the runoff, and those caught and eaten by recreational fisherman infected humans. As a result, the government created the Environmental Protection Agency (EPA) in addition to the Arctic National Wildlife Act, the Wilderness Act, and the Clean Air Act.

At Calvert Cliffs nuclear plant in Maryland, the EPA discovered that the hot water discharged by the plant into the nearby rivers lowered the survival rate of fish in addition to transmitting unknown hazards to people who caught and ate the fish. New governmental regulations were formulated and enforced by federal and state agencies in all of the national and state parks including setting limits on the number of fish caught and specific seasons for fishing.

The application of governmental fishing regulations angered Native American Indians. Fishing rights were part of their cultural heritage, and Native American Indians believed that they alone should have control over fishing rights, recreational or commercial. Therefore, fishing rights became a major concern of the American Indian Movement (AIM).

AIM was formed after World War II to try to end racism, discrimination, and stereotyping of Native American Indians. In August of 1970, AIM began a series of "fish-ins" demanding fishing rights from the U.S. government. In one instance in January 1971, angry whites shot and killed AIM member Hank Adams while he was fishing in protest on the Puyallup River in Washington State. From 1970 through 1973, AIM protests occupied the Bureau of Indian Affairs in Washington, D.C. and in Mount Rushmore and Wounded Knee, both in South Dakota.

In 1976, Congress passed the Indian Self-Determination Act, which gave Indians control of their own education and continuation of tribal customs and assigned fishing rights as protected in the same manner as property rights.

LIFESTYLES

Shopping Malls, Friday and Saturday Nights, and Active Senior Living

By 1967, the country's overall farm population was less than six percent of the total nationwide population, a decrease of more than four million since 1960. A study of small farms documented a lack of recreational and social opportunities in rural areas. Sociologist Gunnar Myrdal reported, "[T]here are few parties, few picnics, few dances, and fewer public meetings." Recreation tended to be informal and included activities such as swimming, hunting, and fishing. Socializing in nearby towns continued at "the barbershop, the street corner, and most frequently the poolroom" (35–37). Many rural inhabitants still relied on mail-order catalogs or traveling to cities for shopping. However, within a few short years a shift in shopping and social trends began with the new, unique, truly American development of the shopping mall.

The shopping mall was a fully enclosed interior shopping environment that first came into being in the late 1950s. Early malls were arranged on a single straight-line axis with a major department store on either end; in-between were many smaller individual chain stores, and located at a central convenient point was usually a food court containing food vendors and restaurants. Consumers could leisurely stroll from store to store and did not have to leave the mall when they were hungry.

Going to the mall (or "malling" as it became known) became a new leisure trend for Americans of all ages. Seniors formed walking groups and usually met to walk around the mall for exercise in the morning or early afternoon hours. Teenagers looked forward to meeting in the mall on Friday evenings, most just to hang out and wile away the hours.

For many working-class adults, Friday evening usually involved bowling. The U.S. Census Bureau reported bowling as the nation's most popular recreational activity with more than 62.5 million participants in more than 150,000 bowling lanes nationwide. In 1976, sociologist Lillian Breslow Rubin reported that over one-third of working-class families regularly bowled on Friday evenings. One young mother said, "Everybody who bowls in a Friday night league brings their kids"; many centers provided baby-sitting services and activities for children (193).

Some Americans simply stayed home; as one young mother reported, "We don't have the money to go out. . . . So once in a while, we invite [friends] over, and we play some cards and have a little beer and a snack" (Rubin, 196). Many others stayed close to home, sometimes going to a movie and dinner. Overall,

Americans reported that at least 25 percent of all their meals were eaten away from the home. A significant number of meals eaten out were eaten on Saturday night.

Saturday night achieved a new importance for social and leisure activity. Susan Orlean, in her book *Saturday Night*, noted that Saturday night was "the biggest night in restaurants, movies, theater, bars, dance clubs, skating rinks, bowling alleys, and video-rental shops" (103). In June 1976, a *New York* magazine cover story titled "Tribal Rites of the New Saturday Night" highlighted a local dance club in Bay Ridge, New York, that catered to disco dancing. The story became the basis for the hit movie *Saturday Night Fever* (see "Music and Theater" later in this chapter).

Saturday nights for a teenager in Washington, D.C., usually meant finding a date and listening to Motown music. Frank Rich recalled, "Motown's rhythm, we instinctively knew set the beat for our Saturday-night couplings; in backseats, in dens with all the lights turned off, [and] in bedrooms when our parents were out" (286).

In 1978, the *Rocky Horror Picture Show* gained notoriety with continuous showings at midnight on Fridays and Saturdays in more than 50 movie theaters nationwide. The film, a musical science fiction satire touching on themes of transsexualism and homosexuality, was first released in 1975 as a film version of a London stage show and was not an instant success. However, a New York theater owner decided to show it at midnight on weekends, and it quickly developed a cult following. Fans, some seeing the show hundreds of times over, sang along with the rock and roll songs in the movie's soundtrack and shouted verbal responses to the on-screen characters. Audiences also began using props at specific points of the movie, for example, throwing rice during a wedding scene or shooting water guns and holding up newspapers during a rainstorm scene. *Rocky Horror* became standard weekend fare as the first audience participation film.

The wealthy developed a disdain for Saturday night and viewed it as reserved for working-class leisure. Ignoring Saturday night became a prominent characteristic of the wealthy class. One New York socialite reported that she would never "think of giving a party on a Saturday night," further stating, "I'm sure it's very important to—how shall I say this—Middle America. But to us dear, it simply doesn't mean a thing" (Orlean, 144–145).

Many of the wealthy maintained exclusivity from middle- and working-class individuals. A significant number of recreation programs were privately owned and required large annual dues of their members. By 1964, more than 3,300 such "country clubs" with a combined total of 1.7 million members existed nationwide catering to golf, tennis, boating, horseback riding, and skiing (Kraus [1971], 95).

With the increased prosperity of the post–World War II period (see chapter 6) and the combination of a longer life expectancy, pensions, and retirement benefits, a significant number of older citizens opted for retirement. By 1970, the U.S. census reported that over 60 percent of Americans (16.8 million) over the age of 65 were in retirement. By comparison, prior to 1947, less than 7 percent were retired.

During this period, many employers instituted a mandatory retirement age of 65 for many working- and middle-class individuals (some municipalities allowed retirement after 20 years of service for sanitation, police, and other civil service workers regardless of age). It was during this period that the idea of planning for retirement took hold among all classes of people.

Surfing, Hippies, and the Summer of Love

In the early 1960s, the Southern California Research Council undertook a major study of the leisure habits of individuals of all classes and age groups in their area, which encompassed a population of well over three million people. The following is a summary of what the council found:

> Leisure is taken in bits and pieces. . . . About one-third of all leisure hours is [*sic*] taken as daily leisure, in small pieces after school or work. About one-fourth is absorbed by family members in weekend leisure pursuits. Vacations and holidays are the settings for yet another one-sixth of the total. The remaining one-fourth is time spent "at leisure" by children too young for school, [and] retired persons. (Kraus [1971], 314)

The southern California lifestyle, as it became known, contained an entire subculture centered on surfing.

Surfing on Waikiki Beach, Hawaii. After World War II, surfing increased in popularity and developed a distinctive lifestyle, especially on the beaches of Hawaii and southern California. Courtesy of Picture Desk.

The surfing craze, which began in Hawaii (see chapter 1), was widespread on the beaches of southern California. In the early 1960s, the introduction of a lightweight fiberglass surfboard made surfing accessible to both males and females of all ages. The leisurely beach lifestyle was romanticized in Hollywood movies such as *Gidget* (1959), *Beach Party* (1963), *Bikini Beach* (1964), *Beach Blanket Bingo* (1965), and *How to Stuff a Wild Bikini* (1965). The most prevalent surfing movie was a documentary titled *Endless Summer* (1966), which glorified the surfing way of life by following surfers who traveled the world in search of the "perfect wave."

Surfing was transposed to the dance floor in the swim and watusi, dances in which the dancers replicated surfing and swimming moves. Numerous bands, including the Beach Boys and Jan and Dean, portrayed the surfing culture in songs such as "Surfing USA," "Catch a Wave," "Surf City," and "Sidewalk Surfing."

In response to the surfing mania, a land device for "sidewalk surfing" was developed—the skateboard. Skateboards were about two feet long, made of wood, and had wheels fastened on the underside, which allowed the rider to replicate surfing moves on the sidewalk. By 1965, millions of skateboards were sold throughout the nation. Surfing, skateboarding, and beaches became synonymous with summer.

Another subculture of this period was the hippie subculture. The term *hippie* was first used in 1965 and applied to a new lifestyle known as the "counterculture." According to Hilmi Ibrahim, the hippie lifestyle rejected the conventional conformist lifestyle "which included passive recreation, consumption, [and] spectatorship." Hippies advocated a participatory leisure lifestyle that included music, expressionistic dancing, sexual relationships, and the "use of mild drugs for mind expansion and for collective consciousness" (219). Hippies also attempted to promote the value of peace, love, and understanding through large gatherings. Throughout the summer of 1967, large gatherings were held in major cities nationwide, prompting *Time* magazine to term the period the "summer of love." In July 1967, one such gathering was held in the Haight-Ashbury district of San Francisco.

Areas such as the Haight-Ashbury district and Greenwich Village in New York City were communities that served as refuges for the hippie lifestyle. Other members of the hippie subculture chose to live collectively in remote communes. By 1970, more than two thousand such communes existed nationwide. Opponents and critics viewed the nonconformist counterculture and the drug use it involved as a threat to traditional American values.

Drug use during the period was widespread, and it was not limited to hippies. In 1970, statistics claimed that at least 20 million Americans had tried marijuana, and at least 7 million had experimented with other types of hallucinogenic drugs such as LSD. Marijuana became widely acceptable and commonplace. Many in the white upper class and suburbia also tried the drug.

The Feminine Mystique and the Sexual Revolution

A survey of thousands of suburban females by Betty Friedan revealed that "[t]here was a strange discrepancy between the reality of our lives as women and the image to which we were trying to conform" (9). Many suburban women reported feelings of loneliness and emptiness and could only describe it as a feeling that they did not have an opportunity to exercise their creative talents. This "problem with no name" was examined in Friedan's book *The Feminine Mystique* (1963), which quickly sold more than one million copies in hardcover and became a national sensation.

Friedan revealed that the problem was indeed real and was also shared by millions of other women. She quoted one young mother of four as saying, "I've tried everything women are supposed to do—hobbies, gardening, pickling, canning, being very social with my neighbors, joining committees, running PTA teas. . . . but it doesn't leave you anything to think about—any feeling of who you are. . . . But I'm desperate. I begin to feel I have no personality" (21).

Friedan blamed the corporate advertisers who were "less interested in ideas to reach women's minds and hearts, than in selling them the things that interest advertisers—appliances, detergents, [and] lipstick" (54). Almost immediately, the major magazines, newspapers, and television programs reported on the "unhappiness of the American housewife." Almost all made light of the "problem" and did not address the problem seriously.

It would take a revolution initiated by women themselves to address the problem, and *The Feminine Mystique* became the impetus for the women's liberation movement. In 1966, the National Organization for Women (NOW) was founded, with Betty Friedan as its first president, to promote the cause of equal rights for women. By 1979, active membership in NOW numbered more than 225,000.

One of the most notable feminist leaders of the period was Gloria Steinem. A product of a working-class upbringing in Toledo, Ohio, Steinem recalled her summers during college when she worked as a Washington, D.C., recreation employee lifeguard at a segregated swimming pool in the all–African American community of Rosedale. As the only white person, she was gradually accepted. On rainy days she learned southern card games and how to "do bones." Steinem recalled, "You sit hunched over and do rhythm on your arms and legs, using your body as a percussion instrument" (Heilbrun, 148). Steinem's experience allowed her to relate similar instances of discrimination faced by both women and African Americans. For women, one of the first steps toward equality was gaining control of their own bodies.

By 1960, the U.S. Food and Drug Administration (FDA) approved Enovid as an oral contraceptive. Enovid, known simply as "the pill" allowed women the freedom of sexual intimacy with almost no chance of an unwanted pregnancy. Within two years, more than 2.3 million women filled prescriptions for the pill. With the pill, Clare Booth Luce stated, "Modern woman is at last free as a man is free, to dispose of her own body, to earn her living, to pursue the improvement of her mind, to try a successful career" (Halberstam, 606).

By 1970, reports indicated that more than 12 million women were taking the pill. The idea of having sexual intercourse for recreation and pleasure, as opposed to procreation, became a heated issue. Many conservatives and religious groups were strictly against any use of contraceptives, especially among unmarried partners. With the debate came concerns over sexual freedom, especially among college students. Universities with dormitories were forced to relax visitation rights in dorms, and an increasing number of unmarried partners were living together. Many conservatives argued that sexual promiscuity would lead to communal living and homosexuality.

Gay Liberation and Disco

In 1948, the Kinsey report (see chapter 6) estimated that at least four percent of the male population was homosexual. The follow-up Kinsey report on female sexuality revealed similar results. At the time, various investigations attempted to disprove the results; nevertheless, the numbers were factual. In 1969, homosexuality, which was long kept a hidden secret, was brought to the public's attention.

For years, New York City police officers routinely harassed and indiscriminately attacked homosexuals. In 1969, in one raid on Stonewall, a known gay bar in Greenwich Village, homosexuals fed up with the continued abuse fought back. Many homosexuals were brutally beaten, and the incident received widespread media attention. The event came to signify a major turning point as homosexual organizations nationwide became public and revealed that similar police raids and harassment were typical in many major cities. By the end of the period, the gay liberation movement included almost one thousand gay and lesbian organizations. These organizations lobbied Congress and attempted to fight discrimination against homosexuals in all areas of life. The general public was slow to accept open homosexuality in society, especially among its sports heroes.

David Kopay, a ten-year veteran of the National Football League (NFL), became the first professional athlete to publicly declare his homosexuality in the publication of *The David Kopay Story* (1977). Kopay wrote, "Sometimes I feel cheated for all the long years I wasted in hiding. . . . There was a time when I felt that it would be the end of the world if people found out about my homosexuality. What I have found is that it is the beginning of a new world for me" (Kopay, fourth cover).

An underground gay lifestyle that eventually became a widespread cultural force in mainstream America was disco. In the late 1970s, disco came to represent a lifestyle that encompassed homosexuality, bisexuality, drugs, and a freewheeling sexual lifestyle associated with such clubs as New York City's flamboyant Studio 54. It became fashionable to openly know and associate with the gay lifestyle.

One of the telltale signs of the disco era was a three-piece polyester suit known as a leisure suit. Unlike the gray flannel suit of business attire, the leisure suit was designed for after-hours use and marketed for wear during activity and entertainment. The brightly colored, usually pastel suit was characterized by an opened collared shirt over wide jacket lapels, a buttoned vest, and bell-bottom pants. By the early 1980s, both the leisure suit fad and disco would fade out of the nation's culture as a result of increased pressure from conservative Americans who viewed the lifestyle as indicative of moral decay.

ENTERTAINMENT

Color Television, VCRs, AM Top-40, and FM Radio

In 1965, color was the catchword for television. At the time, ABC broadcast over half its shows in color. CBS broadcast specials in color, and NBC advertised itself as the first "full-color network." By the end of the period, all programs were broadcast in color, and over 67 percent of all homes owned a color television set.

The most popular show of the early period was *The Beverly Hillbillies* (1962–

1971), which was viewed by more than 60 million people per week (Panati, 356). In July 1969, over 94 percent of all television sets (which represented almost 135 million people) were tuned in to the *Apollo 11* moon landing.

From 1971 through 1975, *All in the Family* was the most watched weekly television program. The show brought to television issues that had never before aired such as racial prejudice, draft resisters, women's liberation, homosexuality, and transvestites. Concerns arose over the television story topics in general, prompting a Federal Communications Commission (FCC) ruling to designate 7:00 P.M. to 9:00 P.M. as "family viewing time." In other words, any program deemed inappropriate for family viewing would not be allowed in that time slot.

In 1977, *Roots*, a 12-hour television miniseries, was broadcast over a consecutive 8-day period and watched by more than 130 million viewers. The following year, a 4-night miniseries titled *Holocaust* that dealt with survivors of Nazi persecution during World War II drew 120 million viewers.

In 1974, the introduction of the videocassette recorder (VCR) created a breakthrough in home entertainment. The VCR allowed individuals to videotape television programs for viewing at a later time at their convenience. The Hollywood film industry saw the opportunity to market movies on videocassette, and the video home rental business was born. By 1985, almost 50 million videocassettes were rented annually for home viewing.

Television simply was the most time-consuming of all leisure activities, and over 95 percent of all American homes had at least one television. Reports indicated that most Americans had the television turned on for an average of 55 to 60 hours each week. In 1976, Robert Armstrong, a California cartoonist, coined the phrase *couch potato* to describe an individual who centered their entire existence on a television set, a remote control, and an easy chair (Kammen, 186). LA-Z-Boy first introduced the lounge chair in 1928, but it achieved prominence during this period and became the couch potato symbol. By the mid-1990s the company had sales in excess of $1 billion per year.

In addition to television, over 99 percent of all homes and over 80 percent of all automobiles had radios. By 1964, radio had achieved a new popularity as a result of the top-40 AM (amplitude modulation, referring to the broadcast mechanism) stations and album-orientated FM (frequency modulation) music formats. The top-40 format played the same forty current hit songs over and over within any given week. The overwhelming dominant force in the top-40 AM format was 77 WABC, a New York AM radio station.

During this time period, New York's 77 WABC consistently had an astonishing 20 percent share of the listening audience (more than eight million listeners). The ratings numbers were unheard of, especially in the competitive radio market where top-rated shows, during the entire twentieth century , averaged around 6 percent. However, that number was only for the New York City area. What was not factored in was that the station's 50,000-watt signal could be clearly heard well over 350 miles away in Pittsburgh, Pennsylvania, and in more than 38 states (Battaglio, "When AM Ruled Music, and WABC was King," 16).

By the mid 1960s, FM radio grew more popular. (FM offered stereo sound and improved reception over AM.) In most large cities a number of underground stations shunned the commercial top-40 format and began playing full album tracks, mostly by rock and roll artists. One notable example was the group Led

Zeppelin and their song "Stairway to Heaven." AM radio usually held strict standards of playing only songs that were between two and three minutes long; "Stairway to Heaven" ran almost eight minutes long. The song became an FM hit and consistently topped polls as the favorite song of the period. Other FM specialty stations emerged featuring formats such as easy listening, oldies, and adult contemporary. By 1979, more people were tuning into FM stations than AM stations.

Newspapers, *Playboy, Ms. Magazine,* and Super Best-sellers

During this period, daily newspaper circulation remained fairly steady at 63 million per year and the total number of daily publications at more than 1,700. A slight shift occurred as morning circulation increased from 25.9 million in 1970 to 29.4 million by 1979, and evening circulation declined from 36.2 million in 1970 to less than 32.8 million by 1979. Sunday circulation increased from 49.2 million in 1970 to more than 54 million by 1979. The change was attributed to the fact that late afternoon publications could not compete with television's evening news programs.

The weekly publication *TV Guide* continued to be the most widely circulated magazine at 20 million copies per week (80 million monthly). Specialty magazines of all kinds continued to be introduced to the market. In 1970, more than 9,500 titles existed, and this number increased to more than 11,500 by the 1980s. Two specialty magazines of note were the popular *Playboy* and the influential and controversial *Ms. Magazine*.

Playboy began publication in 1953 expanding on the titillating concept of the pinup (see chapter 5) by featuring photographs of nude women. The magazine also promoted a leisure lifestyle for young adult men and offered advice on fashion, sports cars, music, stereo equipment, and how to meet women. In 1956, circulation topped 600,000 and would exceed 2.5 million by the mid-1960s. The antithesis of *Playboy* was *Ms. Magazine*.

In 1972, *Ms. Magazine* helped raise the consciousness of American women by presenting issues that were largely ignored by the mainstream press. It carried articles on previously unexplored subjects such as job discrimination, sexual harassment, domestic abuse, and even recreational activities that could be enjoyed during a menstrual cycle or pregnancy. By 1980, the magazine sold more than 500,000 copies per month.

Between 1964 and 1979 sex and controversy were also major reasons that book sales averaged between 1.5 and 1.8 billion per year. In 1966, the medical work *Human Sexual Response* by William Masters and Virginia Johnson (in some ways a continuation of the Kinsey reports, see chapter 6) signified a change to more open discussions of sexual relations. Manuals to assist in relationships published during this time included *Everything You Always Wanted to Know about Sex but Were Afraid to Ask* (1970) and *The Joy of Sex* (1973).

The changing customs of sexual relationships were apparent in Jacqueline Susann's *Valley of the Dolls* (1966), a fictional story of pill-popping women in Hollywood that echoed real-life scandals. The book sold more than 22 million copies, almost all in paperback, and was termed a "super best-seller" (Panati, 347). Other super best-sellers that sold more than ten million copies included *The Godfather*

(1969), *Love Story* (1970), *Jonathan Livingston Seagull* (1970), and *The Exorcist* (1979) (Panati, 406-407).

A series of inexpensive paperback books geared toward young teens called novelizations were written based on a television show or movie as opposed to in previous years when television shows or movies were written based on an already existing book. Titles were published for almost all of the popular television shows including *Voyage to the Bottom of the Sea*, *The Man from Uncle*, and *Room 222*. The book series were numbered consecutively so that the readers could easily pick up the next book in the series without having to remember the complete title.

Freestyle Dancing, the Hustle, and Roller Disco

The counterculture gave rise to freestyle expression in dance. In many of the new dances the partners never touched. Dancers could go on the dance floor solo or in a group and "do their own thing" to the music. Freestyle dancing caught on in all age and class groups. It became common at a social function for individuals to freestyle dance to all types of music, and the trend continued throughout the century. Mainstream partner dancing did return for a short time with the hustle.

A 1975 song, *The Hustle* by Van McCoy, featured a resounding, constant dance beat, which gave rise to the dance of the same name. The hustle dance required dancing with a partner and incorporated turns and moves reminiscent of swing,

Roller disco, a result of the popularity of disco music, combined roller-skating and disco dancing. This photo was taken June 28, 1979 in New York City. Courtesy of Corbis.

merengue, and other Latin dances. The new dance craze hit nationwide with the release of the movie *Saturday Night Fever* (1977) starring John Travolta.

The hustle was prominently featured on the television show *American Bandstand* (see chapter 6). The show's host, Dick Clark, said that "disco is just music with a very heavy beat. It's not listening music; it's dancing music" (Uslan and Solomon, 349). The music and dance were so popular that they spawned regional television dance shows such as *Dancing Disco* in Boston, *Disco Magic* in Miami, and *Disco Fever* in Los Angles. Disco dance clubs sprang up all around the nation. Estimates of the number of these clubs ranged as high as more than 10,000 nationwide, with more than 200 in New York City alone (Panati, 384–388).

The popularity of disco dancing also spread to indoor roller-skating rinks. By 1979, over 70 percent of the nation's skating rinks were equipped to offer "roller disco," roller-skating to disco music (Panati, 388). Many rinks installed additional sound equipment and lights to replicate the disco nightlife setting in a drug-free and nonalcoholic environment for children, teens, and adults.

Hobbies, Frisbees, Slot Cars, and CB Radios

Hobbies continued to occupy a significant amount of leisure time. More than 36 million individuals enjoyed gardening. More than 16 million took pleasure in stamp collecting, and more than 10 million played bridge. Board games were still popular. In 1967, Ouija Boards sold more than 2.3 million games, surpassing Monopoly as the perennial bestseller (Panati, 92).

The Frisbee, first introduced in 1948, was similar to a metal pie pan and was tossed between two individuals. In 1957, the development of lightweight plastic enabled the toy to be made of a safer material and made it more enjoyable to play with, especially among children. Originally named the Flyin' Saucer, Wham-O (the creators of the hula hoop, see chapter 6) bought the idea in the early 1960s and marketed it as the Frisbee. Flinging Frisbees became a national sport on college campuses, beaches, parks, and city streets. By the end of the century, more Frisbees were sold than all other sporting goods toys combined (Panati, 265).

In 1972, Atari marketed the first television video game, Pong, which sold millions and started a new national sensation. The simple game replicated the game of Ping-Pong on a television screen. By the early 1980s, new technological developments would allow for greater improvements in the length of video game play and variations in video games, helping the video game industry to become a multibillion-dollar business (see chapter 8).

In 1959, Aurora manufacturing introduced the first tabletop toy plastic racing cars. The cars, about two inches long, were controlled by a remote handheld device. Two cars were raced side by side on a track that could fit on a kitchen table within the home. In the mid-1960s, larger models (six to eight inches long) known as slot cars were introduced and raced on tracks in excess of two hundred feet in length. The cars were customized and carried in specially designed carrying cases. Unlike the tabletop versions, the slot car tracks were in large storefronts with eight to ten cars racing at one time. By the late 1960s, estimates placed the number of slot car participants at more than 3.5 million in more than 5,000 slot car clubs. The fad died down in the late 1960s, but some slot car clubs persisted throughout the century.

Between 1974 and 1979, a craze in citizen band (CB) radios took the nation by storm. The CB radio was mounted on the dashboard of trucks and cars and allowed drivers to communicate between vehicles on the open road. Frequency of CB use increased as truckers began alerting each other to gasoline availability during the 1970s oil embargo (see "Muscle Cars and Fuel Shortages" later in this chapter). Motorists were initially drawn to the trucker slang such as "10-4" (acknowledgment), "good buddy" (CB friend), "double-nickel" (55 mph speed limit), and "smokies" (police). By 1976, more than 25 million CB radios were in operation in cars, boats, and homes. CB terminology showed up in popular songs, books, magazines, television shows, and Hollywood movies.

Amusement Theme Parks

In 1971, Walt Disney World opened in Orlando, Florida, patterned after Disneyland in California (see chapter 6), and the park averaged more than 15 million visitors per year. Other similarly styled theme parks opened across the country including Busch Gardens (Virginia and Florida), Six Flags (first in Texas and five other states), Cypress Gardens (Florida), Opryland (Tennessee), Knott's Berry Farm (California), and Hershey Park (Pennsylvania).

The new theme parks all had one thing in common: the rides were neat and orderly, and there were none of the risqué rides and customers that had been associated with the early amusement parks (see chapters 1 and 6). The theme parks were also removed from the inner cities and were no longer accessible by public transportation. In addition, higher admissions prices prevented many working-class people from being able to afford to enter the new theme parks. The old-fashioned amusement parks such as Coney Island (see chapter 1) were a thing of the past.

MUSIC AND THEATER

Broadway, Theater, and the Cultural Arts

In 1969, *Oh Calcutta* opened and shocked Broadway audiences as the first Broadway show to feature nudity. The initial run of 1,300 performances was impressive. The revival from 1976 to 1989 ran for 5,959 performances. In 1970, two of the longest running shows closed: *Hello Dolly* after 2,844 performances and *Fiddler on the Roof* after 3,242 performances. In that same year, *Hair* opened as the first rock musical on Broadway and reflected the changing times of the period, with themes including hippies, drugs, and sexual freedom. (Others followed including *Godspell* and *Jesus Christ Superstar*.) *Hair* was so successful that 14 national touring companies performed the musical at the same time it was running on Broadway (1,742 performances). In 1972, the same year that *Hair* closed, the musical *Grease* opened on Broadway and triggered a nostalgia craze for the 1950s. *Grease* closed in 1980 after a then-record run of 3,388 performances ("Longest Running Broadway Shows in History," n.p.). A movie version would be released in 1978 and would also prove to be quite popular. Attendance at Broadway shows numbered ten million per year. By 1979, attendance at nationwide touring company shows was more than 67 million (Statistical Abstract [1986], 221).

Public interest in other cultural institutions involving the performing and visual arts continued to grow rapidly. Many cities undertook major multimillion-dollar building projects for the performing arts, such as Lincoln Center in New York City and the Kennedy Center in Washington, D.C.

Opera companies, which numbered only 77 nationwide in 1941, had expanded to more than 600 by 1970 and 986 by 1980. Symphony orchestras grew from 1,440 in 1970 to 1,572 in 1980 with attendance up from 12.7 million in 1970 to 22.6 million in 1980. Summer concerts of symphony orchestras in New York's Central Park regularly attracted more than 90,000 people for each performance. During the period, attendance at symphony concerts, the theater, and the opera and money spent on attending the performing arts topped attendance at and money spent on all professional sports (Kaplan [1978], 65–68).

In 1966, the Metropolitan Museum of Art in New York City (the Met) provided a new philosophy "that great art should not be the exclusive preserve of a social and intellectual elite." Exhibitions were geared to outreach programs and education of the general public. By 1970, yearly attendance at the Met was more than six million. This outreach and education idea became a national trend that continued throughout the 1970s. Attendance at more than 5,000 museums nationwide amounted to more than 78 million per year; more than half of those 5,000 museums began operation after 1960. During the 1970s total attendance in cultural activities of all kinds topped 300 million per year (Marty, 212).

James Bond, *Jaws*, and Toga Parties

Movie attendance continued its decline from 24 million per week in 1960 to just over 19 million per week by 1964 and remained at that number through 1979. Overall, the total number of motion picture theaters stood at 15,000, of which 4,000 were outdoor drive-ins.

In 1968, the Motion Picture Association of America (MPAA) instituted a voluntary rating system "enabling the parent to make judgments on movies they want or don't want their children to see." The system rated films either G (general audiences); PG (parental guidance suggested); M (for mature audiences); R (restricted, moviegoers under 17 required accompanying parent or adult); and X (adults only) (http://www.natoonline.org). After 1975, the MPAA also began counting the number of screens showing movies instead of counting the actual number of theaters.

The easing of the Cold War was evident in a series of light-hearted spy thriller movies of the time. The James Bond series featured ten movies between 1964 and 1979 in which the title character became entangled in international Cold War espionage with titles such as *Dr. No* (1963), *From Russia with Love* (1964), and *Goldfinger* (1964). The James Bond series would continue through the remainder of the twentieth century. Hollywood also became critical of the Vietnam War through the release of movies such as *The Boys in Company C* (1978), *The Deer Hunter* (1978), and *Apocalypse Now* (1979).

Hollywood movies made a comeback of sorts during this period, at least in box office receipts. Released in the summer of 1975, *Jaws* became the highest grossing moneymaking film up until that time. The movie, based on a best-selling novel (9.4 million copies sold), was set in a New England summer vacation beach resort and told the (fictional) story of a rash of shark attacks. During that same year, the tension and terror created by the movie gave many moviegoers a real-life fear of going into the water.

In 1977, new movie technology and spectacular special effects compelled audiences to see the science fiction film *Star Wars*. Also in 1977, the movie *Saturday Night Fever* popularized the hustle dance and the disco craze. Each became surprise hits that filled the movie theaters.

In 1978, the Hollywood release of *National Lampoon's Animal House* spurred an interest in toga parties. One scene in the movie featured a fraternity house party for which participants were encouraged to come dressed in bed sheets, reminiscent of ancient Roman togas. In September of that same year, *Newsweek* magazine reported that more than one hundred college campuses sponsored toga parties. Throughout the remainder of the century, toga parties would be held at colleges, vacation resorts, and on cruises.

Beatlemania, Woodstock, and Disco

In February of 1964, the musical group the Beatles (John Lennon, Paul Mc-Cartney, Ringo Starr, and George Harrison) appeared on successive Sundays on

The Beatles rehearse for the *Ed Sullivan* television show in 1964. Courtesy of Library of Congress.

More than 500,000 people attended the Woodstock Music Festival in Bethel, New York, in August 1969. Courtesy of Picture Desk.

the *Ed Sullivan Show*. More than 70 million people saw each televised show. Almost immediately, the Beatles were receiving more than 15,000 fan letters per week. Millions of frenzied teenage fans also bought their records.

In 1964 alone, Beatles records accounted for over 60 percent of all the single 45 rpm (revolutions per minute) records sold in the country (Panati, 341). In April of that year, the Beatles had the unprecedented distinction of having the top five singles on the Billboard music charts and also 14 of the top 100 (a feat never before or since accomplished in the twentieth century). They also became the first band to perform live in sports stadiums, playing to more than 50,000 fans at a time. The phenomenon was simply called Beatlemania.

The Beatles' last official live performance on January 25, 1967, was especially significant. The show was the first global satellite television simulcast and was watched by a worldwide audience of more than 400 million people.

In August 1969, the Woodstock music festival, advertised as "three days of peace and music" was held in Bethel, New York. During the festival, the New York State Thruway was backlogged for miles, and many simply abandoned their cars and walked to the festival. More than 450,000 people attended the event. Camping and sharing food and drugs was common as the attendees stayed at the festival to hear a three-day continuous presentation of music. Drugs were openly used, and designated areas known as acid tents were set up for those suffering from a bad LSD experience. After the Woodstock festival, music events of massive proportions became much more common.

In 1973, Elvis Presley (see chapter 6) performed a concert that was broadcast by satellite from Honolulu, Hawaii, and was viewed by more than 1.5 billion people (Super Seventies Rock Site's "Seventies Almanac 1973," n.p.). In August 1977, Presley suffered an untimely death at the age of 42. Within two days of his death, consumers purchased more than two million of his albums (Marty, 210).

In 1975, the disco anthem *The Hustle* by Van McCoy sold more than ten million copies and kicked off a national disco craze of the same name. In 1978, the disco soundtrack by the Bee Gees to the movie *Saturday Night Fever* (1977) sold an unprecedented 25 million copies (more than three times the previous leader) and remained at number one on the album charts for 24 consecutive weeks (Uslan and Solomon, 425). Disco music albums sold at a rapid rate, and by 1980, record sales of all kinds were more than 597 million per year (Statistical Abstract [1994], 578).

SPORTS AND GAMES

Professional Sports Spectators, Monday Night Football, and Intertwined Politics

In 1977, *Newsweek* reported that there were more than 314 million spectators at live sporting events that year. Baseball remained the top professional sports draw with attendance of 24.3 million per year. Statistics from the 1968 baseball season averaged 15,000 spectators per event for 1,620 games (Kraus [1971], 323). During this period, domed stadiums such as the Astrodome in Houston, Texas, added to the spectators' comfort and prevented individual games from being postponed or canceled because of rain. The Astrodome also hosted other events such as football games, concerts, and rodeos, with combined attendance at all events at more than four million spectators per year. The stadium complex also included an adjacent 116-acre amusement park, Astroworld, and a group of hotels (Kraus [1971], 326).

In 1968, attendance at horse racing tracks stood at 61.5 million. Automobile racing attendance topped 40 million. The Indianapolis 500 (see chapter 1), an annual event held each Memorial Day, drew an average of 225,000 spectators, and National Association of Stock Car Auto Racing (NASCAR, see chapter 6) averaged between 80,000 and 100,000 for each event (Kraus [1971], 322).

However, attendance at the actual events was not the main measurement of a sport's popularity; it was the increase in television spectators that represented the significant portion of sports spectators. Television contracts competed and paid millions of dollars for sports event broadcast rights, and sports became big business because of the widespread television coverage.

In 1961, ABC television created the weekly show *Wide World of Sports*, which televised sporting events from around the world as entertainment for Saturday afternoon viewers. The show also introduced Americans to many of the lesser-known winter sports such as bobsledding, luge, and ski jumping.

Football remained one of the top spectator team sports. Between 1964 and 1968, attendance doubled at live football events from 4.1 million to more than 8.2 million. In 1966, the NFL announced a merger with the fledging American Football League (AFL) and announced plans for a championship game to be called the Super Bowl. On January 15, 1967, the first Super Bowl between the NFL Green Bay Packers and AFL Kansas City Chiefs drew a television audience of more than 70 million viewers.

In September 1970, sports and television was successfully merged into a prime-time extravaganza in the broadcast of ABC's *Monday Night Football*. The concept was completely new to sports (even baseball traditionally had Mondays off after a typical Sunday doubleheader). The show was an immediate success with viewers and continued to be broadcast throughout the century. By the end of the period, sports and television were completely intertwined.

Television audiences were exposed to the linking of politics and sports through two Olympic events. The struggle for civil rights reached the international stage during the 1968 Olympics in Mexico City. During the awards ceremony for the 200-meter running event, Americans Tommie Smith (gold medalist) and John Carlos (bronze medalist) each raised a black gloved fist in protest of America's mistreatment of African American athletes. This represented the first instance that athletes had expressed their protests on such a visible stage.

In 1972, at the Olympic Games in Munich, Germany, the nation and the world were stunned as Palestinian terrorists took 11 Israeli athletes hostage. After a tense nine days, the hostages were executed, and German forces killed the terrorists. The Olympics would continue to be the scene of political turmoil and political protest including subsequent boycotts by the United States at the Moscow Olympics in 1980 and by the Soviet Union at the Los Angles Olympics in 1984.

Personal Fitness, Title IX, the Running Boom, and Urban Street Games

A 1967 nationwide survey by the Athletic Institute in Chicago identified swimming and volleyball, each with more than 40 million active participants, as the most popular recreational activities among respondents. Other activities with more than 20 million participants included baseball and softball (25.8 million combined participants), roller-skating (25 million), billiards (23 million), and shooting (20 million). Activities that had between nine and ten million participants included golf, shuffleboard, water skiing, boating, horse shoes, and tennis.

In 1963, the Wilson Company introduced the steel tennis racquet. The T-2000 model was a major improvement over previous wood models. It resisted warping, was lighter than previous models, allowed players to hit the ball at increased speeds, and quickly revolutionized the game.

During this time, many individuals developed a concern for personal fitness. In the early 1970s transcendental meditation (TM), a form of meditation and relaxation, became popular. There was also a fascination and increased interest in the martial arts including judo, karate, and tai chi.

In 1970, YMCA's membership numbered more than 5.8 million in 1,718 branches nationwide. YMCAs around the country maintained a total professional staff of more than 74,000 people. In addition, they serviced 600,000 campers, 46,000 youth clubs, and 17,000 educational classes (Kraus [1971], 83). YMCAs promoted activities such as jogging, cycling, walking, and aerobics.

In the early 1960s, a California dancer named Jackie (sometimes spelled "Jacki") Sorensen created aerobics, which combined fitness dancing and music. Aerobics

A race director tries to remove Kathrine Switzer from the 1967 Boston Marathon. At the time females were prohibited from running marathons. Courtesy of Corbis.

was done indoors in gyms, church basements, and local schools and served as a lively way to stay fit and socialize at the same time. Aerobics was mainly attractive to women (Olson, Historical Dictionary of the 1970s, 10–11).

In 1967, Kathrine Switzer served as a catalyst for the future of women in sports when she became the first female to participate in and complete the Boston Marathon (see chapter 1). Switzer recalled, there was nothing in the rulebooks that explicitly said women weren't allowed to run, stating,

> Four miles into the race, the media flatbed truck loaded with photographers came through . . . and started shouting, "There's a girl in the race," . . . [Jock Semple co-race director] jumped off . . . and screamed, "Get the hell out of my race and give me that number!" I tried to get away from him . . . [My] boyfriend came to the rescue and smacked Jock with a cross body block and Jock went flying through the air. . . . It was this incident as much as any other that made me determined to become a better runner, . . . at Boston I would have finished that race on my hands and knees to prove that a woman could do it. (RunnersWeb.com, "Athletics: An Interview with Kathrine Switzer," n.p.)

Switzer's determination changed the historical view that strenuous sports were an exclusively male domain. However, Boston Marathon officials were slow to react and would not recognize females as official participants until 1972.

In 1972, Title IX of the Education Amendments Act outlawed gender discrimination in education and school sports. As a result, women's participation in college athletics increased from 30,000 female college athletes in 1972 to more than 150,000 by the year 2000. At the high school level, participation increased from 300,000 athletes to more than 4.5 million. Title IX, combined with Switzer's accomplishment and the women's liberation movement, allowed women of all ages to participate in recreation and fitness endeavors. Running in particular would experience a boom in participation by both women and men.

There was an unprecedented surge in running as a recreational activity during this period, especially following American Frank Shorter's win in the 1972 Olympic marathon. Runners were also encouraged by Jim Fixx's *Complete Book of Running* (1977), which was hailed as the "runner's bible." The book showed that any individual could benefit from running and promoted the positive effects that a natural runner's high could provide instead of receiving a high from drugs. By 1979, the running boom was in full force, and the *New York Times* reported that there were more than 20 million active joggers and runners nationwide (Braden, 283). Runners in suburban areas, rural hills, and urban streets became a familiar sight nationwide.

Street games were also common on city streets. Younger children might take out street chalk and scrawl out any number of activities directly onto the pavement. Street games had hundreds of variations, strategies, and rules. The games varied widely between neighborhoods and even between city blocks. The common factor was simple, inexpensive equipment such as chalk, a rope, or a ball.

Girls of all ages were most likely to play hopscotch and jump rope. For the more daring and skilled use of the jump rope, there was double Dutch, which used two ropes simultaneously rotating in two opposite directions, requiring both skill by the jumper and the rope turners. Singing songs and reciting rhymes during jump roping heightened the game. Many neighborhoods competed against each other, and the competitions sometimes became large social affairs.

Games with names such as off-the-point, box ball, ace-king-queen, and hit-the-stick were played using a ball. The ball of choice was the "spaldeen," a smooth, pink rubber ball about the size of a tennis ball. The inexpensive ball was sold in just about every neighborhood dime store, candy store, or toy store throughout the period. The most popular of all street games used a spaldeen and a broomstick and was known as stickball. Stickball was an urban street game that dated from the beginning of the twentieth century.

Stickball was a street version of baseball. The playing field was limited by the curb width of narrow city streets, and manhole covers determined the length of the "field." A game was usually over when a player "roofed" the ball or, worse yet, broke a window. A roofed ball meant the ball was hit onto a building's roof and was irretrievable. However, lack of a complete ball did not deter play. One neighborhood youth remembered that when the spaldeen ball split during play, the children would use the half ball and pitch it like a Frisbee to a batter using a Wiffle ball bat; they would then continue to play until they were called in either for dinner or to go to bed.

Winter Sports and Snowmobiles

A 1967 survey by the Athletic Institute in Chicago indicated that at the end of World War II the nation had only 50,000 active snow skiers. By 1967, there were more than 4 million skiers (Kraus [1971], 321). Increased participation in snow skiing was mainly due to the use of artificial snowmaking machines and the increased construction of ski trails, toboggan trails, and winter resorts. In addition, the introduction of improved equipment such as releasable ski bindings (first introduced in 1937 by Hjalmar Hvam after breaking his own leg in a skiing accident) and metal-edged skis made the sport more enjoyable. The ski trails also quickly became crowded with the increased use of snowmobiles.

Throughout the 1930s and 1950s, companies such as Bombardier and Polaris built prototype snow vehicles combining an automobile engine with a sprocket-and-track assembly. Snowmobiles at first proved to be unsafe and unreliable. During the 1960s, with the addition of lightweight fiberglass and improved engines, one- and two-person snowmobiles became readily affordable. Manufacturers and ski resorts began promoting safety and standardized trail signs. Later snowmobile models featured better suspension and shock absorption than the earlier ones. According to the International Snowmobile Manufacturers Association (ISMA), by 1997, snowmobiling was a $5 billion industry with more than 260,000 snow-mobiles sold annually, more than 3 million active riders, 1.8 million registered snowmobiles, and more than 220,000 miles of designated trails (ISMA, "Facts and Statistics about Snowmobiling," n.p.).

TRANSPORTATION AND VACATION

Muscle Cars and Fuel Shortages

In 1964, the automobile world was abuzz as Ford introduced its Mustang sports car. In the same year, Pontiac introduced the GTO. Both were instant successes, and orders topped one million each and ushered in a new era of "muscle cars." Muscle cars were sports cars and certainly not intended for the suburban family. The cars, with 350–450 horsepower engines, appealed to drag racers and those enamored with speed. In 1966, Pontiac added the Firebird and Chevrolet the Camaro. Some family cars, such as the Dodge Dart for example, were modified with new engines, headers, and dual carburetors to achieve maximum speed.

A 1970 study of working-class individuals revealed that tinkering with cars was still a common leisure pursuit during this time. One individual reported, "About twice a week, my buddy and I get out and fix cars. Between us, we've always got a couple of cars we're working on" (Rubin, 186). Another stated, "I go down into the garage and fix the boat, or just play around with the engine of the pick-up [truck]" (Rubin, 187). It was not uncommon to see a camper or a small boat on a trailer parked in a house's driveway, and Rubin discovered that "most camper owners use their vehicles two or three times a year, usually when the husband [takes a scheduled] vacation [from work]" (Rubin, 200).

The increase in automobile speed also increased the number of automobile-related deaths. In 1970 alone, automobile accidents resulted in more than 55,000 deaths, 170,000 permanent injuries, and 3.5 million other injuries (Southerland and McCleery, 228). A publication by Ralph Nader, *Unsafe at Any Speed* (1965), criticized the automobile industry and helped force the industry to begin constructing safer cars. In 1966, the National Traffic and Motor Vehicle Safety Act required safety features including seat belts that had previously been optional equipment.

High-powered and fast automobiles consumed the nation's imagination, but there was little or no regard for fuel efficiency. In late October 1973 through March 1974, the nation faced a nationwide fuel shortage caused by an oil embargo by Middle Eastern countries (the crisis reoccurred in 1978 to 1979). Long lines at gas stations became common, gas prices quickly tripled, and limits were placed on gasoline consumption. The energy crisis prompted a law mandating a national speed limit of 55 miles per hour. The measure was designed to conserve fuel, but it was also saved lives because highway deaths declined by over 20 percent after passage of the law (54,000 in 1973 to 45,000 in 1974) (Marty, 150).

A direct result of the gas shortage was the increase in the use of bicycles and "people friendly" motorcycles; one example was the Honda 750cc. (People friendly was a term applied by the manufacturer to appeal to all individuals rather than a small specific group that would buy a motorcycle.)

Bicycles, the Ten-speed, and the BMX

A 1967 nationwide survey by the Athletic Institute in Chicago revealed that cycling had more than 59 million participants, making it the most popular outdoor recreational activity. In 1975 alone, more than 7.3 million bicycles were sold, and more than 60 percent of those purchases were made by adults. The lightweight ten-speed bicycle became the most desired model.

The ten-speed, modeled after European racing bicycles, had a lightweight tubular frame, narrow tires, handlebar brakes connected by a cable to both the front and rear wheels, and the ability to change sprocket gears to make going up and down hills much easier. By the mid-1980s more than 82 million bicycles were in use nationwide, including the ten-speed and the BMX bike.

In the early 1970s, Bicycle Motocross (BMX), inspired by the documentary *On Any Sunday* (1971) that featured motorcycle motocross, developed as a new sport. Initially, southern California teens raced around their neighborhoods imitating the motorcycle motocross. They jumped curbs and raced on homemade tracks that they built in vacant lots and in backyards. Soon bikers in other cities copied the homegrown sport.

In 1974, the National Bicycle League (NBL) was formed, which turned backyard and street BMX racing into an organized competitive sport. In 1977, it was joined by the American Bicycle Association (ABA) that also organized competitive events. Any 20-inch bicycle could be used for competition as long as the handlebars had grips and a padded crossbar, frame, and handlebar stem. The kickstand and other unnecessary gadgets were removed for safety purposes, and the rider was required to wear a helmet. By the 1990s, bicycle manufacturers sold models specifically designed for BMX racing and street use. In 1997, BMX bikes outsold all other types of bicycles combined (ABABMX.com "What Is the ABA?" n.p.).

Recreational Flying and Jet Safety

By 1970, flying as a recreational sport showed a marked increase in participants with more than 250,000 private pilots who flew for pleasure (Kraus [1971], 330).

Additional aerial pursuits included skydiving, hot-air ballooning, and gliding. However, the most common mode of flying was as a passenger on a jet.

By 1970, jet travel was commonplace, and the Statistical Abstract of the United States reported that more than 171.7 million people chose to fly during that year as commercial passengers. Americans visited travel destinations in the Caribbean, Mexico, Hawaii, and Europe. In 1970, Boeing introduced the 747, a large four-engine jet capable of carrying 365 passengers. Called wide-body aircraft, models competitive with the 747 included the Douglas DC-10 and Lockheed L-1011.

As early as 1966, jet safety was a major concern and prompted the formation of the U.S. Department of Transportation (DOT) to protect the public's interest and provide policy guidelines. Safety was a continued concern as flights statistically increased the frequency of air disasters. On July 31, 1973, 88 people died in a crash during a jetliner landing at Boston's Logan Airport. On December 1, 1974, 94 passengers died when a Miami-to-Washington jet crashed in the Blue Ridge Mountains of Virginia. On July 24, 1975, lightning struck a jet approaching New York's John F. Kennedy International Airport killing 113 people. In that same year on December 29, 11 passengers died and 75 were injured when a bomb from an unknown source exploded in a passenger terminal at New York's LaGuardia Airport. On March 27, 1977, in the worst air disaster to date, two jets collided on the runway at the Canary Islands, a popular tourist vacation area off the coast of Spain, killing more than 570 people. On May 5, 1979, 275 people died when a DC-10 crashed shortly after taking off from Chicago's O'Hare Airport.

As a result of all of these air disasters, during the 1970s the Federal Aviation Administration (FAA) was given cabinet-level powers and charged with providing policies and safety guidelines. The National Transportation Safety Board (NTSB) was restructured as an independent federal agency reporting directly to Congress. The NTSB was responsible for investigating accidents and providing recommendations to prevent future occurrences (Taneja, 24). For example, one federal restriction mandated that commercial jet aircraft with only two engines could not be farther than one hour's flying time from any commercial airport. Flights over the Atlantic and Pacific oceans were reserved for planes with three or more engines such as the Douglas DC-10, Lockheed L-1011, and Boeing 747.

Some members of Congress had concerns that federal agencies should regulate airline fare pricing and establishment of new airline companies. The subsequent Airline Deregulation Act of 1978 allowed consumers access to discount fares and would create a tremendous increase in the number of airline passengers during the 1980s (Taneja, 28).

Amtrak and the Auto-train

By the mid 1960s, most of the nation's intercity passenger train travel was on the brink of collapse. Railroads were no longer a priority, and a vast amount of public funds were applied to airports and highways. In 1965, the California Zephyr (see chapter 4), running at a loss of more than $1 million per year, filed with the Interstate Commerce Commission (ICC) to cease operations. Other rail lines such as the Twentieth Century Limited had already discontinued service. In

February 1970, the Zephyr had its last roundtrip run from Oakland to Sacramento, California, with less than 50 passengers.

In 1971, Amtrak was formed and took over the nationwide operations of all but three intercity passenger railroads. Amtrak eventually maintained more than 500 stations in 46 states (not including Alaska, Hawaii, South Dakota, and Wyoming). Amtrak had difficulty competing with intercity bus travel, and the public maintained a strong desire to travel by automobile.

Shortly after the formation of Amtrak, the Auto-Train Corporation (ATC) was introduced. The Auto-Train, which originated in Alexandria, Virginia, carried both passengers and their automobiles, offering an economical family option for those in the northeast who were traveling to Florida. During its first full year of operation, the ATC carried more than 51,000 cars and 157,000 passengers.

In 1972, other specialty passenger rail service was initiated such as the Las Vegas Party train between Los Angeles, California, and Las Vegas, Nevada, and the Reno Special between San Francisco, California, and Reno, Nevada. Both of these trains capitalized on the appeal of legalized gambling in Nevada. In its first two months of operation, the Reno Special carried more than 35,000 passengers (Southerland and McCleery, 155–163).

Ocean Travel, Vacation Resorts, and Motels

During this period, the travel industry developed as a full-fledged economic industry. Travel agencies that planned trips and offered package vacations to travelers (see chapter 6) became commonplace. By the end of the period, more than eight thousand travel agencies existed nationwide, many offering cruise ship vacation packages.

According to one travel agent, the cruise ship industry incorporated changes and "concentrated on vacation trips in the Caribbean, and created a 'fun ship' image, which attracted many passengers who would have never had the opportunity to travel on the superliners of the 1930s and 1940s. Cruise ships [also] concentrated on creating a casual environment and providing extensive on-board entertainment." In a short time cruise ship travel increased from less than 500,000 passengers per year to more than 4 million by 1979 (Duke University, "Brief History of the Passenger Ship Industry," n.p.).

By 1970, more than 16 million Americans regularly traveled overseas for pleasure vacations, many opting for the quickness of travel by jet aircraft. Trips to Mexico and the Caribbean became commonplace as organizations such as the French-based Club Med offered the options of a relaxed, sport-filled, or fast-paced exotic vacation.

Club Med also catered to the meeting and gathering of singles. Singles were either unmarried or recently divorced adults who represented a growing portion of American society. Club Med introduced "maverick" seating in their dining facilities. Maverick seating involved randomly seating a single individual or a group of single people at a round table for eight, thereby encouraging socialization and making the single traveler feel welcome.

In 1976, there was a new concept in vacation travel with the introduction of a complete all-inclusive vacation offered by SuperClubs in Jamaica. All-inclusive vacation packages included round-trip airfare and ground transportation to and from the resort. In addition, once inside the resort village, the traveler had to pay no additional cost. All meals, drinks (including alcoholic beverages), sporting activities, and other vacation activities were included. A special added feature was they were never allowed to tip resort staff. Many other resorts and major motel chains copied the all-inclusive concept and began to offer their own special vacation packages.

In 1972, the U.S. Bureau of the Census reported that there were 51,860 motels in operation in the United States with 2.5 million rooms available. (After 1970, the terms *hotel* and *motel* were used interchangeably in census statistics.) Although the overall number of motels was down from 60,951 in 1961, the total number of rooms available represented an increase of over 50 percent (quoted in Jakle, 20). The increase was attributed to ever-increasing construction of larger motel chains offering amenities with which the smaller motels could not compete.

In 1974, Holiday Inn (see chapter 6) was the leading motel chain with 1,703 properties and more than 270,000 total rooms, averaging 130,000 room requests daily. By comparison, Best Western with 1,300 properties offered 90,000 rooms; Friendship Inns had 1,087 properties and 70,000 rooms; Ramada with 669 properties offered 91,000 rooms; and Sheraton with only 370 properties had more than 94,000 rooms. By 1987, the overall number of motels would further drop to 40,420, but the total number of rooms climbed to more than 3 million (Jakle 20–21).

CONCLUSION

On December 8, 1980, during a broadcast of *Monday Night Football*, the nation learned that former Beatles band member John Lennon had been shot and killed outside his home in New York City. To many, Lennon's death signified an end to the turbulent period that began when the Beatles first arrived in America.

During the turbulent period from 1964 to 1979, many of the nation's basic foundations of segregation and inequality were broken down. The participation among minorities, especially females, in recreation and leisure activities represented well over 60 percent of the total active population, and their presence in these activities gained acceptance in American society.

In the following years, however, the counterculture would suffer a backlash from the growing rise in conservative attitudes expounded by the election of President Ronald Reagan. Americans began to work more hours, and a new urban work ethic reduced the number of leisure hours that had been attained in previous years.

CHAPTER 8

YUPPIES, STAR WARS, AND MTV: 1980–1992

CHRONOLOGY

1980   John Lennon is assassinated; the Rubik's Cube becomes popular; *Pac-Man* debuts; CNN is established; Ronald Reagan is elected president.

1981   AIDS is identified as a new plague; MTV debuts; IBM introduces personal computers (PCs).

1982   The ERA fails to receive ratification; compact discs (CDs) first become available; Michael Jackson releases his *Thriller* album; EPCOT Center opens at Disney World in Florida.

1983   Trivial Pursuit debuts; *Jane Fonda's Workout Video* is released.

1984   The movie rating PG-13 is created.

1985   The USA for Africa song *We Are the World* debuts.

1986   The StairMaster is introduced; Pictionary debuts; Bill Cosby's *Fatherhood* sells 2.4 million copies; the Nintendo NES and Sega Master System debut.

1987   The New York Stock Exchange suffers a huge drop on "Black Monday."

1988   Pan Am Flight 103 is bombed over Lockerbie, Scotland.

1989   The Berlin Wall falls; the *Exxon Valdez* spills millions of gallons of oil off the Alaskan coastline; the Recording Industry Association of America issues warning labels on music CDs; Sega Genesis debuts.

1990   Congress passes the Americans with Disabilities Act (ADA).

1991   The Soviet Union collapses.

1992   The number of Americans age 65 and older exceeds 32 million.

INTRODUCTION

By 1980, the memory of the Vietnam War was fading, as were the hippies and calls for social change. A new work ethic was espoused by working professionals who came to be called yuppies and who were willing to sacrifice any amount of leisure time in the pursuit of material gain. Overall, shopping was a major leisure pursuit, and legalized gambling of all types would find acceptance nationwide. Americans traveled at record rates; however, a trend toward shorter vacation stays developed, with pleasure trips sometimes lasting only for a long weekend.

Television (TV) was still the overwhelming activity during leisure hours, but the TV set was more likely to be used for either viewing a videocassette or a cable channel than for watching regular broadcast television programs. Movie theaters underwent revitalizations and transformed from the large palaces into mega multiplexes.

The preceding period of sexual freedom would come crashing to a halt as the newly recognized disease of AIDS captured the headlines, and Americans became concerned about "safe sex." The dominant force of the period was the conservative backlash against the preceding years evidenced and best represented by the election of Ronald Reagan as president of the United States.

PUBLIC INTEREST

The Reagan Era, the Evil Empire, Star Wars, and Age Wars

In 1981, after 444 days in captivity, 52 American hostages being held in Iran were released on the day that Ronald Reagan was inaugurated as the fortieth president of the United States. As one of the most popular presidents in U.S. history, Reagan's appeal to many voters was his proposal to return to conservative middle-class values that many felt the turbulent years of the 1960s and 1970s had undone. In lieu of social programs, the Reagan administration shifted its approach to support big business with a supply-side economic theory claiming that if business did well the economic results would trickle down to the American worker.

The new Economic Recovery Tax Act of 1981 allowed significant tax advantages for businesses that triggered a "merger mania" as large corporations bought up other corporations. In a few short years, more than 20 corporate mergers were valued at over $1 billion each, and the gap between the nation's wealthy and poor citizens began to widen. According to historian Eric Foner, "[b]y the mid-1990s, the richest 1 percent of Americans owned 40 percent of the nation's wealth [including 60 percent of all corporate stock], twice their share twenty years earlier" (322). In contrast, by 1990, more than 33 million Americans were classified as living at or below the poverty level, and almost one-half million were homeless.

In August 1981, Reagan dealt unions a severe blow by exerting executive authority and firing more than 11,400 striking members of the Professional Air Traffic Controllers Organization (PATCO). During Reagan's tenure, union membership decreased to less than 16 percent of the working class as opposed to over 35 percent during the 1930s (Gillon, 1250–1251). Reagan's critics claimed that his administration undid the social changes of the New Deal (see chapter 4) and the Great Society (see chapter 6). Severe budget cuts also reduced the amount of federal aid to libraries, playgrounds, parks, cultural institutions, and arts programs. Reagan also revived Cold War tensions (see chapter 6) and described the Soviet Union as an "evil empire."

In 1982, to combat the Soviet threat, Reagan proposed a $26 billion program to develop missiles and a civil defense system. By the mid 1980s, the United States escalated the nuclear arms race with the Soviet Union, and evacuation plans were developed for all the major cities. Many Americans protested and called for a freeze on nuclear arms. One petition garnered more than 2.5 million signatures. In June 1982, more than 550,000 people protested outside the United Nations building in New York City (Rose, 217–222).

It was the impracticability of large-scale evacuation and low survivability of a nuclear attack that shifted Reagan's priorities from civil defense to a Strategic Defense Initiative (SDI). The program called for a spaced-based defense system, which would supposedly destroy any incoming Soviet missiles using armed satellites in the upper stratosphere. The SDI program was quickly dubbed "Star Wars." The Star Wars initiative was never fully employed because the Cold War came to an end with the tearing down of the Berlin Wall in 1989 and the collapse of the Soviet Union in 1991. Some Americans made arguments to continue defense programs, but concerns arose over the expense of the programs, especially considering senior citizens' distress over the depletion of Social Security funds.

By 1992, the number of Americans aged 65 and older exceeded 32 million (more than 12.5 percent of the total population). For the most part, senior citizens were healthier and lived longer than they had during previous times and were active in all kinds of activities, including marathon running, golfing, and swimming. However, not all seniors lived a lavish retirement lifestyle; many relied on Social Security for living expenses. During the 1980s, a Social Security crisis, mainly caused by the simple fact that so many citizens were eligible for benefits, threatened many Americans' retirement.

Concerns for the elderly prompted the formation of two significant organizations. The first, the Gray Panthers, with 80,000 members, pressured Congress "on everything from health insurance to housing costs." In addition, the American Association of Retired Persons (AARP) sought to provide information on aging, economics, and health to seniors and to the general public; the organization also provided senior citizen discounts for entertainment and leisure opportunities such as restaurants, movie theaters, and vacations to its members. By 1992, the AARP claimed more than 28 million members (TIME.com, "Grays on the Go," February 22, 1988).

AIDS, Safe Sex, and "Just Say No"

In 1981, the Centers for Disease Control (CDC) discovered a debilitating disease in the homosexual community. In July 1982, it was officially classified as Acquired Immune Deficiency Syndrome (AIDS). In its simplest terms, AIDS, a frightening fatal disease with no known cure, debilitated the body's immune system. The highly publicized deaths of Hollywood actor Rock Hudson and Broadway producer Michael Bennett, the creator of *A Chorus Line*, brought widespread attention to the virus, but many continued to believe it was strictly a disease spread among homosexuals. Many conservatives and clergy claimed it was the "work of God" and condemned the homosexual lifestyle, which led to further discrimination against homosexuals. Workplace harassment of homosexuals and denial of medical coverage by health insurance agencies and health maintenance organizations (HMOs) was also commonplace.

It took much education to convince the American public that the virus was not confined to homosexuals; the reality was that AIDS could strike anyone. It could be spread by unprotected sex, a blood transfusion, or an infected hypodermic needle. In 1990, CDC officials said that the AIDS epidemic was spreading throughout all factions of American society at an alarming rate. By 1992, the total number of reported cases in the country amounted to more than 500,000. By the year 2000, at least one in one hundred Americans (2.8 million people) were infected. During the same course of time, more than 380,000 Americans died of AIDS (Pendergast and Pendergast, *Encyclopedia of Popular Culture* Vol. 1: 35-37).

The reality of AIDS changed many Americans' daily practices. People performing simple routine procedures such as dentists doing dental work, a school nurse applying a bandage on a child, or a referee at a boxing match began wearing rubber gloves as a precaution against catching the virus. With the inherent dangers associated with sexual contact, safety when engaging in sexual activities was a concern, giving rise to the "safe sex" campaign.

Safe sex proponents encouraged sex education and the use of condoms. Studies revealed that condoms proved effective not only in preventing the spread of AIDS, but also in preventing the spread of other sexually transmitted diseases (STDs) such as syphilis and gonorrhea. By 1992, the CDC reported that 70 percent of teenagers had engaged in sexual activity by the age of 18 and also reported more than 12 million new cases of STDs each year (Pendergast and Pendergast, *Encyclopedia of Popular Culture* Vol. 3: 299). Some Americans expressed moral concerns and preached abstinence and monogamous relationships within the bounds of marriage to suppress the increase in AIDS cases, the spread of STDs, unwed teenage pregnancies, and drug use.

Cocaine was initially seen as a harmless drug used by the rich, and a 1982 national survey estimated that more than 22 million individuals had tried the drug. However, follow-up studies revealed cocaine to be an addictive, dangerous drug, the use of which sometimes resulted in fatal consequences. The media began reporting on a new drug epidemic and especially on the claim that crack cocaine was a widespread problem among inner-city poor people. (Crack was a cheaper version of cocaine that was smoked rather than snorted.) In 1986, the national concern over drugs caused President Reagan to declare a "national crusade" for a "war on drugs" and prompted first lady Nancy Reagan to institute the "just say no" campaign to combat drugs (Bondi, *American Decades: 1980–1989*, 396).

The ERA, Gender Equality, and the Americans with Disabilities Act

During the 1970s, a major feminist issue was the potential passage of the Equal Rights Amendment (ERA) to the U.S. Constitution. The ERA met stiff resistance, especially among conservatives who argued that the ERA would allow sexual promiscuity, reproductive and contraceptive rights, communal living, and homosexuality. In 1982, the ERA was defeated (the ten-year limit had expired) after it garnered only 30 of the 38 state votes needed for ratification.

Despite the defeat of the ERA, some barriers of female exclusion were finally broken down. In 1983, Columbia University became the last of the Ivy League schools to admit women. Fraternal societies such as the Rotary, Elks, Lions, and Kiwanis Clubs and the Masons were required by the Supreme Court to allow female membership. However, the practice of excluding women and African Americans as full members at many private golf country clubs continued into the twenty-first century.

One previously excluded group that made significant civil rights gains during this period were disabled Americans. In 1992, more than 37 million Americans were classified as permanently or significantly disabled. In addition, almost 450,000 Americans joined the ranks of the disabled each year as a result of birth defects, chronic illness, aging, accidents, and war (Mitchell and Hillman, 190–194). In the cases of those with developmental disabilities such as mental retardation and cerebral palsy, many doctors and family members simply removed them from society and placed them in institutions. In the mid-1970s, widespread abuse at such institutions and lack of civil liberties for all disabled individuals were brought to the public's attention. As a result, three significant federal legislations intended to provide inclusion of disabled individuals into society were introduced: the Education of All Handicapped Children Act of 1975, the Amateur Sports Act of 1978, and the Americans with Disabilities Act (ADA) of 1990.

The ADA, in particular, afforded disabled individuals equal access to public accommodations and facilities. Amusement parks, sports stadiums, and movie theaters were required to remove barriers and provide designated accessible areas. The inclusion of ramps and elevators in many public places allowed equal access to disabled individuals as well as to children in strollers and the elderly.

In addition, nationwide programs for the disabled gained mainstream acceptance. A program known as the Very Special Arts offered programs in music, dance, and acting to more than 1.5 million disabled Americans nationwide. Wheelchair Sports USA (WCSUSA), affiliated with the U.S. Olympic committee, promoted active participation and competition by those using wheelchairs in activities including water skiing, basketball, archery, fencing, and track and field. By 2000, the Special Olympics (founded in 1968) was staffed by more than 500,000 volunteers administering programs in all 50 states in more than 25,000 communities, providing sports competitions for more than one million individuals with mental retardation (Kraus et al., 161).

Planned Communities, Vacation Homes, and Time Shares

In contrast to the planned communities of the past, Pine Ridge Estates near Ocala, Florida, a development of 4,800 homes, was devoted entirely to horse owners. The properties bordering on the community's equestrian trails were middle-class, modest-sized homes with facilities for housing between two to six horses each. One resident said, "Here anytime I want to ride, I just get on my horse and I can travel for miles. . . . There are twenty-eight miles of equestrian trails, ten parks, and a ninety-four acre showplace that features an elaborate riding center, stables, tack room, show ring, and viewing terrace" (Jury, 119).

With the advent of prosperity, both after World War II and during the 1980s, many Americans were able to afford second homes or vacation homes. For those who could not afford a second home, a concept known as time-share developed. Time-shares were usually part of condominium vacation home developments that included leisure amenities. Typically, a time-share buyer would purchase not on an entire home but a share of a home in a two- or four-week per year portion. Later developments in the industry allowed time-share owners to trade weeks in exchange for different portions of the year, stays at other resorts, and even passage on cruise ships.

Parks, Recreation, and the Overcrowded Outdoors

In 1992, the U.S. Statistical Abstract reported that the national parks system contained 76.5 million acres of designated space and recorded more than 270 million annual visitors. In addition, more than 724 million people visited state park and recreation facilities on 11.8 million acres (Statistical Abstract [1994], 251–253). Despite the supposedly vast amounts of allocated space, the state and national parks were severely overcrowded during this period as interest in the outdoors reached record highs.

Time magazine reported, "Everywhere, authorities are having to ration the outdoors with lotteries, permits and reservations for everything from biking to hiking." Beginning in the early 1980s, the national park service began the process of selling campsites in advance through a Ticketron telephone reservation system (a semiautomated, telephone ticket sales service). At Yosemite, campsite tickets were offered for sale eight weeks in advance and were sold in less than five minutes. A very small number of campsite tickets were held back for daily purchase. According to the Sporting Goods Manufacturing Association (SGMA), in 1990, 36.9 million people camped in tents, and 18.9 million in recreational vehicles (RVs). Another 18.6 million individuals went hiking and backpacking (SGMA "Sports Participation Trends" 1995 Press Release, n.p.).

Water permits were also in high demand and short supply. Most of the maximum of 22,000 slots for rafting down the Colorado River through the Grand Canyon were held back for commercial companies and the small number available to the general public had a three-to-five-year waiting list (TIME.com, "Take a Number," July 23, 1990).

In 1992, the U.S. Census Bureau reported a continued increase in the number of recreational boats in America to more than 16.2 million and the total amount of participants in boating activities at 41.7 million people (Statistical Abstract [1994], 259). Many boaters were middle- and working-class individuals who were able to afford a boat based on better financing opportunities available to them as lending agencies expanded services to include long-term boat loans in excess of 10 years, similar to home mortgages.

The air lanes over the Grand Canyon were crowded with more than 50,000 small airplane and helicopter flights for tourists each year during this period. In one incident in 1986, 25 people died when an airplane and a helicopter collided over the Grand Canyon.

Other accidents during this time affected the environment. In 1989, an oil spill from the *Exxon Valdez* tanker off the coast of Alaska killed and contaminated many fish sought after by recreational fishing enthusiasts. Environmental groups such as Greenpeace and the Sierra Club sought to educate the public on environmental issues and maintain a balance between the needs of humans and protection of the environment that humans so much sought to use (TIME.com, "Ah, Wilderness!" July 11, 1988).

In 1992, 37.4 million fishing licenses were issued for saltwater, freshwater, and fly-fishing (Statistical Abstract [1994], 257). Magazines such as *The Fisherman* supported a "catch and release" program in which immediately after catching a fish a fisherman returned it to the water alive. Almost every state maintained a fishing hatchery and set rules and limits to maintain sufficient stock for fishing seasons and protection of the environment (Kraus et al., 96).

In 1992, hunting proponents cited that over $481 million was collected for the sale of 31.3 million hunting licenses, which in turn served to protect the environment (Statistical Abstract [1994], 257). Some antihunting groups protested, claiming that accidental human injuries and deaths (averaging around 150 to 170 per year) in addition to animal extinction made hunting dangerous to the environment. Nevertheless, both the debate and hunting continued well into the following decades.

LIFESTYLES

Leisure during Daily Life and "Shop Till You Drop"

By 1990, the U.S. Census Bureau reported that over 75 percent of the population (more than 190 million people) lived either in urban cities or in nearby suburbs. Those who still lived and worked on farms dropped to less than 2 percent of the total population. Regardless of whether a person lived in an urban, suburban, or rural area some of the leisure activities people participated in remained similar. In 1990, a *Fortune* magazine survey reported that Americans "showed the kinds of typical leisure pursuits that represent family interests and moderate level expenditures: the full range of sports, games, and hobbies including golfing, car repair and restoration, [ocean] cruises for single individuals, family camping and travel to theme parks, and similar involvements" and also "make heavy use of public recreation and park facilities like swimming pools, golf courses and tennis courts, arts centers, senior centers, and other programs" (*Fortune*, August 13, 1990: 107).

For many of the urban working class, leisure still meant inexpensive socializing and recreation. During the hot summer months much socializing and recreation took place on the streets within the working-class neighborhoods. Fire hydrants were sometimes opened and turned on. Municipalities began providing sprinkler caps for the hydrants that would conserve water and also provide a sprinkling spray for children and adults alike to use to cool off. Puddles from the hydrants provided small temporary ponds where some children would improvise by floating small blocks of wood and ice cream sticks as rafts and boats. Children would also play other simple games in the streets or on the sidewalks. Older teens and adults might play cards, dominoes, pitch pennies, or socialize.

Americans, as a whole, embarked on a new spending spree, many buying on credit. According to Juliet Schor shopping was "the most popular weekday evening out-of-home entertainment [and became] a leisure activity in its own right." Between 1980 and 1985, Americans purchased more than 62 million microwaves, 57 million washing machines, 88 million automobiles, 105 million color televisions, 63 million VCRs, 31 million cordless telephones, and 30 million answering machines for 91 million households and "people became accustomed to the material rewards of prosperity" (Schor, 107–112).

A large portion of the consumer market was made up of teenagers and college-age students. Richard Kraus found that they were "a prime target for the marketing of travel opportunities, fast foods, rock music concerts and other forms of entertainment, cars, clothes, and a host of other leisure-oriented products and services. They congregate by the thousands at spring breaks at Florida or Texas beachside resorts, and flock through shopping malls, attending video-game arcades and movie theaters" ([1994], 184).

Yuppies, Work, and Health Clubs

In 1899 in his work *Theory of the Leisure Class*, Thorstein Veblen coined the phrase *conspicuous consumption*, claiming that the Victorian-era idle rich (see chapter 1) consumed in order to display their accumulation of wealth and also displayed their "conspicuous leisure" by not working (TIME.com, "The Superrich are Different," May 23, 1988). During the 1980s, Veblen's observations were reversed as a new class of individuals called yuppies flaunted their wealth and accumulation of material goods mainly through a desire to work excessive hours.

Yuppies were classified as those generally born between 1945 and 1959 who were white-collar professionals living in urban areas and "who thought little of working late at the office, bringing work home, and working weekends if necessary." Careers in investment banking, expensive automobiles such as BMWs and Porsches, designer clothes, upscale health clubs, and chic restaurants replaced the 1960s desire for social causes. By conservative estimates more than 20 million Americans were classified as yuppies and being busy was advertised as a sign of status (Bondi, *American Decades: 1980–1989*, 391–392).

Overall, there was a shift in the number of hours worked. In 1987, a Harris poll reported that the average number of hours worked per week had actually increased from 40.6 hours per week in 1973 to 48.4 hours per week. Although U.S. Bureau of Labor statistics indicated that the average workweek was at 34.9 hours, what was not factored in was the unpaid overtime hours and second jobs that most Americans held or were required to perform. Vacations, when taken at all, tended to be nothing more than long weekends, as "Americans came to worship career status as a measure of individual worth, and many were willing to sacrifice any amount of leisure time to get ahead" (TIME.com, "How America Has Run Out of Time," April 24, 1989).

In 1990, Bureau of Labor statistics reported that "typically after five years on the job" the average American full-time worker received "11 official holidays and 12 days—slightly more than two weeks—of paid vacation." The report also indicated that among American workplaces, extended vacation policies tended to be in unionized companies, which were in severe decline. The overall paid vacation time actually paled in comparison to that received by workers in other industrialized nations. Companies in Great Britain and France each provided 8 paid hol-

Health clubs offered a variety of exercise machines and also served as a place to socialize. Author's archives.

idays, 25 vacation days, and a 39-hour average workweek. Germans worked a 38-hour week and were provided 10 holidays and 30 vacation days (TIME.com, "You Must Be Very Busy," August 20, 1990).

For yuppies "playing hard" became associated with the attitude required for the demanding job environment. Most yuppies found that membership in a private health club offering high-tech equipment could satisfy the need for being able to play hard. By 1987, *Time* magazine reported that there were more than 20,000 health clubs nationwide with over $5 billion spent on membership. Americans also spent $738 million on exercise equipment for their homes. (By comparison, in 1977, sales were only $5 million.) By 1992, 16.6 million Americans belonged to health clubs, and participation in all forms of fitness increased. More than 33 million people trained with weights, 32 million trained by aerobics, and 29.6 million exercised by fitness walking. The most renowned form of dance fitness exercise program was Jazzercise. Founded in the late 1960s by Judi Missett, there were eventually more than 1,700 franchised Jazzercise instructors and 26 million participants nationwide (Kraus et al., 101).

In 1989, the fastest-growing form of aerobic exercise was stair climbing. In 1986, the StairMaster company introduced a simplified stair-climbing machine on which "[e]xercisers push a pair of bicycle-like pedals that move up and down instead of in circles, and a computerized screen gives such data as the number of 'flights' climbed and the 'distance' traveled" (TIME.com, "America Goes Stair

Crazy," December 18, 1989). In 1992, the Sporting Goods Manufacturers Association (SGMA) charted the rapid increase in stair-climbing machines and reported the number of the machines at 18.4 million (up from 1.9 million in 1987). In addition, Nordic Track Ski machines numbered 8.3 million, running treadmills 14.4 million, stationary cycles 38 million, and other types of resistance machines at more than 35 million (SGMA "Sports Participation Trends" 1995 Press Release, n.p.).

In conjunction with the fitness craze, fitness books and videos reached best-seller status. *Jane Fonda's Workout Video* (1983) was the top-selling video (including Hollywood films) for 1983 and 1984. Fonda followed this success with five other best-selling workout videos, spawning a series of exercise books and exercise videos by celebrities such as Raquel Welch and Richard Simmons.

To some people, working out was not nearly as important as wearing the right workout clothes. Specialty sneakers were made specifically for individual activities including aerobics, basketball, running, and walking. By 1989, sneakers were selling at 400 million pairs per year and became a fashion trend that extended beyond the health clubs (Panati, 433). Americans from all walks of life wore sneakers and workout clothes to go shopping or to the mall, regardless of whether or not they actually participated in a fitness activity.

Unique Leisure, Reenactments, and Casino Gambling

Leisure took on some interesting and sometimes unique forms for many in mainstream American life. During the late 1970s and early 1980s, the National Rattlesnake Hunt in Morris, Pennsylvania attracted more than five thousand hopefuls for the "sole purpose of picking up live, lethal rattlesnakes." No previous experience or club membership was required other than paying a one-dollar donation to a local volunteer fire department. Instructions were simple: "To catch a rattlesnake, you pin his head with your catcher, then get your thumb and forefinger and index finger on the head" (Jury, 138–141).

The Barbershop Harmony Society dedicated itself to singing four-part harmony of popular songs dating from 1860 to 1930. The organization claimed more than 40,000 members in more than 800 chapters throughout the United States and Canada and celebrated its fifteenth anniversary in 1988. The Society for Creative Anachronism recreated and lived an eleventh-century Middle Age lifestyle during elaborate weekend and weeklong events. One seven-year member said, "I enjoy the fact that there's an actual life that I'm living. It's not just a simple activity like bowling" (Jury, 113). For those who wished to go back to the eleventh century but only had a few hours, there was Medieval Times, a dinner theater where medieval knights on horseback recreated jousting events at six nationwide locations. Other reenactments included the National Muzzle-Loading Rifle Association reenactments, in Friendship, Indiana, during which participants lived in teepees and tents and dressed in authentic attire from the French and Indian War period of American history. Ian Frazier noted that participants in this reenactment "number in the tens of thousands, and they hold rendezvous all over the country" (144).

Civil War reenactments claimed the largest number of participants. In 1988, the 125th anniversary of the Battle of Gettysburg drew more than 12,000 reenactors and more than 100,000 spectators. Numerous magazines supported the endeavor including *Civil War News*, *Blue and Gray*, and *Camp Chase Gazette* (Pendergast and Pendergast, *Encyclopedia of Popular Culture*, Vol. 1: 521–523). Aside from reenacting Civil War battles, many hundreds of thousands of Americans known as Civil War buffs actively read about the Civil War and visited historic battlefields.

Other leisure activities included dog sledding, ice fishing, lounging at the beach, playing shuffleboard, making handicrafts, attending weekend yard sales or flea markets, cleaning museum artifacts, building elaborate model train setups, or attending outdoor hot-air balloon festivals. Other Americans spent leisure time hunting in local parks with metal detectors, collecting bottle caps or other collectibles, and participating in thousands of other activities.

Gambling became one of the most common forms of entertainment outside the home. In 1985, the U.S. Statistical Abstract reported attendance at horse racing events nationwide totaled more than 73.3 million (at 104 tracks), and attendance at dog racing events was 23.8 million (at 48 tracks) (Statistical Abstract [1986], 216). The tracks also offered offtrack betting (OTB) in which televised simulcasts allowed gamblers to bet on greyhound, horse, and jai alai events from around the country. The most popular form of gambling was gambling done at gaming casinos that expanded well beyond Las Vegas (see chapter 6).

On the New Jersey Shore, a rundown amusement area and boardwalk of Atlantic City was revitalized with legalized gambling. The first casino opened in 1978 and was followed by numerous others. By 1980, moral and social acceptance of gambling was changing. *Time* magazine reported, "Even the most stalwart opponents of gambling [were] breaking down. Louisiana, whose constitution order[ed] the legislature to 'suppress' gambling, decided to call it something else [gaming] and in less than two years has gone from no gambling to riverboat gambling to approving the largest casino in the world on five riverfront acres in downtown New Orleans" (TIME.com, "The Great Casino Salesman," May 3, 1993).

Riverboat gambling was revived along the nation's waterways in replica nineteenth-century showboats (see chapter 1). In 1992, the *Dubuque Casino Belle*, accommodating 2,500 guests, traveled the Mississippi River offering four decks of entertainment and casinos with "over 500 slot and poker machines and 26 gaming tables" (Kraus et al., 209). Although the *Dubuque Casino Belle* itself was short-lived, others followed. The *St. Joseph Frontier Casino* cruised along the Missouri River, and cruise ships converted into gambling boats were docked on Lake Michigan and in nearby rivers within minutes of Chicago.

By 1992, at least 22 states had legalized casino gambling with yearly betting in excess of $286 billion (Kraus [1994], 305). In addition, every state except Utah and Hawaii had at least a legalized lottery and numbers game (see chapter 3). *Newsweek* reported that "Americans [spent another] estimated $278 billion on everything from state-run lotteries to church-run bingo" (quoted in Kraus [1994], 305).

Gambling, however, proved to be an addictive, compulsive behavior on par with alcoholism and drug addiction for some Americans. In 1989, *Time* reported, "A minimum of 15 million men and women routinely bet beyond their means, making them gambling addicts" (quoted in Panati, 438). Some casinos offered to run help lines for gamblers. The Argosy Casino in Kansas City, Missouri advertised the following: "Gambling Problem? [Call] 1–888-BETS-OFF" (*Kansas City*, Vol. 5, No. 2: 2).

Singles and Homosexual Leisure Services

The safe sex campaign did not necessarily send throngs of Americans into the bonds of marriage. In fact, just the opposite happened. There was a trend toward more divorces and single-parent households. By 1992, more than 71 million individuals (over 39 percent of the adult population) were single (either never married, separated, divorced, or widowed). What became classified as a "single lifestyle" was increasingly more common during the 1980s. The Bryn Mawr Presbyterian Church in Pennsylvania provided "a singles council for unmarried adults" offering activities including volleyball, music lessons, and a walking club. Long Beach, California, with a population of 385,000, instituted a progressive parks and recreation aquatic program that offered a specific singles club opened to all unmarried adults over the age of 25 (Kraus [1994], 71, 337). However, the image persisted that a single individual, especially a woman, either could not attract a member of the opposite sex or was homosexual.

Homosexuals tended to self-segregate and developed "a homosexual second society" that existed in every large city and also in many smaller ones. Not unlike the plight of African American segregation, homosexuals faced discrimination in travel and leisure opportunities. Publications such as *Ferrari's Places of Interest* (Phoenix: Ferrari Publications Inc. 1994/1995) and online services such as Gaytravel.com listed safe, "gay friendly" resorts and travel services. Brenda Pitts reported that homosexuals also broadened their leisure base by forming recreation clubs and activities on the local, state, national, and international levels. Activities mirrored those of all other Americans including camping, bicycling, skiing, swimming, volleyball, travel, and running (3).

ENTERTAINMENT

Television, Videocassettes, Cable TV, and MTV

In 1983, a United Media poll reported that over 74 percent of Americans watched an average of more than two and a half hours of television a day, and Nielson surveys reported that televisions were left on for more than seven and a half hours a day while other activities took place. Other leisure activities within the home included reading a newspaper (67 percent), listening to music (50 percent), talking on the telephone (42 percent), exercise (35 percent), spending an evening talking (30 percent), reading a book (24 percent), working on hobbies (24 percent), working in the yard or garden (22 percent), and sexual activities (11 percent) (Ibrahim, 177–179).

In 1980, *Dallas* was the top-rated television show. The "Who Shot J. R.?" episode (1980) was viewed by 106 million people and was the most-watched individual television episode to date. The show would be eclipsed by the two-hour series finale to *M*A*S*H* (February 28, 1983), which was seen by more than 120 million people (Stephen Battaglio, "The Big Business of Fond Farewells," *The*

New York Times, 29 July 2001 AR:23). In 1983, more than 100 million people watched *The Day After*, a made-for-television movie that dealt with the aftermath of a nuclear attack on the United States. The single largest television audience during this period was for an 18-hour miniseries called *The Winds of War* that was viewed by more than 140 million people (Marty, 279). Other popular shows of the period included *60 Minutes*, *The Cosby Show*, *Roseanne*, and *The Simpsons*.

One of the most enduring television shows of the period was NBC's *Saturday Night Live*. It was first broadcast in October 1975 and aired continuously through the remainder of the century. The show aired late in the evening (11:30 P.M. to 1:00 A.M.) and replaced traditional reruns at that hour, quickly making it acceptable for young Americans aged 18 to 25 to stay home on Saturday nights.

By 1992, over 98 percent of all American homes had at least one television, and over 75 percent had a remote control. In that same year, VCRs (see chapter 7) were in over 75 percent of all homes and sold more than 11 million units. In turn, Americans rented more than 3.5 billion videotapes, and network program viewership declined in favor of watching prerecorded videocassettes (Kammen, 206). When not watching videos, viewers could use the remote control to channel surf through the many channels offered by cable television.

By 1980, cable TV was available in about 20 percent of all American homes and had about 600,000 subscribers. Initially, cable channels bought old syndicated television shows to rebroadcast but quickly created original concept networks such as Home Box Office (HBO) that offered movies, a 24-hour sports channel called the Entertainment and Sports Programming Network (ESPN), Cable News Network (CNN) with twenty-four-hour news programming, and Black Entertainment Television (BET) (Hilliard and Keith, 164). Other channels featured programming on weather, comedy, food, travel, history, and home shopping. By 1992, cable claimed more than 50.5 million household subscribers and was available in over 60 percent of all American homes. The most notable cable channel was MTV.

In 1981, the Music Television Video network (MTV) first aired, successfully merging television and music by presenting 24-hour, round-the-clock music videos. (A music video was a short film made to accompany a song that lasted the length of the song.) MTV was an instant success among the 13-to-35-year-old age group. In its first year, MTV's audience numbered 2 million and within a few short years numbered more than 22 million. Conservatives, among them President Reagan, criticized the video productions as morally harmful because of the types of images many of the videos portrayed. By 1990, MTV was available in 50 million households. MTV would prove a viable market for politics during the 1992 presidential campaign when future president Bill Clinton made an appearance on the network and spoke to the young audience on topics from Elvis Presley to AIDS (Pendergast and Pendergast, *Encyclopedia of Popular Culture* Vol. 2: 435–438).

Mall Video Arcades, Pac-Man, and Nintendo

In 1971, the first coin-operated video arcade game was Computer Space, a simple game with a rotating knob and fire button in which the player attempted to hit an attacking flying saucer. Within a few years, home video game units were also available including Odyssey by Magnavox and the Atari game system offering simple video game versions of tennis and hockey. Technological advancements led to better game designs and graphics. As a result, the number of video games increased, and video game arcades opened in shopping malls and other public places. By 1982, *Play Meter Magazine* reported that there were more than 1.5 million arcade machines in operation in more than 24,000 arcades and 400,000 street locations. In 1981, thousands of teens and young adults spent hours in the mall video arcades dropping countless quarters and tokens into the game slots and spending around $5 billion. By 1992, the arcade and video game business made more money each year than Hollywood movies, Nevada gambling, and professional spectator sports combined (Kent, 152).

The perennial favorites among video games included *Space Invaders* (1978) an attempt to shoot off advancing munching aliens, *Asteroids* (1979) a deep space game requiring the blasting of flying saucers, *Donkey Kong* (1981) the lovable stubborn jumping monkey, and *Mario Bros.* (1983) the affable plumber and his brother Luigi who rid the sewers of nasty creatures, and new games appeared almost weekly. Although other games were popular, *Pac-Man* (1980) was simply the most successful video game of all time. John Sellers described the game this way: "Using only a joystick with a red knob, you controlled a fast-moving yellow creature that resembled a block of cheese with a slice hacked out of it. . . . eating 244 dots—no more, no less—while skillfully avoiding four unpredictable and brightly colored ghosts. No shooting, just chomping" (56). *Pac-Man* appeared in

In-home entertainment and exercise was common during the 1980s and continued through the remainder of the century. Author's archives.

cover stories of *Time* and *People*, was the subject of four books on the *New York Times* best-seller list, was the basis of a Saturday morning television cartoon that aired from 1982 to 1985, and even prompted the creation a new breakfast cereal (Sellers, 56–59).

The success of the mall video game arcades began to fade after 1983. The decline was attributed to growing concerns as the arcades were afforded juvenile delinquency status and some parents and mall owners started a cleanup campaign to rid the malls of the video arcades. Others simply dismissed the games as merely a fad that would eventually disappear. The main factor in the arcades' decline was the development of Nintendo.

In 1985, at a time when some wondered whether the video game fad was over, the Nintendo Entertainment System (NES) entered the market and quickly became the top-selling toy—even outselling the long-standing favorite, Barbie. At first, not wishing to align itself with either mall arcades or a defunct fad, Nintendo advertised itself as a family entertainment system (*GameInformer* magazine, June 2002: 102). In reality, Nintendo was played by the same individuals who frequented the mall arcades, only now they played the games alone and "actually wanted to stay home" (Sellers, 150). Nintendo's competitors included Atari, Coleco Vision, and Mattel's Intellivison. However, by 1992 Nintendo controlled over 85 percent of the home video game market with Nintendo systems in more than 30 million American homes.

Board Games, Fads, Baseball Card Collecting, and Dungeons and Dragons

Card games and board games such as chess, checkers, Scrabble, and Monopoly remained favorites for in-home entertainment. In 1985, Monopoly celebrated its fiftieth golden anniversary and staged nationwide tournaments with the final matches held in Atlantic City, New Jersey. The grand prize was $15,140, which was the equivalent of all of the money in a standard Monopoly game. In 1983, a new board game called Trivial Pursuit was the latest rage. At one point, the game was back ordered by one million games (Marty, 286). In the game, contestants collected small different colored pie-shaped pieces by correctly answering trivia questions from a series of random questions in six categories: people and places, arts and entertainment, history, science and nature, sports and leisure, and wild card.

In 1986, another new game that quickly became a home favorite was Pictionary. The game entailed the players competing in teams. One individual would attempt to draw a specified item written on a card selected at random from the game set while the other player or players on that person's team guessed what the drawing was. Points were earned based on which team could guess what the drawing represented in the shortest amount of time. By 1988, Pictionary was the best-selling game in the nation.

Other fads of the period included Cabbage Patch dolls, Teenage Mutant Ninja Turtles, Hacky Sack, Wacky Wall Walkers, and Rubik's Cube. In 1980, Rubik's Cube was marketed in America, and within two years sales of the puzzle topped 100 million worldwide. Charles Panati described the cube as "the six-sided plastic cube [with] nine colored squares in rows of three, and the rows could be rotated to achieve different color configurations" (434). The idea was to rotate the cubes until each side was the same color. The problem was that the face could be rotated randomly in 43 quintillion positions, but only one was the correct solution.

By the mid-1980s, Hacky Sack, a soft leather ball a little larger than a golf ball that was kicked with the side of the foot between players, sold more than 1.2 million units and was considered a national sport on college campuses. In addition, the brightly colored Wacky Wall Walkers, gummy, octopus-like objects that when thrown against a wall would stick and proceed to walk down the wall in a spider-like fashion, sold more than 220 million units in a five-year period (Panati, 434).

During the late 1980s, baseball card collecting became a lucrative business, as did autographed memorabilia. Collectors sought mint-condition baseball cards, the most desirable being an original Honus Wagner card (see chapter1) and a rookie Mickey Mantle card. Sports players, both current and retired, appeared at card collector conventions, and fans waited in long lines after having paid a fee for the players' autographs. Prices varied depending on the status of the player.

An escape from the real world was possible with the role-playing games that were popular during this time. Dungeons and Dragons was unlike any other game of the century in that it was a role-playing game that did not even require a board. One player was the "dungeon master," and other players played the role of another character by rolling a special set of dice, which in turn determined the character's attributes. The game had numerous rules and was a mystery for most of the players as only the dungeon master knew where the game would lead.

Newspapers, Travel Magazines, and Mega-seller Books

Although 70 percent of Americans reported reading a daily newspaper, less than 20 percent actually spent more than a half an hour reading. In 1982, the appearance of daily newspapers changed with the introduction of *USA Today*. The nationwide daily newspaper was the first to use color photographs and feature quick-reading, brief stories similar to television snippets (Marty, 280). Other newspapers copied the format. A significant change was noted between morning and evening newspaper circulation. According to the U.S. Statistical Abstract, by the end of 1992, morning newspaper circulation increased from 387 publications (circulation of 29.4 million) in 1980 to 623 publications (circulation of 43.1 million). Evening newspaper circulation declined from 1,388 publications (circulation of 32.8 million) to 954 publications (circulation of 17 million) (Statistical Abstract [2000], 576). The decline in evening publications was attributed to the fact that more Americans watched evening news programs on television instead of reading newspapers.

Overall, the number of magazines continued to increase and numbered more than 11,500 by 1992. Specialty magazines continued to dominate new publications including new magazines on exercise and video games. *GameInformer*, which was first published in 1990, provided advice and hints on mastering video games. The running boom triggered two mass-market magazines: *Runners World* and *The Runner*, each with a circulation of more than 275,000. In 1987, both magazines were purchased by Rodale Press (a company specializing in health and fitness magazines) and were published as a single magazine titled *Runners World*.

In the mid-1980s, new travel publications appeared including *Travel Today*,

Trips, *Traveler*, and *European Travel and Life*. According to *Time* magazine, these new magazines "pushed out the boundaries of traditional travel writing by including information for impulse travelers as well as careful planners . . . [and] have the latest information for the fast-growing ranks of short-trip takers and long weekenders." The new magazines joined the century-old *Travel-Holiday* (circulation of 800,000) and *Travel and Leisure* (circulation of 1.1 million) an upscale travel magazine that premiered in 1971 (TIME.com, "Telling Readers Where To Go," March 28, 1988).

During this period, the total number of books sold rose from 1.8 billion to more than 2.2 billion. By 1990, bookstore chains such as Dalton and Waldenbooks opened in suburban shopping malls and offered individuals access to mass-market paperbacks and mega-seller hardcover books. (A mega-seller was a hardcover book that sold exceptionally well.) During the period, 12 nonfiction books and 13 novels each sold more than one million copies in hardcover. Ten of the novels were by three authors; romance novelist Danielle Steel wrote four of them including *Daddy* and *Kaleidoscope*. Tom Clancy wrote three of the mega-sellers as the espionage novels *Clear and Present Danger*, *The Cardinal of the Kremlin*, and *Red Storm Rising*, and Stephen King wrote three as the horror novels *The Dark Half*, *The Tommyknockers*, and *It*. Others included *Iacocca: An Autobiography* (1988) and Bill Cosby's *Fatherhood* (1986); each sold more than 2.4 million copies in hardcover (Panati, 466–471).

Concerns about nuclear destruction were evident in Hal Lindsey's publication of *The Late Great Planet Earth* (1970), a mix of apocalyptical biblical prophecies and political and scientific beliefs. The book sold more than nine million copies by 1980, and by 1992, it sold an additional 19 million copies (Rose, 221).

Break Dancing, *Urban Cowboy*, and *Dirty Dancing*

In the early 1980s, break dancing emerged in New York City and quickly spread to the streets of Los Angles. Break dancing was improvised dancing to hip-hop music (see chapter 9) that combined acrobatic spins and was performed on a piece of cardboard on the street.

It was a series of Hollywood films that most influenced contemporary dance styles. In 1980, the movie *Urban Cowboy* (1980) kicked off a renewed interest in country two-step dancing. The movie captured some of the real-life goings-on in an actual Texas honky-tonk—Gilley's in Houston, Texas—and also gave rise to an increase in the number of people wearing western-style clothing and cowboy boots. *Flashdance* (1983) triggered a different fashion trend that included leg warmers, tank tops, and workout clothes. *Dirty Dancing* (1987), a film about a dance instructor at a Catskills resort during the early 1960s, quickly became a cultural phenomenon. The movie's soundtrack album sold more than ten million copies, spurred a Broadway show, a nationwide tour, and a short-lived television series. Nationwide dance studios reported that participation in dance classes doubled. The film also renewed interests in old dance favorites such as the cha-cha and mambo and also sparked new interest in the lambada, a sensual Latin dance involving close pelvic contact between partners.

Theme Parks and Amusement Parks

During the 1980s, Disney expanded its theme park in Florida, adding EPCOT Center (Experimental Prototype Community of Tomorrow) in 1982, Disney-MGM Studios (1989), the Typhoon Lagoon water park (1989), and numerous hotels. Disney-MGM combined the theme park idea with Hollywood movies, creating attractions and rides based on popular movies such as *Star Wars* and *Indiana Jones*. One of the Disney hotels, the Grand Floridian, was the single largest

The world's tallest roller coaster at Cedar Point Amusement Park in Sandusky, Ohio. Amusement parks were favorite pastimes throughout the entire century. Courtesy of Cedar Point Amusement Park.

hotel in the southeast portion of the country. Disney World, Florida, was far and away the top amusement park in the country with more than 30 million visitors per year. In 1990, Disneyland, California, expanded to more than 470 acres, more than six times the size of the original, and attracted more than 14 million visitors per year. At a distant third was Universal Studios, Hollywood, with 5.1 million visitors per year (Fladager, "Amusement Park Attendance Statistics" n.p.).

Sea World parks, for example, which featured live whales, dolphins, and other sea creatures, opened in Florida (4.5 million visitors per year), California (4 million), Ohio (1.5 million), and Texas (1.4 million). Both Opryland in Nashville, Tennessee, and Dollywood in Pigeon Forge, Tennessee (each drawing 2 million visitors per year) offered a country music concept theme park. In Fort Mill, South Carolina, a Christian theme park called Heritage USA attracted more than 5 million visitors per year. The oldest amusement park in continuous operation was Cedar Point, off Lake Erie in Sandusky, Ohio, which attracted more than 3.5 million visitors per year (Cedar Point n.p.). By 1990, total attendance at amusement parks nationwide topped 254 million.

MUSIC AND THEATER

Broadway and Record-Breaking Performances

In 1984, *A Chorus Line* broke the Broadway endurance record set by *Grease* (see chapter 7), and when it finally closed in 1990, after 6,137 performances, it was the longest-running show in Broadway history. *A Chorus Line* featured a very simple stage setting and a story centered on auditioning Broadway dancers. Two other shows would each surpass *A Chorus Line*. In 1982, *Cats* opened and ran until September 2000 for an all-time Broadway record of 7,485 performances. In 1987, *Les Misérables* opened and the following year *The Phantom of the Opera*, and both were still running in the year 2000. *Les Misérables* closed on May 18, 2003 after 6,680 performances and *The Phantom of the Opera* was still running in 2003 at 6,390 performances ("Longest Running Broadway Shows in History," n.p.).

Unlike previous Broadway productions, *Cats*, *Les Misérables* and *The Phantom of the Opera* each were proven stage hits in London before debuting on Broadway. They also featured elaborate sets, technological wizardry, and high production costs, all of which contributed to a sharp increase in ticket prices. By the early 1980s, the average theatergoer was paying two and a half to four times the price that audience members paid five years previously. Although attendance at Broadway shows dropped by more than half (down from 67 million in 1980 to 31 million in 1988), revenues increased, mainly because of the high ticket prices (Bondi, *American Decades: 1980–1989*, 97–99).

A new trend in audience participatory theater also developed. In Los Angeles, for example, *Tamara* took audience members on a chase through a villa. *Tamara* became the longest-running show in Los Angeles theater history and ran for more than ten years (1984–1994). *Shear Madness*, a mystery comedy, also lasted eleven years in Boston, nine years in Chicago, and three years in Washington, D.C. One of the enduring favorite shows was *Tony and Tina's Wedding* where audience members took part in the wedding festivities, including dinner. The show ran concurrently in six cities and spread to many smaller theaters nationwide (TIME.com

"Come to the Cabaret," August 12, 1991). Nationwide theater attendance increased to a total of more than 116 million per year.

Other cultural institutions also charted notable attendance figures. According to the U.S. Statistical Abstract, in 1992, opera companies nationwide numbered a record high of 1,250 (up from 986 in 1980), as did the total number of opera performances (more than 11,000); opera attendance figures topped 15 million (up from 4.6 million in 1970). The number of symphony orchestras nationwide remained constant at 1,570, and attendance was steady at more than 23 million per year. Live musical performances by bands and popular singers totaled more than 104 million. Attendance at other cultural centers and performances included art museums (50.2 million), classical music performances (24.2 million), jazz performances (20.4 million), and ballet (9.3 million). Participation in cultural arts and activities included painting (18.6 million), modern dancing (14.9), creative writing (13 million), and playing classical music (7.4 million) (Statistical Abstract [1994], 263).

Multiplex Movie Theaters, Revised Movie Ratings, *Star Wars*, and Adult Films

During this period, many of the older theaters and drive-ins were either renovated or torn down and completely rebuilt to accommodate new multiplex movie theaters. (By 1990, only, about one thousand drive-in theaters were still in operation.) Unlike previous movie theaters with one large movie screen accommodating thousands of seats, the new multiplex theaters had either 2, 4, 8, 10, or sometimes in excess of 12 smaller individual theaters with 150 to 600 seats on average. Although movie attendance in 1984 averaged 23 million people each week at more than 21,000 movie screens, the number of movie theater sites numbered only about 8,000. The multiplexes also included video arcade games in the lobbies, many based on the science fiction or fantasy movies that were popular at the time.

Nine of the top ten grossing movies of the entire period were either science fiction or fantasy movies, including the highest grossing film of the period, *E.T. The Extra-Terrestrial* (1982) at $228 million; followed by *The Return of the Jedi* (1980) at $168 million; *Batman* (1989) at $150 million; *The Empire Strikes Back* (1983) at $141 million; *Ghostbusters* (1984) at $130 million; *Raiders of the Lost Ark* (1981) at $115 million; *Indiana Jones and the Last Crusade* (1989) at $115 million; *Indiana Jones and the Temple of Doom* (1984) at $109 million; and *Back to the Future* (1985) at $104 million. The one exception was *Beverly Hills Cop* (1984), the ninth highest gross at $108 million. No other movie of the period achieved $100 million gross, only one other earned over $90 million (*Tootsie*, 1982), and only thirteen others exceeded $70 million.

In 1977, the movie *Star Wars* presented a basic premise of good versus evil as Luke Skywalker, Han Solo, and Princess Leia did battle against the evil empire led by the infamous Darth Vader and his storm troopers. The *Return of the Jedi* (1980) and *The Empire Strikes Back* (1983) completed the *Star Wars* trilogy, and both the films and their characters became part of an American cultural phenomenon. Between 1977 and 1984, more than 300 million *Star Wars* toys were sold, and according to the *Encyclopedia of Popular Culture*, the "merchandising became a business unto itself and produced the most important licensing properties in history" (Pendergast and Pendergast, Vol. 4: 512).

After 1984, movie attendance dipped to 20 million per week. In that same year, the Motion Picture Association of America (MPAA), mainly because of mounting pressure regarding film content, revised its ratings system (see chapter 7) by replacing the M rating with PG-13—parents strongly cautioned, some material may be inappropriate for children under the age of thirteen. In July 1986, the attorney general issued a report on pornography and established rules regarding obscenity. Although sexual content was not always the cause for a movie receiving the rating, the infamous X rating became synonymous with pornography and adult films. Therefore, in 1990, the MPAA replaced the X rating with NC-17—no one 17 and under admitted (http://www.natoonline.org).

By 1990, the adult film industry, as "an unforeseen by-product of the VCR revolution," was reported to be earning more than $8 billion per year from video rentals. During the course of the previous years, adults realized that videocassettes allowed them to rent and view adult films in the privacy of their own homes. As a result of the home video business, the movie theaters and drive-ins known for showing adult fare saw a rapid decline. In fact, the adult film industry began shooting almost all of its films directly on videotape, completely bypassing the thought of showing it in a theater (TIME.com, "Romantic Porn in the Boudoir," March 30, 1987).

Compact Discs, Sony Walkman, Music Videos, and Parental Warning Labels

According to the U.S. Statistical Abstract, in 1982, 577.4 million units of music recordings were sold. Vinyl long-playing albums (LPs) and vinyl singles (45s) accounted for 381.1 million units sold, and cassette tapes made up 182.3 million units sold (Statistical Abstract [2000], 573). In 1983, Philips Electronics began mass marketing the compact disc (CD), which had advantages over vinyl in size, weight, and sound quality. With vinyl LPs, the contact made by the stylus on the record itself caused popping and surface noise to be heard through the speakers. A laser light picked up the sound on CDs without surface contact, thereby allowing for better sound quality. Another advantage was that a CD could hold 75 to 80 minutes of continuous recorded sound as opposed to the 25 to 30 minutes per side of an LP. With the advent of CDs, vinyl albums and singles sales dropped to 39.3 million units and would continue a drastic decline to only 8.2 million in 1990. CDs, on the other hand, which in 1985 accounted for a modest 22.6 million units, sold 286.5 million units by 1990 (Statistical Abstract [2000], 573).

By 1990, music recordings of all kinds combined for a total of 865.7 million units sold. Rock music accounted for 37.4 percent of all recordings sales, followed by pop at 13.6 percent, country at 8.8 percent, jazz at 5.2 percent, and classical at 4.1 percent. In 1990, despite the CD onslaught, the sale of cassette tapes grew significantly to an astounding 442.2 million units in 1990. Cassettes proved to be versatile and could record sounds from other forms of media that could then be played back in the home, automobile, and even on a personal Walkman.

In 1979, Sony introduced the Walkman, a small, portable battery-powered unit capable of playing cassette tapes that users listened to through an earphone system. Walkmans not only allowed people to listen to personal music away from the home or car, but many people began wearing them on bus trips, to school, and while exercising on a treadmill or a stair-climber machine. Later versions of the Walkman were both water- and skip-resistant; therefore, runners could use them outdoors. Within ten years, more than 25 million Walkmans had been sold in the United States, and by 1990, they were selling at more than 20 million units per year (Pendergast and Pendergast, *Encyclopedia of Popular Culture* Vol. 5: 66).

In 1990, music videos, which had been a nonentity in the early 1980s, showed sales of 9.2 million units. Two musical artists who thrived in the new music video era were pop singers Madonna and Michael Jackson. Each artist incorporated original choreographed dance numbers with their music into highly stylized music videos, which in turn increased their own music sales. In 1982, Jackson capitalized on using music videos with the release of elaborate music video productions from his *Thriller* album. Sales of the album were boosted by MTV exposure and sold more than 25 million copies, and the *Thriller* album became the top-selling individual album of all time. Another musical artist who also benefited from music video exposure was Bruce Springsteen, who sold more than 13 million copies of his *Born in the USA* album (1984). His subsequent nationwide concert tour attracted more than five million fans. The heavy metal band Guns N' Roses released their album titled *Appetite for Destruction* in 1987, which sold more than 12 million copies. Heavy Metal was a louder, faster version of rock and roll. The bands usually consisted of between 3 an 5 members using electric guitars and resounding drums and bass.

Some musical artists worked to raise awareness for the hungry and destitute and for many other charitable causes. On April 5, 1985 (Good Friday), musical artists from all genres joined in both singing and promoting the song "We Are the World" and the USA for Africa program to help provide food and supplies for starving nations in Africa. The song sold more than seven million copies, and the companion video was in continuous rotation on MTV. At one point, five thousand radio stations worldwide played the song simultaneously.

Other charity concerts included Live Aid and Farm Aid. Live Aid, a 16-hour concert simulcast from both England and Philadelphia, was held to raise money for Ethiopian famine victims and was viewed by an estimated 1.5 billion people. At JFK Stadium in Philadelphia more than 100,000 live audience members witnessed the event featuring 60 musical acts. Also in 1985, country star Willie Nelson organized Farm Aid, a live concert that drew more than 78,000 fans, in a hope "to bring the plight of the American farmer to the attention of the nation" and to support destitute American farmers (Bondi, *American Decades: 1980–1989*, 95–96).

In 1985, the changing reflective moral climate led to attacks on both music videos and popular music in general. For example, the Wal-Mart discount store chain discontinued sales of youth-orientated music magazines including *Rolling Stone*, *Spin*, and *Tiger Beat*. During the same year, the Parental Music Resource Center (PMRC) lobbied Congress to censor album covers and musical lyrics. In 1989, succumbing to pressure from the PMRC, the Recording Industry Association of America (RIAA) voluntarily responded by placing black-and-white warning labels stating "Parental Advisory—Explicit Lyrics" on albums and singles thought to contain music lyrics inappropriate for children. Regardless of labeling, many stores, including Wal-Mart, ardently refused to sell any music with a warning label.

SPORTS AND GAMES

Commercialized Sports, Super Bowl Parties, and Wrestlemania

During this period, baseball and other major professional sports changed the face of their games by negotiating higher television contracts. Athletes' salaries also reached unprecedented highs as long-term multimillion dollar contracts became the norm. The proliferation of large amounts of money paid to televise sporting events translated into more television commercials to generate revenue for the broadcasters airing the games. A large majority of baseball games were televised at night during lucrative prime-time viewing hours. Television, in turn, dictated extended time between innings to air more commercials. The length of time-outs and halftime in televised football games was also increased.

The National Football League's Super Bowl game became an extravaganza, with the halftime show costing millions of dollars to produce and lasting more than 40 minutes (standard halftime was fifteen minutes), and the television audience for the game continued to grow to more than 1 billion viewers worldwide by 1992. In connection with the televised Super Bowl games, there arose a ritual of individuals gathering in their homes and having Super Bowl parties where they watched the game and enjoyed lavish food and beverages.

College football teams also signed lucrative contracts for televised games. Overall attendance at college football games remained steady at more than 35 million per year, and attendance at National Football League games showed a slight increase from 14 million to 17.7 million. Attending a football game itself (professional or collegiate) was not always as important as the pregame tailgate party. "Tailgate party" became a generic term for any parking lot party either before or after a sporting event. It involved a group of fans showing up well in advance of the scheduled start of the game. They would bring barbeques, food, beer, lawn chairs and games to play while waiting for the game to start. The term tailgate refers to the items stored in the back of a station wagon and the tailgate would be left open while the fans ate and had fun. One newspaper reporter wrote, "It's hard to tell if the games come with the parties or the parties come with the games" and found that "[a]t UCLA there were reports of elaborate table settings, with oysters jetted in from New Orleans, as well as clams, prime ribs, sausages, tossed salads and a fully stocked bar" (Jury, 70).

In 1985, spectatorship at all professional sporting events combined reached 223.2 million. Baseball recorded an all-time high of 47.7 million spectators, which further increased to 56.8 million by 1992. Professional basketball attendance also rose from 11.5 million spectators in 1985 to 18.6 million in 1992. College basketball attendance remained steady at 28.7 million per year for men's teams, but attendance at college women's basketball increased from 2 million in 1985 to an impressive 3.4 million fans in 1992. Attendance at professional hockey games numbered 13.9 million. In 1980, professional soccer recorded 6.2 million attendees mainly because of the addition of the North American Soccer League. The league soon dissolved, and attendance dropped to 1.2 million (Statistical Abstract [1995], 257).

According to the U.S. Statistical Abstract, almost one million high school boys regularly played on a football team. More than 514,000 students played basketball, 475,000 participated in track, and 410,000 played baseball. Participatory sports for high school girls included more than 400,000 students who played basketball, 355,000 who participated in track, 270,000 who played volleyball, and 190,000 who played softball. In both high school and other community youth sports programs, more than 30 million participated in an organized sports program, and 6.5 million student athletes participated on the collegiate level (Statistical Abstract [2000], 259).

As more Americans watched sports on television, the sports industry grew into an enormous business, including not only commercialized televised events, but also the retailing of sports equipment and clothing. It was only fitting that by 1980 the Entertainment and Sports Programming Network (ESPN) was available to cable subscribers as a 24-hour all-sports network. The most popular sport shown on cable television was wrestling.

Although televised wrestling was totally choreographed televised entertainment, it quickly became a new fan favorite. The World Wrestling Federation (WWF) marketed weekly hour-long television programs and action toy figures of popular wrestling heroes such as Hulk Hogan and Sergeant Slaughter. Fans were treated to special extravaganzas such as Wrestlemania, which usually ran for three hours and featured special championship and action matches. By the mid-1980s, four of the top ten cable programs were wrestling programs produced by the WWF (Panati, 441). By the end of the century the WWF would be known as the WWE (World Wrestling Enterprises).

Active Participation, Running, Wall Climbing, and In-line Skates

In previous years, it had seemed apparent that as an individual increased in age, active participation decreased. However, a 1987 study by the *Journal of Physical Education, Recreation, and Dance* revealed that in the early 1980s, participation rates at health clubs and in activities such as bicycling, fishing, hiking, skiing, and swimming were higher among those 25 to 55 years of age than they were for teenagers and those in the 18- to 24-year-old range.

In 1990, the U.S. Statistical Abstract indicated that swimming was the most popular activity with participation by more than 72 million people. Between 1980 and 1992, participation in softball increased from 30 million players to more than 41 million players, and the number of adult teams nearly doubled from 110,000 to 202,000. Baseball added another 23 million participants. Golf participation increased from 15.1 million players to 24.8 million players, playing on 13,210 courses nationwide. By 1988, a significant number of urban working-class individuals were entering the sport of golf, and almost half of the total number of new players were female (Statistical Abstract [1994], 259–261).

In 1992, there were 7,183 bowling establishments in the country, down from 8,591 in 1980, and the number of bowling lanes decreased from 154,000 to

143,000. However, during the same year, the total number of participants increased from 72 million to 82 million, this number was evenly divided between female and male participants. Equal participation was also noted in volleyball.

In 1992, the Sporting Goods Manufacturers Association (SGMA) reported that volleyball had 31.3 million players on hard surface and 13.2 million on sand. Other participatory activities of significance were basketball (40.4 million participants) and billiards (37.8 million participants). Activities that had between 10 and 20 million participants included tennis and Ping-Pong (each claimed 18.9 million participants), skiing (18.8 million), touch football (18.6 million), target shooting (16.7 million), and badminton (12 million). Racquetball recorded a high of 10.4 million participants in 1987, but this number declined to 7.5 million in 1992. By the end of 1992, soccer claimed 16.4 million participants, a dramatic increase from 1980, and outpaced tackle football (11.4 million).

Running and jogging claimed more than 40 million active participants nationwide, and many of these people were marathon runners. During the 1980s, the New York City Marathon regularly attracted more than 20,000 runners (more than twice that number were turned away), and more than 2.5 million enthusiastic spectators lined the 26.2 mile route to watch the event. Interest in triathlon com-

Looking up First Avenue in Manhattan, New York, at mile 16 in the 1988 New York City Marathon. The annual run attracted more than 25,000 participants and 2.5 million spectators. Author's archives.

petitions comprised of a 2.4-mile swim, 112-mile bike ride, and a 26.2-mile marathon, spread nationwide and claimed more than 500,000 participants, of which more than 80,000 were women. Participation in women-only running events such as the L'eggs Mini Marathon (a 6.2-mile event) in New York's Central Park regularly attracted more than six thousand participants.

For sheer numbers of participants, the Peachtree Road Race 10K (6.2 miles) in Atlanta, Georgia, took the prize. By 1990, with 40,000 runners, the race was so congested that the final runner started the race a full half an hour after the first runner. By the year 2000, more than 55,000 runners participated, and the event involved 3,000 volunteers and more than 150,000 spectators (www.atlantatrackclub.org).

In the summer of 1976, George Willig made headlines when he climbed up the side of the World Trade Center in New York City. The climb ignited a fad in which college students attempted to climb campus buildings. In 1977, to eliminate the danger, the University of Washington constructed an indoor climbing structure that attracted more than 1,200 students per month (Panati, 382). In 1987, the first U.S. rock gym (an indoor facility where people could replicate the experience of rock climbing) was built in Seattle, Washington, and in 1990, the largest indoor climbing facility opened at Cornell University (TIME.com, "Moving Up in the World," April 2, 1990). By 1992, all sorts of indoor climbing structures were built, which in turn rekindled an interest in outdoor rock climbing; according to the SGMA, participation in outdoor rock climbing numbered 4.3 million mountaineers.

In 1980, more than 25 million Americans roller-skated, and many of them wore the new in-line roller-skates. Unlike earlier roller-skates that had a pair of wheels at the toe and another pair at the heel, in-line skates (sometimes known as rollerblades) had four polyurethane wheels in a straight line attached to a rigid boot, similar to an ice-skate. Ice hockey enthusiasts also began playing roller hockey on hard surfaces, and by the end of 1992, roller hockey claimed more than 2.3 million players. Participation in ice hockey remained steady at two million players per year (Krajick, "Don't look now, but here come the bladerunners," n.p.).

Winter Ice Festivals, Skiing, and Snowboarding

Winter ice festivals (see chapter 1) continued but some not in the same tradition of the past. Mark Jury visited the Perchville Winter Festival in East Tawas, Michigan, in 1985 and noted that the festival regularly attracted more than ten thousand people with "events ranging from a Polar bear swim, to a fishing contest, to a Demolition Derby on the ice of Lake Huron, and nearby snowmobile races at Houghton Lake" (45).

One traditional winter activity that continued to be popular was skiing. In 1992, Colorado Ski Country USA reported that more than 10.4 million skiers visited Vail, Colorado. In 1992, the SGMA reported more than 18.8 million people regularly skied (13.5 million downhill and 5.3 million cross-country) (SGMA, "Sports Participation Trends" [1995], n.p.). During this time, the skiers found new competition for the slopes with snowboarders.

During the 1970s, many craftsmen were shaping various forms of snowboards, including bolting two skis together to make boards known as "snurfers." In 1980, Jake Burton Carpenter combined the bindings and metal edges of ski technology with snurfers to produce the first modern snowboard. However, at the time very few ski areas allowed snowboarders. In 1985 only 39 of the estimated 600 nationwide ski areas allowed snowboarding. By 1990, the SGMA reported that there were more than 1.8 million snowboarders, and the number of snowboarding enthusiasts continued to climb through the 1990s (SGMA, "Sports Participation Trends" [1995], n.p.). In 1998, snowboarding became an Olympic sport and that helped the sport gain mainstream acceptance. By the end of the century, more than 50 different companies marketed snowboards. In addition, almost all ski resorts offered snowboarding instruction and trails.

TRANSPORTATION AND VACATIONS

Auto-vacations and Minivans

In 1990, the Travel Industry Association of America (TIAA) reported that 589.4 million Americans traveled during that year. Of that number, 361.1 million traveled for pleasure and vacation. By 1990, Americans took more than 280 million weekend trips and 422 million individual vacation trips. Seventy-five percent of the trips were taken by automobile and more than 20 percent by airplane (Kraus [1994], 221).

The Chrysler Corporation's introduction of the minivan in 1983 made vacation trips by automobile easier for Americans. The minivan was one of the first vehicles designed with the suburban woman in mind. It was a seven-passenger van built on a car chassis that handled and drove like a car, and it quickly became a symbol of suburbia and filled the shopping mall parking lots. Although the vehicle was well suited for auto-vacations, it was more typically used to drive children to little league baseball practice, dance classes, and the mall. The other car manufacturers quickly followed Chrysler's idea (Pendergast and Pendergast, *Encyclopedia of Popular Culture*, Vol 2: 370).

According to the U.S. Census, highway fatalities in 1980 were at 51,000. By 1992, despite an increase to more than 190 million registered motor vehicles on the American roads (126.6 million of which were passenger vehicles) fatalities were down to 39,250. The decrease was mainly due to most states' instituting mandatory use of seat belts and the institution of the 55 mph (miles per hour) national speed limit. In 1984, New York State became the first state to require all front seat passengers and all children less than ten years of age to wear seat belts (*Rand McNally Road Atlas*, A3).

Airline Deregulation, Airport Congestion, and Hang Gliders

According to the U.S. Statistical Abstract, the rate of air travel continued to increase during this period. In 1980, 296.9 million Americans chose to fly as commercial passengers. By 1992, the number was a staggering 475 million, and the number of people who traveled to a foreign country nearly doubled to 43.9

million passengers. The most popular foreign vacation destinations included Europe, Mexico, and the Caribbean.

The sudden increase in the number of air travelers was attributed to the Airline Deregulation Act of 1978. The congressional act allowed for new competing companies offering no-frills service such as People's Express and New York Air to begin operations. The competition yielded a wide variety of discount fares and increased the number of air travelers, which in turn contributed to congestion and delays at the nation's major airports (Taneja, 28).

In 1986, the top 30 airports accounted for over 65 percent of all air passengers. Chicago's O'Hare International was the nation's busiest airport with more than 25.4 million departing passengers, followed by Atlanta (22.1 million), Los Angles (19.8 million), and Dallas-Ft. Worth (19.7 million) (Taneja, 96). The busy airports were part of a nationwide hub system where smaller aircraft, usually propeller driven, would bring between 10 and 60 passengers from some of the nation's 5,800 smaller airports to the larger airports for travel to nationwide and international destinations (Taneja, 115–117).

The period was not without its share of passenger fatalities. In 1982, 78 people died when an Air Florida jet crashed into the Potomac River. In that same year, 154 people died when a Pan Am jet crashed after takeoff in New Orleans. In 1987, 28 people died in an attempted takeoff by a Continental Airlines passenger jet during a snowstorm in Denver, Colorado. However, on December 21, 1988, a new fear struck passengers when a terrorist bomb exploded onboard Pan Am Flight 103, an American-bound Boeing 747, over Lockerbie, Scotland. All 243 passengers, 16 crew members, and eleven people on the ground were killed.

For a complete sense of freedom that did not include airport congestion, some chose an alternative form of flight—but not for travel. During the 1980s, hang gliding reached new popularity. Most hang gliders used for recreation or sport did not require the operator to have any pilot certification. Other motorized types of gliders and those towed by aircraft had Federal Aviation Administration (FAA) restrictions for pilot certification (Munson, 26). One member of the United States Hang Gliding Association said, "The appeal of hang gliding is unexplainable. Words can't describe the sensation of flying. It's a total sense of freedom, because you're so high. No one's going to bother you. And you're floating there—sitting there watching everything go by and all you feel is the wind. The appeal is the sense of freedom" (Jury, 93).

Mountain Bikes and All-terrain Vehicles

In 1980, 9 million bicycles were sold per year, and this increased to 11.4 million by 1985. Almost 80 percent of all sales were ten-speed bicycles (see chapter 7). By the mid-1980s, there was a trend toward riding mountain bikes. Featuring a lightweight, rugged frame, straight handlebars, and thick all-terrain tires, mountain bikes became popular off-road and in wilderness areas. These rugged bicycles also proved durable on urban streets. By 1992, the SGMA reported more than 7.4 million bikers sought out mountain and wilderness trails on which to ride (up from 1.5 million bikers in 1987) (SGMA, "Popular Trends in Sports and Fitness" [1995], n.p.). Not all bike trails ventured up steep mountain trails. In West Virginia, the Greenbrier River Trail followed an old railroad track and maintained a less than 1 percent grade that extended for 75 miles, crossed 35 bridges, and went through two tunnels (www.pocahontascountywv.com/mtnbike.htm). From 1985 to 1992, bicycle sales still averaged more than 11 million bicycles sold per year; but mountain bikes were responsible for over 50 percent of all sales. Nationwide, more than 6,500 shops catering to bicycle enthusiasts existed; some of these shops chose to carry only bicycle-related clothing and accessories. In 1985, bicycling of all types had 58 million participants and was second only to swimming (72 million) as the most-participated-in outdoor activity (Statistical Abstract [1986], 215).

The competition on the trails among hikers, campers, and bikers was intensified by the presence of off-road vehicles. In 1970, Honda introduced the first all-terrain vehicle (ATV). The ATV was basically a three-wheeled motorcycle designed for off-road adventures. In 1979, Yamaha began ATV production, and in 1982, Suzuki introduced the first four-wheeled ATV. By 1984, sales of all ATVs combined was 535,000 units. By 1985 the number of ATV's sold exceeded 2.6 million. A 1986 study by the Consumer Product Safety Commission raised concerns over numerous ATV accidents and reckless rider behavior. In response, manufacturers began to promote safety awareness, and by 1988, all ATV manufacturers stopped selling three-wheeled models and only sold four-wheeled models ("ATV History," Minneapolis-St. Paul *Star Tribune*, n.p.). Tom Meersman of the Minneapolis-St. Paul *Star Tribune* reported that by 2001 "More than 148,000 ATVs were registered for recreational use in Minnesota . . . ATVs are registered in far higher numbers than off-road motorcycles and trucks, though they use some of the same trails [and] [a]n estimated 830,000 people in the state have ridden an ATV" (Meersman, "Tracks on the land: Nature pays the price as ATVs hit Minnesota's woods," n.p.). Off-road vehicle ridership in areas maintained by the Bureau of Land Management alone increased from 19.4 million in 1982 to more than 63 million in 1990.

Budget Motels, Luxury Suites, and Elvis Week

During this period, there was a noticeable increase in the availability of budget motels offering rooms at lower rates than those offered by other franchised motels. In 1990, Super 8 had the most properties at 672 with 42,200 rooms followed by Econo Lodge at 560 properties with 44,606 rooms. The largest number of budget motel rooms belonged to the Motel 6 chain with 59,900 rooms at its 522 properties. Red Roof Inns was a distant fourth with 204 properties and 22,700 rooms. Other budget chains included Allstar Inns, National 9 Inns, and Friendship Inns (Jakle, 211).

In 1992, Holiday Inn Worldwide had fewer properties than in 1974 with 1,398 sites, but the chain still maintained more than 270,000 total rooms. By comparison, Best Western claimed the most properties with 1,800 and offered 185,000 rooms. During the period, corporate mergers and acquisitions also extended to the motel system. Both Holiday Inn and Best Western were exceeded by combinations produced by the Hospitality Franchise System and Choice Hotels International.

Hospitality Franchise System was the largest motel corporation with an acquired total of 2,291 properties and 283,697 total rooms. The corporation consisted of 1,217 Days Inns, 575 Ramada Inns, and 499 Howard Johnson's properties. Choice Hotels International consisted of a total of 2,158 properties and 195,953 total rooms made up of 764 Comfort Inns, 695 Econo Lodges, 390 Quality Inns, 134 Friendship Inns, 107 Rodeway Inns, 51 Clarion Inns, and 17 Sleep Inns. The Marriott Corporation followed with 690 properties and 150,000 rooms made up of 21 Marriott Hotels, 200 Courtyards by Marriott, 179 Residence Inns, and 99 Fairfield Inns (Jakle, 228). Other than hotels and motels, more than two thousand farm and dude ranch operations (see chapter 4) were available for vacationers to choose from, which attracted an average of between 300,000 and 600,000 visitors per year (Vogeler, 292).

Some vacationers opted for luxury hotels that catered to upscale wealthy clientele and were usually located within the major cities. By 1990, organizations such as Charterhouse Inns, which owned and operated luxury hotels including the Plaza in New York City and the Mayflower in Washington, D.C., expanded within the Northeast from Virginia to New England. In addition, the Hyatt Corporation (which was founded in 1960) expanded to 105 properties nationwide. The oldest name in the luxury hotel chain was Ritz-Carlton. Initially a European chain in Switzerland, London, and Paris, the Ritz-Carlton expanded to the United States and by 1992 operated 25 properties in the country (Jakle, 221–222). Whether considered a budget, moderate or luxury hotel, many of the nation's hotels increasingly booked rooms for individuals traveling to special events such as the Super Bowl, Mardi Gras, Fan Fair in Nashville, the century-old Cheyenne Frontier Days Rodeo in Wyoming, or even to Memphis for Elvis Week.

In 1982, Graceland, Elvis Presley's home, first opened to the public. As one of the most famous homes in the United States, visitation averaged more than 600,000 per year, and it was the second-most-visited home tour in America after the White House. Each August, fans gathered in Memphis, Tennessee, for Elvis Week, "a commemoration of the music, magic and memories associated with the legacy of Elvis Presley." The weeklong event averaged an attendance of 30,000 to 35,000 people, and most of the area's 27,000 hotel rooms were booked long in advance. In 2002, the twenty-fifth anniversary of Elvis's death, the nine-day event attracted more than 70,000 enthusiastic fans (www.elvis.com).

Ocean Travel, SPF, and Scuba

Less than 500,000 Americans took cruises in 1970. By 1982, that number was more than 1.5 million. The increase was considered to be the result of two contributing factors. One was the positive image of the cruise ship and the vacation industry portrayed in the popular television program *The Love Boat* (1977–1986). The other factor was the increased vacation options offered by the industry itself.

Most of the large cruise ships departed from ports in Florida, Los Angeles, and New York. Cruises from New York were limited by weather conditions from April through November, but ports in Florida and Los Angeles offered year-round departures. Cruises began offering more options including airfare and flight connections from additional cities. Cruises could vary in length from three to seven days. By 1992, the cruise ship industry reported more than four million passengers during the year.

Ocean travel did not have to entail an overnight stay. Hundreds of companies

Cruise ships such as Royal Caribbean's *Voyager of the Seas* offered affordable vacation packages and a wide array of onboard activities and entertainment. Courtesy Royal Caribbean Ltd, 1999.

offered lunch and dinner cruises. Lunch cruises lasted about one and a half hours, and dinner cruises extended to two and a half to three hours and typically included entertainment and dancing. Almost every city near an ocean, river, or large lake had one or more companies offering short cruises. Spirit Harbor Cruises offered service in cities including Boston, Massachusetts; Charleston, South Carolina; Chicago; New York; Norfolk and Richmond, Virginia; Philadelphia, Pennsylvania; Seattle, Washington; and Washington, D.C. Other companies offered sight-seeing cruises from areas as far east as Nantucket, Massachusetts, to Oregon on the west coast and in many points in between.

Vacations in the Caribbean and Hawaii were still popular, as were the beaches at Coney Island, the New Jersey Shore, and southern California. Unlike in previous years when obtaining a perfect tan at the beach was desired, studies now began to warn of the harmful effects of the sun's rays because of the depletion of the earth's ozone layer. In response, sunscreen products rated according to a sun protection factor (SPF) began to enter the market. The higher the SPF number given to the product, the better the protection offered by it. For example, an SPF-15 provided minimal protection and allowed a tan whereas an SPF-45 almost totally blocked out all of the sun's ultraviolet rays.

During this period, many people discovered a new interest in scuba (Self-Contained Underwater Breathing Apparatus). In 1959, the YMCA instituted the first nationally organized scuba certification course. The following year, the National Association of Underwater Instructors (NAUI) was formed, and in 1966 the Professional Association of Diving Instructors (PADI) was founded (DivingHistory.com, n.p.). However, it wasn't until the 1980s that scuba became big business, especially among travelers vacationing in exotic resort locations such as the Caribbean, Hawaii, and Cozumel Island in the Gulf of Mexico. Many vacation resorts hired qualified scuba instructors and offered an option for either a resort certification (which allowed limited diving) or full PADI certification. Wreck diving, one of the most popular activities, allowed divers to explore sunken ships. Some divers enjoyed underwater photography, spearfishing, and diving in local lakes. In 1990, according to the SGMA, scuba was a $1-billion-a-year business that involved two and a half million divers. By 1992, an estimated 500,000 new scuba divers were certified each year (SGMA, "Sports Participation Trends," n.p.).

CONCLUSION

In 1988, the election of Vice President George Bush to succeed Ronald Reagan as president continued the conservative mood of the country. With the election of President Bill Clinton in 1992, many considered the 12-year period of the Reagan era over. During the period, commercialism and sports were completely intertwined, and Americans of all sorts were actively involved as either spectators or participants in many new types of activities including snowboarding, mountain biking, and video games.

The following years would provide a cultural change as a minority of the population (less than 30 percent) would pursue healthy and active recreation and leisure lifestyles. Many others would succumb to sedentary leisure lifestyles and embrace television and spectator sports. Leisure habits themselves would enter into a brave new world dominated by virtual reality, the home computer, and the Internet.

CHAPTER 9

GENERATION X, THE INTERNET, AND VIRTUAL REALITY: 1992–2000

CHRONOLOGY

1992   Riots occur in Los Angeles after the Rodney King verdict; Sega Genesis outsells Nintendo.

1993   Use of the Internet grows; the World Trade Center is bombed.

1994   O.J. Simpson is arrested for double murder.

1995   The Oklahoma City bombing occurs; Sony releases the PlayStation.

1996   Nintendo 64 is released in America.

1998   *Titanic* is the most successful movie of all time; the Pokémon craze sweeps the nation.

1999   The shooting at Columbine High School occurs; concerns over the Y2K bug arise.

2000   Sony releases the PlayStation 2.

INTRODUCTION

Until 1970, the major developments that changed the leisure habits of Americans were the motion picture, the automobile, the radio, and the television. After 1992, the computer would join the list. A new generation X adapted well to computers and video games. The music and fashion of grunge and hip-hop were embraced by the young and scorned by the old. Country music and swing music appealed to a large adult audience.

During this time, Barbie was voted the toy of the century, and a new sensation called Pokémon fascinated many youngsters. A president's hopes for national health care and gun control were dashed under a scandal involving a liaison with a White House intern. The nation mourned as a former president's son disappeared in a small airplane crash, and concerns over the Y2K bug gripped the nation.

Cable television attracted a larger viewing audience than network television.

Talk shows, both on television and the radio, dominated the airwaves, as did reality-based TV programs. The surgeon general would issue a warning on obesity and inactivity. At the same time, only about 20 percent of the nation engaged in rigorous activity and frequent participation in recreation and sports.

PUBLIC INTEREST

The Contract with America, Generation X, Gun Control, and Hate Crimes

In 1992, Republican Vice President Dan Quayle spoke on behalf of what was called the moral majority and the new "Contract with America" by denouncing popular culture images on radio and television. In one instance, Quayle said he thought the fictional television image portrayed by single mother Murphy Brown "was an attack on family values" (Hilliard and Keith, 271–272). *Time* magazine questioned the legitimacy of Quayle's attack, saying, "Republicans think they can rack up political points by attacking shows that are watched and loved by millions. . . . Is it all just political posturing? Or has television really crossed the line from entertainment to advocacy?" (September 21, 1992: 44–47). New York governor Mario Cuomo, a Democrat, in his book *Reason to Believe* (1995) challenged the Contract with America, by writing, "[T]he new conservative Republican agenda won't solve our problems" (7). Some of the problems were those of "generation X."

Defined as those 45 million children born between the years 1965 and 1977, generation X represented a group with an extreme amount of purchasing power and was the first generation to have grown up with computers and video games. They witnessed changing family structures that involved high rates of divorce, second marriages, and the reality of HIV/AIDS. By 1999, at least 5.5 million families were composed of remarried individuals with stepchildren.

By 1992, estimates indicated that almost 40 million American adults and families were without health insurance. Early in 1993, Democratic President Bill Clinton attempted to institute a comprehensive national health care system and legislation for gun control. The agenda infuriated conservative Republicans, who in turn launched a bitter media campaign effectively ending any hope of federally guaranteed health care. The National Rifle Association (NRA) was also effective in stalling all efforts at gun control.

During this period, the media highlighted concerns over shootings in public schools. In 1998, at Westside Middle School in Jonesboro, Arkansas, two young students, aged 11 and 13, shot and killed four young female students; a teacher and eleven other students were also wounded. In 1999, 12 students and a teacher were killed in a school shooting at Columbine High School in Littleton, Colorado, further raising vigorous debate over gun control and the intent of the Second Amendment to the U.S. Constitution.

In 1993, the nation was shocked by a terrorist bomb explosion at New York City's World Trade Center. (Terrorists would complete the act in September 2001, taking down both towers of the World Trade Center and killing more than three thousand Americans). In 1995, another horrific act of terrorism occurred in Oklahoma. On April 19, a disgruntled American militia member set a bomb at the Murrah Federal Building in Oklahoma City, destroying the building and killing 168 people, many of them children.

The Contract with America also openly attacked gay rights; one *Time* magazine cover story called it "The War on Gays." Gay bashing both literally and physically was a common occurrence. In 1998, the indiscriminant hate-crime killing of a suspected homosexual named Matthew Shepard in Laramie, Wyoming, raised public concerns. As a result, 42 states passed laws against hate crimes. Although criminal actions were viewed as worthy of inspiring legislation, moral issues were another matter, and 28 states outlawed same-sex marriages (McConnell, *American Decades 1990-1999*, 357).

The American Workforce, New Immigration, and Racial Profiling

In 1992, the U.S. census classified over 60 percent of the American workforce as working in service-oriented jobs. America continued shifting its employment base from an industrialized manufacturing economy (producing a product) to a service-based economy (providing services to consumers). The disparity in wealth also continued to widen. In 1990, a top corporate CEO earned about 85 times the salary of the average worker. By 2000, top CEO executives earned more than 400 times the average worker's salary. In fact the most compelling statistic from a 1997 study by the Bureau of Labor Statistics was that average American workers were actually working longer hours than they had previously worked in the past decades. In addition, at least 63 million adult women worked full-time. Many people both needed and desired to work an extra job in order to merely maintain their earning power because a vast majority of working-class Americans carried huge debts in order to maintain a basic standard of living.

With the need for product manufacturing reduced, the corporate catchword was *downsizing* as many corporations sought to reduce, and in many cases eliminate, middle- and low-wage positions. Also, during this time, many Americans began to worry that the new wave of immigration was taking away Americans' jobs.

The new wave of immigration was largely a result of the Immigration and Nationality Act of 1965, implemented as part of President Johnson's Great Society (see chapter 7), that allowed entry into the United States by immigrants from both the Eastern and Western Hemispheres. Between the years 1965 and 1997, the U.S. census reported a total of 17.1 million immigrants from Asia, Mexico, the Caribbean, and Central and South America were allowed entry, as were more than 19.8 million Europeans. By comparison, between the years 1900 and 1965, immigration from non-European countries was severely limited to only 3.38 million people total while more than 217 million Europeans were allowed entry (Statistical Abstract [1998], 872).

As a result, by 1992, the American population was widely diverse with more than 30 million African Americans, 22.4 million Hispanics, 7.3 million Asians, and 2 million Native American Indians. Many groups claimed that "racial profiling," or singling out an individual as a likely criminal due to their ethnic background, was occurring. The most notorious cases that some people believed relied on racial profiling involved African Americans Rodney King and O. J. Simpson.

In 1991, in Los Angeles, California, four white police officers were unknowingly videotaped beating Rodney King. The following year, those same police officers were acquitted of charges relating to the beating, triggering a wave of protests and riots. In what turned out to be the worst riots in the history of Los Angeles, 58 people were killed, and numerous buildings were destroyed.

In 1994, O. J. Simpson was charged with the murders of his ex-wife and her friend. On June 17, 1994, the police pursuit of O. J. Simpson and his friend Al Cowling in a white Ford Bronco was watched on live television by more than 95 million Americans. The Simpson murder trial was dubbed the "media event of the century," and it was covered in all of the major newspapers and televised live during the day and recapped on the evening newscasts. When a "not guilty" verdict was finally reached, 85 percent of African Americans agreed with the verdict, but only 32 percent of whites agreed—a fact that many pointed to in stating that racial divisions still existed in the country (Geis and Bienen, 113–119).

The Personal Computer, the Internet, and the World Wide Web

The market for personal computers first materialized in 1981 as IBM introduced a tabletop computer, which eventually became known as the personal computer (PC). Although in January 1983, *Time* magazine chose the computer as the "machine of the year," by the end of the 1980s, only about 10 percent of homes had a personal computer. By the early 1990s, the major breakthrough was the availability of the Internet network and the World Wide Web. In its simplest terms, the Internet (often called "the net") linked the personal computer via telephone lines with computer servers all around the world; this international linked network became known as the World Wide Web. In 1991, the networks were available for commercial use, and the Internet opened a vast information superhighway available to a mass market. Millions of people began to use the Internet to communicate, exchange data, distribute information, and sell products via the World Wide Web.

To obtain access to the World Wide Web, an individual was required to purchase direct dial-up access through a telephone line from an internet service provider (ISP). Almost immediately numerous commercial ISP services such as Prodigy, CompuServe, and America Online offered services to consumers beyond the basic Internet connection, adding a wide array of services such as e-mail and discussion groups.

In 1998, the U.S. Statistical Abstract reported that more than 45 million households (42.1 percent of all homes), with approximately 199 million adults, had Internet access either at home, at work, or both. Almost half of those people reported using a computer at least five days per week. The percentage of American households with home computers was distributed about the same among rural (39.9 percent), suburban (38.5 percent), and urban areas (42.9 percent). However, the distribution was not the same among different income levels. Households with a total income of $75,000 or more per year were more likely to have a home computer (79.9 percent) as opposed to those who made less than $20,000 (20 percent) (Statistical Abstract [2000], 568).

The computer quickly became a widespread feature of Americans' daily lives.

A typical personal home computer set-up in the year 2000. Author's archives.

By the end of the century, a common leisure pursuit for Americans was to surf the Web. It was not unusual for a single Web site to receive 40 to 50 million hits, or visits, per year. Within nanoseconds a home computer could search through more than 2.5 trillion Web pages and information sources.

In the late 1990s, the addition of a CD-ROM (compact disc read-only memory) to computers as a storage device allowed users access to a multitude of information. For example, just a few years before, an entire set of encyclopedias would fill up shelves in a home but now the same set could be contained on one compact disc (CD) with room to spare for additional information.

Planned Communities: Leisure World, Disney's Celebration, and Leisure Pools

By 2000, the American Association for Retired Persons (AARP) reported having 31.5 million members. Older adults enjoying retirement on pensions or healthy investments flocked to senior communities, and many opted to live in gated communities.

Leisure World, a gated retirement community in Laguna Hills, California, advertised having more than 200 community clubs, an 844-seat theater, two golf courses, a tennis complex, five swimming pools, a fitness center, a ballroom dance group, its own orchestra, a theater group, and more in a "1200 acre community surrounded by walls, [and] 14 guard controlled gates" (www.leisureworldtoday. com). By 1997, more than 20,000 such gated communities made up of more than 8.4 million residents existed in the United States.

At Disney World in Orlando, Florida, a planned residential community of 20,000 inhabitants called Celebration was an attempt to go backward in time and recreate a small American town. The town included a complete planned community featuring shopping centers, schools, recreation, and a golf course, and it was conveniently located adjacent to the Disney theme parks.

Many cities, especially in the Southwest, sought to attract individuals wishing to relocate or retire by promising attractions beyond the standard golf course. A new concept was the introduction of leisure pools within a multiuse facility. In lieu of the traditional rectangular competitive swimming and diving pool, the pool designs incorporated free-form pool shapes that included wave areas, teaching areas, lagoons, sprays, water slides, rocks, trees, and other amenities (*Athletic Business* magazine, August 2002: 59–65). The Genoveva Chavez Community Center in New Mexico was an example of a multiuse facility that incorporated a leisure pool, a 50-meter competitive pool, a spa, and a therapy pool in addition to a National Hockey League (NHL) regulation-size ice arena with spectator seating and recreational basketball, volleyball, and racquetball courts, indoor soccer, and other amenities.

Outdoor Recreation, Environmental Protection, Caves, and Jet Skis

Federal and municipal budget cutbacks caused the elimination of many urban community programs and the closing of park facilities. For example, in 1980, Baltimore, Maryland, operated more than 130 playgrounds and recreation centers. By 1995, due to budget restrictions, only 77 were still in operation with an additional 10 scheduled for closure (Goodale, "White Paper #2: Leisure Apartheid," n.p.). The national parks also had to make do with very limited resources and deteriorating facilities.

Despite the cutbacks, the parks continued to be crowded. According to the

U.S. Statistical Abstract, by 1999, acreage in all of the state parks totaled 12.9 million acres with a total visitation of 766.8 million people. The national parks accounted for another 286.7 million visitors and 77.7 million acres, and the Army Corp of Engineers managed 4,340 recreation areas at 456 lakes and reservoirs (www.usace.army.mil/recreation).

The question of how to protect the environment without limiting the number of park visitors still lingered. Maryland instituted the Leave No Trace program to minimize the human impact on the environment. Other groups and organizations such as the nonprofit National Resources Defense Council (NRDC) with a staff of 250 environmental professionals and more than 500,000 members lobbied the federal government and sought to educate the public on environmental conservation.

With the advent of the Internet, all of the states and national parks maintained Web sites. The National Park Service Web site provided a state-by-state list of all the national parks and recreation areas within a particular region. In addition, the site featured printable travel guides, as well as other information including costs, seasonal suggestions, photographs, and online booking (www.nps.gov). Every state throughout the country actively pursued tourists, and many states began to advertise unique travel adventures.

Of all the national parks, only one—Isle Royale in Michigan—was not accessible by automobile. The only access was by boat. More than 18,000 people per year traveled to the 850-square-mile park to hike or camp. A small number of intrepid visitors toured it by kayak (*New York Times*, "Paddling to Superior Scenery," August 11, 2002: TR9). In 1999, nationwide, the National Sporting Goods Association (NSGA) reported that kayaking had 3.5 million participants each year (NSGA "Ten-Year History of Sports Participation," n.p.).

The *Missouri Travel Guide* offered "more than 5,000 reasons to be called 'The Cave State.' Caves honeycomb through our hills and valleys, and challenge even experienced spelunkers. For those a bit less adventurous, 19 caves [offered] guided tours, including Springfield's Fantastic Caverns, the country's only ride-through cave" (111).

Caving and climbing were supported by Recreational Equipment Inc. (REI). REI was a cooperative founded in 1936 in Seattle, Washington, that provided a store to purchase climbing gear and equipment for hiking, backpacking, kayaking, biking, and other outdoor sports. By 2000, REI had 1.4 million members with 49 stores in 20 states and also maintained a charitable donation process to protect the outdoors and support conservation projects (www.rei.com).

According to the Sporting Goods Manufacturers Association (SGMA), by 1999, 44.5 million people engaged in freshwater fishing and 14.8 million in saltwater fishing, many of whom fished at least 15 times per year. More than 14 million individuals hunted an average of 18 days per year. Those who simply chose to observe or photograph wildlife numbered 62.9 million, and they did so on an average of 13 days per year. Hikers numbered more than 27.2 million and reported going hiking more than twice a year.

In 1999, the American Camping Association (ACA), a national organization of more than five thousand camping professionals, estimated that tent campers numbered 40.8 million people per year. Recreational vehicle (RV) campers numbered an additional 17.6 million per year. In addition, almost nine million youths participated in summer camps with stays ranging from two weeks to two months. The ACA also estimated that there were 1,430 camps dedicated specifically "to meeting the special needs of campers with physical, emotional, or mental challenges" (Kraus et al., 77).

Outdoor recreational services for the disabled were not limited to camping. The Shake-A-Leg Sailing Center on Biscayne Bay in Miami, Florida, offered sailing and kayaking for disabled adults and children. The program started in 1986 with the development of "an adaptive sailboat specially rigged to accommodate disabled sailors." By 2000, Shake-a-Leg served more than 6,500 individuals with 18,000 outings annually (McCormick, "An Unusual Program for the Disabled," 10, www.shakealegmiami.org).

The U.S. Census Bureau reported a slight increase in the total number of recreational boats from 16.2 million in 1992 to 16.7 million by 1998, with at least 73 million people participating in at least one boating activity per year. Those who participated in water activities on a regular basis included 7.2 million water-skiers, 7.3 million snorkelers, 2.6 million scuba divers, and 2 million wakeboarders (those using a single water ski similar in size to a skateboard) (Statistical Abstract [2000], 261–263). Some people chose a new form of personal watercraft that simply became known by the Kawasaki trademark name Jet Ski. *Time* magazine described these personal watercraft as "small, engine-driven craft that scoot across the water [in excess of 40 miles per hour]. Like their landbound cousins, motorcycles and snowmobiles, they are quick, maneuverable, noisy and a rush to ride." By 1998, the U.S. Statistical Abstract reported more than nine million were in use (Statistical Abstract [2000], 261). Reckless use of these watercraft contributed to many close calls, accidents, and even deaths. In response many states restricted their use to specific waterways and lakes (TIME.com, "Trouble in Their Wake," June 19, 1989).

LIFESTYLES

Fast Lifestyles, Sedentary Leisure, Diets, Coffee, and Routine Participation

For many Americans during this period, speed was essential. Americans embraced same-day mail delivery, fax machines, beepers, and cellular telephones that demanded instant response. It seemed that a large number of Americans were in a hurry to get somewhere quickly, but once there, they did little or nothing in the way of actual physical activity.

Unfortunately, a significant number of Americans succumbed to sedentary leisure lifestyles embracing television, spectator sports, shopping, and the home computer. Many people who led a sedentary lifestyle would wear fashionable jogging suits, designer hooded sweatshirts, and running shoes.

By 1994, it was reported that only 36 percent of all schools within the United States offered physical education classes on a daily basis. A report by the surgeon general claimed that by the end of the century over 60 percent of American adults (more than 150 million people) were overweight, and at least 58 million of those were clinically obese. This sad statistic also extended to 21 percent of all teenagers

Sailing was popular throughout the entire century, and many vacation resorts offered a variety of options. Author's archives.

and 13 percent of children. Weight loss became a national concern, and media advertisements pushed for satisfaction through diets.

The diet craze first became fashionable in the early 1970s, but by the early 1990s diet books and weight loss programs proliferated by the thousands. The Centers for Disease Control estimated that more than 80 million Americans went on a diet each year. Americans also spent $30 billion a year on weight loss products or programs that were for the most part ineffective or that threatened their health. Follow-up studies revealed that at least 95 percent of those who went on diets gained back all of the weight they lost and *more* within a five-year period (TIME.com, "What Health Craze?" December 26, 1994).

Ironically, Americans were actually living longer than they had in the past. The U.S. census reported that the average lifespan by the end of the century was more than 73 years for men and 79 years for women. However, at least 300,000 deaths each year were directly attributed to obesity. In addition, inactivity was a prime contributor to heart disease, the leading cause of death, accounting for over 34 percent of all deaths. Experts claimed that almost all heart disease was preventable through a healthy diet and an exercise program.

By the 1990s, technology had linked rural, urban, and suburban areas to the point that all parts of America were equally exposed to advertising for exercise programs and recreation opportunities. That is not to say that regional tendencies did not exist. Rodeo, for example (see chapter 1), attracted more spectators and participants throughout the Southwest and Midwest than within the metropolitan areas of New York City or Los Angeles. In 1998, 703 rodeos staged 2,213 performances nationwide, attracting 3.5 million spectators (Statistical Abstract [2000], 260). Gardening, taking care of pets, and drinking coffee were common pursuits across many areas of the country.

In 1992, more than 65 percent of all American households engaged in lawn and gardening activities. Total expenditures on lawn care products, household plants, flowers, and gardening equipment topped $20 billion (Kraus [1994], 298).

Americans also spent a significant amount of money on pets. The U.S. Census Bureau classified the total household "companion pet population" at 52.9 million dogs, 59.1 million cats, 12.6 million birds, and 4 million horses (Statistical Abstract [2000], 256). Most households had more than one pet. In fact, in 1992 alone, Americans spent over $8 billion on pet food (Kraus [1994], 298).

Coffee houses also appeared by the thousands across the country. One example was the Starbucks franchise that opened coffee cafés in almost all cities and towns, including in shopping malls and on college campuses. The coffee café also appeared in bookstores including the Barnes and Noble chain. The coffee house became a regular place for socializing, arranging a date, and even meeting a mate.

Americans tended to participate in leisure activities on a regular basis. A tradition that continued throughout the twentieth century was entertaining friends or relatives within their home and 32.8 million adults reported that they did just that at least once a month. Sometimes the entertaining would include playing cards and was reported by 21.5 million. Activities both within the home and outside the home included tossing darts of which 20.8 million played on a monthly basis. 19.1 million Americans dined out; 16.8 million went out to a bar or a nightclub; 12 million went dancing, and 10.5 million played billiards or pool. More than 16 million stayed home for a backyard barbecue and 13 million played board games. Hobbies and activities were reported by 9.5 million that pursued photography as a hobby, 9.8 million regularly enjoyed baking, 6.5 million performed woodworking or home furniture refinishing, 6.5 million cooked for fun, 6.2 million played trivia games, 6 million enrolled in an adult education course, 5.2 million enjoyed crossword puzzles, 5 million played bingo, 4.3 million painted or drew, 3.8 million played word games, 3.8 million played chess, 2.9 million played backgammon, 2.2 million involved themselves in model-making, and 1.8 million partook in bird watching, and for that age-old proverb 4.8 million people did not have to be told to "go fly a kite"—they actually did!

Active Senior Fitness Living, From Fitness to Wellness

Prior to the mid-1990s, the thought of older adults beginning an exercise program or building muscle strength was mostly unheard of. However, in the year 2000, a University of Arkansas medical study revealed that with proper exercise adults could "put off osteoporosis" and build muscle strength to perform routine daily activities in their senior years. A significant number of seniors took note of this, and studies showed that more than five million adults over 65 years of age spent at least five days a week in health clubs performing a wide array of exercises including running, aerobics, and weight training (TIME.com, "Burning Off the Years," April 23, 2001).

The SGMA reported that seniors (aged 55 plus) who spent more than 100 days per year exercising could be divided into the following groups by type of exercise performed: 2.6 million on treadmills, 1.7 million in weight training, and 6.5 million in fitness walking. In addition, 9.7 million seniors walked as a recreational pursuit, and 2 million swam at least 52 days per year. Moreover, 2.3 million golfed, 2.1 million bowled, and 1.7 million fished at least 25 times per year.

In an effort to encourage healthy lifestyles, many companies and college campuses instituted "wellness programs." More than two thousand companies nationwide contracted with the National Employee Services and Recreation Association (NESRA) to formulate fitness and wellness programs for their employees and to implement "a diverse range of employee services." The NESRA focused on "health promotion by offering lunchtime seminars, fitness incentive programs, [and] personal development opportunities." The organization also offered travel services and advised on sports leagues, special interest clubs, company celebrations, and managing on-site health centers (Kraus [1994], 351–352).

The U.S. Statistical Abstract reported that in the year 2000, the total number of adults exercising with equipment at health clubs was 46 million, 26.5 million

Recreational fitness run in Flushing Meadow Park, in 2000, the site of the two New York World's Fairs in 1939 and 1964. Author's archives.

of those on a regular basis. Outside of the health clubs, walking, with 77.6 million participants, replaced swimming as the most popular outdoor activity (Statistical Abstract [2000], 262).

Health clubs and fitness centers also installed computer network units such as FitLinxx, Schwinn Fitness Advisor, and TechnoGym. These systems provided interactive feedback and a connection to the Internet that allowed users to access their fitness information from home. Other health club equipment provided personal television sets and audio CD players (*Athletic Business* magazine, January 2000: 56–58).

Surfing the Net, E-mail, Genealogy, and Home Shopping

"Surfing the net" was a new catchphrase, as well as a dominant activity, for Internet users. E-commerce (doing business on-line), shopping, and purchasing through the use of the home computer and the Internet were new developments. Internet "chat rooms" allowed live, real-time electronic conversations to take place between Internet users who entered the chat rooms to join in a common discussion. Many chose to enter chat rooms under pseudonyms. Computer leisure activities included visiting entertainment sites and playing games. The leading subjects of Internet sites were adult entertainment (pornography), finance, sports, and genealogy.

One of the most widely used Internet features was e-mail. E-mail allowed an individual to type a message and with a push of a button instantaneously send it as an electronic mail message. E-mail was a convenient way to get in touch with people or maintain correspondence with family and friends. A large portion of those in the workplace (over 75 percent) used e-mail to communicate, and the same percentage applied it to home and personal use. A common shorthand language for use in e-mail messages developed that included acronyms and symbols such as LOL for "laugh out loud," BTW for "by the way," and :) for "happy." Typing a message in all capital letters was a symbol for shouting.

With the aid of e-mail, chat rooms, and Web sites, many Americans became interested in genealogy. Genealogy is the practice of tracing a person's ancestors, and it first received widespread public attention with the airing of the 1977 television miniseries *Roots* (see chapter 7). Although countless Web sites offered genealogy services, at least seven Web sites had more than one million paid subscribers for genealogy services. In March 1999, RootsWeb, "a vast electronic trading post for genealogical information," recorded more than 160 million messages in a single month (www.rootsweb.com). In addition to Web sites, genealogical clubs, how-to books, and courses in community colleges aided the genealogist in getting started. In 1999, the Denver Public Library reported that at least 300,000 people visited the library for genealogical research. The Mormon Family History Library in Utah reported an annual visitation of 800,000 people and also began a family search Web site with the goal of providing a repository of 600 million names. Some claimed that the hobby of genealogy turned into a veritable addiction for many roots searchers (TIME.com, "Roots Mania," April 19, 1999).

The most popular American hobby was shopping, and the computer offered its user the ability to shop on-line, as did cable television with the Home Shopping

Network, but they certainly did not take the place of actually going to the mall to shop.

Shopping Centers, the Mall of America, and Lifestyle Centers

According to the International Council of Shopping Centers (ICSC), by the end of the century, shopping malls generated $1.14 trillion in sales (up from $700 billion in 1992). The number of adults (over the age of 18) who visited malls was 197 million each month. Another 10.7 million people worked at the shopping centers. The ICSC also reported that by the year 2000, more than 45,000 shopping centers existed nationwide. By comparison, in 1964 there were 7,600 shopping centers; in 1972, 13,174 centers; and in 1992, 29,000 centers. By 2000, over 20 square feet of shopping space existed for each of the nation's 281 million inhabitants (ICSC Research Quarterly, n.p.).

Most of the malls took on a distinctly familiar look and contained similar franchise clothing, music, and food stores. Malls also became total entertainment packages. According to the ICSC, "consumers [enjoyed] children's playscapes, virtual reality games, live shows, movies in multiplex cinemas, a variety of food in either the food court or theme restaurants, carousel rides, [and] visually stunning merchandising techniques." The National Restaurant Association reported that almost half of all food dollars was spent on eating out in malls (Cohen, 64). *Time* magazine stated, "at least twelve states [ranked] malls among their top three tourist attractions," including Minnesota's Mall of America (TIME.com, "The Mall, the Merrier," November 24, 1997).

The Mall of America opened in 1992 in Bloomington, Minnesota, with 520 stores and twenty sit-down restaurants; it employed more than 12,000 people and recorded an annual visitation averaging 35 to 42 million people. At over 4.2 million square feet it was far and away the single largest mall in the country. (By comparison the Del Amo Fashion Center in Torrance, California, contained 3 million square feet of enclosed mall space, and only nine other malls in the country had between 2 million and 2.9 million square feet.) The mall's unique attraction was a seven-acre indoor amusement park with more than 50 rides including a roller coaster, a Ferris wheel, and a water ride. The top level of the mall was devoted entirely as an entertainment area with a multiplex movie theater, nightclubs, a bowling alley, and video arcades (www.mallofamerica.com).

By the late 1990s, another mall experience attracted shoppers by the millions—fashion outlet malls. Fashion outlet malls offered discount prices in stores marketing one specific designer brand of clothing. Ontario Mills, 40 miles east of Los Angeles, California, contained over 2 million square feet and two separate multiplex movie theaters totaling 54 screens and attracted more than 20 million shoppers per year—making it California's top tourist attraction. In the year 2000, the ICSC reported 278 outlet malls nationwide (ICSC Research Quarterly, n.p.).

By 2000, about 30 regional malls (built between 1985 and 2000) were classified as "lifestyle centers." The ICSC defined a lifestyle center as catering "to the retail needs and 'lifestyle' pursuits of consumers . . . located most often near affluent residential neighborhoods . . . [and] serv[ing] as a multi-purpose leisure-time destination" (ICSC Research Quarterly, 1). An example of a lifestyle center was Flatiron Crossing in Broomfield, Colorado. It opened in 2000, as an "indoor-outdoor center [that included] a 17-acre park with bike trails for the community" (Cohen, 13). By 2000, malls of all kinds had effectively become the new community center.

ENTERTAINMENT

Television, TV Talk Shows, Home Entertainment Systems, and Talk Radio

In 1992, the U.S. Statistical Abstract reported that televisions were in over 98 percent of all American households with each household averaging at least two TV sets. In addition, 84.6 percent of households had a videocassette recorder (VCR), and 67.2 percent were hooked up to cable TV. On any given evening, more than 100 million Americans regularly watched television (Statistical Abstract [2000], 567).

By the end of the 1990s, the longest-running prime-time network television program was an animated series, *The Simpsons*. The success of the show, which first aired in January 1990, led to a host of other animated series geared toward young adults such as *Beavis and Butt-head* (1993), *King of the Hill* (1997), and *South Park* (1997) — all except one of which (*Beavis and Butt-head*) were still running at the end of the century. In 1995, politics and television were completely intertwined as Senator Bob Dole announced he was running for president in the 1996 presidential campaign on *Late Night with David Letterman*, an evening network talk show.

Television talk shows proved to be immensely popular. Some talk show hosts, including Jerry Springer and Geraldo Rivera, turned their television shows into voyeuristic debate that became known as "trash TV" in which guests argued among themselves and with the audience. The *Oprah Winfrey Show* (1984), and the late 1990s introductions of *The Rosie O'Donnell Show* (1996), and *The View* (1997) catered to a predominantly female audience and attempted to provide a sensible alternative to the trash TV talk shows.

In 1992, cable household subscribers numbered 53 million, and that number increased to 66.5 million by the year 2000. Other television developments included Direct TV and other TV satellite dish providers that gave viewers access to literally hundreds of channels. In 1994, the introduction of digital television service provided sharper and clearer television images. Specialty sound systems, large screen televisions, and DVDs (digital video discs) for movies added to home entertainment. A DVD was a CD-ROM that contained a movie. In 1998, only 500,000 DVD units were sold. The following year, more than 2.5 million DVDs were purchased for home use, and DVD sales quickly outpaced videocassette sales (Statistical Abstract [2000], 567, 573).

Virtually every American household (99 percent) had a radio; amazingly, each household averaged almost six radios. By 2000, the total number of commercial radio stations was 10,577 (5,892 FM and 4,685 AM); an additional 2,140 stations were noncommercial FM stations such as college radio stations (Hilliard and Keith, 324). Unlike in earlier years when the radio disc jockey provided the prominent personality and audience draw for a radio station, the shift in music radio was toward homogenous music stations that planned their programming for specific listener markets.

During this period, the dominant radio format quickly changed from music to talk radio. In 1987, talk radio accounted for only about 125 of the more than 9,000 radio stations in the country. By 1998, there were more than 1,350 talk radio stations. A Times Mirror survey "found that 44 percent of Americans named talk radio as their primary source for political information." Conservatives such as Rush Limbaugh, radio therapists such as Laura Schlessinger and Joy Brown, and shock jocks such as Howard Stern, and Don Imus, were each heard daily by more than 20 million listeners. The common trend among many radio talk show hosts was basically to offend individuals or groups, which one radio executive described as "simply more entertaining [than music]." For those concerned with "serious talk" and radio news coverage National Public Radio reached 16 million Americans through 520 station affiliates and established itself "as a dependable voice" (Pendergast and Pendergast, *Encyclopedia of Popular Culture*, Vol. 4: 601).

Newspapers, Best-sellers, Harry Potter, and the Oprah Book Club

The U.S. Census Bureau reported that newspapers declined in circulation from 62.3 million in 1990 to 56 million in 1999. Overall, the total number of daily publications also declined from 1,611 in 1990 to 1,483 in 1999. During the same years, morning newspaper circulation continued a steady increase from 43 million to 46 million, and evening circulation declined from 16.7 million to 10 million. Sunday newspaper circulation remained steady at 60 million. The decline was in part due to fast-action news sources such as the Internet and television programs (Statistical Abstract [2000], 576).

In 1998, at least 78 million adults reported reading at least one book in the previous year, and 45 million of those read at least twice a week. Books sold at more than two billion per year throughout the 1990s. The range of popular books was diverse and ranged from comedy (*SeinLanguage* [1993] by TV star and comedian Jerry Seinfeld) to social sarcasm (*Downsize This!* [1996] by Michael Moore). *The Pelican Brief*, a legal thriller by John Grisham, was the top-selling novel of the 1990s and sold 11.2 million copies. Grisham wrote four of the other top-ten best-selling novels, each selling more than five million copies. Other best-selling titles of the period included John Gray's *Men are from Mars, Women are from Venus* that sold 6.6 million copies, Michael Crichton's *Jurassic Park* at 6.4 million copies, Crichton's *Rising Sun* at 5.6 million copies, Rosie Daley's *In the Kitchen with Rose* at 5.9 million copies, and Robert James Waller's *Bridges of Madison County* at 5.8 million copies (McConnell, *American Decades: 1990–1999*, 400).

In 1999, the allure of reading for children reached an unprecedented high with the introduction of the *Harry Potter* children's book series by J. K. Rowling. Rowling's three novels of wizardry and fantasy—*Harry Potter and the Sorcerer's Stone* (1998), *Harry Potter and the Chamber of Secrets* (1999), and *Harry Potter and the Prisoner of Azkaban* (1999)—sold more than 7.5 million total copies and were on the *New York Times* best-seller list—a rarity for children's books. The Harry Potter series was also read and enjoyed by many adults (McConnell, *American Decades: 1990–1999*, 345).

Television talk show host Oprah Winfrey, whose show was watched by 26 million viewers each weekday afternoon, proved that the power of television could drastically increase book sales. Winfrey created the Oprah Book Club, choosing one book each month as her pick and encouraging viewers to read the book. Five days after the first book was chosen, *The Deep End of the Ocean* by Jacquelyn Mitchard went to the top of the *New York Times* best-seller fiction list on September 22, 1996 (Kirkpatrick, "Oprah Will Curtail 'Book Club' Picks and Authors Weep," 1). Each of Winfrey's 46 monthly picks became best-sellers and sold an additional one million copies after being picked for the club. One publishing executive said, "To my knowledge, there has never been any single person or outlet that has been able to affect book sales in [that] way" (TIME.com, "Winfrey's Winners," December 2, 1996).

Fads, Games, Pokémon, and Video Games

In the early 1990s bungee jumping caught on as a fad. In bungee jumping, a long rubber cable was fastened by a harness to an individual who leapt off a bridge or cliff in a skydiving fashion. The idea was that after free-falling for a time, the rubber cable would prevent the jumper from hitting the ground or water below.

In 1999, several surveys named Barbie as the most popular toy of the twentieth century, and she made her movie debut in the Hollywood movie *Toy Story 2*. In late 2000, Americans purchased more than 10 million razor scooters (similar to a narrow skateboard with a single vertical T-shaped handlebar) as part of a new fad that quickly faded in a few months. Cards and board games also remained popular.

In 1998, Nintendo introduced Pokémon in the United States as a Game Boy program (a game to be played on a small, handheld, electronic game-playing system), trading cards, and comic books that quickly became a billion-dollar industry. Pokémon was described as "a whole world that a kid, or a grown-up kid, can immerse himself in . . . full of quest possibilities, role-playing and interactive challenge" (Kent, 566–567).

In 1993, *Time* magazine reported, "What once seemed like a passing fad for preteen boys has grown into a global moneymaking machine. . . . Video games rake in $5.3 billion a year in the U.S. alone, about $400 million more than Americans spend going to the movies" (TIME.com, "The Amazing Video Game Boom," September 27, 1993).

By 1992, the Sega Genesis System, due in part to the success of the game *Sonic the Hedgehog* (1991), overtook Nintendo in the home video game market. *Sonic the Hedgehog* had the distinction of introducing extreme speed in video game characters and launched a video game competition that lasted throughout the 1990s. According to Steven Kent, *Doom*, (1991), created by id Software, "had the most long-lasting impact on the gaming world" and also set the standard of "the 3D [three-dimensional] first-person shooter genre" (Kent, 430–431, 457–459). A first-person shooter game provided a player with the perspective from the "eyes" of the video game character.

In 1991, *Street Fighter II*, created by Yoshiki Okamoto for Konami, led to an abundance of fighting games. Unlike the original Street Fighter that was a one-on-one fighting game, *Street Fighter II* had "multiple hidden moves" for the ten additional fighters added to the "returning martial artists Ryu and Ken." In 1993, *Mortal Kombat II*, created by Ed Boon and John Tobias for Williams Manufacturing, introduced new characters in a fight to the death. With a push of a few buttons, the player could literally punch "the foe's head off his body, ripping out his spine, causing his head to explode, [and] ripping out his heart." Both Sega and Nintendo sold more than 6.5 million copies of a home version of the game. The Mortal Kombat game was so popular that it led to seven game versions, two Hollywood movies, and a syndicated TV cartoon series (Kent, 445–446, 462, 466).

Critics complained of the inherent violence in many video games, prompting a U.S. Senate hearing in 1993. As a result, the Entertainment Software Rating Board (ESRB) was formed to rate games in a fashion similar to movie ratings. However, only about 10 percent of the games rated were considered violent. The others included skateboarding, football, baseball, golf, and snowboarding games, and players continued to purchase and play video games.

On September 9, 1995, Sony released the PlayStation video game console and sold almost one million units within four months. By 2000, more than 50 million had been sold worldwide. On September 29, 1996, the eagerly awaited Nintendo 64 was available and sold almost equally as well (Kent, 537, 560).

Unlike the other home video game systems, the Nintendo Game Boy (introduced in America in November 1989) was a completely portable, small, handheld system about the size of a standard paperback book. Two AA batteries provided enough power to operate the game for more than ten hours, thereby making it an ideal video game that could be played anywhere that it could be carried. For twelve years, Game Boy remained virtually unchanged and sold more than 115 million units in addition to more than 450 million game cartridges, making it the "most popular game system of all time" (Kent, 322). By the year 2000, the October 26 release of Sony's PlayStation 2 incorporated CD-ROM formats and sold more than 10 million units within 15 months (80 million worldwide). Sega Dreamcasts also sold 6.5 million units in 22 months (Kent, 589–590).

Regarding video games, *Time* magazine reported, "Grownups, as a rule, don't get it." But video games were growing up. In 1980, video game players were mainly 8 to 14 years old (see chapter 8); by 1990, the bottom age stayed at 8, but the top age increased to 24 years old. Then by 2000, the video game age bracket was 8 to 35. Las Vegas and other gambling casinos added huge video arcades. DisneyQuest in Orlando, Florida, was an astonishing "90,000 square feet of high-tech games." GameWorks in Seattle, Washington, advertised "A place where an adult wanted to go and could get good food, get Starbucks coffee, a good beer, have good music playing, and meet other adults in a place that was attractive and appealing." More than 100 video game locations, each location averaging 35,000 square feet, were planned throughout the country (Kent, 528).

Country Line Dancing, the Electric Slide, the Macarena, and Swing Dancing

Line dancing could be traced back to the late 1950s and early 1960s with the Madison and alley cat dances and was even around during the disco dance craze. Line dancing was performed by a group of people in lines, all facing in the same direction and moving in unison to a limited number of choreographed dance steps that were repeated throughout a particular song. From 1984 to 1997, country line dancing was the rage. However, country dancing was not limited to line dancing, and country nightclubs also encouraged choreographed partner dancing and traditional partner dances such as the two-step, cha-cha, waltz, swing, and even the hustle.

In the early 1990s, the most popular line dance of the period was the electric slide, which was danced to a noncountry song, "Electric Boogie," by Jamaican reggae music artist Marcia Griffiths. The dance became a staple at weddings, catered affairs, and on cruise ships. Another line dance that became just as widespread at the same types of events was the macarena. In 1993, the macarena dance to the song of the same name, released that same year by Los Del Mar, began in dance clubs. It was a simple dance that involved almost all hand and arm movements. Many clubs, parties, organizations, and even major league baseball stadiums held macarena nights.

Two popular movies geared toward the teenage audience, *Swing Kids* (1992) and *Swingers* (1996), featured dance scenes that ignited a revival in both swing music and swing dance (see chapter 4). Swing dance societies and clubs became prominent in cities such as Boston, Detroit, Des Moines, Houston, Los Angeles, New York, Philadelphia, and San Francisco. In addition, in the year 2000, Broadway put on a production appropriately named *Swing!* Some said dance was fading by 2000, but dance clubs of all sorts flourished.

By the year 2000, Dancing Classrooms, a 20-class session in 37 New York City public schools, taught more than 3,500 elementary schoolchildren ballroom dancing. Similar programs were offered at Edgewood High School in Madison, Wisconsin; the San Francisco Unified School District; and in Los Angeles, California, and Atlanta, Georgia. Ballroom dancing was also popular on college campuses. In 2000, Brigham Young University not only boasted more than six thousand students involved in some type of social dance instruction, but also that it was the only university in the nation offering a degree program in ballroom dance (TIME.com, "They're Having a Ball," March 12, 2001).

Amusement Parks, Coney Island, Water Parks, and Leisure Liability

Throughout the 1990s, amusement parks continued to report record attendance figures. In the year 2000, the International Association of Amusement Parks and Attractions reported that 317 million people visited amusement parks each year. Disney World, Florida, continued to be the top attraction with 42.6 million visitors a year. Disneyland in Anaheim, California, was second at 13.45 million visitors. At a distant third was Universal Studios, Florida, with 8.1 million visitors, followed by Island Adventures at Universal Orlando at 6 million, Universal Studios Hollywood at 5.2 million and Sea World Florida at 5.15 million visitors per year. Eleven other parks attracted more than three million visitors, 13 more than two million, and 17 more than one million. The large theme parks were expensive to visit, and many required at least a few days' overnight hotel stay to be thoroughly explored (Sterngold, "Fantasy Lands' Ailing Turnstiles," TR:6).

In 1994, *Time* magazine reported that smaller suburban play areas were reappearing "along highways across the country . . . capturing the niche between mega-theme parks and video arcades." Activities included batting ranges, go-cart tracks, and fast-food establishments. Another popular activity was miniature golf, which nationwide averaged more than 30 million players per year throughout the 1990s.

The nation's first amusement park, Coney Island (see chapter 1), was still in operation. The Wonder Wheel and the Cyclone roller coaster (see chapter 3) were still entertaining riders. The Parachute Jump (see chapter 4) was still standing but not operational. In 1991, to encourage people to traverse the boardwalk, the Mermaid Day Parade was instituted and attracted hundreds of thousands of visitors. The yearly parade held each June to celebrate the first day of summer and the official opening of the beach at Coney Island attracted thousands of participants dressed as mermaids, Neptune and other aquatic creatures. The entire event is light hearted fun with competitors vying for the title of Mermaid Queen or King. The parade continued through the 1990s and became an integral part of celebrations in connection with the construction along the boardwalk of a minor league professional baseball stadium to host the Brooklyn Cyclones in 1999.

In 1996, the World Waterpark Association reported that there were 950 facilities operating nationwide with a total seasonal attendance of 58 million. Water slides and tubing were common in the waterparks. Tubing involved sitting in the inner tube of a tire and floating on a river, lake, or even a backyard pool. Schlitterbahn, a 65-acre water park in New Braunfels, Texas (opened in 1979), featured more than 40 rides and activities, including 17 water slides and a 50,000 square foot "lagoon" swimming pool; the park attracted more than 900,000 visitors each season from 1994 to 2000.

With the type of activity involved with amusement park rides, water park slides, and activities on rivers and lakes came a certain number of injuries and accidents.

Adults, children, and families enjoyed water rides at one of the many water parks that provided seasonal family fun. Courtesy of Schlitterbahn Waterpark Resort, New Braunfels, Texas.

With the accidents also came insurance claims and lawsuits. Product liability cases abounded against all sorts of amusement park rides, boating activities, skateboards, ski lifts, ski bindings, bicycles, in-line skates, scuba diving, playgrounds, bicycles, and exercise equipment (Ho, "More than 10,000 people injured on thrill rides in 2000, feds say," A25).

MUSIC AND THEATER

Broadway and the National Endowment for the Arts

In 1991, the show *Miss Saigon* provided a feature unique to Broadway by utilizing a full-size helicopter as a prop and ran for more than four thousand performances. Other long-running shows of the period included *Rent* and *Chicago*. Both opened in 1996 and were still running in the year 2000 at 2,535 and 2,306 performances, respectively. *Smokey Joe's Café* ran from 1995 to 2000, culminating at 2,037 performances ("Longest Running Broadway Shows in History," n.p.).

Two Disney movies were also made into elaborate and successful Broadway productions. In 1994, *Beauty and the Beast* opened and ran for more than three thousand performances by 2000. *The Lion King* opened in 1997 and ran for 1,896 performances by 2000. As with stage productions of the previous decade, they also featured elaborate sets, technological wizardry, and high production costs.

Broadway ticket prices remained high, but Broadway showed an unprecedented increase in attendance. In 1992, the U.S. Statistical Abstract reported attendance was at 7.4 million and increased steadily each year to 11.5 million in 1998. The road tours of Broadway shows accounted for an additional 15.2 million audience members. Non-profit professional theaters nationwide attracted an additional 14.6 million people. In 1998, symphony orchestras nationwide played to 32.2 million listeners (Statistical Abstract [2000], 267). Jacksonville, Florida, was typical of the many cities that offered a variety of theater, which prior to 1970 did not exist. One Jacksonville theater and performing arts location was a "restored 1920s-era movie picture palace [that hosted] more than 300 concerts, theater performances and special events each year." The Jacksonville Symphony Orchestra provided "more than 130 classical, popular, and special events concerts each year" (www. visitjacksonville.com).

In 1998, the U.S. Statistical Abstract reported that opera companies nationwide numbered 1,250 (up from 986 in 1980) and attendance figures topped 6.6 million (up from 4.6 million in 1970). In addition to opera, forty-three million adults reported attending a music performance within the previous year, and 31 million attended at least once a month; 11.9 million adults attended a cultural dance performance (Statistical Abstract [2000], 264).

A 1992 Harris poll found that "60 percent of those polled in the east and south supported federal arts funding [as did a large majority in the West and Midwest]. Clearly, the dominant feeling in this country is in favor of continued federal assistance to the arts" (McConnell *American Decades 1990-1999,* 348). However, right-wing senators and conservative congressional committees disagreed and rescinded federal funding from the National Endowment for the Arts (NEA) for projects that they themselves deemed unacceptable to receive public funds. One such notable example was an exhibit by photographer Robert Mapplethorpe. Mapplethorpe's photographs and displays contained religious images that some critics claimed disrespected the Catholic church. (Some claim that much of the pressure against Mapplethorpe came about as a result of his avowed homosexuality.)

By the mid 1990s, federal contributions for arts programs were down to only $170 million per year; significantly decreased from the more than $600 million allocated each year during the early 1970s. As a result, these programs sought funding from other sources. Individual state funding totaled $273 million, and corporate sponsorship provided more than $630 million. John Rockwell, an art critic for the *New York Times* indicated that these numbers were far short of the total arts expenditures made by other countries (Kraus [1994], 293–294).

Regardless of the funding difficulties, throughout the 1990s, museums continued to tally record numbers of visitors. In 1997, the American Association of Museums estimated that more than 865 million people visited museums during the previous year.

Movie Screens, Highest-grossing Movies, and All-time Attendance Figures

In the late 1990s, the move theater design once again changed. Many new stadium seating theaters were built that incorporated comfortable high-back seats that provided a clear line of sight for each individual viewer as well as better movie projection systems that increased sound and visual quality. During the mid-1990s, more than 50 large IMAX movie screens were also constructed (www. bigmoviezone.com). IMAX theaters are large screens (70 to 80 feet in height) and "feature a giant, flat, silver screen and seating that is steeply pitched between 19 and 25 degrees" allowing unobstructed vision of the movie screen. According to IMAX, the dome theater version, "are 180° encompassing," and "tilted at 30 degrees. . . . completely involving [the audience] in the images projected on the screen" (IMAX.com, "Theaters – IMAX Theater Types," n.p.). Most Hollywood films were intended for widespread release, and an individual film was likely to be shown simultaneously on three to five thousand screens throughout the nation. Movie attendance was also up for the first time since the early 1960s. The chart on the following page indicates the total number of movie screens and admissions nationwide during the 1990s.

With more than $600 million dollars in proceeds, *Titanic* (1997) was both the highest-grossing film of the period and the highest-grossing film of the entire century. Other films of the period that were also among the all-time top ten moneymakers included *Jurassic Park* (1993) at $357 million, *Forrest Gump* (1994) at $329 million, and *The Lion King* (1994) at $313 million.

In May 1999, millions of fans filled the movie theaters for a midnight showing of the most eagerly anticipated film of all time: the *Star Wars* prequel, *Episode I: The Phantom Menace*. It grossed more than $431 million, and when combined with the *Star Wars* trilogy (see chapter 8), it was part of the highest-grossing movie series of all time. The *Star Wars* films were high budget and filled with expensive special effects. For all movies of the 1990s, Michael S. James of ABCNews.com reported that "the average film budget was almost $53 million [and] many films cost over $100 million to produce." However, there was one notable exception.

Number of Movie Theaters and Screens and Total Admissions

	Indoor		Drive-In		Total		Admissions
Year	Sites	Screens	Sites	Screens	Sites	Screens	(In Billions)
2000	6,571	35,627	408	667	6,979	36,264	1.42
1999	7,031	36,488	520	737	7,551	37,185	1.47
1998	6,894	33,418	524	750	7,418	34,168	1.48
1997	6,903	31,050	577	815	7,480	31,865	1.39
1996	7,215	28,905	583	826	7,798	29,731	1.34
1995	7,151	27,843	593	848	7,744	27,843	1.26
1994		25,830		859		26,689	1.29
1993		24,789		837		25,626	1.24
1992		24,344		870		25,214	1.17

Note: Number of sites not available for 1992–1994.
Source: The National Association of Theatre Owners (www.natoonline.org/statistics.htm).

The low-budget independent film *The Blair Witch Project* (1999) "became the most profitable film (percentage-wise) of all time, earning $140 million domestically, but budgeted at only $50,000." The film was a fictional documentary of a horrifying camping trip in which the filmmakers—a group of young adults setting out to make a documentary about a supposedly haunted forest—disappeared one by one.

Higher movie production costs translated to higher ticket prices, which contributed to the ever-changing list of highest-grossing films. In 2000, Exhibitor Relations Co., an Encino, California, box office tracking firm produced a list of the twentieth century's all-time top movies based on attendance figures as opposed to gross receipts:

Movie Title	Admissions
1. *Gone With the Wind* (1939)	202,044,569
2. *Star Wars* (1977)	178,119,595
3. *The Sound of Music* (1965)	142,415,376
4. *E.T.* (1982)	141,925,359
5. *The Ten Commandments* (1956)	131,000,000
6. *Titanic* (1997)	129,201,761
7. *Jaws* (1975)	128,078,818
8. *Snow White* (1937)	109,000,000
9. *101 Dalmatians* (1961)	99,917,251
10. *The Empire Strikes Back* (1980)	98,106,044

All the movies listed above, as was almost every Hollywood film of the entire twentieth century, were available for home viewing on either videocassette tapes or DVDs (ABCNews.com, "Era of Blockbusters?" May 20, 2001).

Grunge, Hip-hop Swing, the Lilith Fair, Country, and Napster

Music recordings of all kinds maintained steady yearly sales increases throughout the 1990s. By 1999, CDs alone accounted for 994.8 million units sold (the music recording industry itself was a $14.5-billion-dollar-a-year business). Cassettes sold an additional 137.8 million units. Vinyl albums (LPs) sold only 8.2 million units sold. Music video sales increased steadily from 9.2 million units in 1990 to 27.2 million units in 1998. Rock music accounted for 25.2 percent of all recordings sales, followed by country at 10.8, rap/hip-hop at 10.8 percent, R and B (rhythm and blues)/urban at 10.5 percent, pop at 10.3 percent, religious at 5.1 percent, classical at 3.5 percent, and jazz at 3.0 percent (Statistical Abstract [2000], 256, 573).

In the early 1990s, an alternative rock music movement known as grunge developed in the Pacific Northwest area of the United States. The music and lyrics of grunge songs reflected the sociological and economical realities of divorce, unemployment, and the apathy and hopelessness of generation X. In addition, grunge espoused a kind of antifashion attitude that characterized the movement with band members and fans of groups such as Nirvana, Pearl Jam, Alice in Chains, and Soundgarden wearing flannel shirts and jeans.

By 1992, hip-hop also became a powerful voice of the young, both black and white that had expanded nationwide. (Hip-hop was the lifestyle culture, and rap was its music.) Many associated hip-hop with negative lifestyle choices, and "gangsta rap" dominated the media's attention, sensationalized by the 1997 shooting deaths of rappers Tupac Shakur and Christopher "Notorious BIG" Wallace. The lyrics in gangsta rap contains violent and explicit lyrics, sexual content, and misogyny. Mainstream rap artists' sampled lyrics and music from many sources including rock and pop. In 1999, one such artist Jay-Z incorporated the chorus of the song "It's A Hard Knock Life" from the Broadway show *Annie* (1977–1983). In 1996, The Fugees used the chorus of the Roberta Flack hit "Killing Me Softly With His Song" (1973). Mainstream rappers such as Will Smith and LL Cool J were major Hollywood film industry stars.

In the early 1990s, swing music also resurfaced. In 1998, the swing band Big Bad Voodoo Daddy made three national televised appearances—at the Super Bowl halftime show, the Macy's Thanksgiving Day Parade, and the Orange Bowl halftime show—that exposed their music to an estimated 400 million viewers. Brian Setzer, former lead of the Stray Cats band, used his electric guitar to front a big band (Brian Setzer Orchestra) and performed the song "Jump Jive an' Wail" to close the televised 1998 MTV Music Awards. During the summer of that same year, no less than six swing CDs were on the mainstream Billboard top two hundred record chart (Badasski, 50).

In 1997, the Lilith Fair music festival featured female musicians appearing in 38 locations nationwide. The initial fair was a success and was expanded in 1998 to 57 shows. By 1999, women purchased more than half of all music recordings (Statistical Abstract [2000], 256). Alanis Morissette's *Jagged Little Pill* album was the top-selling album of the 1990s with more than 16 million copies sold. In 1998, the first Ozzfest, an all-day music festival featuring recording artist Ozzy

Osbourne marked the return of metal music. Ozzfest continued through the end of the decade as the highest-grossing summer tour (McConnell, *American Decades 1990-1999*, 67-68).

The individual musician who sold the most CDs of the period was country music star Garth Brooks. By the close of the century, Brooks's total CD sales topped 100 million, making him the top-selling individual musical act of the twentieth century. In August 1997, one of his concerts in New York City's Central Park (see chapter 1) was performed live in front of one million fans and to a television audience of more than 15 million people.

By the year 2000, the Recording Industry Association of America (RIAA) reported that almost 35 percent of new CD music purchases were by persons over 40 years of age, who represented 18.9 percent of all CD purchasers. By comparison, the number of those 25 years of age and younger who were purchasing CDs dropped from 42.4 percent in 1990 to 33.7 percent in 1999 (Statistical Abstract [2000], 256). The largest drop was among those 15 to 19 years of age, whose purchases dropped by more than a third. Some viewed the drop-off among younger audiences as a direct result of Napster and computer pirating sources.

In late 1999, the Napster program appeared on the Internet, which allowed users to swap music files without having to buy a CD. The music was downloaded by MP3 (technical language ISO-MPEG audio layer-3), which was first developed in 1987 "as a way of compressing CD-quality sound files." The Napster program and Web site quickly attracted more than 25 million users, most in the 15 to 19-year-old age group. Record companies and music artists initiated copyright infringement lawsuits against Napster, eventually shutting it down in the year 2000. Other Web sites such as Imesh and Kazaa quickly copied the music pirating idea, and music swapping on the Internet continued throughout the century (TIME.com, "Meet the Napster," October 2, 2000).

SPORTS AND GAMES

Professional Sports, Spectators, Female Athletes, and Bass Fishing

As more Americans watched sports on television, the sports industry grew into an enormous business, and sports events became widely viewed among Americans as cultural experiences. In response, professional sports teams, in both major and minor leagues, embarked on a massive sports stadium rebuilding programs during this time. Many, if not all, of the stadiums built prior to 1975 were either extensively refurbished or demolished and replaced with new state-of-the-art facilities. Spectatorship at all professional sporting events grew at a terrific rate.

According to the U.S. Statistical Abstract, in 1998, Major League Baseball recorded an all-time attendance high of 71.9 million (up from 55.5 million in 1990). Collegiate football attendance remained fairly constant throughout the 1990s with a slight increase to 37.5 million in 1998, as did professional football at 31 million fans. Professional basketball attendance continued to rise from 18.8 million in 1990 to 21.8 million in 1998. College basketball attendance remained steady at 28 million per year for men's teams, but attendance at college women's basketball games rose from 2.8 million fans in 1990 to a respectable 7.4 million fans in 1998. The National Hockey League attendance figures also grew from 13.7 million to 18.7 million. In 1997, horse racing attracted 41.9 million fans with 11,958 racing days. Greyhound racing attracted an additional 14.6 million and jai alai, 2.1 million fans (Statistical Abstract [2000], 260).

In 1998, NCAA sports participation within the nation's colleges and universities numbered 203,600 male participants on 7,723 teams. Female participation stood at 135,110 on 7,859 college teams nationwide. More than 40,000 female college athletes participated in track or cross-country running. Between 12,500 and 15,900 college females played soccer, softball, basketball, and volleyball. By comparison 55,000 college males participated in football, 24,000 in baseball, 17,000 in soccer, 15,000 in basketball, and 45,000 in track or cross-country running (Statistical Abstract [2000], 258).

In 1999, National Association of Stock Car Auto Racing (NASCAR) events accounted for 17 of the top twenty best-attended professional sporting events. The 38 series corporate-sponsored races attracted 6.5 million spectators, at an average of 164,500 fans per event and a television audience in excess of 300 million (Motor Sports Management "NASCAR Basics," n.p.). In September 2000, a new, redesigned speedway was built at the Indianapolis Motor Speedway (see chapter 1). With the construction of 250,000 permanent seats, it was the nation's largest sporting venue, all for only three yearly events: the Indy 500, the NASCAR Brickyard 400, and a Formula One Grand Prix (*Architectural Record* magazine, May 2002: 258–260). Attendance for all sponsored race car events including Indy cars, stock cars, dragsters, sprint cars, and trucks combined for more than 15.4 million spectators for only 276 racing dates. In addition, NASCAR merchandising exceeded that of the National Football League (NFL), National Basketball Association (NBA), and NHL combined (www.racegoodyear.com).

Sponsorship and commercialization of sports was even more firmly entrenched in American culture as Americans' insatiable desire for spectator sports initiated a search for alternative sports programming. During this period, new sports were created specifically for television viewers, including professional beach volleyball and X Games. The first X Games was a promotion by the ESPN television sports network in the summer of 1995 that included skateboarding, BMX bicycling, wall climbing, street luge, in-line skating, and other nontraditional sports. In 1998, the winter X Games were added, which included snowboarding and freestyle snow skiing.

Another televised sport was bass fishing. Similar to other sports, bass fishing featured a series of scheduled tournaments culminating in a season-end championship. Competitions of the FLW tour (named after Forrest L. Wood, the founder of Ranger Boats and formerly the B.A.S.S. Bass Anglers Sportsman Society tour) aired on cable sports channels. By 2000, advertisers embraced the sport and sponsored tournaments with prizes totaling almost $1 million. Sponsors included outboard motor companies, aluminum boat makers, rod and reel manufacturers, and also companies that made non-fishing products such as restaurants, cereal makers, and national department stores (*New York Times*, "Hooked on Bass Fishing at an Early Age," August 18, 2002: SP12).

Frequency of Activity, Female Participation, Lacrosse, and Cosmic Bowling

Sadly, by 2000, only about 20 percent of the nation's 281 million inhabitants were classified as physically fit. By the end of the century, the surgeon general's office introduced as its "number one goal" the Healthy People 2010 campaign. The idea was to increase activity among Americans on a regular basis and not as a one-time endeavor. The U.S. Census Bureau and the SGMA charted the frequency of participation in sports and recreation activities.

In 1998, the U.S. Statistical Abstract indicated that in 1998 walking, with 77.6 million participants, had replaced swimming (58.3 million participants) as the most popular activity. Basketball (with 39.4 million players overall) was the most popular team sport with 29.4 million individuals playing on a regular basis (more than 40 times per year); 7.2 million basketball players were over the age of 35. The number of female basketball players was 9.3 million (Statistical Abstract [2000], 262).

By 2000, the SGMA reported that golfers numbered 27.5 million, and 9.2 million Americans golfed more than 25 times per year. By 1998, 14,900 golf courses existed in the country, an increase of about 1,500 since 1992. At least 400 new courses were municipal courses for a nationwide total of 2,402 municipal courses. Golf was a predominantly male sport (75 percent) with an average age of 48; however, more than half of all new players entering the sport were either members of a minority group or female. Of all team sports, soccer, with 13.2

Recreational jogging in Clove Lakes Park in Staten Island, New York. Author's archives.

million players, had the lowest average age at 15 and softball the highest at 25 (SGMA, "Golf: Play Is Steady While Sales Struggle," n.p.).

Other activities of regular participation included baseball with 15.9 million players and slow-pitch softball with 17.6 million players (at least 6 million played 25 times a year). Slightly more than half slow-pitch softball players were male. Fast-pitch softball players' average age was 18, and more than two-thirds of them were female. The SGMA indicated that "volleyball and softball are the two main team sports where the number of female 'frequent' players outnumbers their male counterparts" (SGMA, "The American Way to Play," n.p.). Although female participation was greatly increasing, the SGMA noted that after the age of 18, female participation dropped off greatly. At the time, manufacturers also marketed equipment specifically for the female athlete including sports bras, footwear designed specifically for the female foot, and baby jogging strollers (which men also found gave them the freedom to run).

Other regular recreational activities for both men and women included aerobic exercise at 25.8 million participants, in-line skating at 27.9 million, roller-skating at 9.9 million, running or jogging at 22.5 million (many individually in a local park or on a roadway), volleyball at 14.8 million, and tennis at 14.7 million participants who played more than four times per year. Target shooting was reported by 12.8 million individuals; touch football, 9.6 million; tackle football, 7.5 million; and Ping-Pong, 8.4 million. Paintball had 6.4 million participants with almost half of them playing for the first time. Archery and badminton had 4.8 million participants; 4.6 million studied and performed martial arts; 4 million played racquetball; and the surfing culture remained strong with 2.7 million active wave riders (SGMA, "Popular Trends in Sports and Fitness," n.p. and SGMA, "Whassup?. . . . With Extreme Sports?" n.p.).

The fastest-growing team sport was also the oldest sport in American history. Lacrosse, an ancient Native American Indian game, is played outdoors with a netted racket attached to a metal stick used to pick up, pass, or shoot a solid rubber ball that is slightly smaller than a tennis ball. Shooting the ball into the opposing team's net scores a point. Prior to 1990, the sport was confined to regional areas of the Northeast. (Women's rules differed with limited body contact and less protective equipment.) The explosion of the sport occurred in the mid-1990s as more than 1,600 high schools and 400 colleges across the country added the sport for both males and females. By 1998, the sport had more than 230,000 active players. (More than two-thirds of all lacrosse players were less than 17 years of age.) In addition, more than three hundred teams played beyond the collegiate level (www.laxpower.com).

In 2000, the SGMA reported that "more boys aged 6 to 17 went skateboarding (7.5 million) than played baseball (6.9 million)." Overall, skateboarding showed the second-greatest increase with 9.6 million participants in 2000. The SGMA also listed more than six hundred public skate parks that opened between 1998 and 2000 to accommodate skateboarders. At the end of 2000, the SGMA also noted that, "scooters were all the rage. Between 8 and 12 million scooters were purchased in a buying frenzy that lasted only a few months. . . . But the bubble burst in January [2001], and scooter sales fell to almost nothing" (SGMA, "Skates, Boards, Scooters: Sales Down But Participation Steady," n.p.).

Bowling maintained high participation levels. In 1998, the SGMA recorded

During the 1990s lacrosse was the fastest-growing team sport. Msgr. Farrell High School in Staten Island, New York. Author's archives.

Bowling was a consistently popular activity throughout the entire twentieth century. The introduction of "cosmic bowling" provided family entertainment in a "dance club" atmosphere. Courtesy Brunswick Bowling.

that more than 40 million people bowled more than once a year (8.5 million bowled at least 25 times per year). However, overall participation was in decline, and the number of bowling lanes decreased from 148,000 within 7,611 centers in 1992 to 131,000 within 6,542 centers by 1998. The SGMA stated the reason for the decline as "more competition from other activities, more women in the workforce and the relatively long bowling season have also taken their toll on the ranks of league bowlers." In an attempt to increase participation, especially among younger individuals, bowling alleys nationwide introduced cosmic bowling (SGMA, "Bowling Finds Stability Despite Problems," n.p.).

The Brunswick company, that also introduced a glow-in-the-dark bowling ball, described cosmic bowling as "glow-in-the-dark bowling with a dance club atmosphere that rocks the center with a state-of-the-art sound system." Most bowling centers also provided light shows and fog machines. The idea was "a bowling and family entertainment center designed to develop more recreational play and appeal to a more non-traditional bowling demographic" (www.brunswickbowling.com).

Winter Sports, Snowboarding, Ski Equipment, and Ski Accidents

Between 1992 and 2000, regular participation in ice hockey increased slightly to 2.2 million in 2000 up from 2 million in 1992 and remained a favored winter sport in the colder northern areas. The United States Figure Skating Association reported the number of people who ice-skated at least once a year at 30 million and reported that 7.8 million ice-skated on a regular basis (Pendergast and Pendergast, *Encyclopedia of Popular Culture*, Vol. 4: 430).

In 1994, the SGMA recorded 14 million downhill skiers, 4.7 million cross-country skiers, and 2.4 million snowboarders. The ski slopes not only were more frequently used by snowboarders, but also some skiers were giving up their skis for snowboards. By 2000, the National Sporting Goods Association (NSGA) reported "Snowboarding Continues Run as Fastest Growing Sports Activity" with an increase to 5.3 million participants in 2000 up from 2.4 million in 1994 (NSGA, n.p.). At the same time, almost all ski resorts catered equally to both skiers and snowboarders and also offered groomed trails for snowmobiles. One resort, Timberline Lodge on Mount Hood, Oregon, also claimed to offer the longest ski season in North America, with 351 scheduled days per year (Travel Oregon magazine, 114).

Technology changed ski equipment, making recreational skiing easier and competitive skiing faster. Lightweight plastic and titanium metal were incorporated in boots, bindings, and skis. A new hourglass-shaped ski allowed skiers to perform C-shaped turns in the snow. The shaped skis were also shorter, providing added control and flexibility. Integrated binding systems and heel lifts were introduced, allowing the skier maximum leverage. The results of these innovations were faster and tighter turns as well as downhill speeds in excess of 80 miles per hour (mph). Some people blamed the new bindings for a rash of new knee injuries among skiers, and some blamed the excessive speed for skiing deaths (*New York Times*, "Equipment Adds Twists for Skiers," February 10, 2002, 8:1).

The National Ski Areas Association began tracking skiing fatalities in 1985. The largest number of deaths (49) occurred in 1994–95 and the smallest number

(24) in 1989–90. At least nine out of ten deaths were the result of head injuries. In January 1998, a highly publicized fatal ski accident involving Congressman and former entertainer Sonny Bono raised awareness and concerns for ski safety, including the use of helmets (Janofsky, "Record Colorado Ski Deaths Prompt Call for Helmets," L:18).

TRANSPORTATION AND VACATION

In 1998, the U.S. census reported that travel by Americans amounted to 593.3 million trips, averaging two persons per trip. Of that number, 361.1 million trips were for pleasure travel, averaging two people for at least four nights. The most popular mode of transportation continued to be the automobile, and automobile trips accounted for 77 percent of total vacation trips. Seventeen percent of the trips were by airplane, 2 percent by bus, and 3 percent by train or ship.

SUVs, RVs, and Highway Fatalities

By 2000, the U.S. census reported that there were more than 180 million licensed drivers within the United States and 221 million registered motor vehicles (138 million passenger vehicles) traveling over 4 million miles of paved road. More than any other automobile the sport utility vehicle (SUV) was the vehicle of the 1990s. The SUV was a hybrid between a minivan (see chapter 8) and a truck. Most SUVs were capable of off-road travel, but the most desirable feature was the extra room for passengers and cargo and the ability to transport almost any household item, including a boat trailer or a camper. By 1999, more than 20 million SUVs were on the American roads, and more than 3 million were sold per year (McConnell, *American Decades 1990-1999*, 223).

More than 100 million adults took at least one weekend trip each year, most by automobile, and about one-third took five or more weekend trips. A large majority of American travelers opted to travel during a three-day weekend (see chapter 7). Some travelers even chose to auto-camp at Kampgrounds of America (KOA first opened in 1962). With more than 500 properties nationwide, KOA was an open-to-the-public campground franchise that recreated the ease of auto-camping (see chapter 1). KOA did not require an advance registration, advertising "you can simply show up in your car and stay." Most importantly, KOA campsites were inexpensive. The cost was as little as $27 for a full-hookup site for a camper or an RV. Another available option was a "Kamping Kabin capable of sleeping four" (KOA.com and KOAPressroom.com, n.p.).

The Recreation Vehicle Industry Association (RVIA) defined an RV as "a vehicle that combines transportation and temporary living quarters for travel, recreation and camping." RVs were categorized as either self-contained motor homes or campers capable of being towed behind an automobile. By 2000, RVIA statistics indicated that at least 7.2 million RVs were on the nation's roads, and at least "30 million RV enthusiasts, including renters, nationwide". RVs were not limited to camping use. Many were used as a primary vehicle and could be found in mall and supermarkets parking lots and were useful for tailgate parties at sporting events (see chapter 8) (RVIA.org, "RVIA Review," n.p.).

RV and other automobile drivers had the option of traveling on one of the nation's 75 designated National Scenic Byways or 20 All-American Roads in 35 states (Rand McNally Road Atlas, A3). The National Scenic Byway program was established in 1991 by the U.S. Department of Transportation to promote travel along scenic highways, most that were forgotten in favor of the massive interstate highways. The most famous was the "mother road" of all travel roads—Route 66 (see chapter 2). The International Route 66 Festival, held annually in Springfield, Illinois, celebrated America's love of the automobile with music, entertainment, and the "World's Largest Sock Hop" and also displayed thousands of classic cars and motorcycles (Route66fest.com, n.p.).

The U.S. census reported that attending auto shows was popular among 13.9 million adults, and 8.3 million reported attending at least once a month. Although the population increased from 201 million to 281 million between 1990 and 2000, the number of highway fatalities did not rise. The number of highway fatalities occurring each year from 1991 to 1997 hovered around the same number (1992 was 39,250 and 1997 41,967) (Statistical Abstract [1999], 885).

Mountain Bikes, Folding Bikes, and Motorcycle City USA

According to the SGMA, by 1999, bicycling of all types had 56.2 million participants, almost equally divided between males and females. This was down from 62 million in 1992 and placed biking third behind swimming and walking as the most-participated-in outdoor activity. Of particular note was that 17.2 million bicycle enthusiast's claimed frequent participation of at least 52 times or more per year (mountain biking had 7.9 million participants and BMX bicycling 3.7 million regular participants), outdistancing swimming, which was cited by 16.7 million participants at the same frequency rate. Mountain biking had 23.9 million participants (8.6 million off-road). The SGMA reported a large majority of those that mountain biked were males under the age of 34 (SGMA, "Popular Trends in Sports and Fitness," n.p. and SGMA, "Whassup?. . . . With Extreme Sports?" n.p.).

The Travel Industry Association of America (TIA) reported that biking vacations alone attracted "more than 27 million travelers in the past five years and they rank as the third most popular outdoor vacation activity in America (following camping and hiking)" (TIA, "Fast Facts Travel Trends," n.p.). One company, Dahon Inc., promoted a folding bike available for travel that was "[p]erfect for quick errands around town, a jaunt to the nearest Starbucks, or a leisurely ride in the park [and could be] stashed in your car, boat or RV" (www.dahon.com). The folding bike also proved convenient for airline travel, easily fitting aboard as an additional checked baggage item.

Some Americans still preferred a bike with a motor. Once a year, the tiny population (6,700) of Sturgis, South Dakota, swelled to more than 200,000 for Motorcycle City USA, the world's largest annual motorcycle rally. The main attractions were Harley-Davidson motorcycles, but all sorts of show bikes, choppers, classics, and customs made appearances. In 2000, the sixtieth anniversary rally attracted more than 600,000 people and an almost equal number of motorcycles ("Sturgis Bike City USA," 185).

Air Travel and Highly Publicized Air Tragedies

In 1998, the U.S. census recorded that 614.2568 million passengers traveled on the airlines, and at least 70 percent of all Americans had traveled by aircraft at least once in their lifetime (Statistical Abstract [1998], 885). Air travel was so common that at any given moment more than one million passengers were in the air at the same time—a far cry from 1926 when the total for air population did not exceed 112 total passengers in flight at any given time (see chapter 3). In 1998, overseas air travel was the dominant choice with 56.3 million Americans traveling to a foreign country (Statistical Abstract [2000], 269).

Near the end of the century, the outlook for air travel did not indicate any sign of decline, only a projected increase in the number of passengers. The air lanes were still crowded, and airports were congested. One solution for air travel over-crowding was to limit flight departures and maximize each flight to full passenger capacity. Another was simply to build bigger aircraft. In 2000, Airbus, a European consortium, announced plans for the dual level, 555-passenger A380. Slightly larger than the Boeing 747 and accommodating 135 more passengers, the aircraft's distinctive feature was to include a lower deck with lounges, restaurants, and sleeping berths (Airbus.com, "About Airbus," n.p.).

The 1990s were not without their share of airline fatalities. In July of 1996, more than 230 people were killed when TWA flight 800 mysteriously exploded shortly after takeoff over Long Island, New York. Also in 1996, 109 people perished as ValuJet flight 592 crashed into the Everglades in Florida. The most news-worthy air disasters of the period were four separate accidents involving twelve people.

In 1996, 7-year-old "pilot" Jessica Dubroff was killed during an airplane takeoff in Wyoming as she was attempting to become the youngest person ever to fly cross-country. Her father and a flight instructor were also killed. In 1997, famed entertainer John Denver was killed in a crash while piloting an experimental plane over Monterey, California. In 1999, golfer Payne Stewart was among five people killed as his private Lear jet flew over South Dakota. Later that same year, a small single-engine plane piloted by John F. Kennedy, Jr. disappeared near Massachusetts. The highly publicized disappearance became an unprecedented media event that consumed the network and cable news stations for days until the bodies of Kennedy, his wife, and her sister were recovered a few days later in the waters off the coast of Martha's Vineyard.

Amtrak, the Acela Express, Coach USA, and Motor Coaches

By the end of the century, railroad passenger travel on Amtrak reached an all-time high with more than 23.5 million passengers. The majority of passengers originated in the Northeast: New York City/Newark, New Jersey area (10 million passengers); Philadelphia, Pennsylvania (3.8 million); Washington, D.C. (3.5 million); Trenton/Princeton, New Jersey (1.9 million); Boston, Massachusetts (1 million); and Baltimore, Maryland (879,000). Chicago with 2.2

million passengers and Los Angeles with 1 million passengers were the exceptions. However, Amtrak continued to suffer from financial instability and rail accidents.

In 1996, 12 railroad passengers were killed and 39 injured in a collision between an Amtrak train and a Maryland Rail Commuter train. The following year, 156 people were injured during a train derailment in Arizona. Later in the year, the federal government allocated $2.3 billion to relieve Amtrak's financial instability. (During that same year, $32 billion in government subsidies were also provided for the nation's highways and $13 billion for the airlines.) Amtrak also attempted to restore the public's faith and credibility in rail service by introducing new rail lines.

In 1998, the Coast Starlight rail line combined with the American West Steamboat Company to offer "a pleasant alternative to flying" combining a cruise vacation with Amtrak rail access. The Coast Starlight had regular stops between San Diego and Sacramento, California, offering a scenic journey up the Pacific coast prior to boarding a nineteenth-century replica paddlewheel steamboat for a cruise along the Columbia River in Washington state. In 2000, Amtrak initiated the Acela Express, the first high-speed (150 mph) rail service in America, with service from Washington, D.C. to New York and Boston. Amtrak's contract-commuter service for regional authorities in California, Maryland, Massachusetts, Connecticut, and Virginia carried an additional 61.1 million people per year (www. amtrak.com).

Beyond Amtrak, railroad travel appealed to many travelers, and many vacation areas boasted historic train rides. Two examples were the Sumpter Valley Railway in Oregon and the Grand Canyon Railroad, each of which offered a reenactment of a Wild West holdup.

Buses also continued to service travelers during this period. The 2000 American Bus Association (ABA) Motorcoach census reported that more than four thousand private motor coach companies operated in the United States, maintaining 44,000 vehicles in use for charters, tours, and intercity service throughout the United States and Canada, and carried an estimated 860 million passengers. (The buses were renamed *motor coaches* and held 46 passengers each on average.) Sixty-five percent of bus carriers operated fewer than ten buses and serviced 97 million passengers. Only about 50 companies owned more than 100 coaches and accounted for 56 percent of all bus passengers (ABA, "Motor Coach Industry Facts," n.p.).

The largest bus company, Coach USA, formed in 1995, operated ten thousand motor coaches in 120 cities and 35 states (CoachUSA.com "About CoachUSA," n.p.). The Greyhound bus company serviced 2,600 destinations in 48 states with more than 18,000 daily departures serving more than 19 million passengers per year. The New York City to Atlantic City route (serving about two thousand people per day) was the most lucrative bus route in the entire country, followed by New York City to Washington, D.C. (1,300 passengers per day). Other popular travel destinations included Branson, Missouri; Chicago, Illinois; Las Vegas, Nevada; Los Angeles, California; Nashville, Tennessee; New York City; Orlando, Florida; and Toronto, Canada (www.greyhound.com).

Leisure Travelers, Freestyle Cruising, Houseboating, and Barrier-free Travel

During the period, at least half of all travelers booked a vacation through a travel agent. In 2000, more than seven million travelers chose Hawaii as a vacation destination, almost all visiting that state's famous beaches (McDowell, "Hawaii's Tourism Shows Signs of Recovery," TR:3). The Travel Industry Association of America (TIA) reported that on extended vacations of a week or longer, over 35 percent were to the beach, and one in ten of all leisure trips involved going to a beach. Overall, 48.4 million travelers reported going to the beach within any given year, and at least 28.7 million went at least once a month.

One in five people chose a cultural or historic vacation with about one-third of the vacations occurring during the summer months. At least one-fourth of all summer vacation trips involved going to a family reunion. While on vacation, about one-fourth of all travelers (nearly 40 million individuals) also maintained their fitness activities. Regardless of the mode of travel, once at a vacation destination many vacationers stayed at a hotel.

A sample of the many travel brochures from 1999–2000 that were available to aid in planning a vacation. Author's archives.

In 1998, the total number of hotel establishments numbered 51,000 with a total of 3.9 million available rooms. A large portion of these, 33,304 hotels, contained 75 rooms or less, totaling one million rooms. Midsize hotels with between 75 and 150 rooms numbered 12,036, totaling 1.3 million rooms. The larger hotels, having more than 150 rooms, numbered 5,660, totaling 1.6 million rooms. Typically, at least 80 percent of hotel guests made reservations in advance; 45 percent stayed one night, 26 percent stayed two nights, and 29 percent stayed three or more nights (Statistical Abstract [2000], 773).

Cruise ships offered travelers "hotels on the sea." By 2000, cruise lines passed the six-million-passenger-per-year mark (two million of those cruised for five days or less). All of the major cruise lines also offered a combination air/sea package to all major U.S. cities and revamped their offerings. Many cruise lines enhanced staterooms at all price levels, expanded dining options, and offered shipboard amenities and adventures, some never before offered. One Royal Caribbean ship, *Adventure of the Seas*, had a 3,114-passenger capacity and amenities including an ice-skating rink, a shopping promenade, rock-climbing wall, a five-story theater, and a fitness center and spa (www.royalcaribbean.com).

Another new travel offering was freestyle cruising. Norwegian Cruise Line advertised that freestyle cruising "gives you the freedom to choose what you'll do and when you'll do it. Enjoy more dining options, with up to 10 distinctive restaurants per ship, with no pre-set seating times and no pre-assigned dining companions. There's no formal dress code and all gratuities are automated" (www.ncl.com).

Windstar offered high-tech sailing ships with 7- to 14-day luxury cruises to Central America, the Caribbean, Europe, Australia, and the Far East. The smaller ships served a limited number of passengers (between 148 to 308) and advertised "a rare chance to slow down, take stock . . . and recall a bygone era when ocean voyages were long, leisurely affairs" (Windstar Cruises Travel Brochure, "Trans-Atlantic," 59).

Houseboats were another option for travelers who wanted to stay on the water. Lake Powell, with 1,960 miles of shoreline bordering Arizona and Utah, offered more than four hundred houseboats for rent. One renter said, "[H]ouseboating opened up an entirely different world of family vacationing. We could sail as long as we wanted or dock in a secluded cove. We could study the geology by hugging the shoreline or hiking the land. We could swim—or build sand castles on the beach" (TIME.com, "Be Admiral of Your Own Houseboat," December 4, 2000).

By the end of the century, an individual was also much less likely than in the past to find restrictions placed on them either due to ethnic background or disability. Barrier-free cruise ships were commonplace, as were a substantial number of Caribbean destinations including the resort chains Sandals, Breezes, Wyndham, Allegro, and Hyatt Regency. Laurel Van Horn, executive director of the Society for Accessible Travel and Hospitality, said, "While access to the Caribbean is still far from perfect, the warmth of the welcome and the level of service can more than make up for what's lacking. The azure skies and turquoise waters are beckoning" (www.sath.org).

A beachfront at Breezes Resort in Runaway Bay, Jamaica. Note the presence of a wheelchair and a Jet Ski. Author's archives.

Twentieth Century Lists, Y2K, and Millennium Celebrations

At the end of the twentieth century, many created lists to name the top ten in almost any category. A *Time* magazine readers' survey named Elvis Presley (see chapter 6) as the "person of the century" and his "teaching teens to rock 'n' roll" as the "event of the century." In contrast, Prohibition (see chapter 3) was voted the "worst idea of the century" (*Time*, January 1, 2000: 34).

Throughout the year 1999, technicians scrambled to fix "Y2K bugs" (Y2K is an acronym for year 2000), problems that could render computers unusable should their two-digit date systems change years from 99 to 00. Many people warned of the coming of the end of the world. Some resurrected old fallout shelters (see chapter 6) and stockpiled water and food. Books were written and vast amounts of media print and television time were devoted to the "impending doom." Some people feared that airplane traffic control would fail because of the Y2K bugs and would cause air disasters. Others thought stockpiled nuclear weapons would launch.

Time magazine reported, "Americans spent an estimated $100 billion to be ready on all fronts [for Y2K], from telecommunications to sewage treatment." The U.S. military spent almost $4 billion to avert any potential nuclear disasters due to a missile misfire. The Federal Reserve printed an extra $50 billion in cash in case of an ATM or bank failure (*Time*, "Hey, You in That Bunker, You Can Come Out Now!" January 1, 2000: 56).

As it turned out, computers did in fact change over to the new date without major problems. Although at least 72 percent of all Americans opted to stay home at midnight on December 31, 1999, they were not at a loss for television programs airing continuous live coverage of worldwide millennium celebrations that traced the year 2000 turnover as it crossed international time zones.

Millions of other Americans chose nationwide parties, some extraordinary and some quite unique. At least two million people (about four times the usual New Year's Eve crowd) jammed Times Square in New York City to witness the famous ball drop. The worldwide television viewing audience was estimated at 300 million viewers. Traditional parties were sold out months and even years in advance with escalated prices due to the once-in-a-lifetime event. Some couples attempted to be the first married, the first to conceive a child, or, for those who planned well in advance, the first to have a child born in the twenty-first century.

CONCLUSION

At the close of the twentieth century, leisure as an industry had grown in ways that could never have been foreseen just 100 years before. The leisure, entertainment, and travel industry had grown into a multibillion-dollar business, but even though the industry was widespread, it became expensive for Americans to take part in it. Community facilities were no longer available on a nationwide scale. Most required an admission fee or were exclusive to a private membership club or gated community. Widespread fear encouraged by the media made adults afraid to let their children (and even other adults) play unsupervised in a municipal park or playground.

According to the U.S. Statistical Abstract, by the year 2000, the total personal expenditure on recreation (including books, magazines, newspapers, toys, sporting goods, video, audio, computers, musical instruments, flowers, movies, amusement parks, theater, spectator sports, and other miscellaneous items and activities) exceeded $500 billion per year (by comparison, in 1990, the total expenditure was $284.9 billion) (Statistical Abstract [2000], 253). The TIA also reported that in one year from 1996 to 1997 expenditures on all components of the travel industry increased from $489 billion to $502 billion (Kraus et al. [2001] 191).

By 2000, reports listed as many as 79.2 million jobs either directly or indirectly employed in the service of recreation or entertainment. By many accounts, the travel and tourism industry was the largest industry not only in America, but also in the world. Recreation and leisure became a specialty industry, and the prediction for the twenty-first century was that additional employees were required to satisfy this multibillion-dollar industry. More than three hundred colleges and universities offered baccalaureate degrees in recreation and leisure studies, hospitality, and tourism. An additional 280 offered associate degree programs, and more than 100 provided graduate programs (Kraus et al. [2001], 191).

During the entire course of the twentieth century, America was free of a foreign attack on its shores. More tragic than any single event that occurred in the twentieth century was the attack on the World Trade Center (WTC) in New York City. The height and slenderness of the towers made it possible not only for them to be the world's tallest buildings (at the time of their completion), but also allowed for more than half of the seven-acre site on which they were built to be dedicated as a pedestrian plaza. Beneath the sprawling plaza and the WTC towers was a vast underground shopping mall connected by escalators to the street level above and the New York City and New Jersey subway systems below. Unlike other areas in the densely populated urban building sprawl, the plaza was a desirable and unique area for a leisurely lunch or stroll to break up the stressful workday. The trade center plaza represented what the rest of the world did not see about the significance of the twin towers. During the course of any given summer an outdoor music concert series was held on the plaza from Monday to Friday both at lunchtime and immediately after work. Each concert presented a different genre of music and public social dancing including country, swing, salsa, and oldies, among others. The shows were regularly attended by 3,000 to 5,000 people in addition to the estimated 10,000 to 20,000 or so that mingled throughout the plaza and underground shopping mall at any given time.

On September 11, 2001, Middle Eastern terrorists crashed two hijacked passenger airliners carrying both business and vacation travelers into the two towers of the WTC. (Two other passenger liners were hijacked at the same time; one crashed into the Pentagon in Washington, D.C., and the other in Pennsylvania.)

The attacks immediately affected Americans' lifestyles and leisure habits. Almost immediately, all of the national monuments were closed, including the Statue of Liberty and Ellis Island, and would remained closed for some time. The attacks prompted an immediate grounding of all air traffic; millions of passengers (many vacationers) were stranded. A new paranoia swept the country, and anyone remotely resembling a Middle Eastern individual was immediately suspicious in the eyes of many Americans. Some individuals would refuse to board a plane if they thought a suspicious-looking individual was also onboard.

After the attacks, many Americans were afraid to fly, and resort areas such as Hawaii that were highly dependent on air travel were on the brink of bankruptcy. Passengers were not only afraid to travel, but they were also severely hampered by newly imposed security regulations. For a short time, rail travel increased, but for the most part, terror paralyzed the nation as many Americans simply stayed home, riveted in horror to their television sets as this new sensational drama unfolded before their eyes. Some of the simplest pleasures of leisure were put on hold, as Americans were uncertain if more terrorist attacks would follow. Similar to the events surrounding World War I, the Great flu epidemic of 1918–1919, World War II, the Civil Rights movement, and the Vietnam conflict, Americans' leisure habits would once again change. Americans got a glimpse of how their leisure habits would be shaped not only by the political, social, and economic conditions within America, but now in the twenty-first century they would have to reckon with the political, social, and economic implications of global events.

BIBLIOGRAPHY

Albrecht, Donald, ed. *World War II and the American Dream: How Wartime Building Changed a Nation*. Cambridge, Mass.: MIT Press, 1995.

American Heritage Dictionary: Second College Edition. Boston: Houghton Mifflin, 1976.

The Annals of America, Vol. 16, 1940–1949. Encyclopedia Britannica, 1968.

The Annals of America, Vol. 17, 1950–1959. Encyclopedia Britannica, 1968.

Aron, Cindy S. *Working at Play: A History of Vacations in the United States*. New York: Oxford University Press, 1999.

Asinof, Eliot. *1919: America's Loss of Innocence*. New York: D. I. Fine, 1990.

Barson, Michael, and Steven Heller. *Red Scared: The Commie Menace in Propaganda and Popular Culture*. San Francisco: Chronicle Books, 2001.

Baughman, Judith S., ed. *American Decades: 1920–1929*. Detroit, Mich.: Gale Research, 1996.

Benjamin, Robert Spiers. *The Vacation Guide*. New York: Whittlesey House, 1940.

Bondi, Victor, ed. *American Decades: 1930–1939*. Detroit, Mich.: Gale Research, 1996.

———. *American Decades: 1940–1949*. Detroit, Mich.: Gale Research, 1995.

———. *American Decades: 1970–1979*. Detroit, Mich.: Gale Research, 1995.

———. *American Decades: 1980–1989*. Detroit, Mich.: Gale Research, 1996.

Boyer, Paul, S., Clifford E. Clark, Jr. et al. *The Enduring Vision: A History of the American People*. New York: Houghton Mifflin, 2000.

Braden, Donna R. *Leisure and Entertainment in America*. Dearborn, Mich.: Henry Ford Museum and Greenfield Village, 1988.

Brown, Dee. *The American West*. New York: Touchstone Books, 1995.

Buder, Stanley. *Pullman: An Experiment in Industrial Order and Community Planning, 1880–1930*. New York: Oxford University Press, 1967.

Castle, Mr. and Mrs. Vernon. *Modern Dancing*. New York: Harper and Brothers, 1914.

Chicago Recreation Survey, 1937. Vol. 2. Chicago, 1938.

Cohen, Nancy E. *America's Marketplace: The History of Shopping Centers*. Lyme, Conn.: Greenwich Publishing, 2002.

Dodds, John W. "Living in Small-town and Rural America." In *The 1900s*, edited by Myra H. Immell. San Diego, Calif.: Greenhaven Press, 2000.

Doherty, Thomas. *Projections of War: Hollywood, American Culture, and World War II*. New York: Columbia University Press, 1993.

Erenberg, Lewis A. *Swingin' the Dream: Big Band Jazz and the Rebirth of American Culture*. Chicago: University of Chicago Press, 1998.

Faragher, John Mack, Mari Jo Buhle, Daniel Czitrom, and Susan H. Armitage. *Out of Many: A History of the American People*. Vol. 2. Upper Saddle River, N.J.: Prentice Hall, 1997.

Findlay, John M. *Magic Lands Western Cityscapes and American Culture After 1940*. Berkeley: University of California Press, 1992.

Fink, James J. *The Car Culture*. Cambridge: MIT Press, 1975.

Foner, Eric. *The Story of American Freedom*. New York: Norton, 1998.

Frazier, E. Franklin. *Black Bourgeoisie*. New York: The Free Press, 1957.

Frazier, Ian. *Great Plains*. New York: Farrar Straus Giroux, 1989.

Friedan, Betty. *The Feminine Mystique*. New York: Norton, 1963.

Gambino, Richard. *Blood of My Blood: The Dilemma of the Italian-Americans*. Garden City, N.Y.: Doubleday, 1974.

Gargiulo, Vince. *Palisades Amusement Park: A Century of Fond Memories*. New Brunswick, N.J.: Rutgers University Press, 1995.

Garvey, Ellen Gruber. *The Adman in the Parlor: Magazines and the Gendering of Consumer Culture, 1880s to 1910s*. New York: Oxford University Press, 1996.

Geis, Gilbert, and Leigh B. Bienen. "O.J. Simpson and the Trial of the Century." In *The 1990's*, edited by Stuart A. Kallen. San Diego, Calif.: Greenhaven Press, 2000.

Gelber, Steven M. *Hobbies: Leisure and the Culture of Work in America*. New York: Columbia University Press, 1999.

Gillon, Steven M., and Cathy D. Matson. *The American Experiment: A History of the United States Volume 2: Since 1865*. New York: Houghton Mifflin, 2002.

Godbey, Geoffrey. *Leisure in Your Life: An Exploration*. State College, Pa.: Venture Publishing, 1999.

Goldfield, David, Carl Abbott, et al. *The American Journey: A History of the United States*. 2nd edition. Upper Saddle River, N.J.: Prentice Hall, 2001.

Grover, Kathryn, ed. *Hard at Play: Leisure in America, 1840–1940*. Amherst:University of Massachusetts Press, 1992.

Gulliford, Andrew. "Fox and Geese in the School Yard." In *Hard at Play: Leisure in America, 1840–1940*, edited by Kathryn Grover. Amherst: University of Massachusetts Press, 1992.

Halberstadt, Hans. *Classic Trains*. New York: Metro Books, 2001.

Halberstam, David. *The Fifties*. New York: Fawcett Columbine, 1993.

Heilbrun, Carolyn G. *The Education of a Woman: The Life of Gloria Steinem*. New York: Ballantine Books, 1995.

Hilliard, Robert L., and Michael C. Keith. *The Broadcast Century and Beyond: A Biography of American Broadcasting*. 3d ed. Boston: Focal Press, 2001.

Hofstadter, Richard. "The Reality of the Muckraker," In *The 1900s*, edited by Myra H. Immell. San Diego, Calif.: Greenhaven Press, 2000.

Horsham, Michael. *20s and 30s Style*. New Jersey: Chartwell Books, 1989.

Ibrahim, Hilmi. *Leisure and Society: A Comparative Approach*. Dubuque, Iowa: Wm. C. Brown, 1991.

Jakle, John A. *The Motel in America*. Baltimore, Md.: Johns Hopkins University Press, 1996.

Jimenez, Carlos M. *The Mexican American Heritage*. Berkeley, Calif.: TQS Publishing, 1994.

Jury, Mark. *Playtime: Americans at Leisure*. New York: Harcourt Brace Jovanovich, 1977.

Kammen, Michael. *American Culture, American Tastes: Social Change and the 20th Century*. New York: Basic Books, 1999.

Kando, Thomas M. *Leisure and Popular Culture in Transition*. 2nd ed. St. Louis, Mo.: Mosby, 1980.

Kaplan, Max. *Leisure in America: A Social Inquiry*. New York: Wiley, 1960.

————. *Leisure Perspective on Education and Policy*. Washington, D.C.: National Education Association, 1978.

Kennedy, David M. *Over Here: The First World War and American Society*. New York: Oxford University Press, 1982.

Kent, Steven. *The Ultimate History of Video Games*. Roseville, Calif.: Prima Publishing, 2001.

Kolata, Gina. *Flu: The Story of the Great Influenza Pandemic of 1918 and the Search for the Virus That Caused It*. New York: Touchstone, 2001.

Kopay, David, and Perry Deane Young. *The David Kopay Story: An Extraordinary Self-Revelation*. New York: Arbor House, 1977.

Kostof, Spiro. *America by Design*. New York: Oxford University Press, 1987.

Kraus, Richard. *Recreation and Leisure in Modern Society*. New York: Appleton-Century-Crofts, 1971.

————. *Leisure in a Changing America: Multicultural Perspectives*. New York: Macmillan, 1994.

Kraus, Richard, Elizabeth Barber, and Ira Shapiro. *Introduction to Leisure Services: Career Perspectives*. Champaign, Ill.: Sagamore Publishing, 2001.

Larrabee, Eric, and Rolf Meyerson, eds. *Mass Leisure*. Glencoe, Ill.: Free Press, 1958.

Layman, Richard, ed. *American Decades: 1950–1959*. Detroit, Mich.: Gale Research, 1994.

————. *American Decades: 1960–1969*. Detroit, Mich.: Gale Research, 1995.

Lewis, Jon E. *The Mammoth Book of The West*. New York: Carroll and Graf, 1996.

Lingeman, Richard R. *Don't You Know There's a War On? The American Home Front, 1941–1945*. New York: Putnam, 1970.

Lundberg, George, Mirra Komarovsky, and Mary Alice McInerny. *Leisure: A Suburban Study*. New York: Columbia University Press, 1934.

Lynd, Robert S., and Helen Merrell Lynd. *Middletown: A Study in Contemporary American Culture*. New York: Harcourt, Brace, 1929.

————. *Middletown in Transition: A Study in Cultural Conflicts*. New York: Harcourt, Brace, 1937.

Macionis, John J. *Sociology*. 6th ed. Upper Saddle River, N.J.: Prentice Hall, 1997.

Madow, Pauline, ed. *Recreation in America*. Vol. 37: 2. New York: H. W. Wilson, 1965.

Marty, Myron A. *Daily Life in the United States, 1960–1990*. Westport, Conn.: Greenwood Press, 1997.

McConnell, Tandy, ed. *American Decades: 1990–1999*. Detroit, Mich.: Gale Research, 2001.

Mitchell, Helen Jo, and William A. Hillman, Jr. "Disability and the Disadvantaged." In *Recreation and Leisure Service for the Disadvantaged*, edited by John A. Nesbitt, Paul D. Brown, and James F. Murphy. Philadelphia: Lea and Febiger, 1970.

Mock, James R., and Cedric Larson. *Words That Won the War: The Story of the Committee on Public Information*. Princeton, N.J.: Princeton University Press, 1939.

Moss, George Donelson. *America in the Twentieth Century*. New Jersey: Prentice Hall, 1993.

Munson, Robert S. *Favorite Hobbies and Pastimes: A Sourcebook of Leisure Pursuits*. Chicago: American Library Association, 1994.

Myrdal, Gunnar "Recreation." In *Recreation and Leisure Service for the Disadvantaged*, edited by John A. Nesbitt, Paul D. Brown, and James F. Murphy. Philadelphia: Lea and Febiger, 1970.

Nasaw, David. *Going Out: The Rise and Fall of Public Amusements*. New York: Basic Books, 1993.

Nash, Gerald D. *The American West Transformed: The Impact of the Second World War*. Bloomington: Indiana University Press, 1985.

Olson, James S. *Historical Dictionary of the 1950s*. Westport, Conn.: Greenwood Press, 2000.

———. *Historical Dictionary of the 1960s*. Westport, Conn.: Greenwood Press, 1998.

———. *Historical Dictionary of the 1970s*. Westport, Conn.: Greenwood Press, 1999.

Orlean, Susan. *Saturday Night*. New York: Knopf, 1990.

Panati, Charles. *Panati's Parade of Fads, Follies, and Manias*. New York: HarperCollins, 1991.

Peiss, Kathy. *Cheap Amusements: Working Women and Leisure in Turn-of-the-Century New York*. Philadelphia: Temple University Press, 1986.

———. *Rand McNally Road Atlas*. Chicago: Rand McNally and Company, 1998.

Pendergast, Tom, and Sara Pendergast. *St. James Encyclopedia of Popular Culture*. Vol. 1. Detroit: St. James Press, 2000.

———. *St. James Encyclopedia of Popular Culture*. Vol. 2. Detroit: St. James Press, 2000.

———. *St. James Encyclopedia of Popular Culture*. Vol. 3. Detroit: St. James Press, 2000.

———. *St. James Encyclopedia of Popular Culture*. Vol. 4. Detroit: St. James Press, 2000.

———. *St. James Encyclopedia of Popular Culture*. Vol. 5. Detroit: St. James Press, 2000.

Reynolds, Lucile Winifred. "Leisure-time Activities of a Selected Group of Farm Women." Ph.D. diss., University of Chicago, 1939.

Rich, Frank. *Ghost Light: A Memoir*. New York: Random House, 2000.

Rickards, Maurice. *Posters of the First World War*. New York: Walker, 1968.

Rollin, Lucy. *Twentieth-century Teen Culture by the Decades*. Westport, Conn.: Greenwood Press, 1999.

Rose, Kenneth D. *One Nation Underground: The Fallout Shelter in American Culture*. New York: New York University Press, 2001.

Rosenberg, Bernard, and David Manning White, eds. *Mass Culture: The Popular Arts in America*. Glencoe, Ill.: Free Press, 1957.

Rosenzweig, Roy. *Eight Hours for What We Will: Workers and Leisure in an Industrial City, 1870–1920*. New York: Cambridge University Press, 1983.

Rubin, Lillian Breslow. *Worlds of Pain: Life in the Working-class Family*. New York: Basic Books, 1976.

Sanders, Don, and Susan Sanders. *Drive-in Movie Memories*. Middleton, N.H.: Carriage House Publishing, 2000.

Schor, Juliet. *The Overworked American: The Unexpected Decline of Leisure*. New York: Basic Books, 1993.

Sellers, John. *Arcade Fever: The Fan's Guide to the Golden Age of Video Games*. Philadelphia: Running Press, 2001.

Sheehy, Colleen J. "American Angling." In *Hard at Play: Leisure in America, 1840–1940*, edited by Kathryn Grover. Amherst: University of Massachusetts Press, 1992.

Southerland, Thomas C., and William McCleery. *The Way To Go: The Coming of U.S. Rail Passenger Service*. New York: Simon and Schuster, 1973.

Steiner, Jesse F. *Americans at Play: Recent Trends in Recreation and Leisure Time Activities*. New York: McGraw Hill, 1933.

———. *Studies in the Social Aspects of the Depression: Research Memorandum on Recreation in the Depression*. New York: Arno Press, 1972.

Stover, John F. *American Railroads*. Chicago: University of Chicago Press, 1961.

Stowe, David W. *Swing Changes: Big-band Jazz in New Deal America*. Cambridge, Mass.: Harvard University Press, 1994.

Taneja, Nawal K. *Introduction to Civil Aviation*. 2d ed. Lexington, Mass.: Lexington Books, 1989.

Taylor, John M. "The Sinking of the *Lusitania* Nudges America Toward War." In *The 1920's*, edited by John F. Wukovits. San Diego, Calif.: Greenhaven Press, 2000.

Time-Life Books. *Rock & Roll Generation: Teen life in the 50s*. Virginia: Time Life Books, 1998.

Time-Life Books. *This Fabulous Century: 1900–1910*. Vol. 1. New York: Time-Life Books, 1969.

Time-Life Books. *This Fabulous Century: 1910–1920*. Vol. 2. New York: Time-Life Books, 1969.

Time-Life Books. *This Fabulous Century: 1920–1930*. Vol. 3. New York: Time-Life Books, 1969.

Time-Life Books. *This Fabulous Century: 1930–1940*. Vol. 4. New York: Time-Life Books, 1969.

Time-Life Books. *This Fabulous Century: 1940–1950*. Vol. 5. New York: Time-Life Books, 1969.

Time-Life Books. *This Fabulous Century: 1950–1960*. Vol. 6. New York: Time-Life Books, 1970.

Time-Life Books. *This Fabulous Century: 1960–1970*. Vol. 7. New York: Time-Life Books, 1970.

Tompkins, Vincent, ed. *American Decades: 1900–1909*. Detroit, Mich.: Gale Research, 1996.

———. *American Decades: 1910–1919*. Detroit, Mich.: Gale Research, 1996.

Trotter, Joe William, Jr. *The African American Experience, Vol. 2: From Reconstruction*. New York: Houghton Mifflin, 2001.

Uminowicz, Glenn. "Recreation in Christian America." In *Hard at Play: Leisure in America, 1840–1940*, edited by Kathryn Grover. Amherst: University of Massachusetts Press, 1992.

Unger, Irwin. *America in the 1960's*. New York: Brandywine Press, 1993.

U.S. Census Bureau. *Statistical Abstract of the United States: 1987*. Washington D.C., 1986.

U.S. Census Bureau. *Statistical Abstract of the United States: 1995*. Washington D.C., 1994.

U.S. Census Bureau. *Statistical Abstract of the United States: 1996*. Washington D.C., 1995.

U.S. Census Bureau. *Statistical Abstract of the United States: 1999*. Washington D.C., 1998.

U.S. Census Bureau. *Statistical Abstract of the United States: 2000*. Washington D.C., 1999.

Uschan, Michael V., ed. *The 1910s*. San Diego: Lucent Books, 1999.

Uslan, Michael, and Bruce Solomon. *Dick Clark's the First 25 Years of Rock and Roll*. New York: Dell, 1981.

Veblen, Thorstein. *Theory of the Leisure Class*. 1899. Reprint, New York: Dover, 1994.

West, Elliott. *Growing Up in Twentieth-century America: A History and Reference Guide*. Westport, Conn.: Greenwood Press, 1996.

Whitfield, Stephen J. *The Culture of the Cold War*. 2d ed. Baltimore, Md.: Johns Hopkins University Press, 1996.

Williams, Juan. *Eyes on the Prize: America's Civil Rights Years, 1954–1965*. New York: Penguin Books, 1987.

Wrenn, C. Gilbert, and D. L. Harley. *Time on Their Hands: A Report on Leisure, Recreation and Young People*. Washington, D.C.: American Council on Education, 1941.

Young, Lynn. "Open Space and the Inner City," in John A. Nesbitt, Paul D. Brown, and James F. Murphy, eds., *Recreation and Leisure Service for the Disadvantaged*. Philadelphia: Lea and Febiger, 1970.

Zieger, Robert H. *America's Great War: World War I and the American Experience*. Maryland: Rowman and Littlefield, 2001.

MUSEUMS

Ellis Island Immigration Museum, Ellis Island, New York

Newark Airport, Newark, New Jersey

PERIODICALS

ABABMX.com. "What is the ABA?" Internet accessed 30 May 2003. http://www.ababmx.com/about_aba.asp.

Airbus.com. "About Airbus." Internet accessed 30 May 2003. http://www.airbus.com/dynamic/about/index_h.asp.

All-American Girls Professional Baseball League (AAGPBL). "League History." Internet accessed 20 May 2003. http://www.aagpbl.org/history/History_1.html.

American Bus Association (ABA). "Motor Coach Industry Facts." Internet accessed 30 May 2003. http://www.buses.org/industry/.

American Studies Vol. 42, no. 1 (Spring 2001). Mid-America American Studies Association and the University of Kansas.

Attwell, E.T. "Recreation in Colored Communities." *The Playground* Vol. 19, no. 12 (March 1926): 657.

———. "ATV History." *Minneapolis-St. Paul Star Tribune* (24 February 2002) Internet accessed 30 May 2003. http://www.startribune.com/stories/531/1645640.html.

Badasski, Scoop. "The Inside Scoop." *Swing Time*, Issue # 111998, 50–51.

Battaglio, Stephen. "When AM Ruled Music, and WABC Was King." *The New York Times*, (10 March 2002): AR:16.

"Bicycle." *Microsoft® Encarta® Encyclopedia 2000*. Microsoft Corporation, 1993–1999.

BlackBaseball.com. "History of the Negro Baseball Leagues—The Big Years." Internet accessed 30 May 2003. http://www.blackbaseball.com/history/index.htm.

Brown, Ruth. *Rock & Roll: The Early Years*. Time-Life Video, 1995. Videocassette, 55 mins.

Boyd, Lydia, and Lynn Pritcher. "Brief History of the U.S. Passenger Rail Industry." Digital Scriptorium. Internet accessed 7 December 2001. http://scriptorium.lib.duke.edu/adaccess/rails-history.html.

"Boyology: A New and All-Important Study." *The Playground* Vol. 19, no. 12 (March 1926): 670.

Cedar Point Amusement Park. "History." Internet accessed 9 August 2001. http://www.cedarpoint.com/public/news/history/a.cfm.

CoachUSA.com. "About CoachUSA–02/18/2002." Internet accessed 30 May 2003. http://www.coachusa.com/media.cfm?action£ress_detail&press_id.

Crosby, David F. "The Yo-Yo: Its Rise and Fall." *American History* (August 2002): 52–56.

"Cycling." *Microsoft® Encarta® Encyclopedia 2000*. Microsoft Corporation, 1993–1999.

The Daily Aesthetic. "Leisure and recreation in a southern city's segregated park system." http://www.uky.edu/Projects/TDA/narrativ.htm.

DivingHistory.com. "Time Line of Sport Diving History United States." Internet accessed 20 May 2003. www.divinghistory.com/timeline.htm.

Duke University "Brief History of the Passenger Ship Industry" Internet accessed 7 December 2001. http://scriptorium.lib.duke.edu/adaccess/ship-history.html.

"Early Adventures with the Automobile." Eye Witness—History through the Eyes of Those Who Lived It. Internet accessed 10 June 2001. www.ibiscom. com (1997).

Fladager, Darlene. "Amusement Park Attendance Statistics" University of North Carolina 1994. Internet accessed 9 August 2001. www.ibiblio.org/ darlene/coaster/FAQ/FAQ.attendance.html.

Florida Memory Project "Florida During World War II" Internet accessed 20 May 2003. http://www.floridamemory.com/OnlineClassroom/FloridaWWII/ history.cfm.

"GI Bill of Rights." Prentice Hall Documents, Library Online. Internet accessed 9 August 2001. http://hcl.chass.ncsu.edu/garson/dye/docs/gibill.htm.

Glines, Carole. "A Last Hurray for Hollywood: A Saturday in Los Angeles' Last 'Golden Age' Movie Palaces." The Historic Traveler (March 1999). Internet accessed July 17, 2001. http://historictraveler.com/primedia/arts_arch/ last_hurray.adp.

Goodale, Thomas. *The Academy of Leisure Sciences* "White Paper #2: Leisure Apartheid." Internet accessed 9 August 2002. http://www.eas.ualberta.ca/elj/als /alswp2.html.

Gorp.com "Lake Mead National Recreation Area—Activities," Internet accessed 20 May 2003. http://gorp.com/gorp/resource/us_nra/az/act_lm.htm.

Grist, N.R. "A Letter from Camp Devens 1918." British Medical Journal. December 22–29, 1979, pp. 1632–1633.

Ho, David. "More than 10,000 people injured on thrill rides in 2000, feds say," Associated Press *Staten Island Advance* August 24, 2001, A25.

Howe, Neil, and William Strauss. "The New Generation Gap." The Atlantic Monthly (December 1992). Vol. 270, No. 6: 67–89.

IMAX.com. "Theaters—IMAX Theater Types." Internet accessed 30 May 2003. http://www.imax.com/imax_news.html.

International Council of Shopping Centers (ICSC) *Research Quarterly,* Winter 2001–2002 (Vol. 8, No. 4. ICSC 1221), Avenue of the Americas, New York, NY 10020–1099.

ISMA (International Snowmobile Manufacturers Association) "Facts and Statistics about Snowmobiling," Internet accessed 30 May 2003. http://www. snowmobile.org/pr_snowfacts.asp.

Janofsky, Michael. "Record Colorado Ski Deaths Prompt Call for Helmets." *New York Times* March 31, 2002, L: 18.

Jewell, Edwin S. "Adults Play in Omaha." *The Playground* Vol. 19, no. 12 (March 1926): 668.

Johnson, Charles S. "A Survey of the Negro Population of Fort Wayne (Indiana)." Department of Research and Investigations, National Urban League, New York (1928). Internet accessed 24 September 2001. a machine-readable transcription. http://memory.loc.gov/cgi-bin/query/r?ammem/cool:field (DOCID+lit(mu04103).

Kirkpatrick, David D. "Oprah Will Curtail 'Book Club' Picks and Authors Weep," *The New York Times,* April 6, 2002, 1.

Kiwanis.org. "About Kiwanis." Internet accessed 20 May 2003. http://www. kiwanis.org/about_kiwanis.html.

KOA.com, Kampgrounds of America. "KOA Facts—Camping Facilities" Internet accessed 30 May 2003. http://www.koa.com/koafacts/campfac.htm.

KOAPressroom.com. "Company Info—KOA History" Internet accessed 30 May 2003. http://www.koapressroom.com/companyinformation/koahistory.asp.

Krajick, Kevin. Don't look now, but here come the bladerunners," September 1995 Smithsonian magazine September 1995. Internet accessed 30 May 2003. http://www.smithsonianmag.com/smithsonian/issues95/sep95/blading.html.

Library of Congress. "Duke Paoa Kahanamoku: The Father of Modern Surfing." *American Memory* (11 August 2000). Internet accessed 26 June 2001. http://lcweb2.loc.gov/ammem/today/aug11.html.

"Longest Running Broadway Shows in History." Internet accessed 30 May 2003. http://www.geocities.com/auzziek/broadway_list.html.

Maguire, Tom. "Radburn, New Jersey: An Experiment in Urban Form." Internet accessed 9 August 2001. http://garnet.berkeley.edu/cp240/Casestudy/radburn.htm.

McCormick. "An Unusual Program for the Disabled," *New York Times* April 28, 2002, Sec. 8:10.

McDowell, Edwin. "Hawaii's Tourism Shows Signs of Recovery," *New York Times* April 14, 2002, TR:3.

McQuirter, Marya Annette. "A Love Affair with Cars." *African American on Wheels* (Spring 1998). Internet accessed 10 June 2001. http://www.automag.com/AAOWMagazine/1998_spring/love3.asp.

Meersman, Tom. "Tracks on the land: Nature pays the price as ATVs hit Minnesota's woods" February 24, 2002 *Minneapolis-St. Paul Star Tribune*. Internet accessed 30 May 2003. http://www.startribune.com/stories/531/1633242.html.

Missouri Travel Guide 2002. "Outdoor Adventures." Internet accessed 15 April 2002. http://www.visitMO.com.

Mixed Pickles Vintage Dance Timeline. "Early 20th Century Dance." http://www.mixedpickles.org/20cdance.html.

Motor Sports Management. "NASCAR Basics." Internet accessed 4 April 2002. http://www.motorsportsmanagement.com/motorsports/.

National Sporting Goods Association (NSGA). "Snowboarding Continues Run as Fastest Growing Sports Activity." May 2002, Internet accessed 30 May 2003. http://www.nsga.org/public/pages/index.cfm?pageid25.

Page, Ellen Welles. "A Flapper's Appeal to Parents." *Outlook* magazine December 6, 1922. Internet accessed 9 August 2001. http://www.geocities.com/flapper_culture/appeal.html.

Parker, Thomas F. "Recreation for Colored Citizens." *The Playground* Vol. 19, no. 12 (March 1926): 651.

PBS Online, n.p. "Car Camping." Internet accessed 10 June 2001. http://www.pbs.org/wgbh/amex/kids/summer/features_car.html.

Pitts, Brenda. "Beyond the Bars: The Development of Leisure Activity Management in the Lesbian and Gay Population in America." *Leisure Information Quarterly* Vol. 15, no. 3 (1989): 4–7.

Route66fest.com International Route 66 Mother Road Festival "World's Largest

Sock Hop . . . Be There Or Be Square!" Internet accessed 30 May 2003. http://www.route66fest.com/attractions.htm.

"Roy's Letter." *British Medical Journal,* December 22–29, 1979, 1632–1633.

RunnersWeb.com Runner's and Triathlete's Web News. "Athletics: An Interview with Kathrine Switzer." Posted: April 28, 2003. Internet accessed 29 May 2003.   http://www.runnersweb.com/running/news/rw_news_20030428_ KathrineSwitzer.html.

RVIA.org Recreational Vehicle Industry association. "RVIA Review." Internet accessed 30 May 2003. http://www.rvia.org/about/Functions.htm.

Sporting Goods Manufacturing Association (SGMA). "The American Way to Play." September 29, 2000, Internet accessed 4 April 2002. http://www. sgma.com/press/2000/press983389141-13903.html.

———. "Bowling Finds Stability Despite Problems." March 7, 2000, Internet accessed   4   April   2002.   http://www.sgma.com/press/2000/ press983896585-16412.html.

———. "Golf: Play Is Steady While Sales Struggle." February 22, 2002 Press Release, Internet accessed 4 April 2002. http://www.sgma.com/press/ 2002/press1013021504-19389.html.

———. "Popular Trends in Sports and Fitness." 1995 Press Release, Internet accessed   25   May   2003.   http://www.sgma.com/press/1995/ press987339861-18369.html.

———. "Skates, 'Boards, Scooters: Sales Down But Participation Steady." February 27, 2002, Internet accessed 4 April 2002. http://www.sgma.com/ press/2002/press1013784793-1690.html.

———. "Sports Participation Trends." 1995 Press Release, Internet accessed 4 April 2002. http://www.sgma.com/press/1995/press987254056-27067. html.

———. "Whassup?. . . . With Extreme Sports?" October 30, 2000, Internet accessed 4 April 2002. http://www.sgma.com/press/2000/press983385566- 4103.html.

Stanton, Jeffrey. "Coney Island—Horse Racing" (1997). Internet, accessed 21 July 2001. http://naid.sppsr.ucla.edu/coneyisland/articles/horseracing.htm.

Sterngold, James. "Fantasy Lands' Ailing Turnstiles: Parks drawing visitors from afar suffered last year, but regional parks enjoyed an upswing." *The New York Times*, February 24, 2002, TR:6.

"Sturgis Bike City USA." *South Dakota Travel Magazine*, South Dakota Department of Tourism, 2002, 185.

Super Seventies Rock Site's "Seventies Almanac 1973." Internet accessed 30 May 2003. http://www.superseventies.com/1973.html.

Tarrant, Blanche. "For the Girls and Women of South Carolina." *The Playground* Vol. 19, no. 12 (March 1926): 669.

Taylor, Rich. "A Century of Recreation." *Popular Mechanics* (1 January 2000). Internet accessed 7 June 2001. http://www.britannica.com/.

TIA Travel Industry Association of America. "Fast Facts Travel Trends." Internet accessed 4 April 2002. http://www.tia.org/press/trends.asp.

Travel Oregon magazine, Fall/Winter 2002, Oregon Travel Commission 2001, 114.

Vita, Tricia. "Thrill of a Lifetime: Abandoned for almost 40 years, Coney Island's parachute jump rebounds with a $5 million renovation." November 15, 2002 Online Preservation. Internet accessed 23 May 2003. http://www. nationaltrust.org/magazine/archives/arch_story/111502.htm.

Vogeler, Ingolf. "Farm and Ranch Vacationing," *Journal of Leisure Research* Vol. 9, no. 4 (1997): 291–300.

Wade, Judy. "Santa Catalina Island, Southern California's swing-era paradise." *The Historic Traveler Magazine.* Internet accessed 26 July 2001. http://historictraveler.com/primedia/pol_soc/santa_catalina_1.adp.

Windstar Cruises Travel Brochure, "Trans-Atlantic." Windstar Sailing, Inc., 2002, 59.

PERSONAL INTERVIEWS

Dattilo, Dominick. 2 May 2002.
Giordano (nee Dattilo), Phyllis. 26 February 2002.

INDEX

Page numbers in *italics* refer to photographs.

About the Author

RALPH G. GIORDANO holds a license as a professional registered architect in the state of New York, a master's in history from the City University of New York–CUNY, and a bachelor's degree in architecture from the New York Institute of Technology. Professor Giordano is also an adjunct professor of history at the College of Staten Island, City University of New York–CUNY.